LUTHER'S THEOLOGY OF THE CROSS

Luther's Theology of the Cross

Christ in Luther's Sermons on John

DENNIS NGIEN

Foreword by Alister McGrath

Afterword by Carl R. Trueman

CASCADE *Books* • Eugene, Oregon

LUTHER'S THEOLOGY OF THE CROSS
Christ in Luther's Sermons on John

Copyright © 2018 Dennis Ngien. All rights reserved. Except for brief quotations in critical publications or reviews, no part of this book may be reproduced in any manner without prior written permission from the publisher. Write: Permissions, Wipf and Stock Publishers, 199 W. 8th Ave., Suite 3, Eugene, OR 97401.

Cascade Books
An Imprint of Wipf and Stock Publishers
199 W. 8th Ave., Suite 3
Eugene, OR 97401

www.wipfandstock.com

PAPERBACK ISBN: 978-1-5326-4579-2
HARDCOVER ISBN: 978-1-5326-4580-8
EBOOK ISBN: 978-1-5326-4581-5

Cataloguing-in-Publication data:

Names: Ngien, Dennis, 1958–, author. | McGrath, Alister E., 1953–, foreword writer. | Trueman, Carl R., afterword writer

Title: Luther's theology of the cross : Christ in Luther's sermons on John / Dennis Ngien, with a foreword by Alister McGrath and an afterword by Carl R. Trueman.

Description: Eugene, OR: Cascade Books, 2018 | Includes bibliographical references.

Identifiers: ISBN 978-1-5326-4579-2 (paperback) | ISBN 978-1-5326-4580-8 (hardcover) | ISBN 978-1-5326-4581-5 (ebook)

Subjects: LCSH: Luther, Martin, 1483–1546 | Jesus Christ—Crucifixion | Theology of the Cross | Bible. John—Criticism, interpretation, etc. | Spirituality

Classification: BR333.3 N48 2018 (paperback) | BR333.3 (ebook)

Manufactured in the U.S.A. 06/08/18

In Thanksgiving on the 500th anniversary of the Reformation,
for their Friendship, Mentorship, and Scholarship:

Richard Bauckham, Ridley Hall, Cambridge University
Carl Trueman, Westminister Theological Seminary
Oliver Crisp, Fuller Theological Seminary
Timothy George, Beeson Divinity College
Paul Fiddes, Oxford University

Contents

Foreword by Alister McGrath | ix
Acknowledgments | xi

Introduction | 1

CHAPTER 1
St. John's Way of Speaking: The Person and Work of Christ | 15

CHAPTER 2
Divine Hiddenness: The Word of God and Created Forms | 36

CHAPTER 3
Enroll in the Spiritual School: Regeneration, Faith, and Works | 54

CHAPTER 4
Christ, the Bread of Life: The Source and Substance of Salvation | 73

CHAPTER 5
Civil Kingdom and Christ's Kingdom: Judgment,
Grace, and Freedom | 93

CHAPTER 6
Nestle on the Lap of Christ: Close our Eyes and Open our Ears | 113

CHAPTER 7
Jesus, the Master Commentator: Harvesting Divine Things
from Christ | 131

CHAPTER 8
Prayer—Not Our Creation but God's Gift:
The Causative Agency of God | 150

CHAPTER 9
Alternation Between Suffering and Sweetness: The Shape
of the Christian Life | 169

CHAPTER 10
The Glory of the Holy Spirit's Office: The Economic Actions
of the Holy Spirit | 188

CHAPTER 11
Christological Predication: The Usage of *Communicatio Idiomatum* | 208

CHAPTER 12
Bind to Christ's Mouth: No Other Intercessor than Christ | 225

CHAPTER 13
The Power of Christ's Passion: Simplicity of Word
and Magnitude of Substance | 244

CHAPTER 14
Resurrection and Flame of Love: Christ our Brother and His Voice | 271

Afterword by Carl R. Trueman | 289
Bibliography | 291

Foreword

It is a pleasure to commend and introduce this new study of Luther's "theology of the cross." In recent years, Dennis Ngien has established himself as a leading interpreter of Luther, with a most welcome emphasis on the importance of Luther's ideas for the life and witness of the church, as well as for the personal spiritual journeys of individual believers. This important new work will help scholars grasp the fundamental theological themes underlying Luther's approach, while helping a wider readership appreciate how this can inform and enrich the life of faith.

My own discovery of Luther's theology of the cross dates from the spring of 1979. I was working on Luther at Cambridge University, under the direction of Professor Gordon Rupp. At that time, I found its core ideas deeply puzzling. "Living, even dying and being damned, make a theologian, not understanding, reading or speculating."[1] Surely theology was about reading books, and trying to make sense of our world? Surely theology was basically about securing a better understanding of things? Luther seemed to have developed a theological trajectory that bore little relation to the rather academic theology that I knew at that time.

As I read on in Luther, I came across other terse statements emphasizing the centrality of the cross of Christ to faith. "The cross alone is our theology."[2] "The cross puts everything to the test."[3] Luther's words seemed to extend the meaning of the cross far beyond theories of the atonement, suggesting that the cross of Christ was the key to Christian existence—to our knowledge of God, and the dynamics of the Christian life. Happily, I persevered in my engagement with Luther's "theology of the cross," and continue to find it a remarkable source of wisdom in times of uncertainty, difficulty,

---

1. WA 5.163.28–9: "Vivendo, immo moriendo et damnando fit theologus, non intelligendo, legendo aut speculando."
2. WA 5.176.32–3: "Crux sola est nostra theologia."
3. WA 5.179.31: "Crux probat omnia."

and distress. Yet Luther's approach requires careful contextualization and explanation—which is precisely what we find in this new study.

Dennis Ngien has done the academy and the church a great service through this carefully researched study of one of Luther's core theological themes. Its clarity, erudition, and comprehensiveness make it the best resource presently available for those wishing to penetrate to the heart of Luther's early theological vision. I can only wish that it had been available back in 1979, as I began my own reflections on Luther. I have every confidence that it will introduce a new generation of academics and pastors to this distinctive way of thinking, and its implications.

Alister McGrath
Oxford University

Acknowledgments

Since the publication of *The Suffering of God according to Martin Luther's 'Theologia Crucis'* (1995), I became a keen student of the Reformer, according to whom "the cross is our theology." Then I extended the study of Luther's theology of the cross into his pastoral and devotional writings, which resulted in the monograph, *Luther as a Spiritual Adviser: The Interface of Theology and Piety in Luther's Devotional Writings* (2007). In the years that followed, I explored further how the hermeneutical principles of Luther's theology of the cross govern his exposition of biblical texts, both Old and New Testament. This has resulted in *Fruit for the Soul: Luther on the Lament Psalms* (2015); and now *Luther's Theology of the Cross: Christ in Luther's Sermons on John*. The cross, for Luther, is the context for doing theology; it is so central that everything is challenged and tested by it. It has chastised, corrected, and conformed this author to the image of God's Son, though imperfectly. This book is written with the hope that the faithful ones might reap insights from the reformer's sermons that demonstrate an intrinsic linkage between exegesis and theology, preaching and the care of the soul, theology and piety.

This book is dedicated to five renowned thinkers including Richard Bauckham, Oliver Crisp, Paul Fiddes, Timothy George, and Carl Trueman. Their friendship, mentorship, and scholarship have impacted me and aided me in my academic and spiritual journey. I am deeply indebted to Alister E. McGrath, for his generous foreword, and Carl R. Trueman, for his stimulating afterword to this major work; Robert Kolb, an erudite Luther scholar, for making helpful suggestions; and John Pless, a faithful student of Luther, for his frequent encouragement.

I am grateful for the appointment as Fellow at the Centre for Reformation and Renaissance Studies of University of Toronto, during which this book was undertaken; Brett Potter, an able colleague, for proofreading; Kate Wong, for typesetting the manuscript; the Library staff of Tyndale University

College & Seminary, for their unfailing task in securing materials; Timothee Joset, my research assistant, for assisting in German citation; Janet Clark, my dean, for her unwavering affirmation; and pastors and students, for their insightful interactions which have sharpened the focus and call of being a theologian of the cross.

Finally my salutation belongs to my beloved, Ceceilia, whose perseverance and prayer enable me to finish this work, and Hansel, our son, whose incisive help in writing is a source of solace. Praise be unto God!

Dennis Ngien, Toronto, Canada
Professor of Systematic Theology, Tyndale University College & Seminary, Toronto
October 31, 2017, Reformation Day

Introduction

Martin Luther has been primarily received as a biblical exegete whose vocation was to discover and proclaim the living Gospel of God.[1] Nevertheless, a systematic method can be discerned in Luther's theology— one that accords with Joseph Sittler's definition: "If, then, by system one means that there is in a man's thought a central authority, a pervasive style; namely, a way of bringing every theme and judgment and problem under the rays of the central illumination."[2] Many Luther scholars have arrived at the same thesis: the key to Luther's theological method is the theology of the cross (*theologia crucis*).[3]

> The theology of the cross is a principle of Luther's entire theology and it may not be confined to a special period in his theological development. On the contrary, as in the case of Paul, this formula offers a characteristic of Luther's entire theological thinking. Hence our investigation has to do not with a specific stage of development, but with the demonstration of a theological thinking in Luther.[4]

---

1. The English translation of Luther's works, the American edition will be used in the presentation. References from *Weimar Ausgabe*, the original language version will be cited where helpful. Abbreviations used in this book: LW, for *Luther's Works*;, for *D. Martin Luthers Werke: Kristische Gesamtausgabe*; BR, for *D. Martin Luthers Werke: Kristische Gesamtausgabe. Birefweschsel*; WA TR, for *D. Martin Luthers Werke: Kristische Gesamtausgabe. Trischreden*. This monograph is based on Luther's Sermons on the Gospel of John in LW 22–24, and 69.

2. Sittler, *Doctrine*, 3–4. See also Jaroslav Pelikan, *Luther's Works: Companion Volume. Luther the Expositor: Introduction to the Reformer's Exegetical Writings*, 42–43. (Hereafter cited as Pelikan, *Companion Volume*.)

3. Loewenich, *Luther's Theology of the Cross*, 13, 17–18; Prenter, *Luther's Theology of the Cross*, 2; Lortz, *Reformation*, 208–10; McGrath, *Luther's Theology of the Cross*, 1–2; Lienhard, *Luther*, 65–6; Althaus, *Theology of Martin Luther*, 34.

4. Loewenich, *Luther's Theology of the Cross*, 13.

The theology of the cross is the way Luther does theology from the ground up and in its entirety, not just focusing on one doctrine (such as atonement) set alongside others. "The cross of Christ is the only instruction in the Word of God there is, the purest theology."[5] Later Luther stressed: "The cross alone is our theology (*CRUX sola est nostra theologiae*)."[6] Through this, Luther conceives of the whole content of the Christian faith and the task of Christian theology.[7]

The theological themes of the theology of the cross laid down in his *Heidelberg Disputation*—the hidden and revealed God, the paradoxical action of God in contrary appearances, the antipodal relation of law and gospel and faith and works, the priority of God's Word to human reason or experience, the coordinate structure of alien work and proper work, the uniqueness of Christ's atoning efficacy, and the experience of temptation—shape his reading of the Gospel of John. Johann Bugenhagen assumed the primary responsibility for preaching in the Wittenberg parish church of St. Mary. But when he was absent from Wittenberg, Luther assumed the Wittenberg pulpit. While retaining the traditional lectionary readings for preaching on the Sundays and festivals of the Christian year, he proposed John's gospel should occupy a special place in preaching over the course of the week. In *German Mass and Order of Service* (1526), Luther urged that "the evangelist John, who so mightily teaches faith," should constitute the serial text for the Saturday Vesper sermons, a practice adopted at once, and was formally incorporated in the Wittenberg church order of 1533.[8] Between 1528 to 1540, Luther preached on most of John's gospel. He preached on John 1–4 between 1537 and 1540, during and after Bugenhagen's sojourn in Denmark; on John 6–8 between 1530 and 1532, during Bugenhagen's stay in Lübeck; on John 14–16 in 1533 and 1534, not on Saturdays but on Sundays, while Bugenhagen was resident in Wittenberg; on John 16–20:18, during his first assignment for Bugenhagen, in 1528–29; and on John 20:19–31, spanning the years from 1527 to 1540. Hence this study places Luther's sermons on the Gospel of John in the larger context of his whole theology, rather than strictly as a demonstration of his Christology.[9] The chapters in the present

---

5. See "Operationes in Psalms, 1519–1521," on Psalms 6:11 (WA 4.217.2-3) as cited in Kolb, "Luther on the Theology of the Cross," 34.

6. See "In XV Psalmos graduum, 1532/33" (1540), WA 40. III.193.6-7 and 19-20, as cited in Kolb, "Luther on the Theology of the Cross," 34.

7. See Sasse, "Theologia Crucis," 387–88. 6:11.

8. LW 53.68.

9. For studies of Luther's Christology, see Dorner, *History*, 53–115, where he provides a compact summary of Luther's Christology; Lage, *Martin Luther's Christology and Ethics*, where he shows a close linkage between Christology and ethics; Posset,

volume are arranged for pedagogical purposes; they do not reflect divisions within Luther's commentary. This study aims to bring Luther's voice within our hearing, focusing our attention on his interpretation of the major themes of the theology of the cross as they appear in his sermons. As will become clear, there is frequent return to, and elaboration of, these themes, as he works his way through the Johannine Gospel.

Luther's Theology of the Cross in the Heidelberg Disputation (1518)

During his theological education, Luther was very much preoccupied with the search for the "kernel" of truth: "the only theology which was of any value was that which penetrated the kernel of the nut and germ of the wheat and the marrow of the bone."[10] Already in the *Heidelberg Disputation* (1518), a year after the posting of his *Ninety-five Theses* (1517), Luther propounds that the only theology of real value is found in none other than the crucified Christ. The *Heidelberg Disputation* represented the first opportunity for Luther to debate his ideas during the triennial convention of the Augustinian Order in Germany. Johannes von Staupitz, vicar of the order in Germany, exhorted Luther not to become controversial before Pope Leo X, counselling him especially to refrain from attacking the system of indulgences as he did in his ninety-five theses. Instead, Staupitz directed him to present his wider vision of the evangelical faith. The Heidelberg theses are vital in presenting Luther's ongoing theological reflection on such themes as righteousness, grace, justification, law and gospel, alien and proper work, the hidden and revealed God, wrath and mercy, the dialectical character of revelation, faith and works, God's Word versus reason, and the suffering of Christ and the Christian.

Theses 19 to 21 of the Disputation provide us with Luther's theology of the cross, which is essentially a theology of revelation. In keeping with his

---

Luther's Catholic Christology, where he focuses exclusively on Luther's Christology in Johannine epistles; Lienhard, *Luther*, where he traces the historical development of Luther's christological themes from the early to late stages of his career in an illuminating manner; and Siggins, *Martin Luther's Doctrine of Christ*, where he provides an inductive examination of the vocabulary and major themes of Luther's christological doctrine. Siggins' study is imbued with numerous citations from John's gospel. However, this study exclusively based on Luther's sermons on John has not been undertaken as a separate monograph, and will supplement the standard studies of Luther's Christology by Siggins and Lienhard. The theology of the cross as an interpretive principle of Luther's sermons on John will also fill a lacuna in Luther scholarship.

10. WA BR I.17, no. 5.43ff as quoted by Gerhard Ebeling, *Luther: An Introduction to His Thought*, trans. R. A. Wilson (Philadelphia: Fortress, 1970), 248-49.

search for a gracious God, the emphasis in Luther's theology is knowledge of God that is saving. For him, the true saving knowledge of God is to be found in God's self-revelation through Christ and the cross. Referring to Romans 1:20, Luther asserts that whoever attempts to see the invisible things of God, viz., his power, wisdom, righteousness and divinity, through insight into what can be seen in creation, "does not deserve to be called a theologian."[11] God does not wish to be known through his invisible things or through his creation (theses 19–20), as such knowledge is not true knowledge, since it arises out of human speculation. This kind of knowledge of God, which "the theologian of glory" secures through speculation upon the invisible things of God, is not the consequence of God's revelation through the cross and suffering of Christ, and therefore, in Luther's view, is not salvific. Recognition of the traces of divinity deduced from created things does not make one worthy or wise.[12] "Good works," or human virtue, likewise, are misplaced sites for discovering God. Luther argues: "It is impossible for a person not to be puffed up by his good works unless he has first been deflated and destroyed by suffering and evil until he knows that he is worthless and that his works are not his but God's."[13] Thesis 25 states: "He is not righteous who does much, but he who, without work, believes much in Christ."[14] This thesis "rejects the Aristotelian notion of justice (as) that (which) is acquired by developing an appropriate attitude or habit of action," thereby repudiating the attitude of anyone that boasts that he is wise and learned in the law (cf. Thesis 23).[15]

Thesis 20 spells out the paradoxical nature of the cross as revelation: here God's revelation is indirect and concealed. In a sermon dated February 24, 1517, Luther says: "Man hides what is his own in order to conceal it, but God hides what is his in order to reveal it."[16] God's revelation is characteristically veiled and hidden, since human creatures are incapable of seeing

---

11. LW 31.52.

12. "This is apparent in the example of those who were 'theologians' and still were called fools by the apostle in Rom 1:22," in LW 31.52.

13. LW 31.53.

14. LW 31.55.

15. Pannenberg, "Theology of the Cross," 162. Cf. LW 31.277; WA 1.614.17–11 (Explanation of the 95 Theses, 1518): "The theologian of glory, however, learns from Aristotle that the object of the will is good and the good is worthy to be loved, while the evil, on the other hand, is worthy of hate. He learns that God is the highest good and exceeding loveable." See also Luther's "Disputation Against Scholastic Theology," (1517), LW 31.9–10; WA 1.224, where he rejects the efficacy of the will: "One must concede that the will is not free to strive toward whatever is declared good. This is in opposition to Scotus and Gabriel" (Thesis 10).

16. LW 51.26.

God directly, that is, in naked form. If human creatures were to see God's face, they would die. Luther alludes to Exodus 33:23 to grasp this paradox: What Moses was able to see is not God's face but only God's "back" parts.[17] Luther intensifies the paradox, asserting that the invisible God is genuinely revealed and known in the visible humanity of Christ and his cross. He further clarifies in Thesis 21: "He who does not know Christ does not know God hidden in suffering."[18] A true theologian knows God, as he is hidden or clothed in the humanity of Christ, rests on his mother's arms and finally dies on the cross of Christ. "He deserves to be called a theologian, however, who comprehends the visible and manifest parts of God seen through suffering and the cross."[19] A theologian of glory "prefers works to suffering, glory to the cross, strength to weakness, (and) wisdom to folly . . . (It hates) the cross and suffering and loves works and the glory of works."[20] Luther refers to this theologian as an enemy of the cross: "A theology of glory calls evil good and good evil. A theology of the cross calls the thing what it actually is."[21] A theology of the cross is a radical declaration, in that it says that it is God incarnate who suffers death and humiliation on the cross for the sake of humanity's salvation.

To know God aright is to know him in his opposites: in the folly of the world rather than in wisdom, in weakness rather in strength, in suffering rather than in power, in humility rather than in majesty. "God is to be found precisely where theologians of glory are horrified to find: as a kid in a crib, as a criminal on a cross, as a corpse in a crypt."[22] True theology must be concerned with God as he has chosen to reveal himself, not with preconceived or abstract notions of God. Hence any human attempts to know God by way of deductive reflection upon the nature of humanity's moral sense or the pattern of the created order are rejected by Luther as misguided theologies of glory. Philip of Bethsaida, for Luther, represents one such theologian of glory who seeks to know God apart from God's self-revelation in the crucified Christ (cf. John 14:8–9). On the contrary, a theologian of the cross discerns by faith the presence of the hidden God in his self-revelation in Christ. In contrast to a speculative knowledge of God gained by reason, the knowledge of God in the theology of the cross is available only to the

---

17. See Lull, *Martin Luther's Theological Writings*, 43, where the word "back" is used. In LW 31.52, the word "manifest" is used. They share the same meaning.
18. LW 31.53.
19. LW 31.53.
20. LW 31.39–40.
21. LW 31.45.
22. Kolb, "Luther on the Theology of the Cross," 41.

eyes of faith. Luther's theology of the cross is a dialectical principle inextricably linked with faith: "The correlative to *crux sola* is *sola fide*, as it is through faith, and through faith alone, that the true significance of the cross is perceived."[23]

A theologian of the cross does not gape at God in heaven, bypassing Christ's humanity. This is a predominant theme in Luther's sermons on John's gospel, wherein Luther accentuates the unity of God and humanity in Christ, emphasizing Christ's humanity as the instrument of ascent to God. God reveals himself by hiding in the midst of human existence ruined by the fall. A theology of the cross thus seeks God in the way Scripture teaches: to start at the point where God himself starts, namely, in the Virgin's womb, in the manger, at his mother's breasts. It also leads us away from the throne of the Supreme Majesty or the naked God towards the humble manger of Christ the man. Any attempt to execute the opposite movement will either end up in utter ignorance of God or dashing us against the terror of the true God's Majesty. The absolution of the terrifying hidden God is done by Christ—the revealed God, to whom faith clings.[24]

To be safe and saved, one must travel the road mapped out by Christ, and cleave to his Word. For God has covenanted and sealed himself in Christ, certifying that he alone bestows his loving things: grace, forgiveness of sin, eternal life, and the Holy Spirit. Hence all lofty thinking and speculation about God in his majesty, all attempts at obtaining private revelations without external means, and every effort to rid sin through works or holiness, not only err and mislead people but also plunge them into the abyss. Faith in Christ overcomes all miseries of life—sin, wrath, and death—and nothing can undo it!

Another feature of Luther's theology of the cross is that God is known through suffering and the cross, both of Christ and of the Christian. The cross of Christ and that of the Christian must be distinguished, but not separated. The theology of the cross is practical.

> The cross of Christ and the cross of the Christian belong together. The meaning of the cross does not disclose itself in contemplative thought but only in suffering experience. The theologian of the cross does not confront the cross of Christ as a spectator, but is himself drawn into this event. He knows that God can be found only in cross and suffering . . . For God himself is "hidden in suffering" and wants us to worship him as such. . . . If we are serious about the idea of God and the concept of faith in the

---

23. McGrath, *Luther's Theology of the Cross*, 174.
24. Forde, *Theology*, 29–30.

theology of the cross, we are faced with the demand of a life under the cross.[25]

A fundamental contention of Luther's theology of the cross is that God is active in suffering and trials (cf. Thesis 16).

> So far from regarding suffering and evil as a nonsensical intrusion into the world (which Luther regards as the opinion of a theologian of glory) the "theologian of the cross" regards such suffering as his most precious treasure, for revealed and yet hidden in precisely such sufferings is none other than the living God, working out the salvation of those whom he loves.[26]

Trials (*tentatio*) are God's alien work, intended to crush people's self-confidence and reduce them to a state of doubt and despair in order that they might finally turn to God for aid. God creates the experience of temptation and suffering, through which he constitutes us as the beneficiaries of his salvific work. "Through the cross works are dethroned and (the old) Adam, who is especially edified by works, is crucified."[27] Having been reduced to nothing through the cross and suffering, the Christian knows that he is lovely because he is loved by God.[28]

The distinction between the alien work and proper work of God parallels the distinction between law and gospel. The law as God's alien work truly condemns, but only so that we might therefore cling to the gospel, his proper work. It is the same God who performs in us an alien work of humbling, as in law, in order to perform in us his proper work of forgiving, as in gospel. God corresponds to himself in this apparently contradictory activity between law and gospel; the former leads to the latter.

> . . . the law makes us aware of sin so that, having recognized our sin, we may seek and receive his grace. . . . The law humbles, grace exalts. The law effects fear and wrath, grace effects hope and mercy . . . Thus an action which is alien to God's nature results in a deed belonging to his very nature: he makes a person a sinner so that he may make him righteous.[29]

A proper understanding of law and gospel is essential for a proper interpretation of Scripture and the correct way of doing theology. For Luther,

---

25. Loewenich, *Luther's Theology of the Cross*, 113.
26. McGrath, *Luther's Theology of the Cross*, 151.
27. LW 31.53.
28. LW 31.57.
29. LW 31.50–51.

God assaults a person through law to tear him down and thus to justify him through gospel. The reality of a saving relationship is encountered in the paradoxical act of God, the one who works within the dialectic between law and gospel, alien and proper work, wrath and mercy, glory and humility, majesty and shame (cf. Theses 23–27). God himself determines to be divinely loving and good, and is not determined by the attitude or condition of those upon whom goodness and kindness are bestowed. God "gladly waste(s) his kindness on the ungrateful."[30] It is precisely in this sense that God "proves that he is good by nature."[31] The Christian lives under the God whose glory is to give, to act, and to love freely. God's love does not create out of pre-existent salvific materials, but creates strictly out of nothing (*ex nihilo*) a people no longer under divine wrath. This flows forth intrinsically from the cross, as stated in Thesis 28:

> . . . the love of God which lives in man loves sinners, evil persons, fools, and weaklings in order that to make them righteous, good, wise, and strong. Rather than seeking its own good, the love of God flows forth and bestows good. Therefore sinners are attractive because they are loved: they are not loved because they are attractive. That is why human love shuns sinners and evil men. As Christ said, "I came not to call the righteous but sinners" (Matt 9:13) . . . This is the love of the cross, born of the cross, which turns in the direction where it does not find good which it may enjoy, but where it may confer good upon the bad and needy persons.[32]

Major Features of Luther's Sermons on the Gospel of John

In the *Prefaces to the New Testament*, Luther writes of the "true and noblest book of the New Testament," expressing his special love for the Gospel of John. The reasons for Luther's devotion to this gospel: St. John's masterful work on the article of justification and the causative character of Christ's words. Luther sees

> John's gospel and St. Paul's epistles, especially that to the Romans, and St. Peter's first epistle as the true kernel and marrow of all books. They ought properly to be the foremost books . . . For in them you do not find many works and miracles of

---

30. LW 14.106 (Ps 118:29): ". . . God is good; for His steadfast love endures forever."
31. LW 14.106.
32. LW 31.57.

INTRODUCTION 9

> Christ described, but you do find depicted in mastery fashion how faith in Christ overcomes sin, death, and hell, and gives life, righteousness, and salvation . . .

> If I had to do without one or the other—either the works or the preaching of Christ—I would rather do without the works than without his preaching. For the works do not help me, but his words give life, as he himself says (John 6:63). Now John writes very little about the works of Christ, but very much about his preaching, while the other evangelists write much about his works and little about his preaching. Therefore John's gospel is the one, fine, true, and chief gospel, and is far, far to be preferred over the other three and placed high above them.[33]

For Luther, John's gospel, St. Paul's letters, and 1 Peter constitute "the real kernel and marrow of all the books," for they are the outstanding teachers of justification by faith. John's true greatness consists in the fact that he is "the master" of the chief doctrine of justification by faith: "The evangelist John treats of this article of faith more than the other evangelists." Commenting on John 6:52, Luther avers:

> This article of justification is the chief doctrine. St. John expounded it especially. In this he proved himself a master. St. John cannot be sufficiently praised for treating this doctrine of justification. I cannot discourse on it more clearly and more forcefully than John did here through the Holy Spirit.[34]

Luther insists, while commenting on John 6:47, 51, that the whole of Scripture ought to be interpreted in the light of the chief article of justification by faith:

> Consequently when Matthew and the other evangelists speak of good works, we must first give the floor to John. He teaches us how to obtain eternal life and righteousness: righteousness must precede all good works . . . When Matthew and Luke speak about good works, they must be understood against this background. The evangelist Matthew does not emphasize this important and true doctrine of faith in Christ as much as John does; he expounds the other part, the works and fruit of faith. The evangelist John, however, stresses the Christian faith

---

33. LW 35.361–62. Also quoted in Pfitzner, "Luther as Interpreter," 65.
34. LW 23.129 (WA 33.199).

more vigorously than the other evangelists, who have described mainly the miracles of Christ.[35]

John's gospel is "one fine, true, and chief gospel," which Christians must learn by heart, because of its primary emphasis on the preaching and words of Christ that "give life" (John 6:63), rather than reporting Christ's miracles, which is characteristic of the other gospels. This in no way denigrates the other gospels, for there is only one Gospel of Jesus Christ, not four.[36] It is Luther's basic conviction that even though Christ is named, preached, and pictured in various ways throughout the gospel accounts, he remains ever one and the same Christ.[37] Hence Christ's mouth—his own words which are precisely those of the Father—to which Luther binds himself governs his exposition of the text. God's word is causative, determining the way things are. "The basic category for Luther's doctrine of the Word of God was not the category of 'being' but the category of 'deed.'"[38] This is evident in Luther's exposition of Psalm 2: "In the case of God to speak is to do, and the word is the deed."[39] The causative character of God's Word, through which God's deed is accomplished, so thrilled Luther that he never tired of teaching on it.[40] The Word of God possesses an inherent militancy in securing its own followers.

Sermons are, of course, different things than dogmatic disputations and philosophical treatises; hence, Luther, in the context of preaching, avoids the technicalities that characterize his academic and more formal ecclesiastical writings. Hence, polemical discussion of the *filioque* (that the Spirit proceeds from the Son), the Eucharistic controversy with Zwingli (that human nature in Christ is ubiquitous), or the debate with Erasmus over freewill and predestination (that only grace can heal the bound will) do not emerge in his sermons.

Within the Gospel of John, Luther highly favored the farewell discourse of Jesus in John 14–17, and counted his commentary on this periscope as the best of his own writing. As Jaroslav Pelikan points out, at Table in the autumn of 1540, Luther wrote of his commentary on St. John 14–17: "This

---

35. LW 23.108–09 (WA 33.165–66).

36. LW 35.117–18. See Barth, *Church Dogmatics*, vol. 1, part 2, where he argues that Luther's Christology is closer to the Gospel of John, while Calvin's is more closely linked to the Synoptic Gospels.

37. LW 24.50 (WA 45.507).

38. Pelikan, *Companion Volume*, 50.

39. LW 12.33.

40. For a major study of Luther's doctrine of the Word of God, see Kolb, *Martin Luther and the Enduring Word of God*.

is the best book I have written."[41] For Luther, the farewell discourse forms Christ's comforting charge to his followers and provides a set of words which can satisfy human longing in all trials and troubles.

> [These are] the most precious and cheering consolation, the sweetest words of Christ, the faithful and beloved Savior, words of farewell to His disciples as He is about to leave them, words such as no man on earth is able to employ toward his dearest and best friends. They show how He provides for them out of the pure, ineffable, burning love of His heart, and how He is concerned about them far more sincerely than any man is about the greatest need and danger of his most intimate friend. In His concern for them He forgets His own anguish and anxiety, which must have filled His heart at this time, as He Himself confided to His disciples: "My soul is very sorrowful, even to death" (Matt 26:38). Moreover, His battle against death and devil had now reached its highest point. Here Christ highly poured out His great and heartfelt comfort, which is the property of all Christendom and which men should long for in all troubles and afflictions.[42]

Moreover, nowhere else in Scripture than in this closing discourse, Luther claims, are the true, chief high articles of Christian dogma—Trinity, Christology and justification by faith—juxtaposed most powerfully and convincingly so that they become "the highest and most precious treasure and consolation"[43] in Christendom.

From what God does in Christ, we see who God is as God for us (*pro nobis*). Since Luther's theology is about God's ways with us, he particularly focuses on the *pro nobis* aspects of Christ's person. In Luther's accounting, the logic of St. John's gospel can be formulated as such: the "economic

---

41. See Jaroslav Pelikan's Introduction, Vol. 24.x. Luther's favorable verdict on the published sermons is reflected not only in his preface but also in the appraisal of Johann Mathesius (1504-65): "The Herr Doctor often took [his sermons on John 14-17] to church with him and liked to read in it. As I and others heard from his own mouth at table, this was the best book he had written, 'though I did not write it,' he said, 'but Dr. Caspar Cruciger showed his deep understanding and great diligence in [editing] it. After the [translation of the] Holy Bible, this should be [esteemed as] my most worthy and precious book.'" See Johann Mathesius, *Historien von des Ehrwirdigen in Gott Seligen thewren Manns Gottes Doctoris Martini Luthers, anfang, lehr, leben, und sterben*, in Loesche, ed., *Johannes Mathesius: Ausgewahlte Werke*, 3.362 as cited in Introduction to John 17, LW 69.8.

42. LW 24.7 (WA XLV.468).

43. LW 24.8 (WA XLV.468).

actions of God"[44] in Christ through the Holy Spirit stand in the foreground and it is through these that we are told who God is and what he does for us (*pro nobis*). What we experience in the economy of salvation is indeed God in his essence and true relationship to us.

John is, in Luther's estimate, "a master above all the other evangelists, for he treats of this doctrine of Christ's divinity and His humanity persistently and diligently,"[45] but with an emphasis on his office from which Christ receives his name: our Savior, our Salvation, Life, and Righteousness.[46] Like Bernard of Clairvaux, Luther never separated the two natures of Christ from each other, but saw them as united in such a way that the significance lies in the work this one Person came to achieve for us.[47] The Incarnation is conceived of in terms of the central fact of salvation, the passion and death of Christ. "The Incarnation is not only inseparable from the redemptive act; the metaphysical mystery of the hypostatic union is considered solely in the act of salvation of which it forms the very reality."[48] Just as Christology has soteriology as its aim, so also the doctrine of the Trinity is understood in terms of the economic action upon sinners. How God is in and for himself in his immanent life does not concern Luther, but rather how God is for us in his economic action towards us. Luther observes a movement inherent to both St. John's Christology and his doctrine of the Trinity: it is a movement "from below to above,"[49] namely, from Christ as man to Christ as God in the concrete unity of the One indivisible person, who is one being with his Father.

Luther's sermons cover the entire soteriological descent [the incarnation, his suffering, burial and resurrection] and ascent [ascension] for us (*pro nobis*), in which we participate by the Holy Spirit in his life and glory. Henceforth we hold to Christ's words, where the Holy Spirit and his acts are located. This too is St. John's way of speaking about how we might be seized by the paternal love revealed in the Son, the one and same love that flows between the Father and Son, and is communicated to our hearts by the Holy Spirit. Our identity of being God's elect is forged in Christ, known to the

---

44. The technical phrase "the economic actions of God" refers to the salvific actions of God upon us.

45. LW 23.77 (WA 33.116).

46. LW 23.77–78 (WA 33.116). This is evident earlier in Luther's explanation of the Second Article of the *Small Catechism* (1528), where we witness how quickly he comes to soteriology because this is at the heart of his Christology.

47. Posset, *Pater Bernhardus*, 243.

48. Congar, "Considerations and Reflections," 377; Elert, *Structure of Lutheranism*, 68.

49. Althaus, *Theology of Martin Luther*, 186.

Father, and made certain in our hearts by the Holy Spirit; all three persons work together as one God in constituting a people of God translated from God's wrath to God's mercy. To know the Father means not only to know him as the Creator of heaven and earth but as the One who sent the Son into the world for our redemption. The sum of Christianity consists in learning to know the Father, the true name of God, whom Christ reveals and continues to make known to the world through faith and confession, the action of the Holy Spirit.

To amass bountiful sublime things, Luther follows St. John, who teaches us the art and benefit of knowing Christ: that we know how and where to find the true God; how we may be equipped to combat heresies including Arianism, Manicheanism, Eutychianism, and Nestorianism; how we may face the terrifying reality of death; how we may be justified before God; how we may rely on God's mercy to resist all sorts of trials and temptation and conquer the intolerable terror of wrath against sin; how to pray to God with profit; how to differentiate the true Church from the false one; how to reap consolation from the Word and its humble forms; how to find assurance from Christ's priestly prayer; how to make salutary use of Christ's passion and resurrection; how to achieve greater works on earth; how to live within the dialectic of law and gospel; how to live paradoxically between present suffering that is immense, and eschatological joy that is full and complete in yonder life, but only experienced partially now. Faith will behold the matchless glory of God in Christ, now dimly perceived, but there fully grasped without veil and covering. In all this, Jesus is the Master Commentator, in whose lap we must nestle in order that we might harvest a superabundance of power and consolation. Plain are the words with which St. John paints the picture of Christ, but magnitude is the substance from which we reap the fruit and power of the magnificent and innocent person and the efficacious activities of Christ. These themes Luther covers in his sermons on John's gospel reflect considerably his theology of the cross, the organizing principle of his exposition and theological task.

Luther as a Pastor: The Proper Usage of John's Gospel

The Reformation itself was "a movement of applied theology and lived Christianity."[50] Hence one cannot overlook that Luther was fundamentally "a care-taker of souls,"[51] whose ingenuity lies in his usage of the biblical

---

50. George, *Reading Scriptures*, 208.

51. Spitz, "Luther Ecclesiast," 117. See also Wengert, "Introducing the Pastoral Luther," in *Pastoral Luther*, 1–29.

message as a source of pastoral encouragement. His exposition of the text is pastorally motivated, and is in no way a purely theoretical undertaking. The sermons on John's gospel show the intrinsic, close, and causal link between doctrine and consolation. They are an exercise of his vocation as a pastor, or more precisely, as a theologian of the cross who seeks to inculcate the good news of justification by faith in his people, leading them to experience it within the dialectic of law and gospel. For Luther, a true theologian learns to discern in afflictions their opposites—God's marvelous works and his insurmountable comfort. He discerns not as the world does, not through physical but spiritual eyes. He learns to embrace the invisible things and refuses to be overcome by the visible, atrocious circumstances. This requires faith on the part of the wounded souls as well as skill and grace to discern, so that in their manifold afflictions they might behold the oceanic immensity of God's mercy. The whole of the Christian life is to be wrapped up with the golden art of knowing God aright, that is, through his opposites: not in power but weakness, not in majesty but in humility, not in glory but in the shame of the cross. This art should occupy a true theologian, who seeks God where he wills to be found, namely, in the incarnate Christ, even contrary to reason or experience, extolls Christ above all so that his Words, his ways, and his will govern all our thoughts and activities, and permits Christ to be the touchstone, by which we differentiate between Christian knowledge and doctrine and its opposites, civil and spiritual kingdom, Christ's righteousness and human righteousness.

As a faithful pastor who preaches regularly, Luther displays considerable freedom in speaking to his people of the assaults of the devil and the world because of the Word and the office they hold; he shows keen interest in teaching them where they might seek consolation and strength, namely, in Christ's words. Luther was keenly aware of the broken and fragmentary world that needs the hearing and healing of the gospel; the former grounds the latter, that we are healed by opening our ears to his Word, and simultaneously closing our eyes to the horrible appearances. Luther exhorted his sheep to meditate on the Word, for their comfort and strengthening of our faith and for the vexation of the devil and his hirelings. The godly ones must adhere to God's ordained way upon which we must walk: we must despair of everything in us and in the world and cling wholeheartedly to Christ and what he has achieved for us. Christ's voice in John's gospel articulates Luther's deep-felt emotions about his faith, and provides him models with which to inculcate in his parishioners the saving knowledge of God in Jesus Christ.

CHAPTER 1

St. John's Way of Speaking
The Person and Work of Christ

From the very beginning of his commentary on John's gospel, Luther advises that the church must be conversant with the Apostle John, particularly "his way of speaking."[1] We must acquaint ourselves with the Fourth Evangelist's logic and the manner with which he speaks powerfully of the subject and substance of the holy Christian faith, as already enshrined in the Nicene and the Apostles' Creeds. Unless the Son, who is in the bosom of the Father, reveals, no mortal soul can fathom what is said about God and his attitude towards sinners. It is St. John to whom is revealed the person of Jesus Christ, who is fully God and fully man, and together with it the soteriological significance of dual-nature Christology: that Christ who is both very God and very man is the rock on which our eternal welfare and salvation rest. Luther's exposition of John 1 addresses major christological heresies, and his orthodox Christology begins to shine. Not speculation but revelation yields the knowledge of the Trinity and Christology, which he conceives as the central facts of salvation. This is St. John's way, to which we must cling, of apprehending Christ aright: the one indivisible person of Jesus Christ, altogether pure and innocent, has been granted to us by the Father to be our High Priest, redeemer, and humble servant. Christ alone, about whom John the Baptist testifies, toward whom Moses and the prophets point, and through whom God's grace, truth, life, glory, love, and forgiveness are revealed, is the unshakable ground of salvation he achieved for us. Just as the knowledge of sin is a predicate of God's revelation, not human

1. LW 22.5 (WA 46.540).

reason, so is the true and saving knowledge of God. God reveals through the law that we are drowning in sin, a condition only the Lamb of God can overcome. Sin must not remain in our conscience where the law has deposited it, lest despair and damnation are the outcome. Christians must learn the art of extolling these words with a joyful heart: "And the Word became flesh," and praising God for his infinite love bestowed upon the wretched human beings reflected in the self-humiliation of God by becoming one of us.

Chalcedonian Christology Affirmed

Luther quoted the Nicene Creed[2] to confess Christ as "begotten of the Father before all worlds, God of God, Light of Light, very God of very God," and in time also very man, born of Mary. He affirms the orthodox doctrine of Christ formulated at the Council of Chalcedon in AD 451, in which Christ is fully God and fully man, but one Person. The heretics have attacked both natures of Christ. Cerinthius began to assail the second article of faith as early as the apostolic days, denying Christ's divinity; the Manichaeans impugned his humanity. Luther's contemporaries, who followed Kaspar Schwenkfeld,[3] denied true incarnation, averring that because he was conceived solely by the Holy Spirit, Christ did not assume flesh like ours. Christ is a celestial being, and thus his flesh was heavenly, not earthly. Against this, Luther affirmed that Christ, our Savior, was "the real and natural fruit of Mary's vaginal womb," as is borne out in Luke 1:42: "Blessed is the fruit of your womb." Mary gives rise not to Jesus' deity, which he has from eternity, but his humanity. Mary, "the mother of God's eternal Son,"[4] imparts all that she is to Jesus.

St. John, for Luther, was pre-eminent among the apostles in his portrayal of the divinity of Christ. The evangelist affirms the pre-cosmic existence of the Son: "In the beginning was the Word." Cerinthius[5] and other heretics abounded at this time (cf. 1 John 1:18; 4:1). Basing his proof on Moses, Cerinthius denied that the Word was God. The two texts he cited

---

2. LW 22.28 (WA 46.560).

3. LW 22.21, note 19, where Kaspar Schwenkfeld, Luther's contemporary, was cited. Luther also disagreed with his doctrine of the Lord's Supper.

4. LW 22.24 (WA 46.556).

5. LW 22.7, note 2, where Irenaeus, *Against Heresies*, Bk. I, ch. 26 was quoted: "He portrayed Jesus as not being born of a virgin but as the son of Joseph and Mary, born in the ordinary way . . . After His baptism Christ descended upon Him in the form of a dove from the Supreme Potentate and performed miracles. But at the end Christ left Jesus. Then Jesus suffered and rose again, while Christ, as a spiritual being, remained incapable of suffering."

as support of his position are Deuteronomy 6:4 ("The Lord our God is one God") and Deuteronomy 5:7 ("You shall have no other gods before Me"). St. John now quotes Moses in his attack against their heresies and repudiates them completely. Moses began with these words: "In the beginning God created the heavens and the earth . . . And God spoke a word, and there was light" (Gen 1:1–3). The phrase "in the beginning" antedates the creation of the universe and of any other creature. Based on this, St. John offered a far more explicit statement about the eternality of the Word, that "this Word was with God, that God was this Word, and this Word had existed from all eternity."[6] Just as a human person has a thought, or word, or a conversation within himself, so too God from all eternity is pregnant with a Word, a speech, a thought, or a conversation within himself in his divine life. No one knew of this until the Word became flesh and proclaimed this to us. Thus John 1:18 says: "The Son, who is in the bosom of the Father, has revealed him to us." However a wide chasm exists between the thoughts, discussions and words of the mortal beings and those of the eternal and almighty God. Unlike created beings that exist in time, God is from all eternity. Luther articulates this with the medieval scholastic doctrine of divine aseity: "What [God] is, He is of Himself from eternity. On the contrary, whatever we are, we received from Him, not from ourselves. He alone has everything from Himself."[7] The Word in which he engaged with himself in his divine essence and which reflects the thoughts of his heart is "as complete and excellent and perfect as God himself."[8]

In his defense against Cerinthius, Luther latches onto the two words used by St. John: "existed" and "created." That which is created did not exist before; heaven, moon, stars, and human creatures were created in the beginning. But that which was not begun, created, or made, and yet is and has its being must have existed antecedently. Thereby St. John attests that the Son of God, who is the image of the invisible God (Col 1:15), was not created nor made; for before the world, before all creaturely beings were made, and before the beginning of things, the speech or the Word was already in God, without whom nothing was made. Except God the Creator alone, everything was created, and has its being in God. Luther notes that John did not say "'God created the Word.' or 'The Word came into being,' but 'The Word was already in existence.'"[9] And all things were made by the Word, as

---

6. LW 22.8 (WA 46.542–43).

7. LW 22.9, (WA 46.544) note 5, where Anselm of Canterbury, *Monologium*, ch. 6 was cited.

8. LW 22.10 (WA 46.545).

9. LW 22.14 (WA 46.548).

the following verse states: "All things were made through Him, and without Him was not anything made that was made" (v.3). He must be God, if we grant the premise that the Word preceded all creatures. The Word cannot be numbered with the created order, as among the creatures, but with the uncreated order, thus receiving his eternal being in the Godhead.

With Augustine,[10] Luther used the word "Person," as the fathers did too.[11] The word "Person" translates *hypostasis*, "an essence or substance" which comprises a class by itself, namely "God."[12] Verse 2, "He was in the beginning with God," reminds the reader of the distinction of persons within the one Godhead. Where was the Word? "He was with God, and He was God." The Word, which is the Son, is and remains eternal and true God together with the Father. Just as a human son receives his flesh, blood, and being from his father, so the Son of God, born of the Father, derives his divine essence and nature from the Father from eternity. However, the Father can impart his entire divine nature to the Son, constituting him one being with the Father; but a human father can impart only a fragment of it, not his complete nature. Unlike a human father, God's essence is indivisibly One. In the same Godhead, neither is there partition nor division of essence; there is no before or after, thus no chronological sequence; neither higher nor lower, thus no difference in ontological status; neither greater nor lesser, thus no order of rank in being. Though the Son receives his essence from the Father, the Son is co-equal with the Father in deity. He is fully God, just as the Father is. Likewise the Holy Spirit partakes of the one divine majesty and nature with the Father and the Son. These are not two gods, but two persons in the one and same Godhead, along with the Father.

Arius, says Luther, was "the most artful and subtle of all the enemies."[13] In this text, "The Word was God," Arius alleged that the term "God" did not refer to "the true, natural God but to a titular deity."[14] It refers to "the name and the commission: 'Be a god on earth!'"[15] Divinity is Christ's, not by nature but by conferral. The title "God" is not intrinsic to his being; it is honorific, that he was named "God" because he was an unusual person who excelled all others. Whilst Arius acknowledged that Father and Son were two distinct persons, he distinguished between them by relegating Christ to

10. Cf. Augustine, *On the Trinity*, IV, ch. 20, par. 27 as cited in LW 22.16 (WA 46.549).

11. LW 22.16 (WA 46.550) note 13. Luther may have gained his knowledge of this from Augustine, *On the Trinity*, V. ch. 8, par. 9, 10.

12. LW 22.16 (WA 46.550).

13. LW 22.18 (WA 46.552).

14. LW 22.18 (WA 46.552).

15. LW 22.19 (WA 46.552).

a mere Creature. A line of demarcation is drawn between the uncreated order and the created order, and Christ belongs to the latter.[16] However, Arius' position runs contrary to the text. Luther writes: "For, if He existed, then it is impossible that He should have been made or created; but together with the Father He was true and eternal God from all eternity, equal in power and majesty."[17] Arius' blasphemous lie was convincingly refuted by the following verse: "All things were made through Him" (v. 3). With Augustine,[18] Luther affirmed the perspicuity of this text concerning Jesus' deity. By "all," St. John includes every creature so that nothing creaturely is excluded from his creative work. In addition to affirming the Word as the Creator of all things, St. John now draws a negative inference: "Without Him [i.e., the Word] nothing was made." If everything has been created through the Word and nothing exists without him, then the Word cannot be ranked among the created order. He, the Word, who already existed in the beginning, is the Creator of all things. He not only antedated all creatures, but also he was a co-worker and equal Creator of all things with the Father. With respect to divine nature, there is no difference between him and the Father. As one God, both the Father and the Son work together in the economic work of creation. The Son is co-equal Creator with the Father, as is borne out in John 5:17: "My Father is working still, and I am working" (cf. Eph 3:9; Col 1:15–16; Heb 1:2). St. John's deity is not deistic; after completing creation, God does not take leave of absence without any concern for its maintenance. For just as God creates us through the Word without human aid and agency, so also God governs and preserves us without human participation. "For He is the beginning, the middle, and the end of all creatures."[19]

Verse 4: "In Him was life" differentiates between the eternal Creator and other earthly mortal workers. Whatever is temporal and transitory will pass and perish in time, except the Son of God who abides eternally. According to his divine nature, neither can he die nor come back to life. He is sheer life, not only in himself, but also in everything that acquires life from him, especially human beings. Human creatures are created in the image of God and for life eternal; they forfeited this life through the original fall and become subject to death. But they will be quickened through Christ (1 Cor 15:22). St. John writes: "And the life was the light of men." As life, Christ quickens; as light, he imparts light only to his own, that the Word reveals himself to his elect through the Holy Spirit and the oral Word.

16. See Torrance, *Trinitarian Faith*, ch. 4.
17. LW 22.19 (WA 46.552).
18. Augustine, *On the Trinity*, I, ch. 6, par.9.
19. LW 22.28 (WA 46.560).

As early as 1509, Luther noted in the margin of the *Sentences* of Peter Lombard: "It is not so much a physical or logical determination as a theological one. It is as if someone were to say: 'What is Christ?' to which the logician replies: 'He is a person . . .' while the theologian says: 'He is the rock, the cornerstone.'"[20] The article that Christ is both very God and very man, for Luther, is the rock on which our eternal welfare and salvation are founded. The incarnation, the unity of two natures in Christ, is conceived in terms of the central fact of salvation. If the faith is impaired by Arians, who deny the divinity of Christ, we are lost. To divest Christ of his divinity, Luther avers, is to be bereft of all hope.

> If Christ is not true and natural God, born of the Father in eternity and Creator of all creatures, we are doomed. For what would Christ's suffering and death avail me if Christ were merely a human being like you and me? As such He could not have overcome evil, death, and sin; He would have proved far too weak for them and could never have helped us. No, we must have a Saviour who is true God and Lord over sin, death, devil, and hell. If we permit the devil to topple this stronghold for us, so that we disbelieve His divinity, then His suffering, death, and resurrection profit us nothing.[21]

On the other hand, if Christ is divested of his humanity, as with the Manichaeans, we are lost too. "Our sin, misery, and distress are so enormous that they require a ransom too great for angels, patriarchs, or prophets to pay. For this God's Son had to become man, suffer, and shed His blood."[22] For the Manichaeans, the creature is far too filthy for the holy, pure, and immaculate deity to adopt its nature.[23] They consider incarnation the greatest blasphemy and mockery to the divine majesty. Therefore they held that Christ had been born of the Virgin Mary without acquiring her flesh and blood. Others asserted that Christ had fashioned a heavenly body for himself and had caused it to be born of the Virgin Mary. "But if He were not true man," argues Luther, "He could not have suffered and died to achieve our salvation."[24] If Christ is without a real humanity, like ours, we receive no comfort from him.

---

20. See marginal gloss on *Sentences*, lib. III, d. 23; WA 9.91.22–24 as cited in Congar, "Christology of Luther," 376.

21. LW 22.21–22 (WA 46.554).

22. LW 22.22 (WA 46.555).

23. See LW 13.96, note 34.

24. LW 22.23 (WA 46.555).

But in His humanity He must also be a true and natural son of the Virgin Mary, from whom He inherited flesh and blood as any other child does from its mother. He was conceived of the Holy Spirit, who came upon her and overshadowed her with the power of the Most High, according to Luke 1:35. However, Mary, the pure virgin, had to contribute of her seed and of the natural blood that coursed from her heart. From her He derived everything, except sin, that a child naturally and normally receives from its mother. This we must believe if we are not to be lost. If, as the Manichaeans allege, He is not a real and natural man, nothing in common with us; then we can derive no comfort from Him.[25]

Proper Meditation: "And the Word Became Flesh"

Discussing verse 14, Luther fleshes out at length the full salvific import of his two-nature Christology, and instructs us on the proper and improper usage of it. Now the Word acquires a new name. Earlier the evangelist called the Word "God." Now he speaks of the condescension of the Word into our "flesh." He did not become an angel or another excellent creature; he became man, one of us. Against Docetism, he is consubstantial with us in his humanity; he possesses not a seeming humanity, but a real one (John 1:14; Heb 2:16). Christians must learn to prize, esteem and sing these words—"the Word became flesh" (v. 14)—with a joyful heart and thank God for his immense compassion in becoming one of us. In the mass, when the Nicene Creed was sung, the congregation "genuflected"[26] at the words "from the Virgin Mary, and was made man,"[27] and removed their hats, showing reverence.

Angels are much holier than poor miserable sinners, yet God adopted our nature. This elicited awe in St. Bernard, who pondered the incarnation, and composed his thoughts on it, especially found in his devotions.[28] For Bernard, the incarnation has caused the downfall of the archfiend Lucifer and his eviction from heaven. Lucifer foreknew God's eternal resolve to become like us poor bags of worms in time, not a magnificent angel, and

---

25. LW 22.23 (WA 46.555–56).

26. LW 22.103 (WA 46.625). The custom of genuflecting at the words "And was made Man" in the Nicene Creed started very late, in the Middle Ages. 1502 was the year for its official recognition.

27. LW 22.103 (WA 46.625). The words "from the Virgin Mary, and was made man" are from the Nicene Creed.

28. See Clairvaux, *Sermones de tempore*, as cited in LW 22.103 (WA 46.625).

that, Bernard supposed, has provoked his insolence against God. Lucifer regarded himself as more beautiful and noble in appearance than man. So he became envious of mankind, who alone was given the high honor of God's assumption of human nature. Lucifer and his hosts were humiliated by this act, when they recognized that God would bypass them and assume human nature. Thus they fell and were banished from heaven. On the contrary, the good angels rejoiced over God's act of being attired with the human nature; they remained in heaven and recognized Christ as their Lord and God. This is borne out in Matthew 28:6, where the angels say to Mary Magdalene and to other women: "Come, see the place where the Lord lay." Although Bernard's supposition does not constitute an article of faith, says Luther, it is quite plausible.[29] It indeed annoys us to see the divine majesty in the nature of a poor, feeble, and corrupt human nature, rather than in the nature of the holy, glorious angels. If we Christians were to ponder the matter, we too might arrive at the conclusion, as Bernard did, that it would have been far more reasonable and honorable for God to assume the nature of his noblest creatures, the angels, than that of vile human nature. God assumed every aspect of our human nature, except sin and guilt. The great miracle of the incarnation is ineffable, and anyone who believes it cannot help but wonder at the thought that God should deem humans dearer and nobler than an angel, although humans are really wretched creatures by comparison. Like Bernard, Luther took special delight and efforts in contemplating these words with reverence: "And was made Man," from which he had derived comfort and joy.

Luther went further to relate how people could find strength and deliverance in these words: "The Word became flesh," which he considered as equivalent to these words: "I am a Christian."[30] He assigns great value to the proper usage of these words to combat the devil's assault. A brief word spoken in faith such as this is effective to deliver him from his trouble and distress: "I am a Christian, of the same flesh and blood as my Lord Christ, the Son of God. You settle with Him, devil."[31] The devil was unmoved when he heard "In the beginning was the Word." But he cannot stand to hear the words "God became man"; for these words vanquish all his thoughts and he vanishes.[32] The godless misuse these words, supposing that by a mere

29. LW 22.104 (WA 46.626).
30. LW 22.106 (WA 46.627).
31. LW 22.108 (WA 46.629).
32. See LW 22, note 79. This is also recorded in his *Table Talk*, 1540, (Weimar, Tischreden III, No. 3669) where Luther writes: "There is nothing more vexing to the devil than speaking about dear Jesus and His incarnation. Therefore I like it that in church people sing loudly 'And the Word was Made' or 'And was made man.' The devil

repetition of them, though without faith, they could work miracles and charms (cf. Acts 19:13). As an example, Simon Magnus wanted to purchase the gift of the Holy Spirit in order to work miracles without faith (Acts 8:18–19). "But, brother, not that way. You are making it a work without faith,"[33] Luther counters. "If faith is wanting, there is no power in the words."[34] To utter the scriptural words "The Word became flesh" without faith is to abuse it; it also permits the devil to reinforce the error, that there is no difference between words uttered in faith and in unbelief. An unbeliever is impotent to bring about any desirable effects; he parrots these scriptural words of a believer without effect. However, by faith, it will be done to you according to these words; "they cannot but be effective."[35]

The Apollinarists, the followers of Apollinaris,[36] alleged that the true Son of God does not possess a soul, inferring this from the text, where the evangelist did not mention a soul but merely said: "And the Word became flesh." Christ assumed only a human body, but not both body and soul. Such interpretation, Luther avers, does not carry weight, for it would be just as logical to infer that Christ had no body either, for flesh and body are not identical.[37] However, in scriptural parlance, the word "flesh" denotes a complete human being, as in John 3:6: "That which is born of the flesh is flesh." Thus "of a woman both body and soul are born, not an inanimate mass of flesh, a physical being of flesh and blood, designated by Scripture with that one word 'flesh.'"[38] Throughout Scripture, the word "flesh" encompasses "both body and soul, for without the soul the body is dead."[39] The evangelist prefers "The Word became flesh" to "The Word became man." With that word "flesh" he wants to indicate "its weakness and its mortality"[40] in connection with the inexpressible humiliation of the Son, an important constituent of Luther's theology of the cross.

The words "And dwelt among us" speak against the heretical Manichaeans,[41] who took offense at the statement that the Son of God had

---

cannot stand to hear this, and he has to retreat several miles."

33. LW 22.107 (WA 46.629).
34. LW 22.107 (WA 46.629).
35. LW 22.107 (WA 46.629).
36. LW 22.110 (WA 46.632). Apollinaris regarded the divine logos as the soul of Christ's human nature.
37. LW 22.110 (WA 46.632).
38. LW 22.110 (WA 46.631).
39. LW 22.111 (WA 46.632).
40. LW 22.111 (WA 46.632).
41. LW 22.112 (WA 46.633).

become man. They protested that the divine majesty, whose brightness exceeds that of the sun, should not submerge itself into sin-corrupted, impure and mortal flesh. By that they also rejected Mary as the true, natural and physical mother of Jesus. This is illustrated by the analogy of a red glass, which casts a red shadow on the wall, although the wall itself is not red in color. Only a shadow or phantom passed through Mary, like a ghost with no real body or soul. As such Christ had only resembled a human, but not a true human. This means the Romans crucified an incorporeal phantom, not the real Christ. However, by writing "Christ dwelt among us," the evangelist wants to demonstrate the connection between Christ's humanity and his own actions, by dwelling among the people, and assuming human experiences (eating, drinking, suffering) in the feeble and wretched human form and nature. And by writing "we have beheld His glory," the evangelist proceeds to demonstrate the correspondence between Christ's divinity and his own actions. Just as Christ's humanity is discernible in his acts, so also his divinity is found in the acts that he does. The deeds he did by his words were exclusively God's, proving that he was God by nature. For his Word is his deed; by his Word the deed is done. Just as God brought forth heaven and earth through the Word, he too performed all that he wished by a spoken word. As support, Luther cited several texts: "Little girl, I say to you, arise" (Mark 4:41); and: "Lazarus, come out!" (John 11:43); to the lepers: "Be clean!" (Matt 8:3).

This is the first time John introduces these words: "as the only-begotten Son of the Father" (v. 14) as a predicate of the term "Word." The term "Word" may be obscure, lacking clarity in any language; but now it shines, as the evangelist puts it plainly: "This is God's only begotten Son."[42] The evangelist's own interpretation goes like this: "The Word, which was with the Father from eternity and is the Light of man, is called the Son, yes, the only-begotten Son of God. He alone is that, and no one else."[43] Luther provides another version: "The Word, of which I have spoken to you, is the only-begotten Son of God, true God and Creator with the Father, differing only in this, that He was born of the Father, and the Father was not from Him."[44] Christians should treasure this text, from which they could draw comfort; they are lifted out of distress, simply because they are children of the eternal bliss through the only-begotten Son of the Father, begotten of

---

42. LW 22.115 (WA 46.635).
43. LW 22.115 (WA 46.635).
44. LW 22.115–16 (WA 46.636).

him in eternity, and born of the Virgin Mary in time. Luther asserts: "[T]his is our Christian faith. This alone makes us Christians."[45]

The same Word that became incarnate is "full of grace and truth." This expression sets Christ apart from, and exalts him above, all the patriarchs and prophets. The greatness or glory of Noah, Abraham, Isaac, Jacob, Moses, Joshua and others is received from God, who works great miracles through them. "They proved themselves by word and deed, and the glory we perceive in them is divine, not physical and earthly."[46] However, their glory, no matter how brilliant it is, cannot be compared to that of the Word that became flesh. Whilst the other children of God possess only a measure of grace and truth, the only-begotten Son of God alone is "full of," or is "sheer grace and truth."[47] Being the natural Son of God, whose glory is intrinsic to his being, he ranks above all God's adopted children, whose glory is conferred as a token of his grace and mercy. To obtain a better understanding of this phrase, "full of grace and truth," Luther placed Adam and Christ in juxtaposition (Rom 5:12). "As Adam is the fountainhead of sin, misery, and death, and transmits all these to us, so that we now speak of sin upon sin, so Christ is the fountainhead of all grace, truth, and life, from whom we derive a fullness of grace, life, and truth."[48] In Adam we see nothing but God's wrath, damnation and eternal punishment; for the fall of Adam results in lapses: from grace to wrath, from truth to lies, from righteousness into sin, from life into death. The fallen world thus is "a veritable vale of tears, an abode of sadness, a cheerless desert."[49] By contrast, in Christ we see nothing but grace, peace, joy, and favor; all of these are profusely and exclusively his by nature, given that he is "the dear child"[50] of the heavenly Father. Whatever Christ says and does is sheer grace, love, and joy; for He is "the Favourite,"[51] God's only-begotten Son, who can do nothing amiss. His words and acts are well-pleasing to God, as testified by the Father from above: "This is my Beloved Son, with whom I am well pleased; listen to Him" (Matt 3:17; 17:5).

Luther considers the words: "And from His fullness have we all received grace upon grace," one of "the golden texts" in St. John's gospel.[52] For Luther, the phrase "grace upon grace" speaks of two types of grace. The first

---

45. LW 22.116 (WA 46.636).
46. LW 22.117 (WA 46.637).
47. LW 22.117 (WA 46.637).
48. LW 22.138 (WA 46.657).
49. LW 22.119 (WA 46.639).
50. LW 22.119 (WA 46.639).
51. LW 22.120 (WA 46.639).
52. LW 22.130 (WA 46.649).

refers to Christ as the chief fountain of all grace, which he called "Christ's fullness," unfathomable and inexhaustible fullness from which all the saints down the centuries have drawn, and still do. This is "grace upon grace," that we all benefit from Christ's fullness—His righteousness, innocence, and obedience, which Christ imputes to us. The second refers to grace which we receive from him out of his free mercy, by which we are made pleasing to God. There was one verdict that St. John the Baptist pronounced on human creatures from Adam to the end of the world: we are all sinners and liars by nature, devoid of grace or divine favor. But concurrently he offers Christ as a remedy: "Christ alone must be the means. He alone makes us paupers rich with His superabundance, expunges our sins with His righteousness, devours our death with His life, and transforms us from children of wrath, tainted with sin, hypocrisy, lies, and deceit, into children of grace and truth. Whoever does not possess this Man possesses nothing."[53] Thus it is "a terrible and detestable blindness and a demonic presumption"[54] for any sinner to attempt atonement for sin through his works. It too is "a wretched arrogance"[55] for anyone to indulge in bragging and boasting of such things as beauty, riches, noble birth, wealth, honor and glory, when he is nothing but bags of worms or maggots before God. Grace alone, and of superabundance, moves God to be favorably disposed toward us. If we were to acquire grace and truth, "Christ's fullness must perform this."[56] God is pleased with believers, who through Christ's person and work become partakers of this grace and truth. For them grace will not terminate, nor will judgment enter, because of the appealing picture of Christ as "full of grace and truth," which are imputed to "all who received Him."

John the Baptist and His Office

The text says: "John bore witness to Him, and cried: This was He of whom I said: He who comes after me ranks before me, for He was before me. And from His fullness have we all received grace upon grace" (vv. 15–16). As witness, John the Baptist first acquainted the people with the Messiah's advent. This was made necessary because of the mean and inauspicious demeanor the Messiah bore, that is, in such an insignificant and abject form in which he appeared. John the Baptist was sent to preach the advent of Christ so that the people of Israel could not excuse themselves for their ignorance of Christ

---

53. LW 22.131 (WA 46.649–50).
54. LW 22.132 (WA 46.651).
55. LW 22.132 (WA 46.651).
56. LW 22.124 (WA 46.643).

and their failure to recognize him because of his lowly appearance. Even so, his work commanded no respect, as people were awaiting a messiah in some other form. Secondly, John's austere and saintly life should have lent support to his witness to Christ. Yet Christ was not received by the vast multitudes. But John persisted in his mission and faithfully fulfilled the task to which God had called him. Verse 15: "This was He of whom I said: He who comes after me ranks before me" refers to the time now past, before Jesus' public ministry and immediately after the cessation of his own work as a witness. Christ was born six months after John's birth. Christ did not precede John in his humanity; he precedes Christ in office. No one will succeed John, except Christ, who comes after him; no prophet or teacher will intervene between John and Christ. Both he and Christ bore the same content or doctrine. In divine being, Christ precedes, and excels, him. The child antedates his mother, his conception in his mother's womb, or his birth. Surely this has never occurred in nature, from which one could infer that he must be "an unusual child, that He must be God."[57]

God gave John the command and office to preach, to baptize Jesus and usher in a new reign. At the baptism where the Son was standing in the water, the divine majesty manifested itself over Jesus, confirming "not only an inner and private call into the office with which He had been invested before the foundation of the world but also a public and visible call."[58] This is evident in the words spoken by the eternal Father on that occasion: "This is my beloved Son" (Matt 3:17), and in the descent of the Holy Spirit in the physical form of a dove. All three persons of the Trinity, together with the elect angels, were in attendance at Christ's baptism. From this we gather that baptism is not the work of humans but solely of God. Jesus' baptism ushers in a remarkable transformation in which "the Law, the Jewish priesthood, and the kingdom were to be abolished, and a new world was to be established through the Gospel."[59] John was to initiate a new reign, in which not only the Jews but all the nations were to be a people of God through Christ. In accordance with his office, John the Baptist points people away from himself to Christ the Lord, and testifies that he is the Light and Life of the world, the only Savior of the world, the Lamb of God, our shepherd, our abbot, our Bridegroom, and our Messiah. "That proclamation is the sum and substance"[60] of John's testimony and ours too. The testimony of the

---

57. LW 22.129 (WA 46.648).
58. LW 22.39 (WA 46.570).
59. LW 22.39 (WA 46.570).
60. LW 22.53 (WA 46.581).

Light was "most necessary."[61] John was instrumental in our becoming the children of the Light. This is spoken against the Anabaptists who avow that the Spirit could work faith in the people independently of and apart from the external Word. "For God has decreed that no one can or will believe or receive the Holy Spirit without that Gospel which is preached or taught by word of mouth."[62] Though John was not the Light that illumines people to life eternal, the Lord boldly calls John "a burning and shining lamp" in John 5:35. Just as he remains the instrumental light, though people reject him, so Christ is the only Light of mankind in the world, even when only a small minority of people are touched by it. Thus the evangelist issues a terrifying statement: "He came into His own, and His own received Him not" (cf. Isa 53:1–3). God had designated the people of Israel as "his own" through Moses who said in Exodus 19:5: "You shall be My own possession among all peoples." The evangelist here calls them the possession of Christ our Lord, as he says: "He came into his own" (v.11). His own did not accept Christ, for Christ's appearance did not coincide with the image of their imagination. They wanted a Messiah, like an earthly king, who would make them prosperous, great, and mighty lords so that they could have dominion over all the nations. Christ was to appear triumphantly like the earthly emperors, surrounded by worldly splendor, armaments, silver, and gold. Instead he appeared in poverty, as the prophet Zechariah had foretold. Luther paraphrased Zechariah 9:9: "Do not be perplexed and troubled in your minds because He comes in such dire poverty. Rather focus your attention on the fact that He comes to you to save you from sin and eternal death, and to give you eternal righteousness and salvation."[63] They not only rejected John's testimony of him but also Jesus' public office, as had been prophesied in the words of the Lord in Deuteronomy 18:15: "The Lord your God will raise up for you a Prophet like me from among you, from your brethren." The true Light continues to shine for the benefit of those who wish to avail themselves of it and be enlightened as an outcome. Thus the evangelist issues an assuring statement in the next verse: "But to all who received Him, who believed in Him, He gave the power to become children of God" (v.12). Even when few believe the Word, or come to believe and to receive the Holy Spirit, through the Word, this negative outcome does not detract from the efficacy of the gospel.

John speaks of the difference between Christ's baptism and his own when he says in verse 33: "I myself did not know Him; but He who sent me

---

61. LW 22.56 (WA 46.584).
62. LW 22.54 (WA 46.582).
63. LW 22.43 (WA 46.573).

to baptize with water said to me: He on whom you see the Spirit descend and remain, this is He who baptizes with the Holy Spirit." John could baptize with water; he does not give the Holy Spirit nor does he forgive sin. The aim of his preaching is to lead people to repentance and to prepare them for the advent of the Lord, who possesses the power to remit sin. In John's baptism forgiveness is promised, in Christ's baptism it is bestowed. John's baptism was "solely a prelude, as it were, and a preparation for the forgiveness of sin. John preceded Christ; Christ followed him."[64] Accordingly John's baptism is no longer valid, for it has been superseded by Christ's baptism. Christ accepts John's baptism of water, but he adds "the fire," that is, the Holy Spirit. "That is, He imparts the Holy Spirit, who kindles His virtues in us. And thus our baptism in Christ, in which He gives us remission of sin, baptizing us with the Holy Spirit and with forgiveness, remains and continues to be effective."[65] Though we have attained forgiveness of sin through Christ, the Old Adam still abides and therefore sins daily. The devil is alive, and he tempts our flesh to every evil. Therefore the preaching and practicing of repentance are necessary on earth until the Old Adam is dead and until the Last Day, when we will perform the will of the Spirit perfectly. Through the Holy Spirit whom Christ confers on us, we live under the forgiveness of sin, repenting daily and purging and cleansing the evil flesh, which strives against the Spirit.

Moses (Law) and Christ (Grace)

The Old Testament ends and the New begins with John. He no longer proclaims the Law of Moses but the grace that is to come through Christ. Against Antinomianism, Luther qualified: "[T]he Ten Commandments are still in force and do concern us so far as obedience to them is concerned."[66] Yet the law ceases to condemn believers because of what Christ has done. The curse of the law, not its contents, ceases. The law is given for a good purpose, as borne out in St. Paul's words in Rom 7:10–12: "It indeed promised life but it proved to be death to me. This, of course, is my fault, and not the fault of the Law; for the Law is good, holy, and God's glory." St. Stephen, too, asserts in Acts 7:38: "You have received the Word of life from Moses." The law has no capacity to impart life, not because it is imperfect but because we are inept in fulfilling it. The fault lies not in the law, but in us, who do not keep it. The law is holy and good, just as God himself from

---

64. LW 22.177 (WA 46.690).
65. LW 22.179 (WA 46.692).
66. LW 22.39 (WA 46.569).

whom it originates is holy and good. Although the law offers no grace and truth, its purpose was to point to eternal life, not impart it to anyone. "To point and to grant are two different matters, widely separated."[67] The law is "a sermon,"[68] like a hand that points to the right path, that is, to life, but it cannot give life.

The distinction between law and gospel corresponds to the offices of Moses and Christ. Each belongs to its proper sphere, without confounding the office and work of the other. Luther confessed that he was befuddled by this for more than thirty years, stretching from his birth in 1483 till the period between 1516 and 1519, when he had an evangelical breakthrough.[69] Formerly Luther had no delight in the law. But he now realizes that the law is precious and good, given to him for his life. It is "a lesson and a word of life, but only for the person who observes and fulfills all it prescribes."[70]

Just as law precedes gospel, so "repentance precedes forgiveness"[71]— callous sinners must recognize their sins via the preaching of law and learn that they stand in need of forgiveness, which Christ's baptism can bring. To teach and understand the law aright, for Luther, is to lead the people to a realization of their sins and be terrified by the law, and then comfort and cheer them with the gospel. Those who are most profoundly terrified under the law are most profoundly comforted under the gospel, the former leading to the latter. So if we relinquish the law, we shall not long retain Christ and all that he is. Moses is of good use, for he teaches us in the three commandments of the First Table that we love, fear, and trust God. Thus his office is instrumental and his message is blessed, but only forasmuch as it teaches us what we must do and directs us to another man, namely, to Christ. "For after Moses, and beside Moses, Christ, the Son of God, was given to us as a preacher who informs us of what He Himself has done, namely, that He acquired grace and truth for us and He assists us in obeying the precepts of the Law; that is, He obtained remission of sin and a gracious God for us. Christ secured grace, that is, the forgiveness of sins, so that believers in Him would obtain that forgiveness."[72] Through Christ's office, all are perfectly righteous, signified by the word "truth." This is the tenor of St. John: "From His fullness have we all received, grace upon grace."

---

67. LW 22.141 (WA 46.659).
68. LW 22.143 (WA 46.661).
69. LW 22.145 (WA 46.663).
70. LW 22.143 (WA 46.661).
71. LW 22.177 (WA 46.690).
72. LW 22.147–48 (WA 46.665).

Moses' Lamb Vs. the True Lamb of God

With these words, "The Law was given through Moses" (v. 17), John had in mind the sacrifice of a lamb every Passover, which the Jews did, as commanded by Moses. He then juxtaposes Moses' lamb that was butchered and Christ, the true Lamb that was ordained by God to bear on its back the sins of the world. John states: "Behold the Lamb of God, who bears the sin of the world" (v. 29). "God's own beloved Son" was called Jesus, because he was to save his people from their sins (Matt 1:21); this name is exclusively the Son's. This name reflects in essence who the Son is: the Savior of the world. The lambs procured from shepherds never succeed in expiating the sin of the people, a work only the Lamb prescribed by God could do. Christ was a man like all humans, but God made him the Lamb that should bear the sins of the entire world. Not in the law of Moses, but in the cross of Christ are the sins of the world exterminated. Luther advised: "Therefore a Christian must cling simply to this verse and let no one rob him of it. *For there is no other comfort either in heaven or on earth to fortify us against all attacks and temptations, especially in the agony of death.*"[73]

No one can atone for their sins with alms and the like. The Word of God is clear enough: "This is the Lamb of God, who bears the sin of the world." This is not our invention, but God's prescription that this Lamb was the only atoner. God recognizes no other but this Lamb who, in obedience to the Father, assumed the sin of the entire world. As soon as reason is permitted to reign, it eventuates in "a hideous and terrible blindness" concerning the gravity of sin: "Sin is at your throat and it drives you and lies heavy on you."[74] Reason seeks to deal with sin by its own counsel, declaring: "I will reform and become pious."[75] On the contrary, St. John declares that the entire world is polluted with sin, which only the Lamb of God can take away. He shows us through the law that we are sunk in sin, a condition we cannot overcome except by clinging to the Lamb of God. Sin must not rest in our bosom where the law has deposited it. For if it were to remain there, distress and damnation are the outcome. The law places sins upon us; God takes them from us and lays them upon this Lamb. Reflectively, Luther had God say: "I see how the sin oppresses you. You would have to collapse under its heavy burden. But I shall relieve and rid you of the load—and from sheer mercy I shall place the weight of your sin on this Lamb, which will bear

---

73. LW 22.163 (WA 46.678). Italics from original text.
74. LW 22.165 (WA 46.679).
75. LW 22.165 (WA 46.679).

them."[76] Through the law, God exposes our sins in order paradoxically to dispose of them through the gospel. Accordingly we are to ever cherish this thought, that Christ is made a servant of sin, or a sin-bearer, and the lowliest and most despised person. There is no greater bondage than that of sin, and yet Christ undoes it by himself. There is no greater service than that performed by "the beloved Lamb, the Son of the Exalted Majesty,"[77] who descends from heaven to become a servant of all and bears their sins. The profound humility the Son of God displays ought to induce wonder in us. The magnitude of the love of the Son of God for us is revealed precisely in this: the greater the stench of our sins, the more he cleanses, relieving us of the misery and burden of our sins by placing them upon his own back. On account of the humble service of Christ, in which he cumbers himself with our misery and sin, we hear the gospel of a joyous exchange, where God declares: "You are no longer a sinner, but I am. I am your substitute. You have not sinned, but I have. The entire world is in sin. However, you are not in sin, but I am. All your sins are to rest on Me and not on you."[78] Christ has taken "all" the sins of the world upon himself, just as though he himself had committed them since its inception. He has "become the whole world," and has "incorporated all people since Adam into [His] person."[79]

Left-Handed Versus Right-Handed Knowledge

The knowledge of law and gospel corresponds to what Luther called "legal knowledge"[80] and "evangelical knowledge"[81] of God. The former is a "left-handed"[82] kind; the latter is a "right-handed"[83] kind. Reason is confined to the first mode of knowing. It can arrive at the knowledge of God through law; it is conversant with the content of the Law of God; it can tell between right and wrong, as the Law is inscribed in our hearts (Rom 2:15). This knowledge is "natural and universal and was reinforced by the

---

76. LW 22.166 (WA 46.680).
77. LW 22.166 (WA 46.680).
78. LW 22.167 (WA 46.681).
79. LW 22.168 (WA 46.682).
80. LW 22.151 (WA 46.668).
81. LW 22.152 (WA 46.669). Althaus, *Theology of Martin Luther*, 259, where he contrasts between the demonic terror and evangelical terror, the former destroys while the latter saves.
82. LW 22.153 (WA 46.669).
83. LW 22.153 (WA 46.669)

Law of Moses."[84] It is accessible to the heathen, the philosophers and all wise people. But it is not the true knowledge of God, which emerges from the gospel. The heathens progress to a point where they recognize God but they reject him. This is likened unto "sniffing the existence of God without tasting it."[85] Reason possesses only "a left-handed and a partial knowledge of God"[86] through the law of nature and of Moses. But it is totally blind to and ignorant of the evangelical knowledge: the depth of God's purpose, his wisdom, his heart, will and his attitude towards us. Of this John testifies: "No one has ever seen God; the only Son, who is in the bosom of the Father, He has made this known to the world." The proper way to acquire a true knowledge of God is "the right-handed one," which leads us into the inner thoughts and friendly will of God. The knowledge of who we are (that we are steeped in sin and eternally damned) and of who Christ is (that Christ, the Son of God, is the only source of grace and salvation) comes solely through Jesus Christ, and belongs to the domain of divine revelation, not reason. Such knowledge is "not Mosaic or legal knowledge but evangelical and Christian knowledge."[87]

> For this [evangelical knowledge] is a new revelation from heaven, which not only acquaints us with, and instructs us in, the Ten Commandments but also informs us that we mortals are all conceived in sin and are lost, and that no one keeps the Law, but that those who want to be saved will be saved solely through the grace and truth of Jesus. Here is the depth of His nature; here is the will of God. May everyone be apprised, be he who he will—whether he has Moses on his side or whether he is totally submerged in his righteousness—that there is no salvation or knowledge of God outside Christ. No one is approved by God unless he is marked with the grace and truth of the Son. This knowledge is concealed from reason.[88]

There is no inkling of the evangelical knowledge of God in nature, nor trace of it in the books of the jurists and sages or even in the law of Moses. It profits none for the Scholastics to debate the question whether humans, of themselves, can discover that there is a God. The question is not "How can God be known from the Law?" but "How can He be known from grace and truth?" The law by itself, in isolation, terrifies us; grace and truth

---

84. LW 22.154 (WA 46.670).
85. LW 22.152 (WA 46.668).
86. LW 22.153 (WA 46.669).
87. LW 22.153 (WA 46.669).
88. LW 22.156 (WA 46.671).

must accompany it, or else the law profits us nothing. "And the knowledge of God in His grace is the skill and the wisdom which the Son alone has revealed to us."[89] The first mode of knowledge—legal, natural, universal and left-handed—is carnal and earthly and issues from reason; the second mode of knowledge—evangelical, supernatural, specific, and right-handed—is spiritual and Christian and issues from faith. The text clearly informs us that no one has ever seen God; no one, of himself, can know God in the evangelical sense. Verse 18: "No one has ever seen God; the only Son, who sits in the bosom of the Father, He has made Him known." Holy Writ applies the word "bosom" paternally, to a father, when normally the term is used maternally, of a mother holding children to her bosom. The Father enfolds the Son in his arms and caresses him. This peculiar mode of expression "to sit in the bosom of the Father" speaks of the intimacy between the Father and the Son, which constitutes the basis of the reliability and certainty of the self-revelation of God in the Son. The evangelical knowledge of God is a gift which we receive from the only Son of God, who clings to the Father and rests snugly in his arms. The Son is so intimately close to the Father that his knowledge of his Father's heart is absolutely reliable. Though no one has seen God, the existence of God is known to all, without exception, from the works of the creation, as Paul said, "so that they are without excuse" (Rom 1: 19ff). How do we reconcile Paul, who teaches that all humans know God, with St. John, who states that no one has seen God, unless the only Son of God reveals Him to us? Christ also tells the Jews in John 8:54–55: "You claim to know God, but you do not know Him; you call Him your Father but do not know who He is." Here Christ's words were directed not towards the godless or smug scorners, who show no interest in God, but the holy Pharisees, who were seeking God. Christ informs them that had the Son, whom the Father embraces in his divinity, not come to reveal God to us, no one would know him. The phrase "no one has ever seen God" excludes all those who are concerned about God and attempt to find him with their reason. Not by any rational edifice or any fabricated works of human righteousness but purely by the evangelical knowledge are we reconciled to God.

The sinful world by nature disdains God and thus lapses into God's wrath and damnation and subjects to the devil's power. From these contraries—sin, death and wrath—the world cannot break free except through God's Son, who lies in the bosom of the Father. "This is the true and thorough knowledge and way of thinking about God; it is called the knowledge of grace and truth, the 'evangelical knowledge' of God" which nature

---

89. LW 22.154 (WA 46.670).

knows nothing about."[90] The Son of God, who is in God and who himself is God, and whom the Father embraces, is indispensable for the evangelical knowledge of grace and truth. To know God from the law is to know him left-handedly with "His back"[91] turned to us. To know God aright, one must "walk around God"[92] of the left-handed, and look directly into "God's face"[93] of the right-handed, as seen properly in the only-begotten Son. "The knowledge of the Gospel is the face of God."[94] When we behold his true countenance and his salvific plan in Christ, everything in us dies. Thus to know God aright is to come creeping to Christ and be found secured in the Son, attaining everything through his grace and truth. And whoever is drawn into the realm of God's Son is also drawn into the proximity the Son has with the Father, and therefore really knows God in an evangelical sense.

---

90. LW 22.153 (WA 46.669).
91. LW 22.157 (WA 46.672).
92. LW 22.157 (WA 46.672).
93. LW 22.157 (WA 46.673).
94. LW 22.158 (WA 46.673).

CHAPTER 2

Divine Hiddenness

The Word of God and Created Forms

Luther considers it hubris on the part of the human reason to attempt to grasp God above and beyond his revelation in this world, that is, seeking to discover the hidden God.[1] To engage in such speculation is to attempt what he called "a theology of glory."[2] In his *Bondage of the Will* (1525), Luther criticized Erasmus for failing to observe the distinction between God as revealed and God as hidden, between the Word of God and God himself:

> God must be left to himself in his own majesty, for in this regard we have nothing to do with him, nor has he willed that we should have anything to do with him. But we have something to do with him insofar as he is clothed and set forth in his Word, through which he offers himself to us and which is the beauty and glory with which the psalmist celebrates him as being clothed.[3]

To correct such tendencies, Luther insisted that we restrict ourselves to the crucified Christ, that is, to God seen from below. From this perspective, we succeed in grasping the hidden God as well, for they are one and the same God. In his lectures on Genesis (1535-45), Luther has God say: "From the unrevealed God I will become a revealed God. Nevertheless I will remain the same God." Immediately after affirming the identity of the hidden God and the revealed God, Luther continues by having God say:

---

1. LW 22.504 (WA 47.209-10).
2. LW 31.38.
3. LW 33.138-39.

"I will be made flesh, or send my Son. He shall die for your sins and shall rise again from the dead ... Behold, this is My Son: listen to Him (cf. Matt 17:5). Look at Him as He lies in the manger and on the lap of His mother, as He hangs on the cross. Observe what He does and what He says. Therefore you surely take hold of Me."[4]

A theologian of the cross does not perceive the invisible God through created things; rather he discerns God in the visible things seen through the suffering and the cross of Jesus of Nazareth. This is borne out in the patriarchal story in Genesis 28:10–16, where Jacob beheld heaven open and a ladder reaching from the ground into heaven. On top of the ladder was the Lord, our God, and the angels were climbing up and down. Christ applies this story of the patriarch to himself: "(T)he angels of God (are) ascending and descending upon the Son of man" as on a ladder (John 1:50–51).[5] Luther observes in St. John a reversal of direction in our ascent to God: not by way of Christ's divinity, but Christ's lowly humanity, "the holy ladder,"[6] that we ascend to the evangelical knowledge and love of God. This is consistent with what he taught earlier in his *Heidelberg Disputation* (1518): God is found nowhere except in the self-humiliation of the Son. We should not allow the counsels of our natural capacity to dictate what may or may not be said of God, or determine the meaning of sublime divine things, as a theologian of glory does. Rather, we should cling to the divinely-ordained method by which we ascend to God, as a theologian of the cross does: moving from Christ's humanity through his divinity, and then to the Father. In his descent toward us, God hides in Jacob's ladder to reach us; in our ascent toward God, we hide in Jacob's ladder to reach him; both movements presuppose Christ's humanity as God-ordained means of his descent to us and our ascent to him.

We must begin where Scripture begins—begin with "the child lying in the lap of his mother Mary and to the sacrificial victim suspended on the cross—there we shall really behold God."[7] Any attempt to execute the opposite movement will lead us into the terror of true God's majesty, before whom we will be crushed. God has designated a place and person, showing where and how he can be discovered. Hence, we are to encounter him

---

4. LW 5.45 (WA 43.459).

5. LW 22.201–02 (WA 46.711–12).

6. For the image of Jacob's ladder, see Luther's *Lectures on Hebrews* 1:1 (1517–18). LW 29.111 (WA 57.III.9), 111. See Hagen, *Theology of Testament*, 91.
LW 22.201–02 (WA 46.711–12).

7. LW 3.176–77 (WA 1.354.17–18).

where he wills to be grasped, not in his naked majesty but in the incarnate Christ.[8] Just as God hides in Christ's frail humanity, the domain where he awaits us as a friendly God, we too must find him where he wills to hide, namely, in the created forms in which the Word of God comes. God covers us and speaks to us through the humble creaturely forms: preaching, baptism, the Lord's Supper, confession, and absolution, all of which are concrete instances of God's grace. The gospel of Jesus Christ is conveyed by these means that God has ordained as the vehicles of the economy of salvation.

Two Ways of Divine Hiddenness

When God spoke at Mt. Sinai with trumpet blasts, thunder and lightning, and the entire mountain on fire with smoke, as in Exodus 19 and 20, the Israelites found God's majestic and powerful voice unbearable; they did not come before God because the sight was altogether frightful. They pleaded with Moses to be their spokesperson that they might be preserved. Moses said: "The Lord God will give you another Prophet to whom you should cling" (Deut 18:15). Moses here foretold Christ, in whom God had appeared as a human being speaking to us through human speech and words. God has put his words into Christ, through whom God speaks graciously to us. In contrast to the terrifying voice God uttered on Mt. Sinai, Christ will speak so plainly and gently to us that we might endure his words, believe his testimony and cling to them. Luther paraphrases God's reply:

> "Since they cannot endure my voice, I will change my method. Henceforth I will no longer address them from heaven with thunder and lightning and in My Majesty. I will select one of their brethren, who will speak to them gently and sweetly. On the mountain you asked Me to communicate with you in a different way. Now God has fulfilled your request. He will grant you a Prophet in whose mouth He will put His words. And God Himself will take him to task who ignores this Prophet."[9]

Within this reply are two methods by which God converses with us. First, God addresses us in his naked majesty, which causes us to flee, for we cannot endure the language of supreme or angelic majesty. Second, since no one could bear his majesty, God chooses another method in which he addresses us: his incarnate Son. The God who speaks the universe into being

---

8. Althaus, *Theology of Martin Luther*, 186; Siggins, *Martin Luther's Doctrine of Christ*, 84.

9. LW 22.504 (WA 47.209–10).

addresses us in ways that we can bear. Of this, Luther paraphrases God's prescribed method:

> "Well and good, then I shall utterly submerge my Majesty; I shall let My Son become man; I shall let Him be born of a virgin; I shall have Him do good to men and preach remission of sin to them. My Son shall speak most affably to you. Nevertheless, I want you to remember that this Man is the same as He spoke to the Children of Israel at Mt. Sinai in the wilderness. Therefore believe that it is God whom you are hearing."[10]

God hides his supreme majesty in the humanity of Jesus to meet us. He does not appear on the scene amid lightning and thunder, surrounded by myriads of angels but as the son of a poor virgin. Not in his naked majesty, which would have terrified us; instead God addresses us but in plain and humble human form where God awaits us as a merciful God. Both methods human reason denies: on the one hand, we are still less disposed to hear him if God were to speak to us in his majesty, while on the other hand we now trample underfoot him who appears in his poverty and humility. Only the eyes of faith "find both in Christ: the terrifying and sublime majesty, which can save; and the frail humanity, which enables us to approach and cling to Him."[11] John goes to great lengths to describe how Christ acts according to each of his two natures. It is in Christ where sublimity and simplicity coincide, where majesty and frailty meet.

> He is life Himself, and yet He dies. He is all, and simultaneously He is nothing. Since He is all, however, He is surely deserving of worship. Thus these words refer to Christ's sovereign majesty: "He who believes in the Son has eternal life." If He can confer life, He must surely be God; for no creature or angel is entitled to this power, but only the Son of God, who shares equal might with the Father. Therefore whoever believes in the Son and worships Him has eternal life. Yet He is Mary's Son. More than this: here He takes flight, and later He lets Himself be killed. Thus St. John always places the eternal omnipotence of Christ in juxtaposition with His immense frailty. Faith in Christ, the Son of God, saves; and yet it is true, as we read here, that this same Lord Christ flees. Our Christian Creed professes this: Now it is a matter of "take it or leave it" for us, of "believe it or do not believe it."[12]

10. LW 22.504 (WA 47.210).
11. LW 22.509 (WA 47.213–214).
12. LW 22.503 (WA 47.209).

The great Lord raises himself to life, a work that neither human beings nor the devil can do (cf. John 2:19–20). And he who saves all who believe in him, without whom the wrath of God cannot be allayed, now flees from Judea. This Lord, who is God and has all things under his rule, resorts to flight, proving not only that he is very God but also a true natural man, who acts like other humans. This theme Luther picks up in chapter 4:1, where John uses the words "When the Lord learned" to speak of the man Christ. According to his majesty, Christ could have remained, and could have easily said: "Let Me be God in my temple!" For in himself, Christ possesses wonderful power and glory; Pharisees, sin, death, and devil are null before him. But here he acts like a real human being, manifesting himself in lowliness, as low as anyone else. The evangelist describes the significance of this Christology with great diligence: "Proof of His deity lies in the fact that He imparts life; proof that He is not a phantasm or a sham human being lies in this, that He assumes worry, weakness, and fear."[13] In order to draw us to himself, St. Paul declares in Philippians: "He took the form of a servant. He became frail, He ate and drank, so that it was evident that He was a true and natural man" (2:6–8).

Fundamental to Luther's theology of the cross is the revelation of God in opposites: not his majesty, but in humility; not in power, but in weakness; not in glory, but in shame; not in pomposity, but in lowliness. The evangelist teaches us how to know God aright: that this poor, weak, and humble Man is the almighty and eternal God. Since mortal souls cannot gaze upon God in his majesty, God reaches us by burying and concealing his divine majesty. He humbly assumed not only our human nature, that is, flesh and blood, but also all the frailties with which body and soul are afflicted, including fear, sorrow, and anger. Like us, in body and soul, he willingly subjects himself to all human infirmities; he fully identifies with human weaknesses. This shows how God is precisely himself as he acts humanly for me: "For me He humbles Himself; and for me He is finally crucified, although He is at the same time very God, who redeems us from sin and death."[14] The two-fold message concerning Christ is preached to us:

> [F]irst of all, he proclaims His glory and informs us that He comes to us in splendor and divine majesty that we might know that He is truly God, then he tells us that He also comes to us clad in weakness and in the greatest humility. When He died, he tore hell to shreds and removed sin, which is a divine work and reflects sheer deity. Then He also demonstrates that He is

13. LW 22.507 (WA 47.212).
14. LW 22.507 (WA 47.212).

true man, when He decides to leave Judea and take flight before those great prelates, the Pharisees, whom He, of course, could have felled with a breadth.[15]

Instead of coming in his majesty and in the company of angels, God descended in the guise of a poor beggar, suffering hunger and thirst, as we all do. We do not ascend into heaven where Christ is seated at the right hand of the heavenly Father to offer him something as though he has any lack in his being. Instead, he came down to us in humility, placing flesh and blood before our eyes with the plea: Give me a drink! The words "I was hungry" refer to the manner with which he came, that is, disguised in the form of a needy Christian. Luther has Christ say:

> "My poor destitute apostle and Christian is coming to you. This apostle and Christian bears the name 'I.' Now, my dear man, you pay Me court in heaven and are willing to give something to Me there. Rather do that here on earth, because up in heaven I want for nothing. Do not let your pastor and chaplain suffer privation; help to advance my kingdom; look to your destitute neighbor and brother; supply him, lest he suffer hunger and thirst."[16]

The Lord asked a Samaritan woman for a drink. She queried: "How is it that You ask a drink of me?" (John 4: 9). The Samaritans firmly held that they were saved because they worshipped God on Mt. Gerizim. She assumes that she is holy because of the place she had worshipped, and Christ is not. Luther paraphrased her answer: "I would be happy to give you a drink if you are a Samaritan. But You are a Jew, and the Jews had placed us under the ban and have condemned us as heretics."[17] Thus her conscience feared that her purity may be compromised by association with the Jews. But the Lord approaches her gently and continues in John 4:10: "If you knew the gift of God, and who it is that is saying to you: Give Me a drink! You would have asked Him, and He would have given you living water." It is true that Christ asks her for a drink to quench his thirst. But he went beyond her physical need, and looked for something else; he was seeking the Samaritans that they might hear him. He reverses "the order":[18] that he might offer her a drink that tastes better than the water he asked her for. In asking her for a physical drink, that of this world, his aim is to offer her another drink, that of heaven. Hidden in Christ's request is this wonderful reversal: Christ

---

15. LW 22.507 (WA 47.212–13).
16. LW 22.520 (WA 47.223).
17. LW 22.525 (WA 47.226).
18. LW 22.525 (WA 47.226).

offered himself as the gift and the Giver, which only faith could recognize, rather than Samaritan offering him the gift of water. Embodied in the plea "give Me a drink" is the contrary; Christ wants to be recognized as one who wants to offer us the eternal water. In asking the woman for a drink, he intends to instill in her a thirst for the water of eternal life, which only he could give. What Christ wishes to impress on us all, as he does on this young woman, is this marvellous gospel: Christ is not so much concerned that we give anything to him but that he supplies us with his abundant grace, without which there is no hope. This is what Christ wishes to do to us: first we become acquainted with the gift and the Teacher. Then we should be ready not only to give all, but also to confess him as the gift and the Giver, without whom we will surely die of eternal thirst and hunger. This is the meaning of Christ's plea for food: "I am asking you to give Me bread for the sake of God because I want to give you the everlasting bread."[19]

> Our God wishes to impress this on us all, not only on this young woman. Christ wishes to say: "I am not so much concerned that you give Me a drink as that I supply you with living water." It is a disgrace that Christ must go on begging on earth, even among his followers. It is a shame that He must cry: "For the sake of God, give Me bread!" He wants to rouse us to give gladly to those who serve in the ministry. But although Christ pleads and cries: "For the sake of God, give Me bread!" His plea is not fulfilled; for people assume that it is a poor pastor speaking. Verily, Christ does not stand in need of heaven and earth; He could eat and also satisfy his own. But He wants to say: "I am begging that you may obtain food and drink. I use your help to feed Me and My own. In this way you might recognize Him who dispenses the true, eternal drink of water and learn what sort of Word He possesses. After you know that it is I and that the Word is Mine, you will say: 'After all, everything belongs to Thee; we will gladly return all to Thee. Dear Lord, give us who are truly hungry the real bread and drink.' This is the reason why I beg and say: 'For the sake of God, give Me bread!'—that you may recognize Him who is speaking to the young woman."[20]

Luther laments over the fact that schismatic spirits neither recognize this gift nor know the Giver. They despise this ineffably precious treasure, an eternal gem offered to them through the gospel. For some to whom the gift and the Giver are known, they will expend their life, endure tortures, and willingly suffer for it. It is likened unto a man, who having found a pearl

19. LW 22.530 (WA 47.231).
20. LW 22.529–30 (WA 47.230).

in a field, trashes all else to acquire it (Matt 12:45–46). They too will receive the drink from him who offers it. Luther admittedly confesses that he is not as skillful as he should be in the art of recognizing the gift and the Giver. This was partly because he does not possess a profound and strong faith as he would like to. He is keenly aware of the old Adam, which continues to present an impediment so that what he sees or hears is the person of the pastor or brother rather than the Word he speaks. Because we are still in our flesh, we fail to esteem the oral Word and the ministry as a treasure costlier and better than heaven and earth. This impels the Lord Christ to say, which Luther paraphrases in the text: "If you knew the gift of God, and who it is that is saying to you, 'Give Me a drink,' then I would not be obliged to run after you and beg for a drink. You would run after Me and ask Me for the living water. But since you do not know the gift and do not recognize Him who is speaking with you, you despise Me."[21] That Christ is that very gift and the Giver is indeed a treasure above all treasures. He brings with himself another treasure, that is, forgiveness of sin and redemption from death, devil, and hell, if only we believe it. And yet no one could fully express the worth of this treasure. Unless we become God's pupils, the knowledge of the nature of this gift and the Person of the Doctor and Teacher, Christ alone, remains hidden from us. Not flesh and blood but faith alone could perceive the voice of God hidden in Christ's plea "Give me a drink!" Like a stammering child, we begin to recognize that it is not humans we are hearing; it is God who is proclaiming to us an incomprehensively great treasure we have in the divine Word.

We approach God not on our own terms, but on his. "For God will not Himself be found in a place of our own choice and choosing."[22] God confined his presence in the temple in Jerusalem before the advent of the true temple, Christ the Lord. "God had done this, not for His own but for His people's sake, in order that they might have a definite place where they could find Him. For this reason He was not found elsewhere."[23] But this was to terminate now; Jerusalem was no longer the designated abode of God. In the New Testament God established another temple for his habitation: the precious humanity of our Lord Jesus Christ, assumed from the Virgin Mary. "There, and nowhere else, God wants to be found."[24] This is verified in John 4:21–23: "The hour is coming when neither on this mountain nor in Jerusalem will you worship the Father in spirit and in truth." Thus we must

---

21. LW 22.527 (WA 47.228).
22. LW 22.250 (WA 46.762).
23. LW 22.249 (WA 46.760).
24. LW 22.249 (WA 46.761).

place our faith in the person of Christ, whom alone we worship, who sits at the right hand of God in heaven. We should not embark on pilgrimages to Jerusalem, as if God's presence was limited to there. Whoever wants to find God must raise heart and eyes in faith heavenward to the person of Christ, the real and true temple, in whom God is pleased to dwell. For God has established Jesus Christ as the true temple where God would henceforth reside. This is a change in the domain of worship, from the earthly temple to Christ's humanity, in which God hides himself to speak with us. "This same body was God's temple, His castle and palace, His royal hall."[25] Just as in times past those who sought God outside Jerusalem missed God, so also in our times all who seek God elsewhere than in Christ, end up finding no God at all. Whoever finds God outside of Christ will find "the devil."[26] Immeasurable comfort emanates from this, that Christ's body is a temple of God, God's constant abode, and nowhere else. The God with whom we have to do is not God hidden in his supreme majesty but God hidden in the incarnate Son, namely, "God who is proclaimed and worshipped"[27] in Jesus of Nazareth. "There this God, who becomes man, who suffers, dies, and rises from the dead, is proclaimed to me, enters my ears, and by way of my ears enters my heart. Whoever dishonors Christ also blasphemes God, for He is one Person of the Trinity."[28] Luther expressly affirms that in his Word, the one God has lifted his veil, taking a step out of his absolute concealment. God, who is hidden in his naked majesty and nature, does not concern us because God has come in the person of Jesus Christ and therefore has been revealed. The naked God does not concern us because clothed in his Word, he is offered, worshipped, and proclaimed and therefore is accessible. God's essence is accessible insofar as God defines his hiddenness precisely in his self-revelation in Jesus' crucifixion and resurrection. God in his own life corresponds to Christ come and crucified. Whoever wants a gracious God must not bypass Jesus Christ, the proper mercy seat (Rom 5:25); whoever seeks God apart from Christ will end up meeting the God, not of mercy but of wrath, as described by Moses as "a devouring fire" (Deut 4:24).

The distinction between the hidden and revealed God evinces for Luther a paradox in virtue of which, even in God's human hiddenness, God remains the divinely unsearchable and unapproachable majesty in which presence we would be annihilated if we do not take refuge in the love of God that has appeared in Christ. The distinction does not entail two deities

---

25. LW 22.248 (WA 46.760).
26. LW 22.250 (WA 46.762).
27. LW 22.470 (WA 47.181).
28. LW 22.470 (WA 47.182).

or contradiction in God. Both as the hidden deity and as the revealed deity, the one God directs us away from God as he is in himself when we seek to grasp him above his human life, cross and resurrection, toward God as he defines himself in the incarnate Word.[29] Although Luther's emphasis is on God as revealed, he never abandoned the paradoxical doctrine of God who smites to enliven. Integral to Luther's theology is the revelation of anything but salvation—that is, God's impossible and inscrutable wrath before which we are terrified. "From this absolute God everyone should flee who does not want to perish."[30] We must lay hold of this God, "not naked but clothed and revealed in His Word; otherwise despair crushes us," as it did to David.[31] For Luther, the negative aspects of the hidden God and the law are not identical. The hidden God truly condemns the sinner to hell as the sinner's ultimate end, whereas the law sends the sinner to hell as its alien work in order that he might be raised up as the proper work of the gospel. The distinction between God as hidden and God as revealed parallels to the distinction between law and gospel, however, only insofar that the hidden God condemns so that we might cleave to God as he is revealed in mercy. The annihilating knowledge of the hidden God is causally useful if it causes us to flee from its inscrutable terror into the immeasurable grace of God as revealed in Christ. Like the law, the hiddenness of God functions as the alien work by which God keeps us from self-justification through thought and action.[32] Not until we reach the point of utter despair under the hidden God are we prepared to receive God's grace under the revealed God. The certainty of faith lies with the incarnate God: "This God clothed in such a kind appearance and, so to speak, in such a pleasant mask, that is to say, dressed in His promises—this God we can grasp and look with joy and trust."[33] In the face of the utterly dark God, Luther can speak confidently of who God is considering his having spoken definitively in the clothed God. As long as we pry into the forbidden area of the naked God, it leaves us with absolutely nothing, no joy but despair, no liberty but bondage, no consolation but terror. However, as long as we cling to the incarnate God where he is sealed, it leads us into joy, freedom, comfort, and confidence, as we soon find ourselves wrapped in his grace against the wrath of the hidden God.

29. See Gerrish, "'To the Unknown God,'" 263–92.

30. LW 12.312. For a study of hiddenness as a predicate of God, see Lienhard, *Luther*, 255–58; Paulson, "Luther on the Hidden God," 363–71.

31. LW 12.312 (Ps 51).

32. Placher, *Domestication*, 49: "Here the hiddenness of God seems to function . . . as an alien work by which God keeps us from trying to justifying ourselves through reason and work."

33. LW 12.312.

Hidden in the Created Forms of God's Word

God's Word is an instrument of power, which assumes created forms. It is Luther's hermeneutical presupposition that God has chosen elements of his created order, which are intrinsically good, to effect his saving will.[34] Such understanding runs contrary to Western esoteric culture, which, under the grip of the influence of ancient Greece, tends to differentiate the spiritual from the material, and elevate the spiritual above the material. In contrast, Luther, thinking Hebraically, rejects this co-called Platonic spiritualism; he affirms that differentiation occurs between God the Creator and his created order, not between the spiritual and material, since both belong to the created order. God has governed his people through tangible and material signs that so they could recognize him visibly, lest they roam to the ends of the earth in search of him. Animated by this biblical vision, Luther presumed that God at all times bestows external, visible signs so that people might see with their physical eyes that God is disposed to be their benefactor. For instance, Isaiah went naked to demonstrate that Palestine was to be plundered (Isa 20:2–4); Jeremiah wore a wooden yoke about his neck (Jer 27:2); Adam was promised the seed of woman from God, and God dressed Adam and Eve in furs (Gen 3:21); circumcision was instituted as a mark of God's own peculiar people. These are the appointed signs in which the Word of God is hidden, and to which the promise of his presence is attached. Just as in the time of the Old Testament, where patriarchs were given signs of God, in the time of the New Testament, God has given us baptism, the Sacrament of the Altar, and absolution, so that we know where to seize him and take hold of him. God has attached his recreating Word to Christ's flesh, to human language in oral and written form, to the sacramental elements, all of which are the instruments of God's power unto salvation to those who believe (Rom 1:16). Just as God converses with us, by hiding in the incarnate Son, so he continues to meet us, by hiding in humble, insignificant forms: baptism, Holy Communion, preaching, confession and absolution.[35] These are separate instances of the Word of God, which convey to the church God's unwavering promises; and grace is common to them all, bestowing upon the believer forgiveness of sins, life, and salvation.

In all Christendom there is "nothing greater or more sublime" than God's Word, "the principal item."[36] Luther explains this by using a body-soul analogy, in which "the soul [Word] is the chief part, [and] without it

---

34. Kolb and Arand, *Genius*, 176–79.

35. LW 22.202 (WA 46.712). See the Smalcald Articles III: IV (1537), in Tappert, *Book of Concord*, 310, where Luther discussed the creaturely forms of the Word of God.

36. LW 22.304 (WA 47.33).

the body [external signs] is nothing but a foul and stinking carcass."[37] All external signs are nothing if they are devoid of the divine Word; they possess validity by virtue of the strength of the Word of God. It is God, not humans, who preaches and baptizes; it is God, who wants to save us by the Word, which comes to us in a humble form. The preaching of the gospel must be held in high esteem so that our lives be built on solid ground. "For God instituted the ministry of reconciliation and established the Word of reconciliations, that is, the Gospel, among us (2 Cor 5:19) that we should pay diligent attention to it and hear it."[38] For this reason it was necessary for John the Baptist to precede Christ in his mission, to proclaim the external Word and to point at Christ. We must adhere to God-ordained means of the preaching ministry, absolution, and the Sacraments, through which God accomplishes his mighty acts. This is contrary to the sectarians and fanatics of Luther's time, who disdained the oral word, and taught that the Spirit does everything apart from external means.

John wanted to exalt the Word more highly than the Sacraments themselves. Therefore he said in John 4:2: "Although Jesus Himself did not baptize, but only His disciples," to stress that Christ institutes baptism and permits his disciples to administer it. Christ himself dispenses the ministry of the Word, which takes precedence over the holy form of the externals. The efficacy of baptism lies in the Word attached to the element, not in one's faith or lack of it. The Word of God will endure and is true despite contrary appearances. It does not invalidate baptism even if the one baptized is unbelieving and ungodly, just as the gospel would be true even if no one believes, for both are God's work, not ours. This is spoken against the Anabaptists, who aver that baptism is valid only if the baptized person believes. The Anabaptists could not adduce that those whom they rebaptize really believe; nor could they have access to the heart condition of those whom they rebaptize. On the contrary, Scripture informs us that little children believe, as Christ declares: "Let the children come to Me, do not hinder them; for to such belongs the kingdom of God" (Mark 10:14). The baptism administered remains valid even if it could be proved that a child or an adult did not believe when baptized. "For Baptism is not our work; and whether I believe or disbelieve, it remains good and valid in itself."[39] This does not imply that faith is superfluous. Luther clarifies: "If I believe, it benefits me; on the other hand, if I do not believe, Baptism will not redound to my good in all eternity. For Christ says: 'He who believes and is baptized will be saved;

---

37. LW 22.516 (WA 47.219).
38. LW 22.56 (WA 46.583).
39. LW 22.175 (WA 46.688).

but he who does not believe will be condemned' (Mark 16:16). For this is God's Word. Therefore it will endure."[40]

Just as the water of baptism is effective only through God's Word, so it is not the eating and drinking of the eucharistic elements that are effective but the words "for you" and "for the forgiveness of sins." The power and worth of the sacrament lie primarily in the words of Christ which we take to heart. The sacrament is therefore not efficacious being celebrated in itself, but in being believed—this, too, is to be attributed to God's initiative and grace. To draw us to himself, God creates in us hunger for a proper reception of the sacrament. This hunger is generated not by any human compulsion but by a revelation of who we really are before God. This, too, is God's work. Nevertheless, it is an alien work, which he performs by putting us under the law so that we might thereby see our wretched condition and feel the need to be liberated from it as God's proper work. The revelation of sins by means of God's commandment and the believer's willing resolve to get rid of them and longing for godliness constitute the beginning of a hunger that is pleasing to God. God's prior act in the sacrament precedes faith, calls to faith and establishes it so that we possess it. Central to Luther's teaching is the dogmatic assertion that justification occurs not from the sacrament itself but from the faith that it arouses in us. Faith grasps the benefits Christ has acquired for us, which are communicated to us through the sweet, blessed and majestic words of Christ in the mass. For the gift of the Christ's body and blood is a sign which assures us of the promise of God's forgiveness, the very content of the sacrament and the gospel. As Augustine had taught, so Luther conceived the signs of the Eucharist as more than merely symbols of a heavenly reality. He claimed that God had determined to use certain elements of the created order as the vehicles through which he exercised his recreating power to restore sinners to himself, effecting in us the joyous exchange of Christ's righteousness for our sinfulness. Therefore the Eucharist does not merely signify forgiveness of sin and eternal life but actually effects them, if only we believe. The Lord's Supper is not a propitiatory sacrifice offered to God, and thus is not effective on account of the work that is performed (*ex opera operato*). Nor is it effective on account of the work of the one who administers (*ex opera operantis*). The ground of the efficacy of the Eucharist is the causative Word of God, which conveys the grace of Christ. It is God addressing us in the Eucharist: "It is God who has His being here, who speaks here, and is active here."[41] God is gracious to us, "not, of course, in His majesty, which is too sublime for us," but "in his state of humiliation

---

40. LW 22.175 (WA 46.688).
41. LW 22.505 (WA 47.210).

and humanity He speaks to us and offers us His Sacraments."[42] The sacraments are likened unto the Incarnation. Just as God meets us in the human person of Jesus, so he meets us in his sacramental signs. The sacraments are just ordinary bread and wine, but hidden beneath them is the glorious majesty. "The glory of God is precisely that for our sake he comes down into the very depths, into human flesh, into the bread, into our mouth, our heart, and our bosom."[43] This, too, is linked with Luther's theology of the cross in which God reveals himself in what seems weak and foolish, the opposite of power and might.

The same applies at confession when the focus should not be on our confession and contribution but the words by the pastor: "I absolve you of your sins." Against the fanatics or enthusiasts, Luther propounded that God conveys the grace of forgiveness not through the secret working of the Holy Spirit but through the physical, external Word spoken by human beings. Luther refuses to bind the power of the Keys[44] to the professional clergy; rather he includes the absolution spoken by a lay Christian,[45] fully effective as that spoken by the pastor in the stead of Jesus Christ. A series of Eastertide sermons on John 20:19–31 (1522–1540)[46] indicates his break with the penitential system of the medieval church, according to which the sacrament of penance is required to obtain forgiveness. To benefit from the sacramental character of the priest's absolution, the penitent begins with contrition of fear, followed by enumerating all sins committed since the last confession. This ensures him that the eternal guilt of sin was removed by the priestly absolution. But penance of works must be applied to satisfy the temporal punishment due to sin, or else they might suffer punishment in purgatory. Logically, if the church has the power to impose the penalty, it should also have the power to remit it. This line of reasoning paved the way for the abuses associated with the granting of indulgences, resulting in the theology of works-righteousness. This theological understanding became the catalyst, on the one hand, for Luther's repudiation of the system, most evidently taught in the *Ninety-five Theses* (1517), and on the other hand, for an ardent proclamation of the doctrine of justification by faith, the material principle of the Reformation. Though contrition comes necessarily as the assault of the law on conscience, it is ineffective to bring about forgiveness. The heart is incapable of determining when it is contrite enough, and hence

---

42. LW 22.470 (WA 47.182).
43. LW 37.73.
44. For a study of the power of the Keys, see Rittgers, *Power*.
45. LW 69.330 (WA 10.3.96).
46. LW 69.313–436.

contrition offers no certainty of forgiveness. No one knows whether one's pious activities (vigils, studies, almsgiving, fasts, prayers, etc.) are found pleasing to God, in which case doubt remains in one's afflicted heart. Rather than recollecting specific sins, which leads to despair, Luther emphasized the proclamation of grace and forgiveness through absolution and faith. In lieu of the traditional pattern of penance, namely contrition, confession, and satisfaction, in a sermon of 1519 Luther reconfigures the triad as absolution, grace, and faith.[47] The absolution as the Word of God and the faith that received it occupied the focus of Luther's preaching thereafter. In his 1531 sermon on Jesus' words, "Those whose sins you remit, their sins are remitted" (John 20:23), Luther avowed: "The whole world has [thus] been deprived of its work, contrition, and sorrow. If you desire [forgiveness] . . . you will not find it in a cowl or a monastery, but in the mouth of Peter . . . This is where faith belongs, so that it might be believed, so that it might be faith alone that saves and justifies, because I cannot grasp those words of Peter, that sins are forgiven, with my hands, but only by faith, not by fasting or all good works."[48]

In his 1531 sermon on John 20:23, "Those whose sins you forgive," Luther speaks of two-fold sin: "made-up sins," which the papists manufacture, and make out of the small and insignificant matters; "true sin," which is committed against the Commandments and Law of God.[49] The latter is twofold, encompassing "sin lying in wait" (Gen 5:7), sins committed against the Decalogue before they are acknowledged (such is David's sin before Nathan the prophet calls attention to it), and "acknowledged sin," of which David writes in Psalm 51:3: "For I know my iniquity, and my sin is ever before me."[50] Similarly, St. Paul writes in Romans 7:19: "When the commandment came, [sin came alive and I died]." The acknowledged sin, the fruit of the law, will receive forgiveness, the fruit of the gospel. Unless we bring true contrition and show compelling signs that we are sincerely seeking release from sins, our sins will be retained, and damnation is the proper outcome. For God seeks a famished and thirsting soul, and offers such forgiveness; yet forgiveness is offered not because of the contrition, but purely because God has promised that he will remit them. Confession is not to be done away with, but it is the absolution, defined as the proclamation of forgiveness, that is decisive. Confession itself is fruitless unless it is accompanied by

47. See his "Sermon on Penance (1518)," LW 70 (WA 1:319-24); "Sacrament of Penance (1519), "LW 35.11; cf. "Explanations of the Ninety-Five Theses (1518)," LW 31.100-05.

48. LW 69.394, 396, 398.

49. LW 69.375 (WA 48.335).

50. LW 69.375 (WA 48.335).

absolution, just as the law by itself works the opposite of justification unless it is accompanied by the gospel. So we should conduct ourselves in such a manner that we base the absolution on the certainty of God's promise. "God does not forgive your sins because you feel them and repent of them and have contrition and sorrow over them—rather [so long as you do this] you are in them, and it is no merit, [but visible sin]. Instead, sin is forgiven for this reason: the Lord wills to be merciful, out of pure grace. And when the Lord speaks over you the word 'Your sins are forgiven,' say, 'On account of this [my sins are forgiven].'"[51] However, God alone is responsible for both contrition, which God works in us through the law, where sin comes alive and becomes utterly sinful, and absolution, which God works in us through his promise, where such sin is completely remitted. Not only does God promise, but he also fulfills this promise by creating faith in it. When faith obtains a promise, "it finally grasps the object it was made for and in so doing takes leave of itself and clings only to Christ."[52]

Moved by his friendship and love for us, God visits us in the guise of a humble human being for our welfare at heart. Though the pastor may look unimpressive, God hides in him his divine majesty so that he resembles his beloved apostles, the instruments of God's power. The crucial thing to bear in mind is that the treasure [word] must not be given up because of the person [human], and that we might recognize Christ, the gift and Giver of all, who is hidden in a seemingly insignificant vessel. Whether a pastor is endowed with a good and clear voice or not, whether he is gifted and learned or otherwise, or whether he possesses good diction and articulation or not is secondary. One may be tempted to look at the pastor more than at God, in which case he has become "half a Jacob."[53] If we focus on the fact that it is a poor village pastor who is speaking, we will not be thrilled at God's Word. We must become an apt student of the Word that we might hear Christ say: "Give me a Drink!"

We must develop the art of honoring and hearing the precious Word hidden in preaching. For God designates a place where he speaks and we could hear him there: "in church, in books, in your home; and this is God's Word as surely as if God Himself were speaking to you."[54] This reflects how Luther moved from the medieval view of the priest as one who conducts ritual and makes sacrifice in the mass to a creaturely being, namely, the pastor who builds faith in his people through the proclamation of the Word.

---

51. LW 69.392 (WA 34.I.324).
52. Paulson, *Lutheran Theology*, 122.
53. LW 22.529 (WA 47.230). This is an allusion to Gen 27:16–29.
54. LW 22.527 (WA 47.228).

When we hear a sermon, however, we do not hear the pastor. The voice is his but the words he employs are really spoken by God. When we hear words of judgment from the preacher, it is God who is addressing us with hell-fire, as in law; when we hear the words of comfort from him, it is God who does this, as in gospel. Luther elaborates on the hiddenness of God's Word in preaching:

> To be sure, I do not hear this with my ears or see it with my eyes; all I hear is the voice of the preacher, or of my brother or father, and I behold only a man before me. But I view the picture correctly if I add that the voice and words of father or pastor are not his own words and doctrine but those of our Lord and God. It is not a prince, a king, or an archangel whom I hear; it is He who declares that He is able to dispense the water of the eternal life. If we could believe this, we would be content indeed.[55]

The forgiveness of sin Christ won through his suffering and resurrection is distributed through the mouth of apostles and preachers, and grasped through faith in the Word that they bring with them. The preacher speaks, and in his speaking the justifying action is accomplished; the word spoken becomes the deed performed. When his confessor Johann Staupitz assigned him to the task of preaching in the monastery, Luther protested, "It will kill me. I won't last three months." But St. Staupitz's remarkable reply, "When the preacher speaks, God speaks," emboldened Luther to preach with the same boldness with which St. Paul spoke of his preaching office in 2 Corinthians 3 and 4.[56] Thus Luther avowed: "God has opened my mouth, and bidden me to speak and . . . not keep silent as long as I live, until Christ's righteousness goes forth as brightness, and his saving grace be lighted as a lamp."[57] His confidence is solely in the Word that proceeds from Christ's mouth, not in the faith and piety of people, as is borne out in John 2:24: "Jesus did not entrust himself to man." Inherent in such confidence is the promise of God that assures him, "Just go on preaching; don't worry about who will listen . . . You preach and let me manage."[58] Preachers could only assume "the right to speak," though not "the power to accomplish."[59] Preaching is not preliminary to the sacraments, a lower stage of God's grace that we apprehend through sacramental action. Rather, like the sacraments, the apostolic proclamation brings God and all his gifts. Preaching is not a discursive re-

---

55. LW 22.526 (WA 47.227).
56. WA 51.517 as cited in Meuser, "Luther as Preacher," 136.
57. LW 45.347–48 (WA 15.24).
58. WA 10.I.2.51 as cited in Meuser, "Luther as Preacher," 137.
59. LW 51.76 (WA 10.III.15).

flection on God, as is the custom of the university; nor is it a rehashing of the old story, as is done in theatrical dramas. It is a saving event, wherein God attaches the promise of his saving presence. It inculcates the benefits of Christ's Passion and resurrection for us, thereby creating a people no longer under divine wrath.

God's grace descends upon us from the open heaven above us, as we hear his Word in the creaturely forms in which he hides. All these means are revelatory of a gracious God who delights in overwhelming us with these proofs of his mercy and love for us. Each of these is an extension and an application of the gospel. As part of the order of confession before the priest, Luther had the pastor ask the parishioner why he desired to receive the sacrament after he had just received absolution. The parishioner was to answer that he desired to strengthen his soul with God's Word and sign. In reply, the pastor asks whether absolution has not already bestowed grace. To which the parishioner retorts, "So what! I want to add the sign of God to his Word. To receive God's Word in many ways is so much better."[60] Thus all Christians learn for their consolation that they are not forsaken by God. "Truly, what Jacob once beheld in his great distress and need, that you now behold in Me. Indeed, you see this not while asleep or in a vision, as Jacob did, but much more definitely and clearly through faith, namely, through the Word of God."[61] Whoever cherishes God's Word shall feel in his heart the consolation of Christ. Faith will convince us that the God we behold is not a terrifying jailer and judge, but the gracious and loving Father, who surely "converses with us, governs us, provides for us, and Christ hovers over us—but invisibly,"[62] in more than one way.

---

60. LW 53.118 (*A Short Order of Confession Before the Priest for the Common Man*, 1529).

61. LW 22.208 (WA 46.718).

62. LW 22.202 (WA 46.712).

CHAPTER 3

Enroll in the Spiritual School
Regeneration, Faith, and Works

Regeneration has causal priority over human deeds; unless one is given new birth he cannot perform good works. Just as regeneration precedes good works, so does faith. Just as a clean heart is God's creation and handiwork (cf. Ps 51:10), so faith is created in us without our own work. Not reason but grace initiates Christ's descent in order that he might draw us through his ascent. The Holy Spirit works with the Word in baptism to create in us rebirth, implanting new understanding in our hearts, and awakening new and holy impulses towards God in us. Not by flesh but by faith do we reap the fruits of God's salvific actions in Christ: righteousness, innocence, forgiveness, grace, eternal life and heaven. These benefits rightly belong to those who enroll in the "spiritual school,"[1] in which they as pupils of the Holy Spirit relinquish their reason and receive guidance from Christ, the Superior Teacher of the heavenly things: regeneration, faith, and works. All of these are in Luther's exposition of John 3.

Nicodemus, the Paradigm: Regeneration

Luther makes use of the story of Nicodemus to impart his doctrine of regeneration.[2] A pious and influential aristocrat, Nicodemus possessed an irreproachable character, decent and obedient to the Law of Moses. He called

---

1. LW 23.168 (WA XXXIII.265).
2. Pfitzner, "Luther as Interpreter," 65.

on Christ, convinced of his own holy and honorable life, and expected applause from Christ on his blamelessness and piety. Though Christ accepts his confession, he smashes his good works and introduces the doctrine of regeneration, "a far different and greater doctrine"[3] than what was customarily taught in the schools and synagogues, where plenty of attention had been paid to the Ten Commandments, Moses, and the prophets. Nicodemus' piety cannot advance him toward heaven, unless he is born anew. Christ said: "Truly, truly, I say to you, unless one is born anew, he cannot see the kingdom of God" (v. 3). In our fallen condition, we are dead, damned, and doomed; we cannot do anything unless we have life. Parallelism occurs between creation and new creation; both are the result of God's action out of nothing (*ex nihilo*). This is in keeping with God's nature and work, the opposite of what humans do. Whereas humans make something out of pre-existent materials, God makes something out of nothing to accomplish his saving purpose. One must observe the proper order in which good works are placed—not before regeneration but after it. One must be born anew before he can do good works. New birth occurs not by human agency but by the Holy Spirit and by water (John 3:5). All our deeds, even the most pious, done in the old birth are of no account. "In the new birth man becomes something that he was not before; birth brings into existence something that was nonexistent."[4] To have eternal life requires different parents; this is not brought about by a monastic order. He must be made an entirely different person, a new person. "It is necessary to peel off the old skin and the old birth, and to put on the new."[5] Nicodemus fails to grasp the meaning of this new birth, supposing Jesus is referring to physical birth. Thus verse 4: "How can a man be born when he is old? Can he enter a second time into his mother's womb and be born?" Jesus was introducing the doctrine of rebirth by water and the Spirit, apart from which all is lost. "Water," according to Münzer, symbolizes "affliction and temptation."[6] Luther did not deny it, for that indeed was the case, especially in the Psalms such as Ps 18:16 and Ps 69:1–2. But here Christ is referring to baptism, of real and natural water. This water, connected with God's Word, becomes a veritable bath of rejuvenation through the Holy Spirit. "Here Christ also speaks of the Holy Spirit and teaches us to regard Baptism as a spiritual, yes, a Spirit-filled water, in which the Holy Spirit is present and active; in fact, the entire Holy Trinity is there. And thus a person who has been baptized is said to be born

---

3. LW 22.277 (WA 47.4).
4. LW 22.281 (WA 47.9).
5. LW 22.281 (WA 47.9).
6. LW 22.283 (WA 47.10).

anew."⁷ This understanding is verified in Titus 3:5, where St. Paul describes baptism as "a washing of regeneration and renewal in the Holy Spirit;" and is further substantiated by Christ, who taught in Mark 16:16 that "he who believes and is baptized will be saved."⁸ Jesus ushers in a new doctrine that supplants Moses'; he is not speaking of circumcision and of the temple but of a new washing. This is a fulfillment of Moses who pointed to Christ as a new Prophet who will succeed him. Thus Deuteronomy 18:18 says: "God will raise another Prophet like me from among your brethren; Him you should hear." We are to come to this new prophet and are baptized with water and the Holy Spirit, a baptism that causes a new birth and a renewal of being. Nicodemus could not know or believe that Christ died for him, unless this truth had been given to him by the Holy Spirit through proclamation. New birth comes only when people believe that Christ died for them, and through baptism, in which the Holy Spirit is active, making new persons of them. No one can enter the kingdom of God unless, he passes "from the birth of sin to the birth of righteousness."⁹ This is the proper order: "This new birth must precede good works,"¹⁰ that we have been made newborn creatures and are created for good works. "Good works are necessary; but they are performed only by those who have born as new persons, by those who can and must do them."¹¹

To aid Nicodemus in understanding rebirth, Christ teaches him with something known to all, "the wind," an analogy he derives from nature. Thus John 3:8, "The wind blows where it wills, and you hear the sound of it, but you do not know whence it comes or whither it goes; so it is with everyone who is born of the Spirit." The wind is real, constantly surrounding us; and we feel its strong effect when it comes. Yet it is so mysterious that not one movement of it can be discerned. Neither does it blow according to our wish, nor can we control its direction. Despite this, we are content to hear its sound and feel its breath. So it is with regeneration through the water and the Holy Spirit: "The sound of the wind is also heard in this Word of God: 'I baptize you in the name of the Father and of the Son and of the Holy Spirit.' Furthermore, you also have the wind in the baptismal water; the Holy Spirit is blowing here."¹² So a person is born anew by the sound of the divine Word, hidden in the visible signs such as baptism. Regeneration

---

7. LW 22.283 (WA 47.11).
8. LW 22.283 (WA 47.11).
9. LW 22.282 (WA 47.10).
10. LW 22.287 (WA 47.15).
11. LW 22.279 (WA 47.6).
12. LW 22.295 (WA 47.24).

truly happens through the hearing of the Word in the power of the Holy Spirit. Here we must observe the limit of God's revelation; we can neither see nor ascertain how this happens, but it truly occurs. Nicodemus gladly accepts without understanding "far lesser things,"[13] such as the movements of the wind. Now he should gladly humble himself and be taught by Christ of a "far greater"[14] thing, that he must be born anew by water and the Holy Spirit. Nicodemus should follow Christ's testimony, and confess: "I must not see, feel, know, or recognize anything. I must only listen and cling to the Word, basing everything on the Word of God alone."[15] He must behave like a person who is subject to attacks of dizziness, blindfolded, and led across the bridge; lest he falls into deep water beneath it.[16] So, too, if we are to be saved, we must simply close our eyes and follow our guide, the divine Word; we must be wrapped in swaddling clothes and led to the point where we believe without seeing. Christ intends that we stay with the Word, and not torture ourselves with exploring the nature of God to acquire more than what we are supposed to know. To be guided aright, we must be governed by the Word; otherwise we are like a patient who wants speedy recovery but refuses to stay within the confine of the physician's advice. The ungodly goes on his own way, seeing, evaluating, and judging everything according to what he sees and feels—that of the old birth. A godly person is imbued with a capacity to perceive truth in a different light, for he has a reliable and superior Leader, namely Christ. He heeds Christ's words and follows him into the darkness. There he finds himself wrapped in Christ's cloak, through which he ascends into heaven. To be safe and saved, one must remain on the royal way, following the sound of the Word. Even the ecstatic experience of Paul being caught up into the third heaven (2 Cor 12:2-4) cannot be allowed to reign above the Word. Faith rests content with the sound of the wind, "follow[ing] this Word, testimony, and message, depending entirely on it; for God permits Himself to be heard in the proclamation of the divine Word. Set your heart wholly on it, as I Peter 1:13 says."[17]

Just as a distinction occurs between old and new birth, so also a distinction between physical birth and spiritual birth exists. Verse 6 says: "That which is born of the flesh is flesh, and that which is born of the Spirit is spirit." The Hebrews understand "fleshly" as "physical."[18] We are nothing

13. LW 22.295 (WA 47.24).
14. LW 22.298 (WA 47.27).
15. LW 22.305 (WA 47.34).
16. LW 22.305 (WA 47.34).
17. LW 22.307 (WA 47.36).
18. LW 22.288 (WA 47.16).

but flesh or physical being, which will perish unless there is another birth. While whatever is flesh remains flesh, whatever is born of the Spirit is spiritual. These two are irreconcilables. Unlike physical birth, spiritual birth is invisible and intangible. It cannot be perceived by the five senses, nor can it be purchased by anything that is of this world; it can only be believed. The chief treasure the spiritual birth dispenses is forgiveness and eternal life, which faith appropriates. New life will endure when physical life ends; spiritual life will abide when physical birth vanishes and is no longer felt. John expands this in John 6:63: "The flesh is of no avail; it is the Spirit that gives life." Flesh summarizes all the wisest and the mightiest on earth, all their powers. Flesh is "the fruit of reason."[19] Shortly after uttering, "It is the Spirit that gives life," Christ adds: "The words that I have spoken to you are spirit and life" (John 6:63). The latter statement explains the meaning of "spirit." The words Christ spoke were spoken by the Holy Spirit. Christ's words are spiritual, and therefore cannot be grasped by the flesh and its wisdom. The flesh is nothing but dead matter; Christ's words are nothing but life. Reason, flesh, blood or human wisdom are dead; they are not life or spirit. To acquire life for ourselves, we must become a new, spiritual person who begins to believe Christ's words. Faith (not flesh) constitutes a new, spiritual person out of the one who makes Christ's words his own. Fleshly birth is of no use, but is subject to damnation; the spiritual birth, that of the Holy Spirit, is life. If Christ's sermon is to penetrate the heart, something more profound than human wisdom must be added. We must abandon ourselves to Christ and give ear to his words, regardless of whether they can be reconciled with our reason. Whoever seeks to overcome must enter the spiritual school, in which the Holy Spirit is the Schoolmaster and Teacher. "He transforms these words into fiery flames and living thoughts. He needs no pen and ink to write them in your heart for your understanding and acceptance. It is His fire and breath that gives you life and permits you to put these words to good use."[20] Not until the Holy Spirit teaches and blesses us do we ever fathom Christ's words: "Truly, truly, I say to you, unless one is born anew, he cannot see the kingdom of God" (John 3:3). The Holy Spirit must make you his pupil and impress on your heart what reason fails to do. "This is then the work, not of your reason but of the Holy Spirit. It is He who presents it. It is His gift and present, implanted in your heart for you to believe it. Thus the Lord Himself has interpreted the words 'the Spirit gives life' as meaning 'to believe.'"[21] Consequently good works will follow, but for a different reason.

---

19. LW 23.163 (WA XXXIII.257).
20. LW 23.172–73 (WA XXXIII.271).
21. LW 23.170 (WA XXXIII.267).

Just as a person is spirit to the extent he adheres to the Word, so he is flesh to the extent he remains in unbelief. The former is life; the latter is death. To take hold of Christ's Words is to lay hold of "the Spirit that gives life." Whoever hears and keeps the Words will be quickened, for they are life. Hold to Christ's Words, where the Holy Spirit and his acts are located; or else nothing avails. "Whoever hears this hears God's Word and the Spirit's Word. If he believes it, he, too, becomes spirit. Thus faith is obtained."[22]

Witness, Reason, and Faith: Fullness of Christ's Descent and Ascent

John 3:13: "No one has ascended into heaven but He who descended from heaven, namely, the Son of man, who is in heaven," is our faith: that Christ is true God and man. Christ is true God within the eternal Godhead who descended to us, was born of the Virgin Mary. His existence is simultaneously on earth below and in heaven above; after achieving redemption via his death and resurrection, he ascended. Unless he is from heaven, the Son of God could not bear witness to what he himself has seen and heard. Intrinsic to the power of witness is a correspondence between identity and office. The identity, that Christ is God's Son, knows the depth of God's will and wisdom and of the Father's counsel, constituting the basis of his testimony. Characteristic of the kingdom of the Messiah is his prerogative to bear witness of matters never seen or heard before:

> Now the Lord Christ becomes the Father's witness from heaven above all. He is to do nothing else than open His lips. His sermon is to be a testimony of the Father's attitude, of His plan for mankind's salvation and redemption from sin, death, and the power of the devil. To this He bears witness. He submits to becoming man and to dying. He rises again from the dead and says: "My words bear witness to this. If you believe this testimony and these works, then you believe the witness of God."[23]

The phrase, "He bears witness to what He has seen and heard" (v. 32), speaks of the function Christ performs—preaching. He bears witness that he has come as Priest and Lord. But he does this in the form of poverty that reason is offended. The glory of God is precisely that for our sake Christ did not come clothed with the power of an emperor, but he came in lowliness, bearing witness solely of things not seen and heard in law books or

22. LW 23.177 (WA XXXIII.279).
23. LW 22.466 (WA 47.178).

anywhere else on earth. This, too, is linked with Luther's theology of the cross: God reveals himself in what seems weak and foolish. Reason cannot understand how a poor person, like Jesus, could impart eternal life. The logic of Scripture is not reason, which often leads us astray, but witness, which we must hear if we wish to be justified before God. Thus the sermon of the Lord Christ is called "a testimony,"[24] a message to be believed, not rationalized. The nature of witness falls not within the range of rational comprehension. Our task is to honor God, simply listen to the witness and say: "Even if I do not understand this, I still believe it. It is ordained that this should be hidden from sight and reason and should be apprehended by faith alone, let it be so."[25]

The Messiah is portrayed as a Preacher, as all the prophets had prophesied. Preaching marks his realm and rule, with all wisdom, life, and truth as its very contents. God's Word is not to be thought of except as having been sent; it does not come to us through human zeal and investigation. Christ's Word does not spring from the soil of earth, as he is not of the earth. It is the nature of the word to be sent: "The Word does not come unless it is sent from heaven."[26] This is true of the Word in all its forms: made flesh, in Jesus' own proclamation, in Scripture, and sacraments. "Reason is blind; man must hold his ears to Christ's mouth and listen to His Word."[27] Unless God sent his Word, the whole world would have been in total darkness concerning redemption from sin and comfort for conscience. Thus he says: "For He whom God has sent utters the Word of God" (v.34). Without revelation, people are blind to their ailment and cannot detect how corrupt human nature has become through its birth from Adam. They too are ignorant of the remedy for it. Those who consider themselves healthy show no interest in a physician; they either do not believe that they are ill, or they know of no physician for sickness. Not only does reason decline to see our wounds and sickness, but also denies the means of healing and consolation. Because of sin, we fall from Paradise, and cannot ascend into heaven. Our destiny is the abyss of hell. No one can ascend into heaven, except the Son of God and of Mary, who descended from there. The knowledge that Christ is the way to heaven is shared with us by his dear Gospel. Thus we ascend into heaven, not on account of our own person but Christ's own person, to whom we nestle up and press close. By speaking of his descending and

---

24. LW 22.467 (WA 47.179).
25. LW 22.466 (WA 47.178).
26. LW 22.484 (WA 47.193).
27. LW 22.467 (WA 47.178). For a major study of grace and reason, see Gerrish, *Grace and Reason*.

ascending, Christ crucifies human reason, crushing all spiritual pride and reliance on our own righteousness. This text is a thunderbolt against all the "work-saints,"[28] excluding all people and negating all other ways, for they are useless and vain. Because human reason, piety and good works did not descend from heaven, they cannot ascend there again. No one could ascend into heaven by observing the Ten Commandments, for they are too high for sinners to reach and human nature is too corrupt to obey and trust God with all our heart. The world assumes that satisfaction resides within itself, and thus cannot confess: "I believe in Jesus Christ, who died for me." It will hear Christ's verdict: "You are of the earth." However, John the Baptist declares the opposite of what the world denies: "Christ descended from above and dies for me." He shows us how we could rid ourselves of the earthly by clinging to "Him who is from above, to His works, words and suffering. All this is heavenly."[29] Its precise meaning is provided by Christ himself: "This was done for a purpose; for as Moses lifted up the serpent in the wilderness, so must the Son of man be lifted up, that whoever believes in Him may have eternal life" (vv. 14–15). Just as the people were asked to look at the serpent physically so that they may be cured of bodily poisoning, so we are commanded to look at Christ spiritually in order that we might be cured of eternal poison. "This symbolized the fact that God let His Son descend from heaven and be nailed to the cross, where He, too, hangs like a serpent or a worm, the object of scorn and contempt, as Christ Himself laments in Ps 22:6. But whoever believes in this crucified Christ will not be lost and perish but will have everlasting life, just as those who looked at the bronze serpent in the wilderness did not die but were saved."[30] Faith clings to Christ, who not only has the form of a bronze serpent without venom but also a power in him which will cure us of venom. Whoever looks at Christ, this serpent, in faith is assured of everlasting life. Christ is the powerful medicine effective enough to cure sin, death, the old nature and birth. This is indeed miraculous!

God does not "confine Himself to giving us His Son in His incarnation, but He also delivers Him into death for us,"[31] and this should instill in us amazement and awe as we ponder it. For all this is done "especially"[32] for our sakes. To be sure, he was not God's Son for our sake, since he was eternally God's Son before creation; yet it is for us that Christ descended from

---

28. LW 22.330 (WA 47.58).
29. LW 22.460 (WA 47.172).
30. LW 22.340 (WA 47.67).
31. LW 22.354 (WA 47.79).
32. LW 22.332 (WA 47.60).

heaven and ascended again. "Christ's ascending and descending pertains not only to Him; no, they are significant especially for us."[33] Grace initiates Christ's descent to take us through his ascent, to partake of his righteousness and life. Thus to know the Savior aright one must not ignore this article of faith, for "whoever passes [it] by, passes God by; but whoever discovers it, discovers God."[34] Therefore the proclamation of the Son of God is no trivial matter; it is ordained that everything is concentrated in the Son; without him all is lost. "Faith is the engagement ring which betroths us [the bride] to Christ."[35] It lays hold of Christ, saying to him: "You alone ascended." This article of faith, that Christ is our Lord, "is the jewel, the gem, and the golden chain around the neck of the bride, who believes that Christ is true God from eternity, that He descended from heaven and became incarnate of the Virgin Mary, and that He, and no other, ascended again into heaven."[36] Through faith in "the fullness of His ascent and descent,"[37] we no longer remain lost below, but that we, too, may ascend to where Christ is. The entirety of salvation hinges on this Man, who has accomplished everything. Faith accords the honor of declaring that the testimony of this Man is certainly true, and in so doing lays hold of the substance of Our Gospel:

> This Man's work alone accomplished everything. All that we are and have is of the earth, but He who is from above does it all with His death and blood. Even one little drop of His blood helps the entire world; for this Person is very God, begotten of the Father from eternity. He holds the ransom money for me, not for Himself. He was not born, nor did He suffer and die in order thereby to become the Son of God, for He was this already. No, He suffered and died that I might become a son of God through Him and that I might derive my righteousness, wisdom, and sanctification (1 Cor 1:30) from above.[38]

That Christ is the Son of God refers to his essence; he is God himself. That we are sons of God refers to his office and his works for us (*pro nobis*), that we are made such through him. Being holy, Christ requires no salvation for himself; he has always been, and still is, Salvation and Life. The difference between this Son of God and us lies in the fact that Christ gives us eternal life and through himself overcomes death. "He is very God not only in His

---

33. LW 22.332 (WA 47.60).
34. LW 22.331 (WA 47.59).
35. LW 22.334 (WA 47.61).
36. LW 22.334 (WA 47.61).
37. LW 22.336 (WA 47.63).
38. LW 22.459 (WA 47.172). See note 156.

Person but also in His office and His works."³⁹ His works bear witness to his divinity, as he says in John 14:11: "Even though you do not believe Me, believe Me for the sake of the works." The works Christ performs—bestowing eternal life, killing death, and saving all who trust in him—are exclusively divine, proving that Christ is very God in person. "Thus Christ is established in the Godhead not only according to His person and majesty but also according to His work."⁴⁰ We must have a Savior who is more than a saint or angel, or else our salvation is at stake. No mere human could acquire eternal life nor conquer devil and death for us, except "the crucified Son."⁴¹ "But if He [the crucified Son] is God, then the treasure is so heavy that it not only outweighs and cancels sin and death but also gives eternal life."⁴²

The Son transfers his redemptive work to the Father. Their work is identical, for they are one. John distinguishes between the Persons, but identifies the work. In so doing, he repudiates the heresy of Patri-passianism, according to which the Father, who is one person with the Son, was crucified.⁴³ A modalistic doctrine endangers trinitarian distinctions; a perichoretic doctrine, that the Father is in the Son, and the Son is in the Father, establishes the distinction of persons that we should not say that "the Father suffered,"⁴⁴ dying on the cross. For Christ is nonetheless the same God, one undivided Essence with the Father, so that we can say: "God was crucified and died for me."⁴⁵ St. John's deity is not an impossible deity, a God who cannot suffer and die for me. Neither can we fail to find God in the suffering and humiliation of Christ, nor find a God for our comfort and salvation outside Christ. Christ prohibits us from thinking of him as separate from the Father. He directs our attention from himself to the Father, declaring that the Father's Son-giving love is just as strong as his own, reflected in his sacrificial death. Luther has Christ say: "Whoever beholds the Father's love also beholds Mine; for Our love is identical. I love you with a love that redeems you from sin and death. And the Father's love, which gave you His only Son, is just as miraculous."⁴⁶ The Son of man and the Son of God in one Person are delivered up to death for us; the one indivisible Person entered the jaws of death and the devil to conquer them for us. It was impossible for death

---

39. LW 22.364 (WA 47.88).
40. LW 22.364 (WA 47.89).
41. LW 22.367 (WA 47.91).
42. LW 22.363 (WA 47.87).
43. LW 22.365 (WA 47.89).
44. LW 24.99 (WA XLV.550). Althaus, *Theology of Martin Luther*, 197.
45. LW 24.99 (WA XLV.550).
46. LW 22.355 (WA 47.80).

to hold Christ, since deity and humanity were united in him (Acts 2:24). Just as Christ cannot remain in death, we too will be raised as he was if we believe and remain steadfast in Christ. United to him, these negatives—sin and death—no longer accuse and condemn us. Even though we may feel the magnitude of sins, and are frightened or saddened by them, we nevertheless overcome this feeling by swiftly confessing: "I believe in the Son of God and of Mary. He is the devil's venom and death; but at the same time He is my salvation, my remedy, and my life."[47] Not by his exemplary life, but by faith in what Christ has done for him was St. Bernard saved. The realization of this came on the threshold of death when he exclaimed:

> "Oh, I have lived damnably! But heavenly Father, Thou hast given me Thy Son, who has a twofold claim to heaven: first, from eternity, by reason of the fact that he is Thy Son; secondly, He earned heaven as the Son of man with His suffering, death, and resurrection. And thus he has also given and bestowed heaven on me."[48]

The Beautiful Message: Law and Gospel

The inexpressibly beautiful message: "God so loved the world" has no other content than this: "He gives us Himself. He gives us His Son, who is very God. He gives us the very dearest thing He has and is."[49] The first part of the gospel, which informs us that God gives his Son to the world, is "truly the most pleasing proclamation of all; it is the best."[50] There we do not encounter God as an angry judge but a gracious Father, who is so kindly disposed to us that he gave his dearest Son for us so that we might be seized by the power of the inexpressibly glorious words: "you will not perish." The outcome is two-fold: we are not placed under the law; sin, death, devil, and hell are disposed of—but more than this, we are placed under the gospel, that through the Son of God we are his children, to whom God himself has been restored and the gift of eternal life bestowed. Thus Luther saw in John 3:16 Christ's "living words,"[51] "rich, excellent, and salutary words."[52] Not by the

---

47. LW 22.356 (WA 47.81).

48. This story also appears in Luther's *Table Talk* (Weimar, *Tischreden*, IV, No. 4121).

49. LW 22.374 (WA 47.97).

50. LW 22.370 (WA 47.94).

51. LW 22.369 (WA 47, 93).

52. LW 22.370 (WA 47.93).

impartation of the treasury of merits of the holy saints, but purely by clinging to God's Son, "our Gift and our Treasure"[53] are we saved.

After having spoken affirmatively, Christ adds negatively: "Not to condemn the world" (v. 17). Because of original sin, the world has already been judged and condemned; it has always been full of judgment, misery, and death. Romans 1:23 teaches that our conscience condemns and accuses us; there is no need of a judge any more. The Law of Moses, our conscience, and our hearts already declare such judgment. But the judgment is past; the Father and the Son condemn no one. Christ is "the Pledge and the certain token,"[54] which shows that God is not angry with us. Christ was not sent to judge the world, to cause us to escape from him or to repel us as a stern judge. The Father and the Son are one in purpose; it is not the Father's purpose to judge the world, nor is it the Son's purpose. These negative but glorious words, "Not to condemn the world," must be enshrined in our hearts, for they assure us that God does not cast us off. "The negative is always more impressive than the affirmative."[55] The ungodly fear God, flee from God, and cannot approach God joyfully; the believers shall not be condemned or flee from Christ as from a relentless judge. The believers lay hold of Christ who has put an end to judgment, the mission to which he was delegated. Whoever has the Son of God and believes in him escapes the judgment, for the Father has abolished it through the Son. We should apply ourselves like a child to the study of Christ's words: "I did not come into the world to condemn the world," which assure us that "He is a mediator, a Helper, a Comforter, a Mercy Seat, a Bishop, a Shepherd, a Brother, an Intercessor, our Gift, and our Deliverer—not a judge. He was given and presented to us so that we would not have to flee from Him."[56]

Judgment still befalls due to unbelief, the unwillingness to hear and to accept Christ's office: he came to remove sin, bear it on his shoulders, and lock up the portals of hell. The world denies the sorry truth that it is steeped in sin and is damned. It refuses to believe the joyful message that divine wrath, hell, and damnation have been vanquished by the Son, and are no more. Of them, Christ himself declares: "He who does not believe is condemned already" (v. 18). Of verse 19: "This is the judgment, that the light has come into the world, and men loved darkness rather than light," Christ intends to assert that even if we stand in awe of God's judgment, we

---

53. LW 22.369 (WA 47.93).
54. LW 22.375 (WA 47.98).
55. LW 22.375 (WA 47.98).
56. LW 22.377 (WA 47.100).

fear not because the "grand and blessed light"[57] has come into our hearts, vanquishing the fear of divine wrath. Rather than harboring fear of the final judgment, we should yearn for it, the time of rejoicing. Through the Son, all has been changed; redemption has been achieved. At the Last Day death is swallowed up; our bodies will be raised; the devil will be bound; God's disfavor will end. This Day of Judgment will be converted into a happy and desirable Day for those who believe; on the contrary, those who love darkness more than light will dread of the Last Day. At the point of death, when the devil magnifies fear, we should counsel the dying not to recourse to his good works and merits but to Christ's blood, and baptism. Holding the crucifix aloft, we confess: "This Man did everything. I know of no work and merit other than that of this Man."[58] We are to put off the cowl, but put on the baptismal robe as the remedy against dying in great distress and agony.

Genuine faith will openly confess before the world the two statements: Christ is the Son of God and of Mary, and that he became my Savior. "If this Christian confession stands, other good works will follow."[59] True faith makes it impossible for a person to persist in darkness. A healed person finds no delight in sickness nor allows anything to impair his health; he does not remain in sin, but shuns it. Because we retain the old nature, we still feel sin in us. Sin still "remains" in us; it does not "reign" over us.[60] So when vices of the old self torment our souls, we rely on Christ and say: "Thou didst not come to condemn me but to save me." But those who love darkness would not gain comfort from Christ's words, for they live outside Christ and under God's wrath, in law. Christ's words do not apply to them: "God did not send His Son to condemn the world." Whenever Christ speaks a negative word: "Woe unto you!," he intends to save you and lead you to the Father's love, the positive. Even if God grievously afflicts us, he is not bent on casting us off. God's chastening rod is an alien work, which God performs to save us and keep us under his protective care: to ward off and prevent his doom. The negative thought, "Oh, God is angry with me!" could only be put to death by the affirmative words of Christ: God did not send His Son to condemn the world.

Concerning this phrase, "People love darkness more than the Light," Luther speaks of two kinds of darkness: the "subtle darkness," of heretical error and folly, and the "obvious darkness," of open vices and sins.[61] The

---

57. LW 22.384 (WA 47.106).
58. LW 22.387 (WA 47.109).
59. LW 22.393 (WA 47.114).
60. LW 22.394 (WA 47.114).
61. LW 22.389 (WA 47.110).

world is swamped with such darkness, and if they despise the Light, God will chastise them with even greater darkness. They will experience the opposite of the gospel, and share in the verdict which the Lord Christ pronounced upon certain cities: "Woe to you, Capernaum! Woe to you, Chorazin!" (Matt 11:21–24). The world hates the beautiful light of the gospel because the gospel reproaches their darkness. Jesus said: "Because their deeds are evil." When the Light tells us: "You have sinned," we should be wise enough to acknowledge it, as David did: "I have sinned against the Lord." Then he received the forgiveness of sin, through Nathan's declaration: "The Lord has also put away your sin" (2 Sam 12:13). To justify sin reveals one's love for darkness; to repent of sin reveals one's love for the Light. Those who sin and try to be justified in their own words confirm the words Christ spoke in John 3:20: "Everyone who does evil hates the light and does not come to the light." They will not acquiesce to God's judgment; those who resent reproof are bent on doing evil, finding it impossible to say: "Thou art justified and blameless in Thy judgment." It takes a fine skill to concur with God's judgment concerning our sinful condition, as David did: "Against Thee only have I sinned." If sin were to remain in our conscience, it would send us to sheer despair. By contrast, it would be far better for us to cast the sins which our hearts admit into Christ so that God may be justified in his words and we may receive the remission of sin. The God who accuses us will at the same time reassure us. The convicting voice of conscience, as in law, could only be vanquished by the consoling voice of God, as in gospel: "Christ came into the world to take away our sin." Just as he who shuns the light gives reliable proof of his darkness, so also "he who does what is true comes to the Light" (v. 21). Whoever teaches the truth does not evade the light. Whoever does not cover up nor justify his sins does not flee the light, but confesses: "I have sinned." This real confession does not harm him, for he allows himself to be admitted into the light, and be reproved by it.

One Purification: None but Christ

John, according to Luther, delights in allegorical interpretation.[62] The Jordan is the image of the people and the law of Moses. The whole country is called "the land of Jordan,"[63] for the river is the center of the country. The river Jordan symbolizes the law, which was issued in the land and points to Christ, who was to be born in this country. John was fond of baptizing close

---

62. LW 22.414 (WA 47.132); LW 22.422 (WA 47.140). The allegorical interpretation Luther inherited from the late Middle Ages.

63. LW 22.422 (WA 47.140).

to the mouth of the Jordan as well as at Bethabara, the town where the river empties into the swamp. The Jordan flows through Judea until it reaches Bethabara. There it loses its identity as it dissolves into the Dead Sea. Finally the river is drowned, near the town of Bethabara where John baptized. The word "Jordan" means "descent,"[64] that the river descends gradually and follows a downward course toward the sea, where it disappears. Jordan is an allegory for Moses and law. The doctrine of the law shows forth the depth of sin until it leads us to death; it kills and leads us to nowhere except hell. No one can come and drink of this Jordan, that is, the teaching of the law, without being annihilated by it. All is dead there, and all is swallowed up by the Dead Sea. Mystically and spiritually, just as St. John was the last preacher of Jordan, he too marks the end of the law, as Christ says in Matthew 11:13. The law was terminal; and people would have to leave the Jordan and be baptized with the fire from above. Luther has John say: "I am not the true Master; but the Bridegroom will appear, who will accomplish all. I am still part of the Jordan, but He who is to come will not be like this river."[65] In response to John's disciples who debated purification (v. 25), John said that the disciples require a different purification, not by his baptism but by Christ who appears and is now baptizing. Jordan must cease and be drowned in the Dead Sea; similarly his baptism must cease and give way to Jesus' baptism. John did not claim that his baptism could cleanse us, but that we are cleansed by Christ who follows, who purifies us with the Holy Spirit.

All the patriarchs and prophets of the Old were saved and purified through their faith in the advent of Christ, of whom John testified as "the true Purifier."[66] Circumcision was salvific inasmuch as it was linked to the coming Messiah. Because they were circumcised upon their faith in him, they were saved. "God has a different system of accounting," according to which "the one who is nothing must be everything,"[67] and vice versa. Abel, who presumed to be nothing, is everything. He was purified not because of the sacrifice he offered but because of his faith in the promise. Cain assumed that since he was the first-born and the only prince in humanity, he deserved special favor from God. What is missing in Cain is faith, even though his sacrifice is of good quality. He who presumed to be everything, is nothing. The significance of purification has not changed, that one must claim nothing from oneself and expect everything from God. What was formerly observed in the law avails not, for everything points to Christ, who

---

64. LW 22.423 (WA 47.141).
65. LW 22.423 (WA 47.141).
66. LW 22.427 (WA 47.144).
67. LW 22.427 (WA 47.145).

is here now. Since the beginning of the world until the days of John the Baptist, people looked forward to the coming Christ: "Believe in the Seed that is to come." Now that Christ has come, we hear the news: "The Messiah has come." There are not two Christs, but One "who is and who was and who is to come" (cf. Rev 1:18). Whoever is intent upon devising his own method of purifying puts himself outside Christ, and is eternally lost. Even the baptism of the most holy man, John, counts for nothing, except faith in the Christ who was to come.

John 3:27: "No one can receive anything except what is given him from heaven," accentuates God as the origin of all gifts. Baptism is ineffective, unless it is accompanied by faith. Faith springs from God, not from us; this is also true of purification, which has its origin with God and heaven. God had commanded circumcision, which, when enveloped in faith, is a means to the end, Christ. John's baptism, when immersed in faith, points to Christ, whose purification is our crown. Seeking a different purification from the one commanded by God is sheer idolatry. Christ is not introducing a new purification. Christ's and John's purifying are identical, except that Christ himself is the purification from above. Nothing but what heaven has given prevails. Baptism is devoid of value unless Christ, who is purification personified, is present there; he illumines every man (John 1:18), and receives all from his fullness (John 1:16). This verdict of John effaces all canon laws and buries all good works; no one, not even the holiest on earth, can teach anything or take anything unless it is given from God. It behooves us to listen to Christ into whose hands the Father has placed everything—baptism, the Power of the Keys, and Holy Communion—these gifts through which he rules the church. God has ordained and adorned the estates—of parents, governments, burghers, and peasants—for our benefits. Each has its own proper order and sphere, but it does not efface our sin. It is Christ, succeeding John, who is wholly different from him, and who achieves everything. John stands so close that he could point to Christ, the Messiah, whom he is not. The saints may be endowed with splendid gifts, but all this amounts to little. If viewed by themselves, the saints appear fair; but when compared to the Bridegroom, they are nothing. "This calls for a different Man, an only Man, namely, the Bridegroom, whose bed must not be defiled."[68] With theses words: "I must decrease, and Christ must increase" (v. 30), John invalidates all humanly-devised means of purification, including his own. By his own admission that he cannot purify, St. John placed all—his disciples and us—into Christ's arms and bade us abide with him. John rejoices just to be the friend of the bridegroom and hear his voice,

---

68. LW 22.438 (WA 47.154).

for the bridegroom has now come (John 3:29). The groom draws the bride into his arms, baptizes and purifies her. "The Bridegroom, who has a bride, is everything."[69] It is the groom's voice we must hear. He confides all his secrets to his lover. She is one body with her Bridegroom and shares all his goods (Eph 5:25–30). And yet this union does not obliterate the unique identity of the bride, whom the groom sanctifies by placing her under the domain of his purifying grace. This relationship is so exclusive that it leaves no room for a second bridegroom;[70] the church must be subject to Christ or be counted as a harlot. John elevates Christ above all else. To hear another voice than Christ's is to falsify and misplace one's confidence; it is to pollute the bridal bed. By faith we are incorporated into the Man from heaven; for, as his bride, she has everything in common with her bridegroom. In that union, the bridegroom gives the keys and all his goods to the bride. If we remain with him, his heavenly works become ours. "These are not earthly works, . . . No, His Word and doctrine are heavenly and are the Word of God. In this way, you also become heavenly and will ascend to heaven."[71] The heavenly righteousness of the heavenly Man belongs to those who say: "I believe in the only-begotten Son of God, Jesus Christ." Being alone sent from God, Christ brings with himself the Word that contains all. In him dwells the treasures of wisdom; outside Christ there is nothing but sheer blindness, idolatry and ignorance. To Christ alone is the Holy Spirit given completely, for he is full of mercy and truth. Only those who trust Christ partake of the immeasurable liberty of this illimitable Spirit, which includes deliverance not only from the law of Moses but also from its every accusation and condemnation. We have our being from Christ, who is one with God (John 14:9), and not from ourselves. Just as since the Father is in Christ, we have the Father through the Son, so also since the Spirit is in Christ we have the Spirit through him. "All fullness inheres in this Man; God dwells in Him bodily, and the Holy Spirit without measure."[72] By faith we drink from the Son, the inexhaustible spring, for satisfaction, and enjoy him as the chief Treasure. Salvation is to be sought nowhere except in this Man, the Preacher from heaven. Christ is "the chief gift of grace,"[73] in whom we all share in the fullness of our Lord God. The "immeasurable grace" (Eph 2:7) did not dwell in us originally, as they did in him; they are imparted to us by him.

---

69. LW 22.436 (WA 47.152).
70. LW 22.450 (WA 47.164).
71. LW 22.460–61 (WA 47.173).
72. LW 22.489 (WA 47.196).
73. LW 22.489 (WA 47.197).

Christ—The Only Image in Our Hearts

The subject of "For the Father loves the Son and has given all things into His hand" (v. 35) captures the evangelist's attention more than any other. He urges that we keep the Son of God in sight, through whom we look at everything else. "Permit Christ to be the only image in your heart."[74] In the order of being (*ordo essendi*) creation precedes redemption; in the order of knowing (*ordo cognoscendi*), redemption precedes creation.[75] Only when we are seized by Christ the redeemer do we apprehend God as our Creator. Thus to see the Son of God is to see him as the Creator of all the creatures, for God gave him everything on earth. When God moves the Son into our vision, he wishes to show us the Head, under whom all things are gathered; this Head is God's Son. So if we believe in God's Son who became man to redeem us, all creaturely beings—the sun, the moon, the stars, the trees—will appear increasingly "more beautiful" to us than before.[76] The kingdom of heaven and eternal life are obtained for us by sheer grace, not by our earthly works but by this heavenly Man's works. In Christ lies "the superabundance of God's grace,"[77] that even a single drop of his blood could conquer every contrary: sin, death, wrath, hell and eternal damnation. Through union with the Son of God, a Christian has become "a heavenly man,"[78] who can ascend to heaven from the midst of sin and death; the gates of hell cannot restrain him. Faith enables a heavenly person to lay claim to the heavenly works which "Christ wrought for us, presented to us, and still works in us."[79] As heavenly people, we transcend physical nature. We are no longer bound to think, speak, and act in an earthly manner. Hence what is forbidden is not the performance of good works but ugly

---

74. LW 22.499 (WA 47.206).

75. See Thompson, *Modern*, 100. Thompson uses the terms *ordo essendi* and *ordo cognoscendi* to speak of a double movement of the Trinity, "that of God to humanity—from the Father through the Son by the Spirit to our humanity—and that of humanity to God—by the Spirit through the Son to the Father in a reverse direction. The *ordo cognoscendi*, of experience, is not that of the *ordo essendi*, of the Trinity itself, but moves back, as it were, to God from the point where through Christ and by the Spirit he touches and changes life and accepts us as his sons and daughters. The movement of the Son is from the Father by the Spirit, and back again, drawing our humanity up into relationship with the Father."

76. LW 22.496 (WA 47.203).

77. LW 22.459 (WA 47.172). See note 156, where it states that Luther was keenly of the scholastic doctrine of "the superabundance of God's grace in Christ," as expressed in the Eucharistic hymn of Thomas Aquinas, "*Adoro Te devote*."

78. LW 22.461 (WA 47.173).

79. LW 22.462 (WA 47.174).

works, those that are done without faith. "Faith must be a living document, a seal, a signet, a conviction so strong that one is willing to forsake all for it. There God comes to you and makes His dwelling in your heart, converting it into heaven and Paradise."[80] The devil will vacate the heart of those who bear this signet ring; they will not be persuaded out of the ineffable love of the Father. When facing trials and afflictions, we are to close our eyes to them but open our ears to hear and believe this "impressive message":[81] the Father has placed all things under his hands, and we dare not seek it elsewhere. Hearing the gospel rather than seeing the contraries of it, those that seemingly contradict the gospel, is the way to combat these negatives: sin, death, devil and other spiritual afflictions. The enemies of life no longer reign over us because Jesus Christ, who shares equal power with the Father, and in whom alone we put our reliance, is Lord over all; this reality is sealed in our hearts by the Holy Spirit.

---

80. LW 22.474 (WA 47.185).

81. LW 22.500 (WA 47.207). See chapter six on the art of closing our eyes and opening our ears as a viable way to combat all contraries of life.

CHAPTER 4

Christ, the Bread of Life
The Source and Substance of Salvation

The one underlying theme running through John 6 is the christological confession: "I am the bread of life" (v. 35). This too is the startling claim of the one whose voice we hear reverberating throughout the Johannine witness: this man Jesus, who is the Son of God, offers himself as the source and substance of eternal life. The Christology Luther presents as the ground of justifying faith presupposes the conviction that the man Jesus is true God. This conviction is understood in connection with the other unities: (i) the unity of nature of the Son with the Father who sends him; (ii) the identity according to which the Son of God and the Son of Mary are one; (iii) the indivisible union of the two natures so that the flesh Christ assumes is his very own; and (iv) the union of Christ with us by faith. For Luther, the doctrines of justifying faith and Christ are logically linked, mutually implicating and interpreting each other. Luther's Christology is thus "primary and determinative"; as Yeago puts it, "his doctrine of faith spells out the implications 'for us' of the truth about Christ, while the truth about Christ grounds justifying faith in reality and so determines its character."[1] It is in this chief article—justification by faith—in which St. John proved himself to be "the master."[2]

Luther did not deviate from what he taught in his *Babylonian Captivity of the Church* (1520): John 6 is not to be construed as referring to the Sacrament of the Altar,[3] as the language of eating and drinking describes faith

1. Yeago, "Bread of Life," 262.
2. LW 23.129 (WA XXXIII.199).
3. See LW 36.19: "the sixth chapter of John must be entirely excluded from this

as grasping hold of the life-giving bread, Christ's flesh. The saving gift in which we invest our trust must not be abstractly construed, purely in terms of properties such as God's forgiveness or justification, with no reference to the person of Jesus Christ. The logic of faith Luther advocates is just the opposite: faith adheres to the person of Christ, followed by the properties he gained for us. As Christ asserts: "Whoever eats of me shall live" (6:56). Faith, the action of the Holy Spirit, unites us to Jesus Christ as its object and content; it too receives the justifying benefits proceeding from union with Christ.

Seal: No Other but Christ

"God set His seal on His Son, who is man, the Son, who is this Food, who is the Owner of the granary, the Baker, the Waiter, and the Supply."[4] God has affixed his "seal" of authority upon the Son, certifying him as the Chosen One, in whom one must be found to be saved. This is verified by Father's voice from heaven (Matt 17:5): "This is my beloved Son, with whom I am well-pleased; listen to Him." Because God has placed his mercy and will exclusively on him, Christians must be intent on the eternal food the Son offers them, resting content to be fed by Christ. Christ declares, "I am the bread of life; he who comes to Me shall not hunger, and he who believes in Me shall never thirst" (v. 35). Christ employs "unusually direct and well-defined words"[5] to speak of himself not only as the source but also the substance of eternal life, the God-given bread. Luther offers "an incisive commentary" on this verse: "to come to Christ is the same as to believe in Christ."[6] What is in view is not the Lord's Table but believing itself. Thus verse 36: "You see Me and hear Me, and yet you do not believe." Christ here is speaking not of physical eating but spiritual eating, in the sense of believing in Christ. "For to eat . . . and to believe in Christ are one and the same

---

discussion [the sacrament of the bread], since it does not refer to the sacrament in a single syllable. Not only because the sacrament was not yet instituted, but even more because the passage itself and the sentences following plainly show . . . that Christ is speaking of faith in the incarnate Word. For he says 'My Words are spirit and life' [John 6:63], which shows that he was speaking of a spiritual eating, by which he who eats has life." LW 23.46 (WA XXXIII.65).

4. LW 23.15 (WA XXXIII.16). The word "Supply" could be translated "pantry" or "storehouse."

5. LW 23.42 (WA XXXIII.58).

6. LW 23.42 (WA XXXIII.58).

thing."[7] "To do God's work" is equivalent to the term "divine service."[8] "The true service of God consists in faith in Him whom the Father sent, namely, Jesus Christ" (v. 26). The work that we are to perform is to believe in him. Verse 28: "Then they said to Him: What must we do, to be doing the work of God?" reveals how vexed these pious people—the Pharisees and teachers of the law—were when Christ tried to teach them new doctrine. They assume that familiarity with the work of God, since they have the temple, priests, divine worship, and the knowledge of God. Christ calls all this "the transient and vain service of God,"[9] which does not last, and by which people perish. On the contrary, Christ introduces "the true, eternal, and unending service of God,"[10] of which they had been ignorant until now, when the Father placed his seal on Christ. Of good work, Luther is clear that "the first, highest, and most noble good of all is faith in Christ."[11] Yet faith is not one work in the medieval list of virtues, treated as subordinated to love. Rather, everything stems from faith and receives its goodness from it.[12] And yet "it is also called the work of God; for this is the true existence, work, life, and merit with which God desires to be honored and served."[13] Where faith is wanting, true service of God is vitiated. No one possesses faith of himself, unless it is divinely instilled and received as gift: "It is the Father who draws us and gives us the Word, and the Holy Spirit and faith by the Word. It is His gift, not our work or power."[14] Any works that have their sources in humans are of no efficacy before God. We must cling to Christ alone, who lies outside us, so that we may be justified aside and apart from our own agency. "In this manner God wants to be our Father and God, that we believe in Him who is not in us, but enthroned at the right hand of God."[15] There is nothing more pleasing to God than this: "Believe in Christ, whom the Father has sent to you." We are to accept his pronouncements; lest we sin against the First Commandment.

7. LW 23.42 (WA XXXIII.58).
8. LW 23.20 (WA XXXIII.26).
9. LW 23.22 (WA XXXIII.28).
10. LW 23.22 (WA XXXIII.28).
11. LW 34.159–60 (WA 7.72.1–36).
12. Kolb, *Martin Luther*, 81.
13. LW 23.23 (WA XXXIII.29).
14. LW 23.181 (WA XXXIII.286).
15. LW 23.24 (WA XXXIII.30).

The Unity of Father and Son: Salvation

Luther accentuates the significance the unity of nature between the Father and the Son has for salvation. Christ being true God requires a trinitarian explication, for Christ appears before us in Scripture as one who proceeds from and is sent by God. The Trinity is comprehended in the Son: "If you believe in Him who was born of Virgin Mary, and if you believe that He is also the true Son of God, then you also have God the Father and God the Holy Spirit."[16] The confession that Christ is the bread of life is logically dependent upon the assertion, that Christ is God with the Father. "But before we accept (that Christ is food), we must first be convinced in our hearts that He is God and the life, yes, the food and bread of life; and we must not look for God outside this Person."[17] Human thinking tends to devise another way to the Father, as the apostle Philip did. He wanted to bypass Christ and follow "a different route, a detour, to the Father,"[18] when he asked Jesus: "Lord, show us the Father!" (John 14:8). The evangelist John does not separate the Son from the Father, placing the Son on earth alone and the Father in heaven. "No, he *bakes* the two persons, the Father and the Son, together as solidly as possible."[19] Christ henceforth tells Philip: "If you behold Me, Philip, you also behold the Father; and if you hear Me, you also hear the Father." The Father is in Christ; and Christ is "this path, this ladder, master and lantern" to the Father.[20] Luther paraphrases Christ's reply to Philip: "Philip, look at Me. Whither do your wayward thoughts fit? He who wants to come to the Father must come to Him through Me. He grants this. And he who wants to come to Me must do so through the Father."[21] If we remain with Christ and accept him as the bread of life, we know for sure that we have the Father also, thus the entire Godhead.

> Yes, indeed, He is just that [God]; and apart from Christ you will not find God in heaven, in hell, or in the sea. . . In Christ you have the bread of life. He can give you eternal life, deliver you from death, and take the devil captive. You must trust that Christ is the fountainhead of life, and that God has poured all His gifts, His will, and eternal life into Christ and has directed

---

16. LW 23.116 (WA XXXIII.178).
17. LW 23.116 (WA XXXIII.178).
18. LW 23.53 (WA XXXIII.77).
19. LW 23.54 (WA XXXIII.79). The metaphor "*bakes*" means unites: he unites Father and the Son as one God.
20. LW 23.55–56 (WA XXXIII.81).
21. LW 23.54 (WA XXXIII.78).

man to Him. There we are to find all. If you take hold of Him, you have all; you have taken hold of the entire Godhead.[22]

That Christ is God gives "the greatest comfort"[23] to the frightened conscience uncertain about its status with God, living in constant dread of an unmerciful God. A turbulent heart may be stilled, as it reposes and bases its faith on the Person of Christ, in whom the Fatherly heart resides. Both Father and Son are one in being, and thus one in will and grace. "St. John joins and weaves the two wills together, making the being of the Father and the Son one—one will, one mind, one wisdom, one work, yes, one Godhead, and one thing."[24] The Father's will and the Son's will are so interwoven that just as it is the Son's will not to forsake us, so it is the Father's will that he not abandon us. Christ says in verses 38–39: "For I have come down from heaven, not to do My own will, but the will of Him who sent Me; and this is the will of Him who sent Me, that I should lose nothing of all that He has given Me, and raise it up at the Last Day." The fatherly will of which Christ speaks here differs from that demanded by the law: the former centers in the Person of Christ; the latter on good works. These two wills must not be confused nor equated. Faith must not be placed under the rubric of the law and the observation of the Commandments. Rather, whoever clings to Christ has successfully performed the will of God the Father. "[God's] will in Christ is only the gracious will of the Father, which kindly invites us to come to Him."[25] By a community of will between the Father and the Son, God presents his gracious resolve to befriend those who come to Christ and are given to him by the Father. This represents "a beautiful development"[26] of the sublime article of faith in Christ: "The Word which you hear is not Mine but the Father who sent Me" (John 14:24). The Word the Man Christ speaks proceeds from the heart of the Father. A significant difference occurs between the preaching of Jesus, in which we hear God himself, and that of Moses and the prophets, in which we do not hear God himself. For Moses received the law from the angels (Gal 3:19). His commission is not only different from Christ's but a lesser one, for the proclamation of the law merely leads to the performance of good works rather than hearing from God himself. "God's words and His nature and disposition"[27] correspond to each other; the former cannot be different from the latter. God's words

22. LW 23.55–56 (WA XXXIII.81).
23. LW 23.54 (WA XXXIII.78).
24. LW 23.61 (WA XXXIII.91).
25. LW 23.62 (WA XXXIII.91).
26. LW 23.64 (WA XXXIII.94).
27. LW 23.98 (WA XXXIII.149).

emanate from God's nature: "He is goodness, grace, and mercy." Thus when God speaks to us, we hear "only sheer grace, mercy, and goodness. His are fatherly and friendly speeches as He Himself is by nature gracious, merciful, and kind (Joel 2:13)."[28] The voice of the Father is not conveyed indirectly through created instruments, as in times past through a servant or any other medium (such as angels or Moses), but rather through the Son, we hear "a paternal voice proclaiming a message that abounds in unfathomable, ineffable love and grace, uttering nothing but blessing, nothing but what is good, sweet, and pleasant, for that is what it means to be God."[29] Thus whoever wants to be a Christian must be intent on hearing God through the Son, namely, from the mouth of Christ. "Whatever issues from the Son's lips proceeds also from the Father's and is the Word of the Father. In fact, the entire Godhead and the Father's heart is speaking to me when I hear that Man."[30] Christ appears to believers as a gracious and merciful God conforming to the picture of him as taught in the Creed. Christ banishes all wrath, anger, enmity, and disfavor of God, certifying that neither he nor the Father will deny those who heed God's voice. Not only is the promise from Christ's lips his own, it is also the Father's resolve, Word and heart. Luther has Christ say, on the one hand: "This is my Father's order and commandment. This I must do. I must accept you and keep you. This is God's will, and I am glad to fulfill it;"[31] and on the other: "This is your assurance"[32] that you will be preserved for Christ's sake, in whom you believe. The man Christ is the Son of God, who alone can impart eternal life, deliver us from hell, devil, and death. The two statements in verse 39, "I shall not lose him" and "I will raise him up at the Last Day," are proof of Christ's divinity. For to confer life and salvation can be done by none except the Creator. When the Lord declares: "Him who comes to Me I will not cast out," he intends to imprint in our consciousness God's friendly heart in Jesus Christ. "He is the true Bishop of souls, a Teacher, indeed, a faithful Pastor,"[33] who will preserve us from harm.

"No one can come to Me unless the Father who sent Me draws him" (v. 44). Passively, Augustine remarked: "If you are not drawn, you will be drawn nevertheless."[34] Actively, the Father "must draw" us, and does so in two ways: "Outwardly He draws by means of Christ's Word, and inwardly

---

28. LW 23.98 (WA XXXIII.149).
29. LW 23.98 (WA XXXIII.150).
30. LW 23.54 (WA XXXIII.94).
31. LW 23.69 (WA XXXIII.104).
32. LW 23.71 (WA XXXIII.107).
33. LW 23.56–57 (WA XXXIII.83).
34. See Augustine, *In Johannis Evangelium*, as cited in LW 23.94.

through the Holy Spirit."³⁵ The words which Christ spoke he ascribes not to people but to the Father. "Everyone who has heard and learned from the Father comes to Me" (v. 45). As Luther paraphrases them: "When I hear the mouth of Christ the Lord speak, I hear the Father."³⁶ The hearers of the Word fall into two groups. The first kind of disciples merely hear the external Word of Christ, without it penetrating their hearts. They lack confidence in this Word and do not recognize it as the Father's Word; hence they do not come to Christ. They refuse to be the pupils of Christ, and will not accept his direction. They aspire to be masters, exploring the majesty of God. Conversely, the second kind not only hears the Word of God but believes it to be true. They humbly acknowledge: "Reason is too limited to comprehend the Word of God, and in such matters I am a veritable simpleton."³⁷ They appropriate the significance of the words Christ quotes from Isaiah 54:13: "And they shall all be taught by God." The Father teaches you inwardly; then you are drawn. No one can come to the Father, however, unless he is a disciple of the Father and the Father has drawn him.

Luther expounds the significance of this expression of drawing: "When God draws us, He is not like a hangman, who drags a thief up a ladder to the gallows; but He allures and coaxes us in a friendly fashion as a kind man attracts people by his amiability and cordiality, and everyone willingly goes to him. Thus, God gently draws people to Himself, so that they abide with Him willingly and happily."³⁸ Whenever Christ speaks, we hear not only the Son's Word and voice, but also the Father's proclaiming that the Son was sent into the world out of paternal love: "that whoever believes in Him should not perish but have eternal life" (John 3:16). With this message, the Father enchants our hearts and leads us only to Christ. The Father does not draw us away from or beyond the Son; he draws us through the Son, the bread of life from heaven. Yet we do not become Christ's "pupil but the Father's, for it is not [Christ] who is speaking; it is the Father."³⁹ Nor is Christ a schoolmaster; but we both, Christ and the listener, share one Schoolmaster and Teacher, the Father, who instructs us. But "there is only this difference, that God is speaking to you through [Christ]. That is the glorious power of the divine Word, through which God Himself deals with us and speaks to us, and in which we hear of God Himself."⁴⁰ Christ wants us to stay with his

---

35. LW 23.94 (WA XXXIII.142).
36. LW 23.94 (WA XXXIII.143).
37. LW 23.95 (WA XXXIII.144).
38. LW 23.86 (WA XXXIII.131).
39. LW 23.98 (WA XXXIII.148).
40. LW 23.98 (WA XXXIII.148).

words in order that we might advance to the point where we conclude: "It was indeed a good sermon; I heard God, the heavenly Father."[41] Henceforth all questioning stops, for nothing is wanting. "Now you are a believer and a disciple of Christ, and you have come to Him; for the Father has drawn you and has brought you to Christ."[42] We are to gaze on Christ's lips, trusting the efficacy of his Word given him by the Father, that all will come to pass in the power of Holy Spirit.

> And when he hears the Word of God this Man Christ, he is persuaded that he is hearing the Word of God the Father. When the heart can arrive at the conclusion that God the Father Himself is conversing with us, then the Holy Spirit and the light center, and man is illumined and becomes a joyful master who can now test and judge all doctrines. For he is imbued with the light and has faith in the divine Word; and in his heart he is convinced that his doctrine is God's Word. These are the righteous, who not only hear the Word, as the vulgar mob does, but also regard it as the Word of God. . . The only method is to hear [Christ's] Word, to listen to [Christ], to let yourself be persuaded that [Christ's] Words are also [His] Father's Word. For the Father has His Word proclaimed from [Christ's] lips, and He enlightens your heart that you may realize that it is His Word. Thus the Father draws him whom He wishes to bring to [Christ]. We must let the Son proclaim the Word, and we must listen to Him. Thus He gives faith.[43]

The Son of God and Mary: One Son

Jesus Christ, the Son of God, is true man; we can see that he speaks like a human being: "For this is the will of My Father, that everyone who sees the Son and believes in Him shall have eternal life" (v. 40). Reason considers as insufferable heresy the doctrine that Christ's humanity could impart eternal life. The fanatics, including Zwingli, exclude Christ's humanity from his divinity, declaring that his humanity is of no avail (cf. 6: 53), with only Christ's divinity imparting eternal life to those who believe. In so doing, they divide Jesus Christ into two, divorcing the Son of Mary from the Son of God, teaching that we must not place trust in humans but in God alone. This Luther regards as contrary to the Creed, which knows "nothing of a

---

41. LW 23.95 (WA XXXIII.145).
42. LW 23.98 (WA XXXIII.145).
43. LW 23.96 (WA XXXIII.146).

Son of God who is not also Mary's Son who suffered, the God enveloped in humanity who is one Person."[44] Just as Father and Son are one in being, so the Son of God and Mary's Son are identical, and thus it is improper to separate one from the other and say that the humanity is of no use, but only the divinity. This was the error of many teachers, including Luther himself, who admitted his former neglect of Christ's humanity and overemphasis on his divinity. For to overlook Christ's humanity is to tumble from "the ladder"[45] that leads to Christ's divinity. Reconciliation with God occurs not through Mary but her son, Christ, the only God and the only Son of God, who descended from heaven and assumed human nature. Whoever receives Christ as Man receives him as God, for they are one Person. Whoever touches him, sees him, and crucifies him also touches, sees and crucifies the Son of God. "God is in Him personally, though hidden and concealed."[46] This Luther illustrates by an example: "If I steal someone's pocketbook and declare that I did not purloin the money but only the purse, would the other person say: 'You did not steal the purse, but you stole one hundred florins from me?'"[47] Such a distinction does not hold up. When Christ interprets himself as the Savior, declaring: "He who believes in Me has eternal life" (v. 47), it is exclusively his prerogative to speak about himself in such an illustrious manner, for the bestowal of eternal life is God's work alone. But this does not negate that the Son was born man from the Virgin Mary. "God is, to be sure, hidden from sight, but He is nonetheless present. In this light we must view the doctrine of Christ."[48]

"My Flesh" — Life-Giving Bread

Of John 6:51: "And the bread which I shall give is My flesh, which I shall give for the life of the world," Luther reiterates what he taught earlier (vv. 35ff), that this chapter refers to spiritual nourishment and eating, and does not apply specifically to the Sacrament of the Lord's Supper.[49] Here Christ is speaking of himself, "His own flesh."[50] Christ is speaking here of the chief

---

44. LW 23.102 (WA XXXIII.154).
45. LW 23.102 (WA XXXIII.155).
46. LW 23.104 (WA XXXIII.159).
47. LW 23.104 (WA XXXIII.159).
48. LW 23.105 (WA XXXIII.160).
49. LW 23.118 (WA XXXIII.182). See Boehme, "John 6," 13–14, where he argues that Luther and the Lutherans reject a Eucharistic interpretation of John 6. See also Mueller, "Notes," 802–28.
50. LW 23.118 (WA XXXIII.181).

doctrine of the Christian faith: believe in his flesh and blood, or else we be lost. "This is not simple, ineffectual flesh; as Christ says, it is His flesh. Here human flesh is united with the Godhead; it is made divine."[51] Yet the belief that this flesh is "a divine flesh"[52] is not derived from human reason; it is communicated to our hearts by the Holy Spirit. "This text is a thunderbolt against the fanatics,"[53] who fail to distinguish between the word "flesh" and the words "My flesh."[54] The word "flesh" requires no great skill to know what it means. When we hear the voice of him who declares: "My flesh is food indeed, and My blood is drink indeed" (John 6:55), these words take on an entirely different significance; the strength of the words "*My* flesh" lies in the identity of the speaker. Christ distinctly stresses: "My flesh," "My blood," for he wants us to take note of him who speaks and who teaches that this flesh is not the kind of flesh from which sausages come, but his very own. By means of a crude illustration, Luther speaks of a physician who takes pure water and makes sugar water. "It is water, yet not pure water, but sugar water. It does not act like water; for it is sugar water, and I cannot properly consider it water."[55] Though water indeed, it is now so permeated with sugar that it has been changed into "a different essence," with "a new quality and taste."[56] This shows that Christ is indeed one of us, of flesh and blood like us; yet he is more than that, that he is God. "We are nothing but water, bones, and flesh. But a sugar was added to Christ's flesh, so that he who sees His flesh and tastes and drinks His blood sees and worships God. On the other hand, he who desecrates these, crucifies and dishonors God. Thus one eats the Godhead in the human nature."[57] Just as whoever touches the water also touches the sugar, so whoever touches his flesh also touches his divinity.

Jesus is fully human, not according to the Old Adam, but the new.[58] The doctrine of the virgin birth is of one piece with the doctrine of salvation; both are purely by grace. Sinful humanity could not prepare for its salvation. Christ our Lord is not our creation; his mother became pregnant with him without carnal agency but by the Holy Spirit and his co-operation. Sinful humanity made no contribution to this; it did not carve him out of wood

---

51. LW 23.125 (WA XXXIII.193).
52. LW 23.125 (WA XXXIII.193).
53. LW 23.118 (WA XXXIII.182).
54. LW 23.119 (WA XXXIII.182). See Hendel, "Finitum est capax infiniti," 164, where he discussed the meaning of flesh and "My flesh" in relation with Zwingli and Oecoclampadius.
55. LW 23.119 (WA XXXIII.184).
56. LW 23.119 (WA XXXIII.184).
57. LW 23.120 (WA XXXIII.184).
58. Schneider, "Intimate Connection," 11.

or bake him with dough; he is solely provided by the Holy Spirit as both God's and Mary's Son. Though personally guiltless, he experienced all the weakness and curse that humanity incurred through sin. Christ's flesh does not possess the qualities of sinful flesh. It will not give rise to sin, or to a bad conscience or death, as other flesh does. Being Christ's, it will endow believers with godlike power, virtues and works. It will wipe out sin, deliver us from the devil and death, and will liberate us from all wretchedness. This is spoken against those who divorce Christ's humanity from his divinity.[59] For Luther, Christ's flesh is "godlike flesh,"[60] by which he impels us not to find God, in heaven or on earth, except in the flesh of Christ. By "godlike flesh," Luther is not a Docetist, for he truly affirms Christ's real humanity. By this phrase, he affirms that Christ's flesh acquires a new power through its union with his divinity; the divine power is present bodily in the flesh of Christ, and naturally acts in it. Luther avows: "These words of Christ, 'My, My, My flesh,' should be imprinted into man's hearts with large and bold letters . . . Here 'My flesh' means 'I am God and God's Son. My flesh is *divine, the flesh of God*'."[61] The flesh which Christ offers to be our true food is "more than mere flesh and blood, but [is] invested with greater strength by virtue of the word 'My.'"[62] God did not wish to offer us his divinity unconcealed; this is borne out in Exodus 33:20: "Man shall not see Me and live." Hiddenness is essentially God's; it is divine that God should hide, cover, and conceal himself in the flesh of Christ so that we might touch and apprehend him. It is not any flesh but Christ's alone to which God wants to draw us and bind us. Christ's flesh and blood, though real, not only have the qualities of flesh and blood but "partake of the Divine,"[63] as explained with the illustration of the sugar water. In addition, Luther resorts to the Patristic analogy of the glowing iron,[64] to expand on the soteriological import of the dual nature of Christ. When fire and heat are added to the iron, it glows. Though it remains iron, it is so diffused with fire that it acquires a new power that when one

---

59. LW 23.122 (WA XXXIII.189). The Valentinians were a Gnostic sect that emerged in the second century. On Luther's view of the Manichaeans, see LW 13.96.

60. LW 23.123 (WA XXXIII.189).

61. LW 23.126 (WA XXXIII.194). Italics are Luther's.

62. LW 23.119 (WA XXXIII.183).

63. The phrase "partake of the divine" is not a reference to Eutychianism: Christ's humanity becomes absorbed into the divinity and loses its distinctiveness. Rather it is to emphasize that the flesh the Son takes on is God's, and thus acquires new power on account of the union so that whoever touches the flesh touches God.

64. LW 23.123 (WA XXXIII.191). See footnote 95, where it indicates that the analogy of heated iron has its origin in Origen and Basil, which finds expression in John of Damascus, *The Orthodox Faith*, Book III, ch. 17, 1069.

touches it, one cannot call it merely iron on account of the heat. The red-hot iron could burn a hole through a barrel; a cold iron, not aglow with heat, could not brand anything. On the other hand, the fire itself is ineffectual in bringing about the same result apart from the iron, where the fire burns. "Thus divine power is present bodily in the humanity of Christ and does what God naturally does, or does what the fire in the iron does. Only flesh and blood are visible. But faith sees a Man, sees flesh and blood which is like fiery iron; for it is permeated with the Divine."[65] Luther does not locate the union in two substantial natures in Christ, a classic statement of the Eutychian error which robs the constituents of their integrity, making Christ into a *tertium quid* (third thing) between God and man.[66] Just as sugar water is sugary, or as a glowing iron is hot, so here one who encounters Christ's flesh encounters more than mere flesh but God himself. With Chalcedon, Luther affirmed the dual nature of Christ: "in the first place, that He is real flesh and blood, just as the water is real water in the sugar and the iron is real iron when diffused with fire; secondly, that the word 'My' imparts the divine element to the flesh and blood, and these are now no longer mere flesh and blood, but are now God's flesh and blood. Indeed, the flesh and blood remains, but the word "My" imparts the divine element."[67]

Luther lamented that this text "The flesh is of no avail" (v. 63) had suffered severe torture, especially under the Sacramentarians, who misconstrued the text as referring to the Lord's Supper. They attempted to prove that Christ's living and true body is not present in the Eucharist, but that mere bread and wine are found there. They also contended that Christ's flesh and blood in the Lord's Supper is mere flesh, and thus is devoid of any saving purpose. Their understanding, Luther contends, runs contrary to Christ who declared: "My flesh is food indeed" (v. 55), which gives life to the world. But here Christ is contrasting Spirit and flesh, the former quickens life and the latter reaps destruction. "Flesh is of no avail" relates to all that is born of the flesh, all the children who stem from flesh, all except Christ's body who was born of the Holy Spirit. This is clearly taught in the Creed: "I believe in Jesus Christ, who was conceived, not of flesh but of the Holy Spirit." The word "My" sets his flesh apart from all other flesh, that his is holy, blessed and endowed with the Holy Spirit. "By nature, of course, He

---

65. LW 23.123–24 (WA XXXIII.192–92).

66. Siggins, *Martin Luther's Doctrine of Christ*, 229: "But here Luther is not addressing the scholastic problem of unitive Christology, and he has abandoned substantial categories. Once again, he is simply asserting that this true and natural flesh and blood, born of Mary, given and crucified for the life of the world, is unique, because it belongs to the person in Whom God alone is to be sought and found by faith."

67. LW 23.124 (WA XXXIII.192).

is Mary's child. Still He has spiritual flesh, a true, divine, and spiritual body, in which there resides the Holy Spirit, who begot Him and spiritualized His flesh through and through."[68] The contrast reveals this: flesh by itself profits nothing; Christ's flesh profits everything.[69] Flesh by itself is of no avail, but flesh united to Christ, constituted as his own, shares in all God's glory via the doctrine of communication of properties.[70] The hearts which enroll in the school of the Holy Spirit will inevitably cling to this doctrine, that Christ's crucified flesh helps and saves us from death. "Thus the Lord Himself has interpreted the words 'the Spirit gives life' as meaning 'to believe.'"[71] While the doctrine of Christ's flesh as food for life is offensive to the heathens, it is "the greatest and the chief doctrine"[72] for the Christians. "This is the Christian's golden art"[73] and we must learn and believe the doctrine that our salvation and life are grounded in the flesh and blood of Christ, his suffering and crucifixion rather than in the law or its performance.

Shortly after uttering these words, "It is the Spirit that gives life," Christ adds: "The words that I have spoken to you are spirit and life" (v. 63). The latter statement explains the meaning of the word "spirit"—the words Christ spoke were spoken by the Holy Spirit. To take hold of Christ's words is to lay hold of "the Spirit that gives life." Christ himself states that it is by divine order that "the Spirit must not be sought elsewhere than in and by the words which Christ speaks. His words assure us that the flesh is given and the blood is shed for us. Whoever hears this hears God's Word and the Spirit's Word. If he believes it, he, too, becomes spirit. Thus faith is obtained."[74] Christ's words are spiritual, and therefore cannot be grasped by the flesh and its wisdom. Just as a person is spirit when he believes the Word, so he is flesh when he remains in unbelief. The former is life; the latter is death.

Faith Alone: Cornerstone of Justification

St. John joins three items, distinguished but inseparably one: first, the deity and humanity of Christ; second, faith in Christ, our Savior who atones for sin; third, the good works which attest to faith in God and love of our neighbors. God must begin his salvific work in us by the preaching of the Son

---

68. LW 23.167 (WA XXXIII.262).
69. See LW 37.145.
70. See chapter 11 on Luther's usage of the doctrine of *communicatio idiomatum*.
71. LW 23.170 (WA XXXIII.267).
72. LW 23.171 (WA XXXIII.269).
73. LW 23.171 (WA XXXIII.269).
74. LW 23.177 (WA XXXIII.279).

through his Spirit. His message rings in our ears and later penetrates into our hearts, causing us to both hear and believe. This occurs without any human actions, for these do not induce God to descend upon us; grace has descended from heaven when the Father sends the Son and draws us through the Son to himself. Salvation by faith in Christ alone is in conformity with Christ's explicit assertion that this food—Christ's flesh and blood—is an outright gift. "This is not your work; you did not perform or effect it. It is God's exclusively, and it comes into being without any cooperation whatever on our part."[75] Luther insisted that "we must first give the floor to John,"[76] who teaches us that Christ alone, not good works baked with Christ, as if the two together might obtain for us forgiveness of sins, is our salvation. Faith alone justifies, without human preparations. Yet "faith dare not be unfruitful,"[77] as it shall be accompanied by good works as the consequence. Though all is done when we believe, we do not forsake good works. Goodness toward our neighbor is an outward expression of the inner faith of our heart. But we must maintain that good works do not enact anything; faith has already accomplished all: "(Our) faith finds and imparts the bread of life and eternal life to you."[78] Christ did not swear an oath attesting this: "He who believes in Me *and performs good works* has eternal life."[79] Not so! Instead he swore by this, that "Truly, truly, whoever believes in him has eternal life" (v. 47). St. John honors the doctrine of justification, in which Christ's flesh and blood are endued with the power to conquer all miseries—sin, death, devil, hell, and world—and confer all blessings—forgiveness of sins, righteousness and eternal life.[80] Thus it is folly to undertake through good works to achieve what is already given to us through Christ. The comparison between faith and good works is likened unto that of the sun and a taper;[81] they are like a little candle compared with the great bright sun. Not a single good work we perform can atone for a single sin. By contrast, "a single work of Christ excels the works of all men, and I would rather call one work of Christ my own than all the works and holiness of all the saints."[82] Faith possesses "an authoritative significance,"[83] as it transmits Christ's works on the cross to

---

75. LW 23.159 (WA XXXIII.249).
76. LW 23.108 (WA XXXIII.166).
77. LW 23.159 (WA XXXIII.249).
78. LW 23.110 (WA XXXIII.168).
79. LW 23.110 (WA XXXIII.168). Italics are Luther's.
80. LW 23.141 (WA XXXIII.219).
81. LW 23.182 (WA XXXIII.288).
82. LW 23.182 (WA XXXIII.288).
83. Lohse, *Martin Luther's Theology*, 61.

us, and makes them our own. Christ's flesh is our life, and all that he has accomplished with it are ours by faith in exchange for our sin, wrath, and death. The ground upon which a bad conscience can stand is not good works: "I have lived a holy life," but faith: "I believe in Christ," that is, the words of Christ, that of God himself.

Christ is of no avail unless we get him into our mouth, to eat him, or to adhere to him by faith. Justification is founded upon no other god than this God, whose flesh and blood we cling to if we want to be saved. God places before our sight not the Divine Majesty but the Man Christ, who dies for me. This doctrine the Lord confirms with a strong oath: "Truly, truly." These words convey power, and confer comfort, that all voices—devil or conscience—cease their power over us. Neither should we despair due to our evil life nor boast due to many good works. We must avoid the ditches on both extremes; we are to hold to the middle of the road and declare: "There stands One who says that His flesh is the food for my soul. I shall let Him rule."[84] Good works will inevitably fail the test; the flesh and blood of Christ withstand it. "If you remain loyal to this flesh and this blood, you need not worry. But if you abandon it, as the devil urges you to do, you are doomed, lost, and already overcome."[85]

Believers possess eternal life and Christ "in faith and not in fact;"[86] here on earth they still feel sin, and the oppression of death and hell. All negative forces—sin, death and hell—still present a perpetual struggle which might deprive believers of Christ and all his benefits. Yet they do not reign over or hold us, for Christ, in whom we believe, is Lord over all. Just as we possess him, so we too possess all in him. "He is pure righteousness, life, and eternal blessedness, and Lord over death as well. Christ is free from every flaw and failure. He is eternal life, joy, righteousness, and blessedness. This treasure is all mine in Christ; He is all, without defect, and lacking nothing."[87] It suffices for this life to hear his Word until that day when faith shall be sight, when we behold it with body and soul and with all our faculties. Christ declares that "he will raise him up at the Last Day" (v. 54). By faith we are most assured of possessing eternal life through Christ. Christ is most certainly present, though in an invisible and hidden manner. In the meantime, we do perceive death, the devil, sin, and all sorts of distress; but Christ we do not see. We must not be guided by senses or external appearance but by the Word, which promises and confers upon

---

84. LW 23.139 (WA XXXIII.217).
85. LW 23.140 (WA XXXIII.217).
86. LW 23.107 (WA XXXIII.163).
87. LW 23.107 (WA XXXIII.163).

us everlasting life. Even when death, perils, and sin assail us, they will not devour us. "This doctrine of the flesh and blood of Christ is the power and the strength to rise from the dead."[88] The negative news, that death is most apparent, remains; the positive news, that Christ will raise us up at the Last Day, is most certain. The expression "raise up" is thus deliberately chosen by Christ to encourage us to remain constant in our faith, especially when threatened by death. Yet hidden in the destructibility of death lies the power of the promise, that Christ is our life and our true food which preserves us. He will raise us up again, so that we will see before our very eyes that we will live forever, just as Christ does. No difference occurs between the hour we begin to believe and that of the Last Day, except that eternal life is still hidden and concealed in faith.

Union with Christ: Life in Him

Faith unites us with the Son, and all that God is for us in him. Verse 56: "He who eats My flesh and drinks My blood abides in Me, and I in him," has been interpreted, Luther averred, as referring merely to a thought or meditation on Christ's suffering, instead of construing faith in Christ as the true spiritual indwelling of Christ in us and our indwelling in him.[89] Some have reduced the contemplation of Christ to a mere thought, perverting the suffering of Christ and rendering it ineffectual. The Hebraic word "abide" means "to remain" or "to dwell" in a person.[90] Luther renders Christ's words as follow: "[Not] Your thoughts of Me are in Me" or "[Not] My thoughts are in you," but rather: "You, you are in Me, and I, I am in you."[91] The Lord demands that the entire person "I" is in him with all my properties: body, life, soul, piety, and righteousness; on the other hand, the person "Christ" is also in us with all his properties: holiness, righteousness, wisdom, and salvation. This mutual personal indwelling thus goes beyond just cognitive discourse on Christ, which profits us nothing. "Contemplation and shadowy and erratic thoughts, which are but an imaginary indwelling and nothing but thoughts, will not do here."[92] A plain conversation about Christ's sufferings does not bear good fruits; their lives offer no proof that Christ is dwelling in them, for they remain steeped in wickedness, sins, and errors. Faith is not simply intellectual assent, or bare thinking of God, in which case it is

---

88. LW 23.141 (WA XXXIII.220).
89. LW 23.144 (WA XXXIII.224).
90. LW 23.145 (WA XXXIII.227).
91. LW 23.144 (WA XXXIII.224).
92. LW 23.144 (WA XXXIII.225).

nothing but "a cold concept in the heart."[93] True faith "dare not be an idle thought";[94] rather it goes beyond it and lays holds of the person of Christ. It is not enough to recall doctrinally how Christ was crucified; it must move beyond these thoughts and allow them to penetrate our heart, persuading us that Christ was given for me (*pro me*). "Thus faith . . . cannot be a mere thought of our Lord God; for thoughts are not sufficient. . . My heart must take hold of and apprehend Christ; I must cleave to His flesh and blood and say: 'To this I cling to this I will remain faithful. I would rather surrender life and limb. May I fare with it as God wills.'"[95] Basic thoughts about Christ's suffering are ineffectual in conquering the enemies of life: trials, the devil's temptation, a terrorized conscience, and frightful reality of death. Divine power is required to subdue the terrors of a bad conscience, repel the darts of the devil, and overcome the fear of death. "Something else must reside in you, so that your enemies will have to cope with a power which will prove too strong for them, a power which they fear from which they flee, and which will permit you to carry off the victory."[96] Satan, an angry adversary, does not worry much about thoughts but about a divine force in us that is too strong for him. This was evident in the martyrs, in whom God's power resides, which emboldened them to confront the judges, fully aware that their life is at stake. "Such conduct calls for consolation, not for a mere thought."[97] It is "a matter of the heart"[98] that a person can face trials and death. To remain in Christ, to make our dwelling in him, to confess him with heart and lips when facing life's storms is "no child's play or trifle."[99] This is not something human strength could achieve, except by Christ who lives in us; it is "a fruit of the tree of Christ's presence and His residence"[100] in us. This is borne out in Galatians 2:20, where St. Paul writes: "It is no longer I who live, but Christ who lives in me." That which lives in Paul is not the thoughts he entertains, but Christ. This is where he is: "I am in Christ, and I am certain that there is where I shall remain."[101] Union with Christ constitutes us "an entirely different person,"[102] one who is not easily fooled

---

93. LW 23.127 (WA XXXIII.198).
94. LW 23.128 (WA XXXIII.198).
95. LW 23.128 (WA XXXIII.198).
96. LW 23.145 (WA XXXIII.226).
97. LW 23.145 (WA XXXIII.226).
98. LW 23.145 (WA XXXIII.227).
99. LW 23.145 (WA XXXIII.227).
100. LW 23.145 (WA XXXIII.228).
101. LW 23.147 (WA XXXIII.230).
102. LW 23.147 (WA XXXIII.230).

or terrified, for Christ really abides in him with his power. The significance of mutual abiding between Christ and the believer is wrapped up in Christ's words: "It matters not if you are still somewhat weak, for I am in you. If you lack anything, I have an abundance of righteousness, holiness, and wisdom. I have no weaknesses. But if you are weak, your weakness is in Me, and I will see to it that I help you, that I drown your weakness in My strength and power, that I delete your sin in My righteousness, that I devour your death in My life."[103]

To further elucidate, Christ said: "As the living Father sent Me, and I live because of the Father, as he who eats Me will live because of Me" (v. 57). Just as Jesus abides in the Father, from whom he has his life, so we too abide in Christ, from whom we receive life. Christ lives because of, and from the fact, that the Father abides in him and he in the Father. Likewise whoever believes in Christ will live because of him, the one in whom he abides. Whoever believes in him and remains constant will live because of the mutual indwelling—he abides in Christ and Christ in him. Just as Christ has his life from the Father from eternity, so we, too, shall derive life from Christ, but with this difference: he is God's Son from eternity by nature, and we are his by mercy. By mercy we are made heirs of his possessions and "partakers of his divinity."[104] Believers benefit from Christ's flesh, which is permeated with divine strength and glory via the doctrine of the communication of properties (*communicatio idomatum*). Believers possess Christ (the person) and all that he has (properties): righteousness, life, and eternal blessedness, and Lordship over death as well.

Just as God and man are one indivisible person in Christ, so Christ and we also become inseparably one in body and flesh. "His flesh is in us, and our flesh is in Him, so that He also abides in us with His essence, etc."[105] Just as the two natures in Christ remain distinct, so the personal union with Christ does not abolish the distinction between Christ and us. Christ, with his flesh and blood, becomes one body with us, that we are his. Since we have been joined with Christ into one body and being, the good or evil that happens to us happens also to him. The pain a member experiences is predicated of the entire body, Christ's and the believer's. Union with Christ is hidden, invisible to the world; it is apparent to faith. Faith perceives Christ in

---

103. LW 23.148 (WA XXXIII.230).

104. LW 23.150 (WA XXXIII.235). The phrase "partakers of His divinity" does not refer to the Eastern doctrine of *Theosis*, according to which our humanity is deified as a result of union with Christ. It simply refers to the benefits that are accrued to believers on account of union with Christ. For a new discussion of this doctrine, see Braaten and Jenson, *Union with Christ*.

105. LW 23.149 (WA XXXIII.232).

his invisible life and being, receiving Christ and the Word of God, the very contents of his proclamation against the lies. Union with Christ is not by means of will, likened unto two friends joined together by a mutual agreement, sharing one will and mind. Such union is only external, and is a "unity in law" (*legalis unitas*), a phrase Luther borrowed from late medieval jurisprudence.[106] The union between Christ and believers is much more intimate than any friend. Christ is so constituted in us (and is truly one body with us) that he abides in us mightily with his strength and power. "The name which might be given this union is quite immaterial and unessential."[107] It suffices to adhere to the text, that it is not by dreams and contemplations that we are in him and he is in us. Should this union be achieved by human will, actions, and the law, it would amount to "preaching works in opposition to faith."[108] Instead Christ must first come to us and instill his knowledge, wisdom, and power in our heart. "Then He can find voice in me, and I can speak and confess the divine Word and be so emboldened in my heart to risk life and limb and cast aside every other consideration for such a confession. Christ must be the Cornerstone, and He must lay the foundation, not we."[109] We are to hear the gospel, and allow ourselves to be taught, without resisting the message. Then the Holy Spirit works efficaciously in us through the Word, inculcating Christ in our hearts. Only after Christ comes to us are we able to do what the law prescribes, and suffer for the sake of God's Word.

Luther purposely stresses this doctrine—Christ in us by faith—so diligently that one reaps its effectiveness when it prevails, and incurs harm when it disappears. Faith grasps the power of the comparison: As the Father is in Christ, namely, that this indwelling was born into the Son from eternity, without any merit through works, so we too, do not acquire merit through good works. Instead Christ's indwelling was born into us by faith, understood as eating and drinking Christ. How does Christ enter into us? The text indicates the way: "He who eats My flesh and drinks My blood has eternal life." This food and drink is not our work; it is "a gift or a present or a benefit"[110] accrued to us by faith. Unlike the fathers who offer to feed the people with manna, Christ is the "unusual Feeder,"[111] in whom is eternal life (cf. v.58). Christ in us by faith alone is efficacious in purging away every remnant of sin, thereby making good works superfluous. Christ's actual

---

106. LW 23.150 (WA XXXIII.235).
107. LW 23.150 (WA XXXIII.236).
108. LW 23.151 (WA XXXIII.236).
109. LW 23.151 (WA XXXIII.237).
110. LW 23.153 (WA XXXIII.238).
111. LW 23.153 (WA XXXIII.238).

presence, not the mere contemplation of him, overcomes sin, death, and damnation. It prevails, especially at the hour of death, when one realizes Christ's life, his holiness, and his righteousness abide with him. Believers enjoy the justifying benefits that flow from union with Christ:

> If you have sin, He has righteousness. If you have an abscessed or wounded conscience, He is the healer, an almighty Physician who can cure you indeed. If you are sick and at death's door, He will restore you to health and life. Even if you are thrown into purgatory—if this were possible—it will not harm you. If a body endowed with life, health, strength, and power has an injured, weak, infected member, it can be helped and healed in them. Thus Christ abides in us and daily cures all our infirmities. Therewith this sermon is concluded, and this is its Christian interpretation. May God help us to grasp it. Amen.[112]

The indispensable pre-requisite of such victory consists not anthropologically in subjective contemplative thought about Christ nor polemically in an intellectual discursion about him but christologically in a personal abiding in him by faith. Through justifying faith in the life-giving flesh of Christ, we become one with him and share his life; Christ and all he possesses are ours. This is the ground of Peter's confession: "Lord, to whom shall we go? You have the words of eternal life" (v. 68). In Luther's rendering: "These are living words, not the language of the Law."[113] No flesh can appease the wrath of God and vanquish death and devil but Christ, "the Holy One of God" (v. 69), sent from heaven to be the eternal food.

---

112. LW 23.154–55 (WA XXXIII.242).
113. LW 23.196 (WA XXXIII.312).

CHAPTER 5

Civil Kingdom and Christ's Kingdom
Judgment, Grace, and Freedom

As formulated in Luther's teaching on authority in relation to the Peasants' War in his *Tract on Temporal Authority* (1523), God "ordained two governments: the spiritual, by which the Holy Spirit produces Christians and righteous people under Christ; and the temporal, which restrains the un-Christian and wicked so that—no thanks to them—they are obliged to keep still and to maintain an outward peace."[1] The Kingdom of Christ and the secular government are not to be confused, or else the pure gospel and the true faith cannot be preserved.[2] In the spiritual sphere the word rules; in the secular realm it is the sword. Luther makes clear where the boundaries of secular power lie: "No one shall or can command the soul unless he is able to show it the way to heaven; but this no man can do, only God alone." He further qualifies: "for God cannot and will not permit anyone but himself to rule the soul."[3] The preacher's task is to direct the church with the Word of God, the sword of the spoken word—he should not accomplish anything by use of violence. The secular government, however, must be faithful to its own domain, and it wields a different sword, that of iron. Whilst the sword of the princes and lords inflicts physical punishment, the preacher's smites only consciences. With Bernard of Clairvaux, Luther

---

1. LW 45.91 (WA 11.251.15–18).
2. For a major study of Luther's two-kingdom theory, see Bornkamm, *Luther's Doctrine of the Two Kingdoms*; Wright, *Martin Luther's Understanding of God's Two Kingdoms*.
3. LW 45.106 (WA 11.263.3–5; 261.9–10).

insists: "These two rods and swords must be kept apart and separate, so that the one does not infringe on the province of the other."[4] God works in different ways within the distinct realms of these two governments, but with the same goal, namely, to resist the realm of Satan and redeem human beings from it.

The occasion of transforming the house of God into a house of trade (John 2), and the story of the woman caught in adultery (John 8) are instances for Luther to speak of the clear distinction between Christ's kingdom and the civil kingdom. A theologian of the cross does not deprive Christ of his office to bear witness to himself as the Light of the World, whose judgment is just, and as the Savior of the World, whom the Father sent. He sticks to this Man, as commanded by the Father; he hears the proclamation of Christ to be informed of God's will and mind. Everything that is from below, or of this world, is condemned. All hinges on God's Son, whose words are efficacious enough to banish all assaults sourced either from the devil, or the world, or the flesh. Just as there is sheer darkness, without Christ's preaching, so too there is no real freedom without the truth Christ brings from above, by which we are liberated from all that enslaves us: sin, death, the devil, and hell.

Spoken Word and Clenched Sword

The priests in Jerusalem neglected what God had commanded them to do. They transformed the house of God into a house of trade (John 2:16). The Lord thus came to the defence of the temple; with anger "He made a whip of cords" (John 2:15) against the disorderly conduct and rid the temple of the buyers and sellers. The key question in view is why the Lord resorts to a violent exercise of might, seemingly out of character with his previous acts. Elsewhere he prohibited his apostles from using the sword (Matt 26:52); they were to leave the use of physical force to princes and rulers. But here he himself resorts to physical action, a characteristic feature of the secular kingdom in which a worldly sovereign seeks to establish a reign of might and dominate others by force. Contrary to this kingdom, controlled by the force of weapons, the Lord came to establish a spiritual kingdom, governed by "the rod of His mouth" (Isa 11:4). In Christ's kingdom, the spoken sword of God would reign supreme, not a clenched sword.[5] For Christ's kingdom is not of this world and cannot be administered with physical power.

---

4. LW 22.225 (WA 46.735). See Bernard of Clairvaux, *De consideratione*, Bk. IV, ch. 3, par, 7, 776, where he argued for a distinction between the two swords.

5. LW 22.223 (WA 46.732).

In this scene, however, it seems that Christ moves beyond the constriction to jeremiad in dealing with the priests in the temple; he intervenes with brutal weapons and quickly. Yes, we might see in Christ's harsh and hostile treatment of the priests a prophetic action coordinate with and illustrative of the Mosaic rule amongst the people of Israel. In many instances, Christ comported with the demands of the law of Moses, including the acts of being circumcised, sacrificing in the temple, and going to Jerusalem three times per year for the feast as others did. The law of Moses was in this regard fulfilled by Jesus. It might also be said, notably in this particular instance, that Jesus could embody the law's demands—its promises and threats. The actions of Jesus, then, illustrate the wrath warranted and opened up by the breaking of the law.[6] On the other hand, "Christ did not act like a pupil of Moses but as one who now belonged to the New Testament, where Moses' Law was to be abrogated and a new spiritual order was to be established in the entire world by means of the Gospel message."[7] As support of this, Luther cited the episode of Christ's disciples plucking ears of grain on the Sabbath, whereupon the Pharisees challenged Christ for this and complained: "Lo, John's disciples observe the Sabbath, but Yours do not!" Here Christ did not assume a stern position, but nevertheless came to their defence of his disciples in a way that gestured to the sublation of the law itself: "The Sabbath does not concern Me. I am its Lord, and the Sabbath cannot lord it over Me" (Matt 12:1–8). Christ here acts according to the gospel, thus in violation of the Mosaic law.[8]

Because Christ reigns over both realms, the secular and spiritual, he performs both duties, one of instruction and the other, like Moses, of punitive action. In accord with the law of Moses, which was still operative, Christ resorts to force in countering idolatry in the temple. However whichever method he implements, it is always good, since he is the Lord of both—the Law and Sabbath. Luther writes:

> If He chooses to follow Moses, it is right. If He prefers not to do so, it is not wrong; for He owes the Law nothing, since He is the Lord of the Law and the Sabbath. He has the right to follow His own will and pleasure, for He is king and baron. At times He used the Law and kept it strictly, as one subject to Moses.

---

6. If Moses, David, Elijah, or any pious Jewish kings and prophets had entered the temple at that time, they, too, would have used their fists and stoned these Jews to death, thereby fulfilling the law of Moses prescribed for idolaters (Lev 20:2). And now, since the priests failed to fulfill what was required of their office, the Lord does not act in his capacity as Christ but as Moses, and as a subject under his realm.

7. LW 22.223 (WA 46.732).

8. LW 22.223 (WA 46.732).

Christ was not bound to go up to the temple in Jerusalem three times a year; but when He did, He did it gladly and voluntarily. Whenever He refused to keep the Law, this is also meet and right. Therefore the Lord is doing nothing amiss here and is not acting as an insurrectionist, for He has the Law of Moses on His side, which orders death for idolaters. Nevertheless, if Christ had remained passive and had refrained from scouring the Jews, He would also have been within His rights. For Christ lived during the transition from the Old to the New Testament and was part of each. Here He keeps the Law of Moses, as He often did. By His occasional disregard of the Law of Moses Christ wanted to intimate His gradual abolition of it.[9]

Spiteful and Proper Zeal

The evangelist John adds in John 2:17: "His disciples remembered that it was written: zeal for Thy house will consume Me." The temple in Jerusalem occupied an eminent place among the people, in which they convened frequently to hear and learn the writings of the prophets and the psalms. It was particularly the Psalter with which people in that day were familiar. The disciples thus remembered this verse recorded in Psalm 69:9: "Zeal for Thy house consume Me"; they applied the words specifically to Christ. It is customary that "as long as it does not violate the article of faith, a passage with general significance is given specific, individual, and personal application."[10] Accordingly the disciples apply the rule here and refer the verse of the psalm to what Christ did. Thus these words "Zeal has consumed Me," are predicated specifically of Christ who cannot do otherwise than display such zeal for God and his people. The term "zeal" designates the vigorous emotion of jealousy or anger born out of friendship and affection. "Thus zeal is an angry love or a jealous love,"[11] which renders any unchaste attitude toward a wife unbearable to her husband and any infidelity of a husband intolerable to his wife. Should there be true love among husband and wife, there would be proper jealousy and wrath arising from it. For jealousy and anger belong essentially to the meaning of love; indifference is the opposite of love. So if the wife treats the improper action of her husband with indifference, she does not act from a motive of pure love. It is only proper for angry love or jealous love to be alive between lovers; indifference is a sign of the absence

---

9. LW 22.224 (WA 46.733).
10. LW 22.230 (WA 46.740).
11. LW 22.233 (WA 46.743).

of true love. However, we must express a modicum of jealousy, without carrying it to excess, lest it endanger a healthy loving relationship. We must also beware of an evil, contemptible and spiteful jealousy that arises when others enjoy greater good or popularity than we do. Such jealousy is "nothing else than sheer malevolence,"[12] one of the demonic sins and vices on earth to which the devil himself is addicted.

"Just as spiteful jealousy is a despicable vice, so proper zeal is a precious and noble virtue."[13] The former we ought to shun; the latter we ought to cling to. It not only angers us but also saddens us that a beloved person falls into sin and shame. To feel otherwise becomes a vile and shameful vice. "To begrudge a person becomes a virtue which inheres in God alone and in the hearts of those especially moved by God. For this deep grief over a good friend's sin and shame, this begrudging of such sin and shame, still indicates the presence of a divine spark in the human heart."[14]

In a Hebraic way of speaking, God derives his names from the works he performs. The name "the God of vengeance" (Ps 94:1) is not to be treated as a statement of God's being, but about God's way of being in relation to his world, the way in which he acts. God's true nature is love, not wrath. "Wrath is truly God's alien work, which He employs contrary to His Nature [i.e., love] because He is forced into it by the wickedness of man."[15] God's wrath is not God's nature but God's way of acting in response to evil. Wrath does not define God's essence; it remains no more than a potentiality. "Unlike holiness or righteousness, wrath never forms one of the permanent attributes of the God of Israel."[16] God pours out his wrath against sin as his alien work through which God's redeeming love as his proper work is expressed. Hidden in Christ's anger is his love for God and his concern for their salvation. Wrath is Christ's severe love against evil through which he might bestow his sweet love. Watson wrote of Luther's understanding of the wrath of a loving God:

> For the God whose nature is revealed in the Gospel as pure love and grace is no mild sentimentalist . . . Love's wrath, however, is neither the evil passion of offended self-esteem, nor the cold severity of violated justice, but the intensely personal reaction of the Father's all-holy will against evil. Wrath represents the purity

---

12. LW 22.234 (WA 46.743).
13. LW 22.234 (WA 46.744).
14. LW 22.234 (WA 46.744).
15. LW 2.134 (WA 42.356). See Barth, *Church Dogmatics*, vol. 1, 104–05; Brunner, *Mediator*, 445, 520–21. Both maintain that wrath is God's alien work.
16. Eichrodt, *Theology of the Old Testament*, vol. 1, 262.

of the Divine love which, while it freely and fully forgives sin, never pretends that it is not sin and does not matter.[17]

That God is wrathful against evil is proof that he cares. Hence God's wrath is most terrifying when the sinner is not punished but allowed to continue in his sinful condition. "When God speaks, shows his wrath, is angry, punishes, gives us into the hands of the enemies, sends plague, hunger, the sword and the other troubles, it is a certain sign that He is gracious to us."[18] The God of the Bible is not some wildly abusive deity who punishes out of sadistic pleasure but a good God, who cannot stand by idly and allow evil to triumph. God's wrathful opposition against sin is generated not by an abstractly conceived divine justice, which demands unmitigated retribution for the broken law, or by a wounded self-esteem turned vindictive, or by a frustrated love turned bitter. God's love expresses itself in wrath, in a vengeful opposition against evil so that good and its love might shine forth. Thus Luther could speak of God's love as "wrathful love": "For when love is angry, it does no injury; but when hatred and envy is angry, it corrupts and destroys as far as it can. For love's anger seeks and wills to sunder the evil that it hates from the good that it loves, in order that the good and its love may be preserved."[19] Similarly, this is the type of zeal Christ the Lord displays in the temple. His anger does not spring from hatred, but from a love of God, who founded the temple to his own honor and wished it to be used properly, namely, to instruct people in the ways of salvation and in the service of God. Of this, Luther writes reflectively of Christ, who wants to say: "I begrudge the beautiful and fine temple this disgraceful abuse, and I begrudge the people the damnation into which they are being led."[20] These vigorous emotions—holy zeal and indignation—eat and gnaw at Christ's heart, consume him, torture him, and finally move him into dedicated and fierce action, as we saw him lashing at the money-changers in the temple. His was no self-seeking jealous ire; this is evident in Matthew 23:37, where he wept with zeal over the fate of Jerusalem: "O Jerusalem, Jerusalem, how often would I have gathered your children together!" These words do not emanate from a laughing heart but a grieving heart. This befits Christ's "office of concern, of solicitude and zeal imposed on Him by His Heavenly Father, and this zeal of His ceased only on the cross."[21] At the cross, God

---

17. Watson, *Let God be God*, 159.

18. See WA TR 1.117 as cited in Lage, *Martin Luther's Christology and Ethics*, 66.

19. LW 20.175 (WA 23.517.2ff). Also quoted in Watson, *Let God be God*, 182. See also Köstlin, *Theology of Luther*, vol. 2.190ff.

20. LW 22.235 (WA 46.745).

21. LW 22.237 (WA 46.748).

suffers his own wrath in himself and conquers it, thereby creating a people no longer under God's wrath but his mercy. As in law Christ performs the alien work to lead us to his proper work: that ultimately God's Word and his salvific activities must shine, and be prized above all else. The cessation of wrath occurs when the gospel reigns; the continuation of it occurs insofar as we let unbelief, sin, and the devil reign.

God's wrath is thus his response to something alien to himself; it reflects the outworking of his character in response to sin. This is already borne out in his *Small Catechism* (1528), where Luther furnished his use of the "jealous God" passage in Exodus 20 and Deuteronomy 5 in his conclusion of the Ten Commandments: "He says, 'I the Lord your God am a jealous God, visiting the iniquity of the fathers upon the children to the third and the fourth generation of those who hate me, but showing steadfast love to thousands of those who love me and keep my commandments.'"[22] Here the commandments are framed with the paradoxical distinction between law (God punishes all who transgress these commandments), and gospel (he promises grace and every blessing to all who keep them). Though he uses his left hand to judge, he is right-handed, for mercy defines God's being. Christ sets the boundary for the expression of wrathful love, which must not be done for one's personal gain but for one's neighbors' interest, just as Christ did—not by virtue of his person but his office and the word of God. The disciples cannot aspire to this; no one but Christ retains the prerogative to act in accordance with Moses' law.

Different Judgments: Christ's and Moses'

The woman caught in adultery in John 8 is another instance for Luther to speak of the clear distinction between the law and the gospel, or between Christ's kingdom and the civil kingdom. The Pharisees suspend their own laws and place before Jesus the woman caught in sin, asking Jesus to render a verdict upon a legal matter on which they themselves are well-informed. Their intention is to trap Jesus so that either way, yes or no, they may silence him. If he should say no, they could cite the law of Moses, which requires death by stoning. In this case Jesus would have been charged with impugning Moses' authority, thereby stamping him a rebel. On the other hand, if Christ would agree with Moses that she be stoned and killed, they would have succeeded in conducing a contradiction. In each case, he is trapped: if his answer is yes, he is contradicting his own public teaching; if no, he is opposing Moses.

22. Luther, "Small Catechism," in Tappert, *Book of Concord*, 344.

Jesus was aware of the Pharisees' trickery, thus verse 2: "Jesus bent down and wrote with His finger on the ground." The Lord was silent, and did not deign to speak to them. But they persist in pressing him for an answer to this legal case. In verses 7 and 8, Christ administers a masterful rebuff: "And as they continued to ask Him, He stood up and said to them: Let him who is without sin among you be the first to throw a stone at her. And once more He bent down and wrote with His finger on the ground." Christ does not dispute the jurisdiction of the latter nor oppose Moses; but in a skillful manner, Luther writes of the implication of Christ's answer as follows:

> "Why do you not do as Moses commanded? But if you want to judge her according to My rule, do not harm her. My verdict is: This adulteress does not stand alone, for there is not one among you who is not as bad and evil as this poor harlot may be. If you comply with Moses' Law, then stone her; but according to Mine, let her go. I can infer from your question to Me that you do not propose to condemn her according to Moses' law. Therefore I say to you that there is not one among you who is not as base as this poor harlot."[23]

The content of Christ's proclamation is grace and forgiveness. In Christ's kingdom, all have sinned and come under God's wrath; none are excepted but rather all deserve eternal death, hell, and everlasting fire. "Where this is preached, there sword, judge, judgment seat, town hall, jurists, and executioner are all abolished."[24] Proper to the rule in Christ's kingdom is this: "Let him who is without sin among you be the first to throw a stone at her." With this Christ silences them. Because the Pharisees meddle in Christ's realm, he strikes back at them like lightning, thereby flashing their sins before all eyes. Christ's words take on the function of the law, which laid bare their hearts and revealed a record of their sin, causing them to forget the sins of others. Of the reaction of those who come under the negative effect of the law, Luther wrote imaginatively:

> As God addresses them, their sins loom so big and they become so alarmed and frightened that their own sins now occupy them and cause them to forget about others and to begin to think that in comparison other sinners are pure saints. Thus they stand thunderstruck. They feel as though the lightning had shone and flashed into their hearts, filling them with pure light and revealing their innermost thoughts. As their hearts are open like a book, they forget about this woman entirely and begin to

---

23. LW 23.312–13 (WA XXXIII.500).
24. LW 23.313 (WA XXXIII.502).

imagine that their sins are inscribed on their foreheads and that everything they have ever done can be seen on their noses. Not one of them has the courage to look at the other. They imagine that the very stones are staring at them. Time seems endless, until they find the escape and can slink out through the door. They cannot lift up their eyes and look man, house, sun, or a dog cheerfully and squarely in the face. They are dispirited, cowed, and bereft of their senses. They can stand it no longer. They can look no longer in the face but must turn tail and stealthily sneak out of the temple, slinking out as a dog with a burned snout slinks from the kitchen.[25]

The character of life under Mosaic Law is anger and judgment, which is proper to the law's office. God governs the world through the ordinances, the law, the office, the sword, the gallows, and the wheel; all these are God's methods by which he punishes numerous vices and evils. It is God who put the sword of justice into our hands; those invested with such an office, whether scoundrel or noble, are to use them, and pass sentence regardless of circumstances. "An evil judge has God's gift, office, and command, just as much as a pious judge who bears the sword."[26] The Pharisees should have remained within the domain of their own office and position, just as Christ has remained within the bounds of his office and kingdom. They claim to be holy, and they crawl into God's domain, but only find themselves under the lightning of God's law, which shines brightly into their hearts, revealing their innermost evil, the precise opposite of what they claim to be. It is as if Christ says: "Before the world I acknowledge your piety, your jurisdiction, and your office, even though you are rogues and rascals. But here in My realm you must surrender your office, your jurisdiction, and your sword like a wretched knave; here you are condemned to hell."[27] In Christ's kingdom, he reduces all to sinners without distinction. Yet he does not stop there; for then he absolves them. Before the Jewish law, the woman stands accused and condemned: death by stoning. This was enough cause for fear, for there is nothing but bitter death staring at her in the face. Then she found great comfort in Jesus' words: "Let him who is without sin among you be the first to throw a stone at her." There are two kinds of sinners. There are those who realize that they have sinned but who do not admit it, nor feel it. But the kingdom of Christ is directed towards the second kind: sinners, like the adulteress, who feel their sins and are struck down by a sense of guilt. To

---

25. LW 23.314 (WA XXXIII.502).
26. LW 23.314 (WA XXXIII.502).
27. LW 23.315 (WA XXXIII.504).

these, Christ applies the second part of his message, namely, the forgiveness of sins. Before Christ performs the second function of his office, he performs the first, that of law, which makes all people sinners, for the Holy Spirit is to "convince the world of sin" (John 16:8). As in law, Christ speaks the negative word, that all stand condemned to hell; as in gospel, Christ speaks a positive word, that he will lift us up. In Christ's words, "Let Him who is without sin," the adulteress first hears the negative word by which she is condemned. But transition occurs only when she also hears the positive word of consolation, as Christ says to her: "Neither do I condemn you" (John 8:11).

All who enter Christ's kingdom must feel and recognize their sin; they must consent to God's judgment that they are sinners. The Pharisees did not have to become sinners; they are sinners already. They became even greater sinners when Christ exposed of their sins to them with his words: "Let him who is without sin, etc." Despite this revelation, they hid their sin and would not await Christ's second statement, his absolution: "Neither do I condemn you." Hence they have no share in, and are not admitted into, Christ's kingdom. Only those sinners who recognize their sin, feel it, and lay hold of Christ's words, "I do not condemn you," constitute the membership of Christ's kingdom. No saint nor those who lay claim to holiness belong to Christ's kingdom; justification occurs within the pradoxical action of law and gospel: "If you have tasted the Law and sin, and if you know the ache of sin, then look here, and see how sweet, in comparison, the grace of God is, the grace which is offered to us in the Gospel."[28] They are living saints on account of Christ's absolution, though sin still abides; they are covered in Christ. "If sinners enter (Christ's kingdom), they do not remain sinners. He spreads His cloak over their sins... To be sure, sin is there. But the Lord in this kingdom closes His eyes to it, covers it, forgives it, and does not impute it to the sinner."[29] The story of an adulterous woman, who had been infested with sins but whose sins Christ covers and does not impute to her, is indeed a fine illustration of Christ's mercy. This is Christ's way of proving his power over the law, leading her out of the kingdom of death into the kingdom of life.

Christ's Boast: The Light of the World

After having spoken of his power over the law, Christ now proceeds to speak with authority about his ministry, elevating it above the proclamations, doctrines, and ways of the world. Christ wants to be known as "the Light of

28. LW 23.318 (WA XXXIII.510).
29. LW 23.318 (WA XXXIII.510).

the world" (John 8:12), not just the light of a certain area. Darkness reigns where Christ is not; where Christ is extinguished, there is sheer darkness. Christ alone wants to be the "Teacher, Master, and Leader of the world."[30] With this office, Christ abolished all other doctrines, including Moses' law, the Ten Commandments. All others are pupils who sit at this Man's feet, and they, under his illumination, now see the Sun. Thus Malachi calls Christ "the Sun of righteousness, with healing in His wings" (4:2). By itself, the message of Moses does not lead us to the light. We need another doctrine, namely, that of the gospel, which declares: "I, Christ, am the Light." The law is detrimental, for it demands what we are to do, and is ineffectual in leading us to the light; the gospel is delightful, for it does not teach us what we are to do for God but what we are to take and receive from him. Those who abide under Christ's wings will gladly hear, see, and feel this brightness. "To him who crawls under her wings salvation, eternal life, and forgiveness of sin are promised; he will lack nothing, for the Sun will shine for him."[31] The message of the gospel lies in this: Christ is the light and the true brilliance of the sun, which radiates through the entire world, and without which we will lapse into ignorance of who God is, or what life, righteousness, salvation, and freedom are. Luther elaborates by way of a creaturely analogy of the moon and the sun:

> The doctrine of the Law, or the first light, is the moon. It teaches our obligation to bear fruits, as a good tree should. The other light is the sun. It speaks of the new man, of a different tree, telling us that we receive the Gospel from Christ. There we hear whence and how a man becomes good, namely, through faith. Thus the Gospel deals, not with our works but with grace and gifts, with the good that God does for us and presents to us through Christ. The Ten Commandments tell us about our duties toward God. Now, to be sure, the moon shines at night, but still it does not turn night into day. Christ, however, is the true Sun. He ushers in the morning and the day. He teaches us how to be saved and how to be delivered from death and sin. Therefore He says: "I am the Light which illumines the whole world"; for He alone liberates from sin, death, the devil, and hell.[32]

John 8:12, "He who follows Me will not walk in darkness, but will have the light of life," does not refer to works we do or the example of the

---

30. LW 23.325 (WA XXXIII.521).
31. LW 23.325 (WA XXXIII.521).
32. LW 23.324 (WA XXXIII.521).

saints we imitate to be transposed from darkness to light.[33] Not so! Christ draws the pupils to himself; thus he says: "Follow Me!" meaning "Keep My doctrine!" To follow Christ means to obey his words by faith. In his *Brief Instruction on what to look for and expect in the Gospels* (1522), Luther wrote: "The chief article and foundation of the gospel is that before you take Christ as an example, you accept and recognize him as a gift, as a present that God has given you and that is your own."[34] What is in view is not Christ as example, in which we are called to follow, doing his works, and suffering as he did; this will follow only after Christ as sacrament is accepted. What Christ demands is that we adhere to his doctrine, abide by it, and depart from doctrines of delusive lights and fluttering spirits which do not herald Christ as the Light. To follow him, Christ explains, is "to see a light that gives life."[35] Christ says: "He will not walk in darkness." Just as the sun cannot be apprehended with the other senses but can only be beheld with the eyes, which can see the brilliant light, so Christ too cannot be apprehended by good works, except by the eyes of faith, which enable us to know him, hear him, permit the Word to shine into our hearts and acknowledge it. Hidden in a boastful claim of Christ: "I am the Light of the World" is his illumining of the good road which leads us to eternal life, not by means of good works but by Christ's life-giving passion and death.

> Humility accomplishes nothing. You will not get to heaven unless you are proud and arrogant. This dare not be an unchristian arrogance. We must brag and boast of this art; we must be arrogant in the Lord. He who brags otherwise and is haughty is a conceited ass. It is forbidden to praise oneself or what one has. Fools are proud and conceited. It is wrong to indulge in self-praise.[36]

Christ glorifies in the truth when he says: "Therefore My testimony is truth. It is the truth, for I know whence I come and whither I go" (John 8:15). Christ needs not brag about himself, for he knows the purpose for which the Father sent him, and He who sent him cannot lie. He is certain of his calling, and of his office, in which he is entitled to glory. "He knows the beginning, the end, and the outcome of His office and His nature."[37] His boasting rests on a precious foundation: "For I know whence I have

---

33. LW 23.325 (WA XXXIII.521).

34. LW 35.119. Augustine, *De Trinitate* 4.3, as cited in Lohse, *Martin Luther's Theology*, 47–48; 222. For Augustine, Christ as sacrament (gift) precedes Christ as example.

35. LW 23.326 (WA XXXIII.522).

36. LW 23.328 (WA XXXIII.527).

37. LW 23.332 (WA XXXIII.534).

come and whither I am going." He knows of his origin, that he comes from his Father, and his destiny, that he is returning to the Father who sent him. Neither did Jesus come "according to the flesh" (John 8:15) nor will he return to the Father according to the flesh. He can and must act in accordance with his call from heaven; this he does according to the spirit. Just as Christ glories in this, that he comes from God and returns to God, so a believer glories in this, that he comes from Adam to Christ by baptism. Baptism, Christ's death and resurrection, the Word of God, and the blood of Christ are holy, and on that account, we are made holy by faith. We are given this holiness, the substance in which we glory, and we confess: "This is not mine; it was given me in Baptism."[38] There are no defects in the gospel, in baptism, and in Christ's blood; they can render satisfaction for sin. Baptism changes Adam's children into new beings and puts them in a new estate. "This certainly is a strong and mighty fortress; this certainly makes a man boast."[39]

It befits him who claims, "I am the Light of the world," to be a judge of the world. Christ says in John 8:16: "Yet even if I do judge, My judgment is true." Christ alone could judge that the world lies in blindness and darkness, and openly condemn that which lies under sin, death, and devil. Christ's primary mission, however, is not to judge but to save. This was already borne out in John 3:16: "For God sent the Son into the world, not to condemn the world, but that the world might be saved through Him." But if someone rejects his chief function, he will not attain salvation. It is his office to pronounce a righteous judgment that this one remains in his sin, and must bear death as the consequence. "And this, though the office was really not established for judgment but for help and comfort, it is forced to judge nevertheless."[40] Genesis 22:18, "In your Seed shall all the nations of the earth be blessed," speaks of Christ, his title and his office, namely, to bless or comfort. But hidden in "the sweet word bless" is the bitter word "curse," just as the consolation of the gospel lies hidden in the intolerable curse of the law.

> Christ is to be a comforting Preacher, a friendly Man and Helper, who will spare no effort and do nothing but teach and work, help and bless. With Him is pure help and consolation. Yet these same words include condemnation, judgment, and sentence. Whenever a blessing is rejected, there a curse follows. He who will not be well must remain sick. He who will not go to heaven must go to hell. Although it is not part of Christ's office

---

38. LW 23.331 (WA XXXIII.531).
39. LW 23.333 (WA XXXIII.534).
40. LW 23.339 (WA XXXIII.545).

to consign to hell, to curse, or to condemn, but to help and to rescue, it is equally true that he who scorns this help must remain in hell.[41]

It is not Christ's office to judge; rather he is compelled to do so, because of wickedness. "That He must be a judge is not because of His Person but because of others, who despise Him and force Him to judge."[42] He who will not have Christ and his ministry of comfort will have the devil, in whom there is nothing but curse, darkness, and damnation. This judgment is just, and will ever stand, as it is substantiated by two witnesses: John the Baptist, and now God who also bore witness to Christ: "For it is not I alone that judge, but I and He who Sent Me" (John 8:16). He is delegated to be a Witness, a public ambassador and Preacher, and so his judgment is lawful. His heavenly Father bears witness on his behalf (Matt 17:5): "This is My Beloved Son, with whom I am well pleased; listen to Him." No one could deprive him of his office, which was conferred upon him by command. His office is not his to give away; he is bound to it, just as an official pastor has no other obligation than to baptize, preach, and administer Holy Communion.

John 8:21: "I go away, and you will seek Me" is a dreadful sermon, an appalling word of farewell. He repeated what he said in John 7:53: "I shall be with you a little longer; you will seek Me, and you will not find Me." With these words, Christ stresses that he has been preaching the Word of God and offered to all what the Father commanded him to offer, namely, eternal life, remission of sin, and deliverance from death and hell. If the world turns a deaf ear, then they will remain what they are, namely, in sin, while Christ will remain what he is, a Judge to them. It is dreadful when Christ goes away, as eternal life and salvation and all the gifts of God also depart from them. What he leaves behind is nothing but death, the devil, sin, and every misery. When he goes away, he takes with him the knowledge of God and the proper understanding of baptism and of the Lord's Supper. And it will only become worse when Christ adds: "You will seek Me, and you will not find Me." Nowhere in Holy Scripture than in this verse, Luther asserts, is a more fearful statement. He has Christ say: "Now that I am here and offer you this, now that you have the fair at your very door, you renounce Me. You crucify Me, and you thrust Me out of the city. But after I am gone, you would gladly dig a hundred wells to disinter Me; but you will not find so much as a hair of Me."[43] To know Christ is to know him as our Redeemer, and all that Christ came to offer: help, grace, life, consolation, blessedness,

---

41. LW 23.339 (WA XXXIII.545).
42. LW 23.341 (WA XXXIII.548).
43. LW 23.355 (WA XXXIII.573).

and deliverance from these enemies—death, sin, the devil, and hell. When Christ is gone, all things which are Christ are gone too. For what is left are the strenuous human endeavors with which one seeks to be reconciled with God. If Christ's Word disappears, it will be supplanted by pious human deeds. Yet all the noble and pious efforts fail to reach God; the outcome is damnation, the opposite of salvation, as Christ announces: "You will die in your sin; and where I go you cannot come" (John 8:21). Luther thus admonishes his congregants to impress Christ as sacrament—that is, Christ's life-giving passion and death—upon their hearts so that they might advance to the point where they despair of their own piety, and confess Jesus Christ as their savior.

His Words: Carnal and Spiritual Freedom

With his words in John 8:24, "I am He," Christ separates from himself all the holiness and wisdom of earth so that he might offer them something other than the law of Moses and good works. Nothing from below or of this world—wisdom, power, might—can capture God. "This will always miscarry."[44] To communicate with God, Christ first draws all away from mere thoughts to his words. In the eyes of reason God appears foolish when he seeks to accomplish his purpose by means of his tongue, not his fists. Being from above, Christ does nothing of himself but repeats what his Father taught him. Christ says: "In the first place, I am He who is now speaking to you." He simply wants them to hear him first; he repudiates any fluttering about outside his word to approach God. Yet no one can know who Christ is unless he acknowledges him as the preacher, whom the Father sent.

> These words carry this emphasis: "I am not only your Creator but also your Preacher, and you must accept Me as such. I am He who, according to the promises of the prophets, was sent to preach to you. Now if you follow My message and give ear to Me, you will find out who I am. But if you refuse to hear Me, this will not be revealed to you. If you heard Me, you would know Me." . . . Christ says: "I am He. All depends on Me. You will not know or have God and the Father unless you hear My Word."[45]

Thus he says: "If you know me, you will know the Father also" (John 8:19). The significance and intent of Christ's self-inclusive words consists in this: without Christ we know nothing about God, nor can we know

44. LW 23.367 (WA XXXIII.595).
45. LW 23.367 (WA XXXIII.596).

anything if we do not first know Christ. Christ defiantly declares his reliance on his Father, saying, "I tell you that if you do not believe in Me, you will all perish. I do not say this of Myself, nor is this the invention of My heart; but the Father says it. He taught Me, and He commanded Me to speak this way. And He who sent Me is with Me and not with you. Therefore beware!"[46] Despite the malice hurled against him, Christ takes comfort from the seal: "He who sent Me is true, and I declare to the world what I have heard from Him" (v. 26). Christ knows the Father who will not lie; he is faithful, upright and truthful. "The Father is with Me; He will not lie; He will aid Me" (v. 29). The Father has commanded him to preach, and will not let him be discredited. "Otherwise I (Christ) would have remained in heaven. But now that God has commanded Me to preach and has sent Me for that purpose, He will indeed protect His Word and fulfill its threats."[47] But the people despise the content of Christ's preaching, that the Son was sent by the Father into the flesh to preach to them. Thus John 8:27: "they did not understand that He spoke to them of the Father." Christ's preaching will deal with the scoffers; it will be called "great and effective."[48] The godly will incur eternal life according to the Father's promise; the ungodly will incur eternal death according to the threats made to them. Christ's message must run its course, that Jerusalem and every one of its wall will be destroyed; not one stone will remain upon the other (Matt 24:2). Whoever opposes Christ opposes God; he becomes God's mighty enemy. The world seeks to please God apart from Christ; all their words and actions are nothing, compared to great profit believers derive from Christ who says: "Whatever I do and preach pleases God. He has not left Me alone" (v. 29). This means: "Until Judgment Day I [Christ] constantly do what is pleasing to God. My Word, message, Baptism, and Sacrament shall endure, in spite of everything."[49] The efficacy of Christ's words in his kingdom so thrilled the evangelist that he adds: "many believed in Him" (v. 30).

Not an initial acceptance of Christ but fidelity to Christ's doctrine is the mark of true disciples. As Christ says in verse 31: "If you continue in My Word, you are truly My disciples." At first people might accept the gospel, only for their own advantage and gain. They aim to seek something in Christ that they will not find. "These are disgraceful disciples; they flock to the Gospel for carnal freedom and temporal benefits."[50] The peasants, for

46. LW 23.384 (WA XXIII.624).
47. LW 23.372 (WA XXXIII.602).
48. LW 23.369 (WA XXXIII.598).
49. LW 23.392 (WA XXXIII.638).
50. LW 23.397 (WA XXXIII.647).

one, disdain the gospel, for they find out that the gospel brings them no earthly goods. When things go contrary to their wish, they refuse to remain as Christ's pupils; neither will they perceive God nor taste spiritual comfort.

> They hear and learn much, yet they never come to a knowledge of the truth. They do not understand the truth. They do learn to speak the words, as a parrot or parakeet repeats words spoken by people. But their heart does not feel them; they remain unchanged and do not taste and perceive how faithful and true God is. I suppose one tenth of the people really perceives God, while the other nine tenths begin to believe but do not perceive, for it is difficult and trying to remain faithful. Such people have no solid foundation.[51]

To be numbered amongst this Man's disciples requires perseverance till the end. "Such steadfast people are the true disciples."[52] They will be rewarded and comforted: they will find the true God; they will be endowed with strength and power to remain with God's Word. True disciples do not remain at the beginning of faith; they move beyond the phase of novices and reach a point when they may taste and experience that "God is a Man"[53] who can deliver them from their needs. They progress to the point where they declare: "God has promised."[54] They stake all on the power of God's Word: "The divine Word alone is the cornerstone, the I-beam, the girder, the stanchion, and the pillar undergirding our constancy. Therefore it is imperative that we hold to the plain Word of God, that we cling to the words of Christ. Then we will experience God's help in the midst of danger and upheaval."[55] Victory is hidden, even where one could neither see nor feel how things would end or where help or counsel might come. Contrary to all reason and wisdom, the Christian is constrained to say: "It all depends on God's power, and it is all staked on His Word."[56] Here Luther cites Abraham who had the Word of God: "I am your Lord and your God." But where was his protector when his wife, Sarah, was taken from him in Egypt (Gen 20:2)? In the circumstance when the honor and chastity of Sarah were at stake, he had neither the strength nor the skill to find counsel amid his distress except to cling to the Word: "The Lord is my protection." Then he experienced and

---

51. LW 23.400 (WA XXXIII.651).
52. LW 23.398 (WA XXXIII.649).
53. LW 23.400 (WA XXXIII.651).
54. LW 23.400 (WA XXXIII.653).
55. LW 23.400 (WA XXXIII.651).
56. LW 23.400 (WA XXXIII.652).

apprehended the truth. For God had afflicted Pharaoh until he was willing to return Sarah to Abraham and present him with large gifts.

John 8:34: "Truly, truly, everyone who commits sin is a slave to sin," speaks of our ailment, namely, bondage to sin. Christ's words in verse 32: "You will know the truth, and the truth shall set you free," and in verse 34: "So if the Son sets you free, you will be free indeed," specify the remedy against slavery to sin, that Christ will truly redeem us, and free us from sin. The false disciples begin to believe, but they defect, so they do not know the meaning of the word "truth"; the true disciples continue on the hard path, and learn to cling to the Word, from which they draw freedom, comfort and strength. Truth consists not merely in hearing Christ or in being able to speak about him at length, but also in believing and experiencing in our heart that Christ wants to liberate us. "Not only to know, learn, read, and hear the Word but also to experience it—this makes you a genuine disciple."[57] The freedom of which Christ speaks is two-fold. On the one hand, there is a carnal freedom that is eager to receive things, and to possess what might profit, such as temporal riches, honor, might, and pleasures; but it can never lead to the gospel. On the other hand, there is true freedom that belongs to those who remain loyal to God's Word, endure it, suffer it, and bear it. Christ's conception of freedom is not a physical kind, but a true, eternal and spiritual kind, that he will liberate us from sin. Christ does not concern himself with external matters, and does not alter secular kingdom or abolish serfdom. But the freedom Christ has in view lies outside and above the outward existence of life. Christ deals with freedom from sin, death, and God's wrath—those bondages cannot be set free by earthly means but only by God, and the truth. The freedom we have before God is given us, when God pronounces us free from sin. This is "an eternal freedom"[58] Christ came to offer to all, by which he steers people away from their carnal conception of freedom, although they repudiate it as though they are lords, and are not in need of it.

With these words, "Everyone who commits sin is a slave to sin," and "If the Son makes you free, you are free indeed," Christ speaks of true Christian freedom, setting it in opposition to the Jews, who wanted to pervert it into a physical freedom according to the flesh. They should aim for a different freedom, "a higher and loftier freedom,"[59] which only the Son can offer. Luther summarizes the content of Christ's sermon:

---

57. LW 23.400–01 (WA XXXIII.655).
58. LW 23.414 (WA XXXIII.668).
59. LW 23.409 (WA XXXIII.664).

"Your boast of being Abraham's children does not suffice; to obtain Christian liberty requires more than to be Abraham's child, his flesh and blood. That will never make you free, for Abraham himself was not freed by the fact that he came from the lineage of his father—though the Jews set great store by their physical birth—but his freedom stemmed from God's promise made to him of the Blessed Seed (Gen 22:18). Therefore forget about Abraham and cease boasting of all that you have from him, and see to it that you are made free only through Me. Otherwise you will not be free but remain in bondage forever."[60]

The Jews suppose that Christ will establish a physical empire in which they will become kings, princes, and grand lords on earth. Instead, Luther has Christ say: "If you want to be free, to have your own king, to be rid of all tribute, and to shake off your yoke and bondage, you must believe in the Son."[61] Christ wants to usher them into a kingdom in which truth reigns, with real freedom as its outcome. His is a "genuine kingdom, in which there is real life. Its life is different from this temporal life. In it truth will really make you free."[62] Christ directs their minds away from their earthly rule and their ambition to occupy high and mighty positions on earth to the heavenly realm, where they become great lords, true kings, and powerful princes on account of Christ. We should first be concerned with the chief doctrine, namely, being pious and righteous before God and being liberated from that which holds us in the firmest and closest bonds, namely, from sin. This is the real freedom, which Luther calls "the first freedom,"[63] which comes about not according to the flesh, as the world would like, but solely through Christ's words: "If you keep My words, the truth will make you free" (John 8:32). Faith grasps God's indisputable promise, that none who trust in him will be disappointed.

Earlier Christ said: "I know you are Abraham's descendants," (John 8:37); but he now says: "I speak what the Father commanded Me to say" (v. 38). Here is a shift from Abraham as the father of the Jews to the heavenly Father, whose Word Christ brings is the basis of spiritual freedom. Though the Jews are of Abraham's seed, they are not free for that reason. They are slaves to sin and seek "to kill Christ" (v. 40), because his Word—the truth—which he heard from the Father, finds no place in them. They are bent on being imitators of the devil, their father; thus they are not free from this

60. LW 23.414 (WA XXXIII.668).
61. LW 23.394 (WA XXXIII.642).
62. LW 23.394 (WA XXXIII.642).
63. LW 23.407 (WA XXXIII.662).

father. "According to their flesh and blood, they are Abraham's seed; but according to their works, they are the devil's seed."[64] Physical birth, even that of the Jews' privileged descent from Abraham, is no basis for becoming children of God. Sin, a predicate of divine revelation, is too powerful, and no humanly devised means could subdue it and its concomitants: death and the devil. Only one weapon and device is efficacious: "If the Son makes you free, you will be free indeed."

The great glory and ineffable eternal treasure of being God's children is given "not to all; but to all without limit and to the exclusion of none who believe in His name."[65] The singular privilege of being God's children is made effective only in, and limited to, those who accept his Word in faith. The true Christian must be startled and awestruck by such "a grand and overpowering thought,"[66] that we sinners are singled out for such a great honor to call the eternal and almighty God our Father, and for such a magnificent offer to be his children. Real freedom is obtained *ex nihilo* (out of nothing): nothing we could do or possess contributes toward justification, except by clinging to Christ as sacrament. This is contrary to the Bielian premise that we can "obtain grace by doing what lies in us," a widespread notion that is at odds with thesis 16 of Luther's *Heidelberg Disputation*: "The person who believes that he can obtain grace by doing what is in him adds sin to sin so that he becomes doubly guilty."[67] Everything depends on God's Son, who ranks above all convents, cloisters, cowls, sects, and tonsures. His declaration is causative, bringing real freedom from all that enslaves us. Anything that is not God's Son has no power to make us free. Whatever else human beings may undertake is of no effect. The will is bound to sin, which nothing but grace can heal and break free. The force and beauty of grace lies in this: that we rest from our labors, repose in Christ's life-giving passion and death, and let him who is called the Son of God do his redeeming work. "This Jesus Christ, our Lord, alone imparts this birth, granting believers in Him, the privilege, the right, and the power to become God's children. He alone bestows sonship."[68]

---

64. LW 23.417 (WA XXXIII.671).
65. LW 22.87 (WA 46.611).
66. LW 22.88 (WA 46.612).
67. LW 31.50.
68. LW 22.101 (WA 46.623).

Chapter 6

Nestle on the Lap of Christ
Close our Eyes and Open our Ears

In his sermons on John 14, Luther employs the image of little children, cuddling and nestling on the lap of Jesus to hear his teaching on the second article of faith, "the one thing needful" mentioned by Christ in Luke 10:42 and chosen by Mary, "which shall not be taken away from her,"[1] to reap from it the fruit of assurance and consolation. This article teaches aright that we look solely to Christ—his hands and lips, and apply it to our good as the doctrine upon which our salvation and happiness rests. We learn from Christ how to differentiate the voice of the devil and that of Christ; when and to whom we apply the terrifying words of judgment and the comforting words of grace; how to face life situations such as distress, despair, illness, and the loss of earthly treasures; how to face death and dying, and how to stay on course until our journey of faith ends at the eschaton; and how to accomplish greater works than Christ did. It is "a Christian art"[2] to close our eyes to what we see and feel surrounding us, and open our ears to hear the glorious and heart-warming promises of Christ. Through the Word, we reap the assurance of being included in the inner circle Christ forges between the Father, himself, and us, in which there is nothing but sheer grace and sweet comfort.

---

1. LW 24.97 (WA XLV.548).
2. LW 24.16 (WA XLV.474).

Discerning the Voices: Christ and the Devil

It is central to biblical faith that there is only one true God, the right object of faith. Only God is entitled to faith in himself, just as only God is entitled to bestow eternal life, a thing no creature could do. Jesus Christ, to whom faith is directed, must be God himself. Jesus said: "Believe in God, believe also in me." The idea of faith as adherence to Jesus Christ as the exclusive giver of life is logically dependent upon the confession of Christ as true God. Only in the context of this confession does faith possess any meaning. Christ makes himself equal with God and demands the same honor that rightly belongs to God. "Not that He adds another god to the one God; no, He wants to point out here that He is about to establish His kingdom on earth, that He is leaving them to assume His real office and reign."[3] As God, he is one in whom we believe as surely as we believe in God. Faith in God and faith in Christ are identical—this is the heart of Luther's gospel.[4] God is ours only through Christ. "For here is my Lord, in whom I believe. And if I trust in Him, I am trusting in God; for He Himself is true God."[5] Thus Christ is the subject of the First Commandment: "I am the Lord thy God: thou shalt have no other gods but Me." Christ's words, "Believe in God, believe also in me," teach us this: not only are we taught to trust in God, but also we are to be shown where we will surely find him, lest our thoughts continue to spill out idols bearing the name of God. To believe in God, thus, is not about giving an intellectual assent to certain doctrines, nor about engaging in a discourse about Christ; rather it is to cultivate a heart that grows strong and fearless in the face of whatever may oppose or confront us. In Christ, in whom we rely, we too partake of the benefits of their [His and His Father] indwelling with us: "We [His Father and He] will love, adopt, and protect you: We will quicken you and dwell with you forever."[6] No terror could overwhelm and subdue people with faith, for unto them is given "a far different, surer, and higher comfort and support than all the world has, and greater strength and power on which (they) can rely than that of the world and the devil."[7]

The Christian life lies in the daily battle against the devil, the mortal enemy of Christ's followers. Thus it takes skill to differentiate in the heat of battle between the voice of the devil and Christ's. Just as law and gospel

---

3. LW 24.21 (WA XLV.489).
4. Siggins, *Luther's Doctrine of Christ*, 87.
5. LW 24.25 (WA XLV.483).
6. LW 24.25 (WA XLV.484).
7. LW 24.18 (WA XLV.476).

exists in a constant struggle, so the devil's work and Christ's are in contention against each other. Christ does the opposite of what the devil does, just as the gospel does the contrary of what the law does. The devil's aim is to ruin and destroy; Christ's aim is to build up and restore. The devil speaks terrifying and threatening words only to create in the believer despair and despondency. This is contrary to the voice of Christ, who bids us and all believers to be of good cheer. We must observe the right time and the proper place in which to apply Christ's words, and the right person to whom Christ's words pertain. The Christian knows that the real function of the law is to work in us the knowledge of sin not so that it might condemn us but that it might rescue us from it. In Christ, there is no sign of disfavor. "Now that would be true knowledge—if only we could attain it—to control, bridle, restrain, and curb our thoughts so as not to know, think, or hear anything but how Christ is disposed towards us."[8]

The devil is skillful at perverting the usage of Christ's words, and transforming truth into a lie, adorning himself with Christ's name and works, when in reality he is the archenemy. When he terrifies a person, he keeps him in permanent sadness without relief. The cultivation of despair is one of the primary tasks of the devil, whose ultimate aim is destruction. "He does not let a single proud and impenitent person despair; or when a person finally does lapse into terror and fear, as happens in the end, to all such, then he deserts him. Even then he does not put an end to his terrorizing but oppresses and distresses him so severely that he must despair eternally unless he is restored by Christ."[9] The satanic strategy is to shift our focus from Christ to self, change our confidence in God to ethical conduct, and undermine assurance of God's free grace in Christ so that we put our reliance on our works. And if we let him succeed, he would have converted us, so to speak, from a theologian of the cross to a theologian of glory.[10] However if Christ frightens a person from unbelief into faith, or from a sinful life into penitence, it is for a short duration, just as he frightened Paul prior to his conversion. Christ's work bears a salutary purpose—he terrifies us not so that we might remain in grief but that we may be freed from it and enjoy relief in God's embrace. Despair can only be healed by clinging to Christ's words: "Let not your hearts be troubled."

---

8. LW 24.62 (WA XLV.517).
9. LW 24.16 (WA XLV.475).
10. Trueman, *Luther on the Christian Life*, 127.

Consolations Hidden in Contrary Appearances

As an art of consolation, Christ has us think in contrast: all the loss we suffer on earth is insignificant and slight, compared to all the gain and blessings that are ours by faith. This is borne out in John 14:2–4: "In My Father's house are many rooms; if it were not so, would I have told you that I go to prepare a place for you. And when I go and prepare a place for you, I will come again and will take you to Myself, that where I am you may be also. And you know the way where I am going." St. Augustine, for one, ingeniously interpreted Christ going to heaven to prepare these rooms as having no other meaning than that believers were being prepared to dwell there. "This is, to be sure," Luther remarked, "a fine and masterly interpretation and a good catachresis."[11] However Luther prefers interpreting these words plainly, as they appear. He came up with consolations against the devil, the world, and every evil that may beset his beloved disciples.

First, Christ compares the dwelling here on earth, in which the devil resides and rules as Lord, to many more abodes for the believers with the Father in heaven. In accord with the title given to him in John 8:44, the devil carries out only two activities: as liar, he misleads people with false teachings or ideas, and as murderer, he fills everything with murder, war, and all sorts of cruelties. As long as we dwell on his property, we expect nothing of him except deception and murder. "This is his nature and office."[12] If the devil and his tyrants rob us of house and home here, rest assured that we shall have ample room for our dwelling in heaven. "The rooms of life are far more spacious than the abodes of death."[13] For what is lost here will be richly reimbursed there. Comfort is hidden in its opposite, that if they lack anything here, they will be abundantly supplied in heaven, in the place which Christ calls "My Father's house," where we will dwell eternally with the Father and with Christ and never suffer separation from them. The second consolation is derived from Christ's words: "If it were not so, I still tell you that I go to prepare a place for you." Even if the supply were not enough, Christ promises that he will create a sufficient number so that there will be no lack or scarcity of all sorts of dwellings to satisfy the desires of their hearts. Even when the world now grievously tramples us underfoot and torments us, we do not lose but remain blessed of God. A more horrible fate the wicked incur for the persecution they inflict on the believers is enough cause for us not to judge nor avenge but intercede for them so that they might be

---

11. LW 24.26 (WA XLV.484). Cf. LW 12.346, n. 16.
12. LW 24.26 (WA XLV.484).
13. LW 24.27 (WA XLV.484).

rescued from eternal misery. The third consolation is contained in Christ's words: "And when I go and prepare a place for you, I will come again and take you to Myself, that where I am you may be also." He inculcates in them the thought that his departure from this world and his going to his Father are indeed good news, for they are assured both of the dwellings in heaven and Christ's eternal company. Yet this is hidden from sight and remains disputable here on earth, but it is crucial we open our eyes properly and look not at what is apparent, attuning our ears to Christ's words: "I will not abandon you, but will come and take us into myself." With St. Paul, Luther interpreted this to mean that through our new identity in baptism, we have Christ dwelling in and with us, and have been transposed from the wicked dominion of darkness into the spiritual, heavenly existence of light, where we are "fellow citizens with the saints and members of the household of God" (cf. Col 1:13; Eph 2:19). In addition, Luther adds the fourth one, that it is Christ's will to grant us the privilege to know now where Christ is heading and also to know the way. The "way" here refers to the way of his holy passion, about which Christ has taught his disciples at length. Christ is the way, and there is no other way they should pursue. "Everything is here,"[14] despite contrary appearances. That is more than enough to offset the loss we have experienced here, for we would still possess the Master who provides for us, since we have him with us forever. All the loss a Christian suffers here he will be restored with a hundredfold. This radical contrast is the source of comfort.

Christ is All—Beginning, Middle, and End

We must cleave to the beautiful voice of Christ who says: "I am the Way, the Truth, and the Life." These christological terms are synonymous; they are different names, reflecting the various distinct experiences one has when clinging to him and finally reaches the end. A theologian of the cross adopts a spiritual way of looking at Christ, which differs sharply with the way the world does and the disciples did up to this time. The same road Christ travels is now laid upon his disciples, as Luther confessed: "And if I remain steadfast in this faith, I take the same way and road, through cross and suffering, and reach the same place to which He has gone."[15] Just as Christ goes through weaknesses, cross, death, and everything in order to come to the Father, Christ also draws his disciples in the same way with and through himself to reach the Father. It is indeed a real art to appropriate the beautiful

14. LW 24.30 (WA XLV.488).
15. LW 24.35 (WA XLV.493).

voice of Christ, "I am the Way," through which we may deafen the alluring voice of the deceiver, who tries to remove Christ from our sight. There is no way or road we could create or provide which we might call our own, except Christ's. For no one has ever descended from heaven or ascended into heaven on his own. The express purpose of Christ descending from heaven and ascending to heaven is to show us the way and take us up into heaven through himself. Christ has preceded us on this way, and could lead us on it. Faith clings to the Word, boldly trusting in this Man as the way to heaven.

To inculcate "proof and perseverance in the faith" (1 Pet 1:7), Christ assumes the other aspects in our experience: "I am Truth and the Life." All these terms apply uniformly to the one Christ, although they must be distinguished. "With a view to the beginning He is called the Way; He is the Truth with regard to the means and the continuation; He is the Life by reason of the end."[16] The very content of this verse is contained in this brief form: Christ is "all"—"the beginning, the middle and the end of salvation."[17] As in Gen 28:12, he is the beginning, the middle, and the last rung of the Jacob's ladder to heaven. Once we begin with Christ as the Way, we must remain and continue the road with him as the Truth, lest we deflect from Christ and seek other and erroneous ways to heaven, resulting in death. Luther illustrates this by the story of the crossing of the Red Sea, in which the Jews embarked on the way through the sea in obedience to God's command, continued on it, and did not waver. Not a drop of water could fall, and the sea had to let them pass through dry-footed, which, in the judgment of reason, is a perilous, frightful, and impassable way. The proper and exact way to face danger and the uncertainty of death is not by means of a final resolution, in which we confess Christ as Our Life when we are about to give up our ghost, while meanwhile living as we please. We should consider him soon enough, and not wait until such time when it may be too late. In the whole time on earth, from the beginning to the end, Christ is Our Life. Here Luther resorts to the sacrament of baptism, the single great act of grace in the Christian's life, as the basis of the assurance of faith, and as a defence against the temptation. Baptism is the Christian's personal exodus from Egypt, which constantly brings to mind: "I am a Christian and therefore the Devil cannot have me."[18]

Then Christ goes on to declare: "Yet a little while, and the world will see Me no more, but you will see Me; because I live, you will live also" (John 14:19). Resurrection marks the beginning of his life, and theirs. Christ holds

---

16. LW 24.48 (WA XLV.505).
17. LW 24.48 (WA XLV.505).
18. Trueman, *Luther on the Christian Life*, 139.

life so firmly in his grip that no death could devour his person, although he dies physically. Christ drowns death in himself and swallows it up in his life; he overcomes the devil through his power. Those who are frightened by death and all kinds of misfortunes could defy the devil and the world, and say: "When you kill me, you really do not kill me; you help me gain life. When you bury me, you lift me out of ashes and dust up into heaven. In brief, your wrath and rage is nothing but grace and help; for you merely give me reason for, and the beginning of, Christ's bestowal of life on me, as He says: 'I live, and you will live also.'"[19] Christ is sheer life by which we live in him, just as Christ lives in the Father and the Father in him. Through union with Christ, we will become lords over the world, the devil, hell, and all their defiance; they no longer thwart us. We remain confident of victory, which Christ gives us through his Spirit. We too experience in our hearts the force of being in the Father: that Christ has devoured everything deadly in him, and that by being in Christ, the power of sin, death, and the devil is dead in us, as it is in him, and in the Father. By faith we experience Christ's power, co-equal to his Father's, one and the same power which assures us that pure life prevails.

To apprehend and believe that death is dead, both for Christ and us, always requires "a knowledge of a high order,"[20] that is, an experiential knowledge of the cross—afflictions and assaults from within and without. The consolation Christ bequeaths to his disciples does not take root until trials come to bring it home; we must learn it when afflictions, be it from the devil, death, and the world, oppress and frighten us. Luther thus says: "It will be difficult and will cost many a hard battle."[21] God permits the devil and death to assault us, not so that he might devour us but test us, to purify us, and manifest himself ever more to us. Affliction is a form of God's alien work, through which we will not remain in our early, incipient faith; it too preserves us against indolence and idleness. Trials work good for us, for they produce in us the certainty of Christ's love for us and of his self-disclosure as an outcome. In our darkest moments when it appears that we possess neither God nor Christ, as though we are completely forsaken and without help, Christ will not remain at a distance but return to us with a clearer revelation of his and the Father's love. Our experience bears this out: God is manifest in the opposite of appearances and feelings; though it seems that Christ has completely deserted us and that the devil has thoroughly overpowered us, we remain in the Savior's grip, proving that he loves us;

---

19. LW 24, 136 (WA XLV, 585). See Sauter, "Luther on the Resurrection," 99–118.
20. LW 24.137 (WA XLV.586).
21. LW 24.137 (WA XLV.586).

when we feel most cursed, we are most cuddled, as we nestle on Christ's lap where his comfort lies.

The Article of Faith: Christ and Father are One

The true identity of Christ and his intimacy with his Father constitutes the basis of his counsel for aggrieved hearts. For Christ is God, and he himself supplies the contents of God's deity. With these words: "I am in the Father and the Father in Me" (v. 11), Christ intends to drum into our ears the chief article of faith, that Christ and God are one in being. The whole verse, "Believe Me that I am in the Father and the Father in Me; or else believe Me for the sake of the works themselves," attests to a correspondence between the works of Christ and his identity. Such works done publicly before all eyes—healing the blind and the deaf, forgiving sins, casting out devils, and raising the dead—are not human but are exclusively divine, exposing his identity as God. By his works, Christ has aptly demonstrated to us that the Father is in him and wants to be known through him. Christ's identity is further substantiated in verse 13, where Christ says, "Whatever you ask of Me, I will do it." Christ assumes all the power and might of the Divine Majesty to do what we ask of him. The phrase, "Whatever you ask," means barring nothing, since Christ bids us to pray for all this and he will grant it as a fulfillment of his promise. It would have been proper to apply the glory to himself; yet he transfers the honor to the Father, and in doing so he includes both the Father and himself. This is evident in verse 13: "That the Father be glorified in the Son." Neither did he exclude the Father with the preceding words, "Whatever you ask . . . I will do it," nor did he separate from him with the proceeding words, "that the Father may be glorified." Christ joins the two by rearranging the words "I will do what you ask, that the Father may be glorified in the Son." When He says "I will do it," he indicates that it is he who is entitled to the glory for the deed he does. Yet in the words that follow, he is silent about his glory but transfers it to the Father. So if the glory is rightly the Father's, it follows that the work he does must be identical to Christ's. On the other hand, if the glory is predicated of the Father, Christ, who does the same work, must also share the same honor that the Father has.

Knowing that his bodily absence would create unrest, Christ asks the Father to grant them the Comforter, who will remain with them forever. John 14:16: "And I will pray the Father," assures the disciples that they will not suffer lack; nor will they be forsaken. The preceding statement, "Whatever you ask in My name, I will do," is an assertion of his identity as true God, who is able to give and do all things, for his nature demands it. Here the statement, "I will pray the Father," pertains to Christ who spoke here as the lowliest man on earth, as a servant amongst all people, although he is true God and Lord over all, worthy of our worship. Thus it is not to be understood as the true God, petitioning someone else, for God cannot be subject to someone else and be obliged to him for things received. To gain the proper meaning of Scripture, Luther prescribes a rule: "For how can one express in any words that He speaks as God and as man at the same time, since He has two distinct natures? If He were to speak as God at all times, one could not prove that He is also true man. And if He were to speak as true man at all times, one would never be aware that He is also true God."[22] The same Person who said: "Whatever you ask, I will do it," also declares here: "I will pray the Father." The former relates to his divinity; the latter relates to his humanity. Since Christ is one Person, fully God and fully man, it is appropriate to speak of him as each nature requires, with certain words reflecting his human, others his divine nature.

John 14:28: "If you loved Me, you would have rejoiced, because I go to the Father; for the Father is greater than I" has given rise to all sorts of errors and fallacies concerning the identity of Christ. By his admission that the Father is greater than him, some argue, Christ cannot be the same eternal God as the Father is. To counter this, Luther quoted St. Hilary, who argues that because the Father is the first Person, it is only proper to call him greater than the Son. The Father is greater than the Son, not in terms of the order of being, for all three are One being, but order of relation, that the Father is the first, and prior to the Son. The Father is greater, "not by nature or essence but by authority," that is, not by virtue of divine essence but solely because the Son proceeds from the Father, not the Father from the Son.[23] On this text, Augustine said: "The Son is the lesser according to his humanity,"[24] not according to his divinity. Regardless, what is in view is not how Christ is God or man, or what his nature and essence is, or whether in his being he is greater or less than the Father. Rather, it is Christ's express purpose to console the disciples not to be frightened by the prospect of his impending departure from them, for he is going to where he shall attain greatness. The immediate context is indicated in the words: "Because I go to the Father," whose meaning consists in nothing other than occupying the Father's kingdom, in which he will reside with his Father as his co-equal and will be acknowledged as having the same majesty. It does not refer to

22. LW 24.104 (WA XLV.555).

23. Hilary, *On the Trinity*, Book IX, par. 51–55, 321–27. Also cited in LW 24.187 (WA XLV. 632), n. 101.

24. Augustine, *On the Trinity*, Book VI, ch. 9 as cited in LW 24.188 (WA XLV. 632), n. 102.

Jesus being born of the Father, but refers to his glorification, to the kingdom to which he is returning from this house of bondage to assume openly his divine and omnipotent power and rule, which he has with the Father from eternity. He cannot enter this heavenly reign before he had fulfilled the office of a servant, to which he was sent. As St. Paul says in Phil 2:7, in the humiliation in which Christ came, he "emptied Himself" of all divine glory and took the servile form, so that, in keeping with this, he is not only less than the Father but also less before all people. This is integral to Luther's theology of the cross, in which God works out the salvation of the world in the efficacious activities of the Son, not through might and power but in the weakness and suffering of the cross. Of John 14:30–31: "I will no longer talk much with you, for the ruler of this world is coming. He has no power over Me; but I do as the Father has commanded Me, so that the world may know that I love the Father. Rise, let us go hence," Christ speaks of his victory over the devil's might. Though the devil wants to devour Christ, he will find out that this will tear his belly apart;[25] for he has no jurisdiction over Christ, and Christ owes him nothing. The God who is known in Christ is the God who comes in lowliness or humility. The being of Jesus Christ in humility, suffering and dying on the cross is being in self-humiliation and the atonement effected by him is the act of Christ's self-humiliation. The Son of God is our servant, who so utterly debases himself that he assumes the burden of the world's sin, and died a real death. Nestling on the lap of Christ, we reap the sublime substance of the gospel: the righteous and innocent One—Man Christ—must suffer like a poor condemned sinner, feel God's wrath and judgment against sin in his gracious heart, and taste eternal death and damnation.[26] The theologian of the cross must not look away from the horror of Golgotha, and speculate about things beyond, guessing about how atonement works in heaven. For him, there is no other way than this: "[Christ's] obedience and humility in the utmost weakness, by cross and death, by [his] submission to his Father, and by surrendering his right and might."[27] The Father is greater than the Son, not in terms of his immanent Being but of Christ's economic mission on earth. In humiliation, he is a poor, wretched, suffering, and dying Christ, but in his glorification, with the Father he will be a great, glorious, living, and almighty Lord over all. He shall become greater, as great as the Father is, so that he shall reign with him in equal power and majesty. The context deals with Christ's passing from this life

---

25. On the metaphor of the devil's belly for the atonement, see Pelikan, *Companion Volume*, 185–86.

26. Forde, "Luther's Theology of the Cross," 55.

27. LW 24.192 (WA XLV.635–36).

into the realm of the Father, and thus Luther sees no need to engage in a sharp dispute on the divine essence of the Father and of the Son. In being, Christ is and remains equal with the Father, the eternal God, who humbled himself, descended to our flesh, assumed the lowliest and most menial office for us, and died. But by doing this he conquered death and drew us up to where his kingdom, identical to the Father's, is.

The Three Foundations: Greater Works than Christ

Christ speaks of the Christian works, which exceed that of his own. The general sense of "greater works" lies in this, that the apostles and Christians had a wider field than Christ did, and that they were able to preach to more people to Christ than he did during his sojourn on earth. While Christ's activity was limited to a certain locality and to a short duration, the apostles and their successors, however, have extended their activities over the entire history of Christianity and to all the world. The work initiated by Christ was extended and expanded by Christians till the Day of Judgment. To fortify the disheartened disciples, Christ laid three foundations for the efficacy of the works that Christians do. This is borne out in his own words: "He who believes in Me," (John 14:12) and "Because I go to the Father," and "whatever you ask . . . I will do it" (v. 14).

The first foundation is faith in Christ. He says: "He who believes in Me will also do works that I do" (v. 12). Christ performs the divine work, making the disciples believe that the Father is in him and he is in the Father. Verse 11: "Believe me for the sake of the works I do," applies to the time before we become Christians, as Christ speaks of the works by which we are made Christians. Now Christ extends this and says that the disciples, too, should perform such works—works that demonstrate that they are in Christ and that Christ is in them. Faith in Christ is a necessary condition for the performance of the selfsame works, and even greater works than Christ does, that is, "more work and more extensive works than Christ Himself did."[28] Yet their works are identical, the same as his, except that the works we do must issue from him as the fountainhead, as we adhere to him in faith. Not of ourselves, the works we do are wrought in us by his power and might. Through us he works and manifests his power, which effects conversion to God. Just as the Father who dwells in Christ does his works, so also we who dwell in Christ do his works, namely, through his power. The "very greatest works"—the demolition of the devil's realm, the deliverance of souls, the conversion of hearts, the preservation of peace for land and nation, and

---

28. LW 24.78 (WA XLV.531).

salvation in all sorts of distress—are continuously done by Christians, because they believe in Christ, their head from whom they derive everything. Consequently, the Christians are lords and gods of the world, as God says to Moses in Exod 7:1: "See, I make you as God to Pharoah." Every Christian is an emperor and lord over the masters of the world, not by virtue of his person as a human being, but because of his faith in the Lord Christ. This is evident in Ps 8:8 which says: "Thou hast put all things under his feet." Whatever power and possessions the world has is given to it because of the beggarly Christian, whom St. Paul described in 2 Cor 6:19, "as having nothing, and yet possesses everything." Unlike other people, the baptized Christians are elevated to the status as lord over all, just as Christ is Lord over all. This is something which Christians could "boast of greatly; it is glorious,"[29] that they, whom the world despises and regards as filth, are so highly praised by Christ and esteemed by God.

The second foundation is Christ's ascension, because of which believers could perform greater works. Christ says: "Because I go to the Father" (v. 12). His going to the Father means his entrance upon his reign and his kingdom he obtained, being made Lord and placed on the royal chair on God's right hand. Luther has Christ say:

> "And now I must let Myself be crucified and put to death. But afterwards—after my crucifixion, death, and burial—I shall first leap from death to life; from the cross and the grave into everlasting glory, divine majesty, and might. Then—as Christ states elsewhere (John 12:32)—I will draw all men to Myself, and all creatures will have to be subject to Me. . . Thus it will become apparent that you are doing far greater works than I am now doing."[30]

Christ is crowned with power, co-equal in majesty and publicly exalted as true God and Lord over all creatures. Christians will accomplish great works that Christ himself accomplishes only a small fraction, because of Christ's exalted status in heaven in which we share. This is also taught by St. Paul who wrote in Ephesians 2:6 that God has already "made us sit with Him in the heavenly places," meaning we reign with Christ, though this heavenly status is hidden from us now. Sin, death, devil, the evil world—prostrate before Christ's feet, and cease their power over us. Just as Christ is Lord over all sin, death, and the devil, so we shall also be lords over them. The same power in which we glory is ours, not because of our own worthiness or strength but solely because of God's grace. Though the Christian may

29. LW 24.83 (WA XLV.536).
30. LW 24.85–86 (WA XLV.538).

appear as a beggar, owning nothing here on earth, they still own a great treasure in heaven, in and with Christ: power and authority over the enemies of life. This is stated in Luke 10:19: "Behold, I have given you authority to tread upon serpents and scorpions, and over all the power of the enemy; and nothing shall hurt you." Of this verse Luther has Christ say: "For I have placed into your mouth the Word which is My Word, and have given you the Baptism which is My Baptism; and through these I want to demonstrate My almighty power."[31] Christ continues to work via the external and his ordained means: his Word, Baptism, and Sacrament.[32] These are the ministries Christians perform to convert people, snatch souls from the jaws of the devil, deliver them from hell and death, and usher them into heaven. These works which are done with God's power accomplish everything, and no one can boast of himself. The Word of God Christ preached was handed down to the Apostles, and then transmitted to us, through the agency of true bishops, pastors, and preachers. So what they (and we) proclaim is none other than the Word that comes from Christ's lips, which is the Father's. The words and the works of their ministry must proceed from Christ alone, regardless of whether their own person is good or evil; they must also point solely to Christ. The Baptism and Sacrament they administer is not theirs; it is Christ's. The apostles and pastors are nothing but instruments of divine power, through which Christ speaks and transmits his gospel from the Father to us. Here on earth we perceive God, as St. Paul indicates in 1 Cor 13:12, "in a mirror dimly," enveloped in Word and Sacraments. "These are His masks or His garments, as it were, in which He conceals Himself."[33] The mortal soul cannot bear to see and look at his brilliant Majesty without being crushed by it. We apprehend him through the Word and through the works Christ performs by means of the ministry and other offices. God has earnestly enjoined these two—God and his work, and Christ and his Word, which must be kept together most firmly. The Holy Spirit, whom the Father sends (John 14:26), will come and dwell with us and sanctify us through the Word and sacrament, the tools and means through which he works faith in it and impresses upon our hearts the knowledge of Christ. "This also makes Christian holy before God, not by virtue of what we ourselves are or do but because the Holy Spirit is given to us."[34] There is no lack in him, true God together with the Father and the Son in One divine Essence yet distinct in person, and thus we will not lack for comfort, courage, and wisdom. The

---

31. LW 24.84 (WA XLV.537).
32. On the created forms of the Word of God, see chapter 2 of this book.
33. LW 24.67 (WA XLV.522). On the metaphor of masks, see LW 14.114, n. 9.
34. LW 24.168 (WA XLV.614).

world, the devil, and the conscience will frighten and torment us; neither would the Father nor the Son aggrieve us. This is established, for Christ will ask the Father, not to terrorize us or cast us into hell but "to send us another Comforter, who will abide with us forever" (John 14:16). Both the Father and the Son are of one heart and mind. Nor does the Holy Spirit do the opposite of what the Father and the Son do, for all three share the same Godhead. Christians must be skillful at the art of learning to know and believe what Christ depicts about the Holy Spirit, that when sin, death, hell, the devil, or the world confront us, the Holy Spirit will adequately comfort us. The Holy Spirit is "not the Spirit of anger and terror but a Spirit of grace and consolation, and that the entire Deity reflects sheer comfort. The Father wants to comfort, for it is He who grants the Holy Spirit; the Son likewise, for He prays for this; and the Holy Spirit Himself is to be the Comforter."[35] Then our hearts rest assured that Christ loves us, that the Father loves us, and that the Holy Spirit, who is sent to us, loves us.

The third foundation is prayer, as Christ says, "Whatever you ask in My Name, I will do it" (v. 13). We inherit the power through faith and through his ascension, that we can do the same works that Christ has done, and even greater ones. As part of the consolation, Christ adds his promise: "I will do it." We benefit from Christ's going to the Father the power, which not only avails but also prevails over the devil and the world. Just as God hides in the Word and Baptism to effect his saving grace, so he hides in the prayer of the Christians to achieve his work. Prayer is one of the greatest works that helps and preserves the world, even if we did nothing else. So greatly can a whole nation be benefited from the prayer of one pious man, for whose sake all are blessed. This is illustrated in the story of Lot in Gen 19:22, where Sodom and Gomorrah were spared while Lot still dwelled there. Because of Naaman alone, God bestowed prosperity and victory on the entire idolatrous kingdom of Syria (2 Kings 5:1). All Egypt were helped because of one pious man, Joseph (Gen 41:46ff). Fortune and victory were accrued to the Romans, the Persians, and others not by virtue of human effort but solely for the sake of Christians, through whom God performs much greater works. Any victory that kings, lords, and princes incur is proof that they have been supported by another power, namely, God who upholds their reign through the prayer of the Christians. "Hence these men receive a hidden help, a help that is unseen by them and unknown to them, namely, God's Word and order and the prayers of the Christians."[36]

---

35. LW 24.111 (WA XLV.561).
36. LW 24.81 (WA XLV.534).

By his command to pray, Christ reveals to the disciples their impotence, and that of themselves they cannot achieve greater works than those he himself has done. With this he forestalled pride, presumption, and self-reliance, as though they were complete and no longer in need of him. The more they exercise their faith in Christ by prayer and petition, the more they will experience God's power in weakness and in suffering, as they are impelled to call upon him. Prayer is a "Christian's true office and function,"[37] through which we reap "a spirit of compassion and supplication" (Zech 12:10). Christ will effect in all Christians these two things: First, he will assure their hearts of a compassionate God, with whom they are reconciled, and thus possess all they need for themselves; secondly, when they have this, they will become gods and saviors of the world by their supplication. Through the spirit of compassion, they, as children of God, will mediate between God and their neighbor, and will help others attain this estate too. God so "completely permeates"[38] a Christian that he is compelled to help others acquire the same benefits, that of being redeemed from death and brought into his dominion and inheritance. "For his greatest delight is in this treasure, the knowledge of Christ."[39] Where the Christian is in "the greatest calm," namely, in God's grace and peace, "a spirit of restlessness"[40] surges from within, causing him to confess his treasure openly, and pray that others might receive the same mercy. Where the spirit of grace resides, he cannot sit still or idle; he feels compelled to boldly confess Christ with all his might, as one whose sole object in life is to praise God's honor and glory among the people that others may also receive such a spirit of need for themselves for whom supplication is made. Christ highly extols the Christian estate of prayer, "the true work characteristic only of the Christians."[41] Prayer in Christ's name gives him heartfelt pleasure; it is "the glory and consolation of Christians,"[42] for only they possess the grace and spirit to apprehend what God has given them in Christ, and for that reason they accomplish greater works than Christ himself has done. The Christians function as the legs that sustain the entire world until the Last Day. Because of the Christians' prayers, by means of which they obtain and receive spiritual gifts and physical goods on earth, the world is indebted to the Christian and his prayer for whatever they own. Through faith, his Word and prayer,

---

37. LW 24.87 (WA XLV.539).
38. LW 24.87 (WA XLV.540).
39. LW 24.87 (WA XLV.540).
40. LW 24.88 (WA XLV.540).
41. LW 24.88 (WA XLV.540).
42. LW 24.89 (WA XLV.542).

we possess such abiding treasure that we can show others how to remain steadfast in the hour of death and uphold them in every trouble—this is something the world with all its wealth, crown, and splendor cannot do.

Enclosed in the Circle: Nothing but Sheer Grace

Finally Christ cements the faith of the troubled disciples by drawing them into the inner circle of the triune life. Of verse 20: "In that day you will know that I am in My Father, and you in Me, and I in you," Christ wants to teach that on the day when he rose and ascended to the Father, the disciples will be persuaded of his being in the Father in such a manner that everything the Man Christ says, does, and suffers is indeed God himself who says, does and suffers it. Here Luther underscores the all-important truth of a double movement of God: descending to us from above, from the Father through Christ; and ascending to God from below, through Christ again to the Father. The Son descends from the Father and attaches himself to us; we, in turn, attach ourselves to the Son, through whom we ascend to the Father. Christ was sent to draw us up to the Father, just as he is in the Father. "Christ forges these links between Himself and us and the Father, thus enclosing us in this circle, so that now we are in Him and He in us, just as He is in the Father and the Father is in Him. Through such union and communion our sin and death are abolished, and now we have sheer life and blessedness in their stead."[43] Whoever has this knowledge has everything.

This text contains the two facts, "the highest and the most necessary for our consolation":[44] that Christ is in us, and that we are in him. The former points downward, the latter upward. We must first be found in him with all our being, with our sin, death, and every trouble, and know that we are liberated from these before God and are pronounced justified through Christ. Our being is found in Christ, just as his being is and remains with the Father. That is our proper place. Not only must we see ourselves in him, we must also seek to be found in him, and be his own. To be found in him is to vault "above ourselves and beyond ourselves," and "become completely merged into Him."[45] In us, we stand condemned on our account; in him, we are blessed on his account. If we feel death in us, we have life in Christ. Sin, the devil, death, and hell are all in him, and that is its proper place; in exchange, righteousness, God, life, and heaven are ours if we remain in him. We must practice, as a true Christian and perfect person does, remaining in

43. LW 24.139 (WA XLV.587).
44. LW 24.142 (WA XLV.591).
45. LW 24.143 (WA XLV.591).

Christ, and experience this, that it is truly the work of him who is in us and in whom we are. The devil works hard to sever our thoughts from Christ and Christ from the Father. He wants us to let both the Father and Christ keep residing in heaven, as though he were far removed from us, not in us and did nothing in us. We must be certain that Christ is in us, speaking and working from us: "that whatever we do and perform in Christendom, He calls His own activity; and that our tongues, eyes, ears, hands, and hearts are all His."[46]

To know Christ is to love him in such a way that we are drawn into the inner circle of grace. Luther paraphrases Christ's saying: "He who wants to know Me must love Me, hold to Me, and not to be ashamed of Me. If they do this, they will experience that I will manifest Myself to them. Then they will notice in themselves that they have believed aright and have not been deceived."[47] This is where the way of the world parts with Christ's. The world cannot and will not love Christ, and because of it, God does not manifest himself to them, but remains at the distance. On the contrary, Christ's words still stand: "If you love Me, you will keep My commandments" (v. 23), that Christ is hidden in those who love him, and who have and adhere to his Word. It is they, as true church, in whom the Father and Christ will dwell. While the devil gains mastery over us by means of the picture of an unmerciful and angry God, Christ dispels it and leads us to the picture of the fatherly heart of God. Thus Christ said: "And My Father will love him." For the love with which Christ loves us is identical to the love with which Father loves us. "This is indeed a beautiful and charming message": "[You] have Christ the Lord as your friend and not only Him but also the Father, who assures you and testifies through the mouth of His Son that He loves and cherishes you because of your faith in Christ, and your confession of Him."[48] Christ continues to comfort with these words: "Not only will I and the Father love him who loves Me; We will also come to him and make Our home with him" (v. 23). This means not only are we safeguarded from the future wrath, and from every foe of life but we shall also have Their dwelling with us here on earth. "We [Father and Christ] will be his daily guests, yes, members of his household and his table companions."[49] Only Christians would enjoy such "a rich comfort and an exceedingly high honor" to be the "Divine majesty's dwelling, pleasure-ground, and paradise, yes, His

---

46. LW 24.144 (WA XLV.592).
47. LW 24.156 (WA XLV.603).
48. LW 24.158 (WA XLV.605).
49. LW 24.158 (WA XLV.606).

heavenly kingdom."[50] All the raging and renting of the devil and the world fail to conquer the Christians, unless the Father and Christ cease to be their God, which is inconceivable. They who cling to Christ and keep his words are kept in the providential care of the Father and Christ, who already prepare a sure dwelling in heaven; they shall also be Their castle and home on earth, as Christ promises. Christ remains our Guest; we his inn and dwelling. The devil and the world may rob us of our life, but cannot deprive us of this Guest. Because we possess him we certainly possess everything through which we are able to combat the enemies of life.

---

50. LW 24.158 (WA XLV.606).

CHAPTER 7

Jesus, the Master Commentator
Harvesting Divine Things from Christ

In his sermons on John 15, Luther portrays Christ as "the Master Commentator,"[1] from whom we harvest divine things. Christ interprets the meaning and purpose of afflictions, the basis of election and friendship with God, the need of appropriating Christ as sacrament to ground embracing Christ as example, the close linkage between faith and love. St. John furnishes a christological lens on divine things, through which we may perceive God's friendly heart hidden in its opposite, and receive abundant consolations from Christ amidst the horrible picture of the devil and the world. No other interpreters save Christ are reliable, as only he leads us with precision and promise. He who creates out of nothing (*ex nihilo*) could bring good out of evil; he could employ the devil's and all the world's evil as instruments with which to serve his good purpose, an art at which he is most skilled. Faith grasps the Word of God, the purifying catalyst through which we are clean before God. The Word of God continues to cleanse us of residual sins through cross and suffering. We too harvest God's love from the love of the cross—a right perspective (christological) on how to look at others. All goods—eternal and temporal—we obtain from Christ by faith we now share with others; this is done for their good, not for our own gain.

---

1. LW 24.194–95 (WA XLV.637).

Suffering as God's Alien Work

Any attempt to invoke Christ's suffering to ensure one's exemption from personal suffering denatures the cross and the Christian life.[2] Cross-bearing is intrinsic to the Christian life. "For God has appointed that we should not only believe in the crucified Christ," argued Luther, "but also be crucified with him."[3] To expound the purpose of affliction and suffering, Christ dramatizes himself as a vine and the Father as a Vinedresser, with us as the branches. In an exceedingly fine parabolic picture, Christ says: "I am the vine, and My Father is the Vinedresser. Every branch of Mine that bear no fruit He takes away, and every branch that does bear fruit He prunes, that it may bear more fruit" (John 15:1–2). This is "a very comforting picture and an excellent, delightful personification,"[4] in which Christ interprets all the suffering, which both he and they are to endure as something that causes them to bear fruit abundantly. Christians are not afflicted without God's counsel and will; they should see affliction as a sign of grace and fatherly love, not of wrath and judgment. Whatever hurts and distresses us does the opposite of its aim; instead of working hurt and harm in us, it ultimately redounds to our good and profit. The suffering we endure is compared to the work of a vinedresser who hoes and cultivates his vine without ruining it, so that it might yield more and better fruits as the outcome. The vine might revolt against the Vinedresser, and say:

> "Ah, what are you doing? Now I must wither and decay, for you are removing the soil from my roots and are belaboring my branches with these iron teeth. You are tearing and pinching me everywhere, and I will have to stand in the ground bare and seared. You are treating me more cruelly than one treats any tree or plant." But the vinedresser would reply: "You are a fool and do not understand. For even if I do cut a branch from you, it is a totally useless branch; it takes away your strength and your sap. Then the other branches, which should bear fruit, must suffer. Therefore away with it! This is for your own good."[5]

The cross and afflictions—characteristic of Christ, the Vine—will also be imposed upon Christ's followers, the branches. Christ interprets the suffering that he and his beloved encounter as a benefaction rather than bane.

---

2. Clark, "Martin Luther's View," 337. Also cited in Parsons, *Martin Luther's Interpretation*, 272.

3. LW 51.198 as cited in Clark, "Martin Luther's View," 337.

4. LW 24.193 (WA XLV.636).

5. LW 24.194 (WA XLV.637).

Affliction and suffering are God's alien work, via fertilizing and pruning, which serves God's proper work, that we might grow and yield all the better fruit. Without fertilizing and pruning, the vine might degenerate into an unfruitful specimen, which would finally perish entirely. But the Father (Vinedresser) wills that it be well-cultivated, fertilized, pruned, and rid of its superfluous leaves, so that it develops its full strength and yields an abundantly delicious wine. The cross and death Christ undergoes is God's alien work, through which his proper work might shine: that he shall come to his glory, inaugurate his reign, and be confessed throughout the world. Here Christ is surely "a master commentator": "But the fertilizing and pruning I suffer will yield a richer fruit: that is, through My cross and death I shall come to My glory, begin My reign, and be acknowledged and believed throughout the world."[6]

Happy is the Christian who can interpret this picture and apply it in hours of distress and trial. Then she learns that the contraries of life—death, the devil, and the world—are only God's hoe and clipper; they are the alien work God performs, not intrinsic to divine nature, which prepares the way for a reception of God's grace. Thus disciples may praise God, who uses the devil and his vile deeds to serve our good. For instance, the patriarch Joseph declared in Gen 50: 20: "As for you, you meant evil with me; but God meant it for good." What was intended to take Joseph's life served to preserve it. In this art God is "a great Master,"[7] who knows how to employ the devil's and all the world's evil as divine tools with which to cultivate the vine. God controls the extent of these assaults to which we are exposed, not vice versa. They must cease at God's command, and they cannot go any farther than our welfare requires. The world's misfortune and wickedness are God-ordained tools; they are merely the forks and the clippers, not the Gardener. Whatever would cause misery and harm in us must aid to strengthen our faith and hope, as we are drawn to pray more fervently and enjoy more richly God's comfort. Though the world intends to do us harm, faith perceives the opposite, that trials usher us from the world's misery into the eternal joys. Luther cited the two martyrs, Agnes and Agatha,[8] who, though they were led to imprisonment and torture, felt as though they were led to heaven as a bride escorted to a dance. They regarded the torment and death accrued to them by the world as no different from a wedding, an occasion for the greatest joy. For they believed in God, who always works the opposite of what the world intends and puts its evil schemes to good use. God, the one

---

6. LW 24.194–95 (WA XLV.637).
7. LW 24.195 (WA XLV.638).
8. LW 24.118 (WA XLV.569).

"calling into being the things that do not exist" (Rom 4:17), reverses and renews all things. Thus there is no cause for fear, for God will not permit them to exceed what serves our best interests.

Christ presents a complete picture of the various kinds of branches, and specifies how he deals with each. "Every branch of Mine that bears no fruit He takes away" (v.2). The first kind is what Luther calls "schismatic spirits and false brethren."[9] They are illegitimate shoots, which bear no fruit, but only consume the sap the truly fruitful branches should possess. These are cut off and thrown into the fire. Though they come from the vine, they do not remain there. As time goes on, they degenerate into unruly shoots and are Christians in name only. They may even develop into large branches, and expect to be treated as the best of Christians. They use God's Word, and make use of and enjoy the sap of others. They bear an appearance that outdoes all the rest, but they are decayed, bereft of the reality of the true sap and strength. The second kind are nominal and indolent Christians, possessing the Word and pure doctrine, but not living in conformity with it. Like the first kind, they are fleshly. Being so loose and lazy, they are susceptible to factions and false teachers; they are docile pupils who easily are predisposed to heresy, since they become weary of true doctrine. The two classes finally collapse into one: the wild and useless branches. The third kind is the true little flock, whom Christ distinguishes from wild branches. He will not allow the first two to ruin the true vine. He thus pronounces the judgment that they must be cut off and thrown into the fire. God does not cut off the wild branches immediately as they emerge from the stalk; he permits them to grow until it becomes obvious what they are. The true branches are those who "are already made clean by the Word which Christ has spoken to them" (John 15:3). This is how to recognize who are the true Christians, the ones who have and retain doctrine as it is established in Scripture, as the apostles and prophets had it. They remain in the vine, even if they are weak and thin branches; they often produce beautiful grapes, something that a lazy and thick energy-sucker is unable to do. Those who adhere to Christ and have the Word will survive; the unruly branches, intent on overgrowing true branches by their size and strength, will be exterminated. Faith shall abide as long as there are Christians. True-branch Christians must persevere in faith among false saints, in order that they may be found genuine.

The Vinedresser is not content with a good vine and true branches, but wishes that they bear much fruit. To achieve this, he hastens to work on the branches, trimming and pruning them. He does not let Christians be idle; he sends them trials to make them stronger and better. He allows the devil

---

9. LW 24.201 (WA XL.643).

and the world to assail them with external and internal persecutions, which compel them to exercise their faith. As a result, they may praise God all the more. The Word and its power will increase everywhere, and there will be abundant fruit. All trials and sufferings are instruments of divine power, given not for Christendom's harm, as the devil and the world intend, but for its welfare, so that it may be purified and improved, bearing abundant fruit for the Vinedresser. This is the meaning of verse 2: "Every branch that does not bear fruit He prunes, that it may bear more fruit."

The Purification Agent

We are not clean by virtue of our deeds and the suffering we undergo, nor are we clean by the fruit which comes as a result of Christ's pruning. Mature Christians' fruit and works, instead, proceed from the heart-cleansing power that they already receive from the Word. "But in order that it may have power in you, be surely apprehended and firmly retained by you, the Father sends you many kinds of suffering, peril, anxiety, distress, and affliction, to humble you and to teach you that the cleanness does not proceed from you and is not of your own doing."[10] Likewise suffering exists not as a condition of justification, that we are declared clean before God because of it, but as a condition of discipleship, leading us to lay hold of God's Word with a firmer grip in order that faith might grow and the remainder of indwelling sin might diminish in its power over us. "Therefore your suffering is not the cleanness itself," says Luther, "but [t]he Word is itself the purification of the heart if the heart adheres to it and remains faithful to it."[11] This is the meaning of Christ's sermon: "You are already made clean by the Word which I have spoken to you" (John 15:3). The "you" refers to the apostles who have been grasped by his purifying Word. Faith alone grasps the Word, through which we are reckoned completely pure and holy before God, even though we struggle with residual sins, requiring continual purging. But how can Christians be unclean and clean at the same time? This is made possible solely by the Word, by which God effects in us justification and continues to cleanse us of the residual uncleanness by cross and suffering. Justification is prior to sanctification; both are the work of the one and same Word. "[M]an is first declared clean by God's Word for Christ's sake, in whom he believes. For by such faith in the Word he is grafted into the Vine that is Christ and is clothed in His purity, which is imputed to him as his own and is as perfect

---

10. LW 24.211 (WA XLV.653).
11. LW 24.211 (WA XLV.653).

and complete in him as it is in Christ."[12] Impurities and sins that remain are not imputed to us; God closes an eye to the uncleanness that still clings to us. Christ constantly prunes and cleans the branches on the vine that are now clean by the Word; he proceeds to improve and perfect the justified saint by cross and suffering, so that faith may develop and remaining sins are daily purged until death.

Christ writes: "Abide in Me, and I in you. As the branch cannot bear fruit by itself, unless it abides in the vine, neither can you, unless you abide in Me" (v.4). We have his Word, by which we are clean and through which our fruits are good; everything pleases God. If we were to retain this cleanness and continue to bear good fruits, we must remain in him through faith. Christ warns against letting trials sever us from faith so that we spoil the fruit, forfeiting the cleanliness that springs from him. The fruits Christ has in mind are not natural fruits that proceed from natural talents, but those that proceed from Christ, which remain eternally and are acknowledged by God. It refers to a life conducted in a manner that pleases God both here and yonder, a life so rooted in him that bears "enduring fruit" and will not be forgotten.[13] Christ repeats this in verse 5: "I am the Vine, you are the branches. He who abides in Me, and I in him, he it is that bears much fruit." With these words, Christ seeks to impress on his disciples the necessity of adhering to him solely and firmly. God has ordained that Christ is the only Vine there is; we who are grafted into him are true branches in God's sight. Raging tyrants and false teachers try to be the vine and branches, leading many astray. They gleam and glitter in outward appearances and fine words, far more attractive than Christ with his true branches. In comparison, Christ appears not so much as a vine but as the stalk of a wild thorn bush, and his followers as a thorn hedge. Thus Christ repeats his foregoing words in order to impress into our hearts, that he alone must be the One planted by God himself as the Vine, and we who remain in him shall be the only true branches.

Christ speaks these words "He who abides in Me, and I in him" against false Christians, instructing us that a person becomes a true branch not by his natural strength and works, but purely by abiding in Christ. Our abode is in Christ, and this is given to us. It is not by our efforts that we endure and stick to our place in Christ, but Christ establishes our place in him and keeps us there. The branch is not manufactured or assembled; it grows out of its relationship with the vine, sharing the same nature or species as Christ has. Only those who remain in Christ as natural branches on the vine could

---

12. LW 24.212 (WA XLV.654).
13. LW 24.214 (WA XLV.655).

produce good fruits, since "like begets like."[14] The mere name does not constitute a Christian, nor does the fact that they dwell among Christians, as Judas the apostle and others did. They are withered twigs of thorns amongst the grapes, though they excel in outward performance. "A Christian and true saint must be a divine work and creation, the creature of a Master who with a single word can make everything out of nothing, and make it complete and perfect. No human effort, rule, or order can do this."[15] Only the Creator can make of us a new creature, without human aid, just as the sap flows from the stalk to the branches. "[T]he essence of my heart is renewed and changed. This makes me a new plant, one that is grafted on Christ the Vine and grows from Him. My holiness, righteousness, and purity do not stem from me, nor do they depend on me. They come solely from Christ and are based only in Him, in whom I am rooted by faith."[16] Christ and Christians merge into one loaf and one body, so that the Christian can produce good fruit–not Adam's or his own, but Christ's. When a Christian speaks God's Word and does his Word, he does not do this as one descended from the stream of Adam; it is Christ who performs this in him, for Christ is in him, and he is in Christ. True Christianity does not consist in putting on a new garment over the old clothes, nor does it consist in the adoption of a new manner of living. It is not brought in from outside; rather it is a new birthing by God's Word and Spirit. Any attempt to fabricate something out of works fails to issue forth a new and true nature, the requisite for good fruits. Not until the heart is born anew in Christ do fruits such as the confession of the gospel, works of love, and obedience follow naturally. Christ's words: "For apart from Me you can do nothing" do not pertain to physical or worldly life, for they are within the grasp of human beings. Christ is speaking of the fruits of the gospel–that is, his spiritual kingdom and government in which God himself dwells, reigns, and works through his Word and Spirit. This is God's domain: to baptize, to preach the gospel, to administer the Sacrament, to comfort the aggrieved and strengthen timid consciences, to terrify and punish the wicked. In this spiritual kingdom, we can achieve nothing unless we are and remain in Christ. Christ condemns all the great and arduous works of the saints as sin committed in idolatry and unbelief. "Thus a fearful judgment is decreed here against all life and activity—no matter how great, glorious, and beautiful—if it has no connection with Christ."[17] The works the world highly esteems as excellent and precious are truly naught

---

14. LW 24.227 (WA XLV.668).
15. LW 24.226 (WA XLV.667).
16. LW 24.226 (WA XLV.668).
17. LW 24.229 (WA XLV.670).

before God because they have not sprung out of him and do not abide in him. A work that is judged worthy and pleasing to God is determined not by outward shape and form but by the nature of its origin. It all hinges on the fountain-source from which the works come. The knowledge of the difference between works performed outside of Christ and that done by a new person in Christ is hidden to the world. Previously because he was a thistle and a thorn, not part of the Vine, his works are null and void. But now that he is a Christian, the same work produces a fine and precious grape, simply because it flows from the good Vine, which is Christ.

There are two verdicts Christ pronounces: those who remain in faith will bear true fruits that give heartfelt pleasure to God; those who do not abide in Christ will share the fate of the unproductive branches, cast into the fire. Christ pronounces a curt and terrible verdict upon the latter. John 15:6: "If a man does not abide in Me, he is cast forth as a branch and withers; and the branches are gathered, thrown into the fire, and burned." Christ mentions several disastrous consequences of all life and activity that does not grow from and remain in him. First, they must be removed from the assembly of God and separated from those who preach and believe the truth, as summer is from winter. This is stated in Ps 1:5: "The wickedness will not stand in the judgment, nor sinners in the congregation of the righteous." True and false Christians, true and false preachers, cannot co-exist; the Word divides the hearts. False Christians cannot remain with the righteous, nor with the Word; they must be cast out so that all may know that they have been false and sterile branches. They suffer these tremendous losses: the Word, of Baptism and the Sacrament, the intercession of Christ, his blood, his Spirit, and everything there is in Christ. The branch may suffer a break or a tear, or some other hurts, but it can be healed if it remains on the vine. Likewise, though a Christian may fall short in his conduct and thereby suffer harm, he is not bereft of all the comfort, mercy, help, and salvation if he returns to Christ in repentance and faith. Second, not only is a branch not remaining in Christ removed and cast away, it will also wither. This refers to those who not only defect from Christ but also become so callous and hardened, like sap-drained branches that they end up in unbelief and sin. In the first instance, he is not beyond redemption if he returns soon enough to the Vine. However if he allows the negative condition to deteriorate until he is entirely withered, persisting in error, he has committed a mortal sin for which there is no help. Third, these useless and withered branches are gathered, thrown into the fire, and burned. Since they do not remain in Christ and refuse to repent, their final verdict is nothing but punishment. The word "gathered" signifies that they cannot break free from the penalty, by embarking on pilgrimages to Rome or Jerusalem, or by some pious activities.[18] Their fate is the same as the hardened Pharaoh, Judas, Caiaphas, Herod, and all other sects, who are seized and bound in a bundle; he will be punished along with them. "They will be burned," says Christ. This fire into which they are thrown is not purgative but punitive. They will remain in the fire forever and be reduced to powder. Christ speaks the ominous words: "The fire is not quenched" (Mark 9:48).

How does one abide in Christ? Christ offers his answer in John 15:7: "If you abide in Me, and My words abide in you, ask whatever you will, and it shall be done for you." Everything depends on whether Christ's Word remains in us, that is, whether we believe and confess the second article of faith. Then our roots are intertwined and joined, so that Christ's Words and our heart have become one. How this occurs is hidden from us; it shall be revealed in yonder life. In addition, whatever we ask of him, it shall be granted to us. When afflictions occur, we come to him as a little child speaks to his father, who is pleased with everything he does. The "Spirit of grace and supplication" (Zech 12:10) will be poured out over him, making him acceptable to God. Though he is still sinful, he receives forgiveness through this grace and is covered with it. The same Spirit urges him to cry to God in every distress and need, assuring him that his prayers will be heard. Only those who remain in the Vine enjoy the glorious comfort of the Christian estate to which the divine promise is attached, that whatever they ask of and desire from God shall surely be granted. Existence apart from faith is surely wretched. They receive no comfort or assurance that their prayers and labor will reach heaven. "Prayer is solely an act of faith,"[19] which only Christians can perform. For they pray not in their own name, but in the name of the Son of God in whom they have been baptized. With this they are certain that such a prayer is efficacious, since he commanded it and promised to hear them. As a Christian undertakes to pray, he does not wait until he has amassed good works and has prepared himself sufficiently worthy. Rather he prays "in compliance with God's command and in reliance of His promise,"[20] offering it in the name of Christ, and knowing that whatever he asks for is fulfilled without a doubt. Even when he is not immediately liberated from his troubles, he knows nonetheless that God is pleased with his prayer, enabling him to bear and overcome his trials. "This ability is tantamount to the removal of the trouble."[21] Only Christians, who by prayers perform all kinds of good and overcome every misfortune, are

---

18. LW 24.237 (WA XLV.678).
19. LW 24.241 (WA XLV.681).
20. LW 24.241 (WA XLV.681). See chapter 8 for Luther's theology of prayer.
21. LW 24.241 (WA XLV.681).

the ones highly honored by the Father. Verse 8: "By this My Father is glorified, that you bear much fruit and so prove to be My disciples." Like Christ, Christians engage in the highest and foremost service of God. Christ makes us who abide in him priests and servants of God, offering holy and acceptable sacrifices to his Father. Thus Psalm 110:4 declares: "Thou art a Priest forever." We become Christ's disciples, not by tormenting ourselves to death with our own works, but by abiding in him and remaining in his Word.

Faith and Love

After we come to faith, Christ admonishes us to love above all else. He fixes in our minds both himself and his Father as the noblest and perfect example: "As My Father has loved Me, so have I loved you; abide in My love" (John 15:9). God the Father loves the Son so much that he transmits all his power and might to him. Whatever Christ does and suffers is predicated of his Father, as though it were done to him, for the Father and the Son are one being.[22] Luther asserts: "To be sure, He (Father) lets Me (Son) suffer now; but He takes to heart all that I [the Son] do and suffer as though this were happening to Him, and He will raise Me from the dead, make Me Lord over all things, and completely glorify His divine majesty in Me."[23] The Father loves us through Christ, and bids us abide in his love. This is how Christ loves us: he does not leave us in our sins and in death, but stakes his life to rescue us. We should reflect Christ's love for us in our love for each

---

22. The question of whether the Father suffers in the suffering of the Son did not arise in Luther's sermons on John. This question, a contemporary one, has been dealt with extensively by Jürgen Moltmann, who asserts that the Father and the Son suffer, each in his uniquely different way: "Jesus suffered death abandoned by God. The Father, on the other hand, suffered the death of his Son in the pain of his love. The Son was 'given up' by the Father and the Father suffered his abandonment from the Son." Based on Pauline thought, Moltmann sees in the event of the cross a double *paradidonia* and a double passion. "The grief of the Father here is just as important as the death of the Son. The Fatherlessness of the son is matched by the Sonlessness of the Father, and if God has constituted himself as the Father of the Jesus Christ, then he also suffers the death of his Fatherhood in the death of the Son." However Moltmann's assertion does not fit Luther's logic of Scripture, which puts the emphasis on the economic actions, rather than the immanent life of the Trinity. With Augustine, Luther accentuated the unity of the immanent and economic Trinity, but with the stress on the economic Trinity. One must bear in mind that these materials presented are sermonic, not dogmatic exposition or abstract discursion of christological themes. Luther's sermonic presentation dwells on the economic actions of God, not on speculating how God might be in and for himself. Specifically, Luther did not preoccupy himself with how the cross might affect the immanent relationship of the persons within the same Godhead.

23. LW 24.246 (WA XLV.686).

other, thereby completing the other aspect of the Augustinian pair: Christ as example.

Christ says in John 15:13: "Greater love has no man than this, that a man lay down his life for his friends." Christ's self-sacrificial love is surely the greatest one. All other loves pale into insignificance when compared with the love of the cross, where the Son of God suffers and dies for us, to redeem us from death and hell. To imitate Christ, we must let his love be "stronger, greater, and mightier" than the pain we feel.[24] Just as Christ does not allow any suffering to frighten him away from the Father's love, so he does not let any torment deter us from his love for us. So if the world inflicts harm and pain on us, look to Christ, and see what Christ did and suffered for us. Then in exchange we will be ready to suffer for him. Even if the world rages against us, we will nonetheless remain with this Man and be content that we are seized by a love that flows between the Father and the Son, one and the same love, in which we abide. Not only Christ loves us but also the Father. "This is the first love, our love for Christ,"[25] which we must maintain over against the hatred of the world. Yet Christ demands not that we surrender life for our neighbor, but only that our life gives tangible evidence of our love toward them in return for his great and effable love of the cross. Then from the supreme example that Christ places before us, we show our love for others. The pair—Christ as sacrament and example—must be inculcated daily, lest we be misled by alien doctrine and be severed from Christ. As we recognize Christ as our Savior, we are motivated to respond to our neighbors' needs with the same favor with which we are blessed.

> Thus we must now learn to follow this example of Christ and observe this injunction in our mutual relations, each one in his own calling toward his neighbor. For without this example which Christ put before us it would be too difficult, yes, entirely impossible to keep this commandment and to endure. But now, as I consider what He suffered for me, I can take courage and say: "very well He did this for me. Therefore I will also suffer this or something else for Him. And even if the world should become furious and foolish in its raging, I will nonetheless remain with this Man and be content that He loves me and the Father also loves me through Him and bids me hold firmly to His love."[26]

24. LW 24.247 (WA XLV.686).
25. LW 24.248 (WA XLV.687).
26. LW 24.248 (WA XLV.687).

Christ urges the disciples to take the love commandment to heart: "If you keep My commandments, you will abide in My love, just as I have kept My Father's commandments and abide in His love. These things I have spoken to you that My joy may be in you and that your joy may be full. This is My commandment, that you love one another as I have loved you" (John 15:10–12). If we are in Christ and remain in him, then we must be intent on keeping Christ's commandment; we must love in a way that we will be recognized as Christ's branches and as his disciples (John 13:45). Just as Christ remains in his Father's love by keeping his commandments, so we remain in Christ's love, by obeying his commandments. The Augustinian pair of concepts, Christ as sacrament and example, links closely the pair of faith and love in Luther's theology. "For where there is no love but its opposite manifests itself, there certainly is no faith."[27] He who believes loves; the opposite of this is proof of the absence of faith. Therefore Christ says: "You are my friends if you do what I command you." Through Christ's self-giving love, he has made the Father our friend and has proved himself our friend above all. All of us who are his friends must also extend this friendship to others. "This is a fine and an easy commandment,"[28] for it is given not as coercion, as a slave beaten into obedience (John 15:15). The obedience of which Christ speaks is not a slavish kind, but friendly in character. "This is the lightest and sweetest of tasks,"[29] for Christ does not demand love as a payment, as though he needs this as a sort of appeasement. "God has no need whatever of such service and help, nor does He give this command for His sake. But we, of course, need it in our inmost hearts."[30] Through Christ, we receive all that is necessary for salvation from above; out of gratitude we proceed to share this with our neighbors from below. We do this, not for the sake of amassing merit, but wholly for their sake, in accordance with the example of Christ. As stated in his *The Freedom of the Christian* (1520): "I will therefore give myself as a Christ to my neighbor, just as Christ offered Him to me: I will do nothing in this life except what I see as necessary, profitable, and salutary to neighbor, since through faith I have an abundance of all good things in Christ."[31] Neither do we serve the neighbor's needs for the purpose of transmuting their enmity to friendship, nor for the sake of enlightened self-interest, but purely as Christ serves us. We are to "become

---

27. LW 24.252 (WA XLV.691). For a treatment of love, see Mannermaa, *Two Kinds of Love*.

28. LW 24.252 (WA XLV.691).

29. LW 24.252 (WA XLV.692).

30. LW 24.252 (WA XLV.693).

31. LW 31.367. Kärkkainen, "'The Christian as Christ to the Neighbor,'" 101–17; Moseman, "'Becoming Christ to One's Neighbor,'" 93–105.

a Christ to (our) neighbor and be for him what Christ is for me."[32] Ample supplies of good, both eternal and temporal, are given us so that we can easily help others. Thus Christ says: "I appointed you that you should go and bear fruit." Just as Christ was appointed to love us, so we, his elect, are appointed to love others. Christ chose us and spent all on us that we might bear much fruit and live in a manner that people might recognize as Christ's true branches.

Love does not beget friendship with God; it follows as an external sign of it, which Christ as sacrament has already established through his blood and life. Works of love for others must be there, or else it falsifies this friendship. It is a token of the treasure that is accrued to us by faith. To prove this point, Luther cites Adam, who was created with "original righteousness," and did not need to merit innocence by his obedience to the commandment. "[Adam] knew God, obeyed him with purest delight, and understood his works without prompting. . . Adam loved God and his works with devoted and absolutely pure devotion."[33] Original righteousness was a gift integral to the image of God to love, trust, and know God, rather than a gift added to human nature, as understood in the scholastic view.[34] Just as we already have vision by birth or nature, without any need of ignition from elsewhere, so Adam already has innocence by nature, without any need of imputation from elsewhere. He was sinless and perfect, for his nature had been created as such. He did not have to become holier than he inherently was, for he already possessed what he should have. Yet the commandment was given to him in order that he might demonstrate his obedience and piety before God. Through Adam's fall, we fled from God; we lost innocence. But through Christ's redemption, our innocence is restored, and we are now as pure as Adam when he was originally created. So this love commandment is given to us, who are reborn and cleansed through Christ, in order that we may show our obedience. He gives us his blood and his life, through which we receive exemption from the laws of Moses and many onerous commandments imposed by others. To refuse to keep this one commandment is to insist on eating only from the forbidden tree, and thus is to be guilty of disobedience as Adam was. Many still pattern themselves after Adam, allowing themselves to be estranged from obedience. "They fall away from their regeneration."[35] Just as a living, productive tree yields fruit, true faith manifests itself in life. Where the opposite is in evidence, Christ

---

32. LW 31.368.
33. LW 1.113 (WA 42.86.1–16).
34. Kolb, *Martin Luther*, 99.
35. LW 24.256 (WA XLV.694).

will certainly be absent: "(A) false faith bears the same name, employs the same words, and boasts of the same things; but nothing results from it."[36] The works of love are not hidden, as they are done among the people. Such fruit we bear in ever-increasing abundance through which we might be sure of our election. They are fruits that abide and are eternal; they will be praised by God also in future, when they will shine in all glory.

Luther has been looked upon as a theologian of justification; that faith alone justifies. What is often neglected is that he was also a theologian of love. The 28 theses of his *Heidelberg Disputation*, in which Luther outlines his theology of the cross, culminate in the distinction between two kinds of love: *amor Dei* and *amor hominis*, God's love and humanity's: "The love of God does not find but creates, that which is pleasing to it. . . Rather than seeking its own good, the love of God flows forth and bestows good."[37] God pours his love into the believer's heart as a result of Christ living in him through faith. God's love finds lowly objects to lovingly create a new creature out of nothing: "This is the love of the cross, born of the cross, which turns in the direction where it does not find good which it may enjoy, but where it may confer good upon the bad and needy person."[38] Just as God's love seeks not its own good but others' deepest needs, so true love, born of the cross, moves toward the direction where it shares with others, not for self-gain. "Since Christ lives in us through faith, he arouses us to do good works through that living faith in his work, for the works which he does are the fulfillment of the commands of God given us through faith."[39] Faith makes us act the same way Christ does, loving those in need. It is not love but rather faith that transforms the human will or orientation in a way that seeks others' highest good. Glory thus belongs not to the Christian, but to Christ; Christ is the "operator," the Christian is one "operated upon."[40] Thus the works the believer performs are pleasing to God, not in and of themselves but strictly because of the grace of Christ's operation.

Christ's Verdict on the Elect

Christ offers the beautiful and comforting words to his disciples by calling them "friends," as opposed to "servants." John 15:15: "No longer do I call you servants, for the servant does not know what the master is doing; but I

36. LW 24.265 (WA XLV.703).
37. LW 31.57.
38. LW 31.57.
39. LW 31.56.
40. Forde, *On Being*, 112.

have called you friends, for all that I have heard from my Father I have made known to you." Christ initiates this friendship, accepting us and transforming us from enemies into friends. Thus verse 16: "You did not choose Me, but I chose you." Christ speaks of the way in which we are constituted his friends, namely, by being the passive recipients of his benefits. "For we gave Him nothing previously, nor did we merit His friendship."[41] A servant does not know of the master's plan and secrets; he has no share in the Master's property, except his stipulated wages. He is at the disposal of his master, who could pay him off and discharge him at any time. But the revelation of all that Christ has heard from his Father is given not to any servant but his friends whom he chose. Christ entrusts and gives all his knowledge and secrets to them; he discloses both his heart and the Father's heart to them—their friendly hearts. The comfort lies not so much in answering all questions that beset us but in this: we are given the knowledge of God's whole plan and counsel, by which our faith is made immovably certain. Nothing that serves our salvation is hidden from Christ's friends. Thus Christ repudiates all attempts to soar heavenward with our thoughts or to seek a secret revelation from God; Christ has transmitted to his friends all that he's received from his Father. We can be assured of this: the Father in heaven has no other purpose than to befriend us with all his grace and eternal life. "This is a decision arrived at in heaven. No creature, devil, or adversity can alter or annul it."[42]

Friendship with God is not self-chosen nor self-achieved. We have it because Christ chose us through his suffering and death and acknowledges us as his friends. Forgiveness and eternal life lie beyond human power; they belong solely to the domain of Christ's election and friendship. We are friends of God, not because of any merits, but solely because he loved us so dearly and unconditionally. Sinners do not do the choosing and initiate the friendship; they flee from God. Apparently Luther broke with the nominalist concepts of merit and grace, which he already taught in his famous *Disputation Against Scholastic Theology* (1517) that "on the part of man, however, nothing precedes grace except ill will and even rebellion against grace."[43] "This is said in opposition to Scotus and Biel,"[44] according to whom doing what lies in us prepares us for a reception of grace. He draws us to himself and gives us everything. We did not "find Jesus"—he came in search of us and brought us to himself when we were alien to the knowledge of

---

41. LW 24.256 (WA XLV.695).
42. LW 24.256 (WA XLV.694).
43. LW 31.11.
44. LW 31.10.

God, sunk in sin and condemnation (Eph 2:12–13). Having been called and chosen through his Word to be his beloved branches, liberated from and made lords over sin, death, and the power of the devil, we now are to be his servants, lending a hand in spreading his kingdom, "bearing much fruit, fruit that abides" forever before God. Christ adds a third dimension, saying: "So that whatever you ask the Father in My name, He may give it to you" (John 15:16). The efficacy of prayer lies also in "the power and the result of His election."[45] Not only does God's electing grace permit us to be God's friends through Christ and receives God as our Father, but also assures us that our prayer will be answered.

Consolation is found in Christ's verdict on the elect. First Christ comforts us, by pointing out the inefficacy of the world's malice, wrath, and mockery, from which he was left unscathed to the present day. Because of this, we are roused to despise the arrogant raging of the world with a proud faith, leaping for joy and praising God against the hurt and vexation of the world. The second reason with which Christ seeks to comfort us is contained in Christ's verdict: "You are not of this world" (John 15:19). Election is not based on monasticism and any human accretions, but purely by Christ's verdict, which we grasp by faith. This is a comforting and heart-warming word to Christians, compared to the terrifying pictures with which Christ has painted the world to be. The world possesses the virtue of mutual hatred, envy, and opposition—prince against prince, neighbor against neighbor. The world is "the mortal enemy of all who speak about Christ."[46] Though they are opposed in other matters, they are united in what pertains to Christ and his Christians, for no other purpose than suppressing the doctrine of true faith. Nevertheless we have every cause to be comforted in the highest degree because of the divine judgment that we are not of the world. This is so, not because of anything we bring or do, but simply because we believe in Christ, confess his Word, and, as a result, suffer the world's vices. All the hatred and all our sufferings at the hands of the world are proof that we do not belong to this throng, but have been separated out from their midst and saved in Christ, who asserts: "For if you were of the world, the world would love its own "(John 15:19). We suffer on behalf of the gospel, the Word, and the sacrament, a "sure sign"[47] of our election. The world's rejection, though it may depress us, is not the last word. Christ's election, which inspires our courage, is. When confronted by real threats and terrible doubts, we should

---

45. LW 24.263 (WA XLV.702). See chapter 12 of this book on Christ's priestly prayer in relation to election.

46. LW 24.266 (WA XLV.704).

47. LW 24.275 (WA XLV.712).

not look inside ourselves (*in nobis*) to see if we are worthy or holy enough to approach God; this only presents an occasion for the devil to terrorize us into sheer despair. Instead we look outside ourselves (*extra nobis*) to the external word of grace in Christ's verdict in which we place our confidence. Assurance rests not on the strength of our grip on Christ, but rather on the strength of his verdict on us–the power of his election. We stake all on faith's object, Christ, not on the level or strength of our faith.[48] In trials and turmoil, Christ must be presented as sacrament, so that we may have a mirror in which to contemplate how much Christ loves sinners, knowing for sure that though we are hated on account of him, we are already chosen by him and declared to be separate from the world. Whoever hates or harms Christ's members has done this to Christ himself. God consoles his own through the prophet Zechariah: "He who touches you touches the apple of My eye" (Zech 2:8). Christians thus have the consoling knowledge and the sure sign that they are not of the world but have been chosen by Christ.

The third reason with which Christ comforts his own is contained in an illustration: "Remember the word that I said to you: A servant is not greater than his master. If they persecuted Me, they will persecute you; if they kept My Word, they will keep yours also" (John 15:20). The servant should not be nobler than his master; nor should he enjoy better life than his master. Luther wrote illustratively: "It is incongruous for the Head to wear a crown of thorns and the members to sit on a velvet cushion."[49] Christ augments this in Luke 6:40: "A disciple is not above his master; but everyone, when he is fully taught, will be like his teacher." It is both right and proper that a true and faithful servant incurs both good and bad in his master's house. Both the master and his servant will receive the same treatment, for what is accrued to the Master is not relieved of his servant. The devil has a very high opinion of himself, as he wants to be revered for his power and wrath. We must be bold and of good cheer, and learn to sneer at him and most proudly despise the devil and the world, for they are not worthy of one sigh from us, nor even a single gray hair on this account. Using himself as a pedagogical tool, Luther showed how he conquered the devil and his tricks: "Because of my sins and my life the devil can indeed frighten and terrify me; but where I find that this Christ is the issue, I am not at all worried about the devil's terror and wrath. If he wants to devour me, let him first devour Him who is up there."[50] All torments from the devil and the world should not deter us either in terms of our persons, who really deserve nothing but damnation,

---

48. Olmsted, "Staking All," 156.
49. LW 24.278 (WA XLV.714).
50. LW 24.279 (WA XLV.715). On the metaphor of *scales*, see LW 13.280, n. 47.

or our office, which inevitably incurs the world's wrath as an outcome of proclamation. There is no cause for complaint, since we not only incur the world's wrath with our proclamation but also deserve this wrath in view of our person as a sinner. Hence we are suffering no injustice, even though the devil and the world assail us.

> This is our just due in a two-fold aspect: first, by reason of our office, which really is not ours but Christ's; and then also because of our persons. Thus accounts are balanced with us both because we have richly deserved it and still deserve it, and because of our office, since we want to preach to the world and help it. It is not fitting for the world to reward its faithful servants in any other way.[51]

But the really terrible enmity occurs not between the world and us but between the world and Christ. Christ says: "If the world hates you, you know that it has hated Me before it hated you" (John 15:18). In his person Christ is holy and innocent; in his office, he has gone to the extent of sacrificing his precious life to redeem the wretched poor from sin and death. In return for this benefaction, the world becomes so hostile to him that they do not desist until they have killed him and murdered his Christians. Therefore there is no other definition of the world than this: "[I]t is a mass of people possessed of a hundred thousand devils,"[52] since it commits an unspeakable and diabolical blasphemy to hate. We must cultivate an art of contempt for the world's defiance and arrogance, so that we will not become what the world and the devil would make of us. If the devil brings us to the point when we immerse ourselves in grieving and lamenting day and night over the world's raging and ranting against the gospel, he wins. There is no greater and more dreadful penalty than being struck with blindness and madness, as they hinder the persecutors from hearing or wanting to hear how they may be saved. God's anger is poured upon them, by first closing their eyes, causing them to walk blindly from one pit to the other, as occurred to Pharaoh in Egypt, until they finally drowned in the Red Sea. They bypass the Mediator sent by God and repudiate the humble form in which the Supreme Majesty appears. The gospel has been preached to the world often enough, and has been attested sufficiently by miracles, "not to give them excuse but to convict them out of their refusal to accept it."[53] They impenitently choose to retain their blindness, and thus they cannot escape the

---

51. LW 24.268–69 (WA XLV.706).
52. LW 24.269 (WA XLV.707).
53. LW 24.286 (WA XLV.721).

wrath of the Last Day. Not the world, due to blindness, but God's elect alone, due to revelation, possess the knowledge of his salvific way with people: the omnipotent God and Creator wills to hide in his opposite to reach us: not in power but in weakness, not in glory but in the lowliness of the incarnate Son. Concerning such knowledge, we have no other way but to be taught by Christ, the great Master.

CHAPTER 8

Prayer—Not Our Creation but God's Gift

The Causative Agency of God

The key motive for prayer is God, since it is God who draws us to himself. "Just as God was in Christ reconciling the world unto Himself, so in prayer God condescends into the world of human asking and thinking and draws man into his own world."[1] Luther's theology of prayer is centered wholly on the infallible Word of God, from beginning to end. However, the Word of God appears in various forms: as command, promise, Christ's own words, and other portions of Scripture. These are the selected instruments of divine power, which God uses to achieve his saving purpose. Fundamental to the Divine nature is God's extravagance and generosity. Prayer does not cause God to do anything but is an occasion for us to receive what God lavishly gives. God is the causative factor moving us to pray, and seek what we need from him rather than from ourselves. God does this through his four ordained avenues: God's command, God's promise, Christ's words, and faith—all are God's gifts to us. This is summarized in Luther's exposition of the opening phrase of the Lord's Prayer—"Our Father"—in his letter to Master Peter the Barber, *A Simple Way to Pray* (1535):

> O Heavenly Father, dear God, I am a poor unworthy sinner. I do not deserve to raise my eyes or hands toward thee or to pray. But because thou hast *commanded* us all to pray and hast *promised* to hear us and through thy *dear Son Jesus Christ hast taught us*

1. Marty, *Hidden Discipline*, 65–66.

both how and what to pray, I come to thee in *obedience to thy word, trusting* in thy gracious promise. I pray in *the name of my Lord Jesus Christ* together with all thy saints and Christians on earth as he has taught us: Our Father who art, etc., through the whole prayer, word for word.[2]

The same idea occurs in his sermon on John 16:23–24 (1534), where Luther prays:

> "Dear Lord, Thou knowest that I certainly do not come before Thee on my own authority and presumptuously, and I am not impelled by a sense of my own worthiness, for if I were to consider my worthiness, I would not dare lift up my eyes to Thee, and I would not know how I should begin to pray. No, I am approaching Thee in obedience to Thy own *command*, to Thy earnest request that we should call upon Thee, and also to the *promise* which Thou hast added. Furthermore, Thou hast sent *Thine own Son*, who *taught us what we are to pray and even recited the words for us*. Therefore I know that this prayer is acceptable to thee. And be my audacity in boasting of being God's child, as great as it may, I must be obedient to Thee. Thou dost want it so, in order that I may not call Thee a liar, thereby adding a graver sin to my others both by disregarding *Thy command* and by not *believing* Thy promise."[3]

Theo-Logic of the Order: Ten Commandments, Creed, and Lord's Prayer

Distinctive to Luther's theology of prayer is the sequence in which he placed the Lord's Prayer after the Ten Commandments and the Creed, viewing it as the exercise of faith to the law-gospel distinction. This stands in opposition to the most common medieval order from 1450 to 1500: the Lord's Prayer, the Creed, and the Ten Commandments, this rationale consisting in that "the Lord's Prayer in the rosary was useless without the faith of the Creed, and the faith of the Creed was of no effect without the keeping of the commandments."[4] Luther consciously reversed the order, accentuating the priority of the gospel as the source of life and power for morality. However, this does not imply that he was constructing a new vision

---

2. LW 43.194–95. Italics are mine.
3. LW 24.388 (WA XLVI.80). Italics are mine.
4. LW 43.13.

of salvation in which keeping the law is denied its rightful place. Rather, the law, whose function is to expose our powerlessness to fulfill God's will, finds its fulfillment in the gospel. Luther's thinking on the structure and substance of prayer reflects the way in which God's revelation comes to us, moving from the Decalogue (law) to the Creed (gospel), and ending with the Lord's Prayer (the appropriation of the Creedal benefits by faith). There is in Luther's thinking a movement from crushing power of the Decalogue (law) to the summary of the triune God's gracious activities for us in the Creed (gospel), culminating with the Lord's Prayer (the appropriation of the Creedal benefits procured for us by faith). Whereas the command to pray takes us back to the Ten Commandments, the promise that God hears us and is "our dear Father" leads us to the Creed. The Ten Commandments teach us what we ought to do; the Creed teaches what God does for us and bestows upon us. We are first confronted with the Ten Commandments and their stern demands. God's wrath and displeasure still condemn us because we, by ourselves, could not fulfill the law's demand. But the Creed comes, bringing us "pure grace and making us upright and pleasing to God."[5] The Creed draws us into God's triune life, forgiveness and love, which we embrace in faith. The Lord's Prayer teaches us to pray for the full actualization of our new status as God's beloved. This order succinctly echoes that of Luther's earlier *Personal Prayer Book* (1522), where he claimed that the Ten Commandments, the Creed, and the Lord's Prayer constitute "the essentials of the Bible." They summarize the total content of Scripture with such brevity and clarity that we are without excuse regarding the things necessary for salvation. "God's particular order of things" is thus woven in the fabric of the Christian life, as indicated in Luther's foreword to his prayer book:

> Three things a person must know in order to be saved. First, he must know what to do and what to leave undone. Second, when he realizes that he cannot measure up to what he should do or leave undone, he needs to know where to go to find strength he requires. Third, he must know how to seek and obtain that strength. It is just like a sick person who first has to determine the nature of his sickness, then find out what to do or leave undone. After that he has to know where to get the medicine which will help him to do or leave undone what is right for a healthy person. Third, he has to desire for this medicine and to obtain it or have it brought to him.

---

5. See "The Large Catechism," in Tappert, *Book of Concord*, 420.

Thus the commandments teach a man to recognize his sickness, enabling him to perceive what he must do or refrain from doing, consent to or refuse, and so he will recognize himself to be a sinful and wicked person. The Creed will teach and show him where to find the medicine—grace—which will help him to become devout and keep the commandments. The Creed points him to God and his mercy, given and made plain to him in Christ. Finally, the Lord's Prayer teaches all this, namely, through the fulfillment of God's commandments everything will be given him. In these three are the essentials of the entire Bible.[6]

Law and Gospel: God's Command and God's Promise

The law-gospel schema is Luther's hermeneutical key to reading holy things fruitfully, including prayer. First, God's command to pray is contained in, "Truly, truly, I say to you, if you ask anything of the Father, He will give it to you in My name." In his exposition of the Second Commandment in *The Small Catechism*, Luther saw the command to pray embedded in the prohibition not to use the name of God in vain: "We should not use his name to curse, swear, practice magic, lie or deceive, but in every time of need call upon him, pray to him, and give him thanks."[7] It is pre-eminently in this Commandment that Luther found the "ought" of prayers. Just as it is required of us to praise God's holy name, so it is "our duty and obligation to pray if we want to be Christians."[8] This "creaturely obligation [to pray] grounded in our nature as human creatures"[9] is understood in the same light as the obligations to honor our parents, obey civil authorities, love our spouses, and help neighbors in need. As with all the Commandments, the command to pray (the Second Commandment) is an outflow of the First Commandment. "Prayer, therefore, is as strictly and solemnly commanded as are all the other commandments, such as having no other God (the First Commandment), not killing, not stealing, etc."[10] We should not take this command lightly. Just as God punishes those who blaspheme or misuse the name of God, so also he incurs his greatest disfavor on those who ignore

---

6. LW 43.13–14. Cf. Krodel, "Luther's Work," 374–75.
7. See "The Small Catechism," in Tappert, *Book of Concord*, 342.
8. See "The Large Catechism," in Tappert, *Book of Concord*, 421.
9. Arand, "'The Battle Cry of Faith,'" 47.
10. LW 43.29; See "The Large Catechism," in Tappert, *Book of Concord*, 420–21. See Lehmann, *Luther and Prayer*, 18.

this command and go their own smug way, as though they have no obligation to pray.

The key point is not whether we are worthy or unworthy, or whether we are ready or not to pray, but whether we are ready to render an obedience owed to God. Even when the devil is intent on making us doubt the efficacy of prayer, it is of utmost importance that we keep God's commandment and do not tolerate any hindrance. The solemnity of Luther's advice on this command cannot be ignored:

> Consider this command well, and impress it on your consciousness, so that you will not think that you may pray or not pray at your discretion, as though it were not a sin if you did not pray but were sufficient to let others pray. No, you must know that God has earnestly enjoined prayer under pain of incurring His greatest disfavor and punishment, just as He has commanded you not to have any other gods, not to blaspheme or misuse the name of God but to confess and proclaim, to praise and to extol it. And he who transgresses this command must know that he is no Christian and no member of God's kingdom.[11]

Just as he did in his interpretation of the Ten Commandments, so Luther framed the command to pray within the context of God's terrible threats and comforting promises:

> God will not have this commandment treated as a jest but will be angry and punish us if we do not pray, just as he punishes all other kinds of disobedience. Nor will he allow our prayers to be frustrated or lost for, if he did not intend to answer, he would not have ordered you to pray and backed it up with such a strict commandment.[12]

The command to call upon God parallels the paradoxical action of God in performing an alien work under the law to achieve his proper work under the gospel. As alien work, the command to pray carries the force of a threat: "You shall and must obey," or you incur God's wrath; as proper work, the command takes on the force of promise which impels us to pray. In these contradictory activities, God performs an alien work of humbling us by means of the law so that we might be drawn to him for grace and help through the promise.

God's threats and promises are the two ways in which the command is heard. When only the negative aspect of the command is heard, we meet

---

11. LW 24.389 (WA XLVI.82). Cf. LW 24.88 (WA XLV.540).
12. See "The Large Catechism," in Tappert, *Book of Concord*, 421.

a terrifying God who would annihilate us for our sin. But when the negative aspect of the command is heard alongside the positive aspect, it leads us to seek grace by our prayers. To those who are struck down by the law, the word of promise comes as a powerful consolation, causing them to approach God for grace. God desires to help and therefore requires that we ask for it. Abiding in these two words is God's determination to remain the God to whom we look for all good in whom we find refuge during every hour of need. Prayer, which flows from the First Commandment, ultimately takes us back to it. By calling upon God, we make known the peculiar significance of his place and standing as God in our lives. We allow him alone to be our God, worthy of trust and praise. Any thoughts of deferring prayer take us away from the First Commandment, and thus from the One who wishes himself alone to be our God. In prayer, we indicate how much God is worth to us (Is he alone worthy of our trust?) as well as how much we value the First Commandment (Do I take it as seriously as I take God?). In Arand's apt words: "In prayer, the hegemony of God is at stake in our lives."[13] By prayer, we extol the pre-eminence of God's ontological status as God in our lives. In the command to pray (the Second Commandment), as in the First Commandment, God declares his sovereignty over all creation and remains the true God to whom our hearts cling for all good. This concurs with what Luther said in his commentary on Psalm 118 (1530): "He who does not call on God or pray to him in trouble certainly does not consider him as God."[14] Prayer is thus a practical way of performing the First Commandment. Whoever considers the First Commandment considers God alone as God. If God is God in our lives, prayer is the outcome. Those who do not call on God when trouble strikes do not consider God as God, and hence disobey the First Commandment.

God's promise is also contained in Christ's words: "Truly, truly, I say to you, if you ask anything of the Father, He will give it to you in My name." Just as we are to impress God's command on our hearts, so also we lay hold of God's promise, inculcating these words in our hearts.[15] Not only does God give us the promise but he also strengthens us and confirms it with a twofold oath. We are motivated to pray because God's promise rings true. God's promise elicits our appropriate response of prayer and praise; it is no empty solicitude; what he promises, he truly fulfills. The command and promise are bound together, not to be seen in isolation from one another. In every instance, command is accompanied by promise; what he commands,

---

13. Arand, "'The Battle Cry of Faith,'" 50.
14. LW 14.61.
15. LW 24.390 (WA XLVI.82).

he too promises. Yet his promise is unconditional; our sole duty is to ask. In his exposition of John 16:24, "Ask, and you will receive, that your joy may be full," Luther again links command and promise together:

> And just as it is the purpose of Christ's promise and assurance to make us eager and willing, so this command should constrain and compel us. If I want to show my love of Christ and be obedient to Him, I have an obligation to pray, no matter how unworthy I may be.[16]

In Christ, God's gracious promises and bountiful blessings reach their consummate expression. Thus we must consider Christ's promise that if we ask anything of the Father he will grant it in Christ's name. Christ's promise enables us to combat our sluggishness and apathy, impelling us to begin to pray from the heart:

> [In] all fairness we should blush with shame before ourselves and really fear God's terrible judgment if we attach so little importance both to His command and to His solemn promise and allow them to fall on deaf ears. It will do no good to excuse yourself and say: "I really did not know whether I was worthy" or "I lacked the desire, and it was inconvenient for me" or "I had to attend to other business."[17]

Failure to pray is, therefore, the result of our unwillingness to be earnestly motivated and rightly empowered by the infallible promise of Christ. Prayer is both a privilege and a responsibility. It is because of God's promise that we are drawn to pray; it is because of God's command that we dare not disobey. Promise without command is empty, as is command without promise.

Invoke by His Mouth: Words to Use for Prayer

God not only commands us to pray and promises to meet us in our prayer; he also supplies the words to use in our prayer. This was already stated in the opening address of the Lord's Prayer in *A Simple Way to Pray*, where Luther wrote, "thy dear Son, our Lord Jesus Christ, has taught us both how and what to pray."[18] Based on Matthew 6:9, Luther taught that "we should be

---

16. LW 24.398 (WA XLVI.89).

17. LW 24.390 (WA XLVI.83).

18. LW 43.194. For Luther's study of the Lord's Prayer, see Thielicke, *Our Heavenly Father*; Nestingen, "Lord's Prayer," 36–48; Pless, *Praying Luther's Small Catechism*, 51–77.

encouraged and drawn to pray because, in addition to this commandment and promise, God takes the initiative and puts into our mouths the very words we are to use."[19] The same truth occurs in his Sermon on John, where Luther writes: "Thou hast sent Thine own Son, who taught us what we are to pray and even recited the words for us. Therefore I know that this prayer [the Lord's Prayer] is acceptable to thee."[20] We invoke God by his mouth.[21] More precisely, we are given the way to pray and the words we are to utter. Luther thus treated the Lord's Prayer with highest regard: "This in short is the way I use the Lord's Prayer when I pray it. To this day I still suckle at the Lord's Prayer like a child and as an old man eat and drink from it and never get my fill. It is the very best of prayers, even better than the Psalter, which is so very dear to me."[22] Prayer is our response to God's drawing nigh to us in his Word, reflecting God's voice back to God as his overflowing love is echoed in our praise and pleadings. It is Luther's basic conviction that the Word of God can open an entire world of meaning, providing an agenda for both praying and living.[23] Without the Word of God both faith and prayer to him are impossible. The heart needs to be nurtured and shaped for prayer; this is accomplished not by means of pre-existent salvific materials within us but by the Word of God. This God-ward desire is not a human invention but God's creative work. The Lord's Prayer is one means God uses as "flint and steel to kindle a flame in the heart" for him.[24] Enough time for recitation and thoughtful reflection is given, until the heart is rightly stirred and inclined toward God. It is the devil's trick and guile to keep us busy with other duties; our faint and sluggish nature also affords him an advantage to divest us of prayer. To counteract the false suggestion of the devil and our own thoughts, Luther advised that we should pray an "Our Father" before we become less ready:

> Cultivate the habit of falling asleep with the Lord's Prayer on your lips every evening when you go to bed and again every morning when you get up. And if occasion, and time permit, pray before you do anything else. In this way you get ahead of the devil by surprise and without warning, whether you are ready or not, before he catches up with you and makes you wait. For it is better to pray now, when you are half-ready, than later,

19. "The Large Catechism," in Tappert, *Book of Concord*, 423.
20. LW 24.388 (WA XLVI.80).
21. See Boulton, "'We Pray by His Mouth,'" 67–83.
22. LW 43.209.
23. Kolb, *Teaching God's Children*, ch.5.3–4.
24. LW 43.209.

when you are not ready at all, and to begin to pray only to spite and vex the devil, even if you find it most difficult and inconvenient to do so.[25]

The Word of God awakens faith and kindles in us a love to pray. For this reason, Luther took very seriously the discipline of daily recitation and meditation. In his *A Simple Way to Pray*, he disclosed his personal practice of prayer in his catechism's rhythm of the Ten Commandments—the Creed—the Lord's Prayer:

> First, when I feel that I have become cool and joyless in prayer because of other tasks or thoughts (for the flesh and the devil always impede and obstruct prayer), I take a very little psalter, hurry to my room, or, if it be the day and hour for it, to the church where a congregation is assembled and, as time permits, I say quietly to myself and word-for-word the Ten Commandments, the Creed, and some words of Christ (including the Lord's Prayer) or of Paul, or some psalms, just as a child might do.[26]

There is a doctrinal logic behind the order of Ten Commandments-Creed-Lord's Prayer, that we first encounter the moral imperative of the law and are struck down by it before being made ready to hear the word of grace in the gospel. The Lord's Prayer leads us to an appropriation of the Ten Commandments' fulfillment through the Creed. Luther never intended this procedural approach to be a rigid formula, however, but instead as an aid to contemplation. External gestures such as standing, singing, kneeling or prostrating are of no avail if the heart and soul are totally absent. But whenever such postures help in enkindling the heart and awaking desire and devotion for prayer, then it is profitable and good. That too is the reason that from ancient times the Psalter was daily sung and read, so that through the hearing and use of the Word of God, devotion, crying and sighing to God might be stirred up. Praying and outward recital of Scripture, the external words and actions, are helpful and necessary, as they enable the heart to be focused rather than distracted, fastening its thoughts to the Word rather than being led astray by its own inclinations. Once the heart is rightly warmed to prayer, certain formula or words or syllables may be laid aside. Not the natural desire of the heart, but the desire of the kindled heart is the springboard for prayer. In the moments when we are fully engaged with

---

25. LW 24.387 (WA XLVI.79).
26. LW 43.193.

God, attention is held; the mind does not wander off; the heart is enflamed and made ready to express its yearnings, joys, and sorrows to God.

We come to God because of his infallible promise, that he gladly hears our pleas. But what are we to do when the promise is left unfulfilled? Here, Luther addresses the agonizing question of unanswered prayers, referring to the case of David pleading in vain for his son's life (2 Sam 12:16ff). In response, Luther outlines how prayer must be formulated not according to our wish but according to God's will. We hold to God's promise that we are heard. But how he should help us and grant our prayers is outside our knowledge. "We must not stipulate for God the measure, the term, the manner, the place, or the person. No, we must leave this to His knowledge of what He should give and what is useful for us."[27] Prayer must be offered so as not to violate the ordained order in the Lord's Prayer: God's name be hallowed, his kingdom, and his will.

> Therefore God Himself has established the order in the Lord's Prayer and has specified three goals which must always take precedence: that His name be hallowed, His kingdom, and His will. Then come our daily bread, deliverance from temptation and all trouble, etc. Preference must be given to God's name and to His kingdom; if this is done, then our interests will surely follow. Therefore St. John says in his first epistle (5:14): "And this is the confidence which we have in Him, that if we ask anything according to Him He hears us." And St. Paul declares in Rom 8:26ff.: "We do not know how to pray as we ought, but the Spirit intercedes for us with sighs too deep for words" according to the will of God.[28]

We are unable to determine and define what hallows God's name, promotes his kingdom, and fulfils his will, nor how God should provide our daily necessities, or deliver us from sin and temptation. The knowledge of what we should ask for and how we should pray is clearly known to us; the knowledge of how God comes with fulfillment is sublimely hidden from us. The time (when), the person (by whom), the manner and measure (how), and the place (where) according to which God should come with aid are not revealed to us.[29] We should leave this to his divine wisdom and pray nevertheless; for God is well-pleased with our prayer. God acts as he considers best; everything is done for our benefit. The expression of God's fatherly love through his Son assures us that he cannot bestow anything but the very

---

27. LW 24.390–91 (WA XLVI.83).
28. LW 24.390–91 (WA XLVI.83).
29. LW 24.390–91 (WA XLVI.83).

best. God gives us something that is not only different from what we have asked, but far better than we can comprehend. God's disposition towards us is that of a loving father toward his child. Though he may withhold what the child has asked for, he does this, as everything, for their improvement, so that they may learn to apprehend their father's heart and be obedient to him. God also strikes us with his rod, not in a punitive way but in grace as a child by his father.[30] The discipline God administers will be without fruit while there is only wrath; it serves to make us more pious, after which he wraps us all the more with his mercy and favor. God's wrathful discipline does not stop at once; it causes us to cry out and lament, which will not go unnoticed. Pious children perceive God's goodness and friendship hidden in their opposite; they do not wish to be relieved of God's chastisement (his alien work), but submit to it and mend their ways as they want to remain good children.[31]

Trinity and Prayer "In My Name": The Spirit of Grace and Supplication

The third part of verse 23, "in my name," is the foundation on which prayer must rest. True prayer is contained in the simple words, "in My name." With these words, Jesus radically distinguishes between his forerunners of the Old Testament and his advent in the New Testament. Before Christ's advent, the dear patriarchs and prophets prayed in faith but only in reliance on the Christ who is yet to come; now they pray in the name of him who has already come, fulfilled the Scriptures, and is reigning with power. Prayers not addressed to God in the name of this Christ are condemned and vain. Luther has Christ say:

> "This type of praying will now be initiated after My passion and ascension, where the Gospel about Me will be revealed and proclaimed throughout the world, namely, the message that I have come and have carried out all that was prophesied of Me, that I have wiped out sin, have killed death, have destroyed hell, have unlocked heaven, and through this new proclamation now institute a new divine worship. In this new worship all differences of external manner, place, gesture, etc., are abolished; here all is drawn to Me, and all is directed toward Me, with the result that hereafter no other prayer or worship will be valid than that

30. See St. Augustine, *Confessions, Book IV* as quoted in LW 14.141 (WA 18.481). George, *Reading Scripture*, 97; Rittgers, *Reformation of Suffering*, 102.
31. LW 24.391 (WA XLVI.84).

which is performed in faith in Me, that no prayer is acceptable but that which is offered in My name. I have now come and have been revealed through the Gospel."[32]

"I have said this to you in figures; the hour is coming when I shall no longer speak to you in figures but tell you plainly of the Father," Christ says in John 16:25. Due to the pastoral context in which he wrote, Luther had no intention to elaborate on the profound meaning attached to this text by some of the fathers,[33] although that would be proper in academic circles; he merely accentuated with them that Christ wanted to proclaim to his disciples that he, together with the Father and the Holy Spirit, is true God. For Christ himself stated earlier in John 16:14, the Holy Spirit's role is to glorify him, establishing that he is the Son of God in eternity (cf. Rom 1:4). Since Father and Son are one God, everything Christ said and did proceeded from the Father's premeditated and firm counsel. Everywhere in the gospel Christ in his own Person relates all his words and works to the Father's will. He does this to draw us to the Father, certifying that there is no other God than Christ, through whom we may know of God's desire to be our gracious, dear Father. "And just as we look to Christ for all love, for every good thing, and for help and comfort, so we should look for the same things and for nothing else from the Father."[34] The Father is just as kindly disposed toward us as Christ, who mercifully and willingly dies for us in obedience to the Father's will and command. The clear revelation and proclamation of what Christ on the cross does forms the contents of faith; it too grounds our prayer in Christ's name. "In that day you will ask in My name," Christ stressed in John 16:26. By way of imputation, Christ's holiness and worthiness is reckoned unto us. We are to come in Christ's authority and his name, not ours. A prayer not spoken well but made in Christ's name is found pleasing to God. Prayer, when spoken in the name of some saints, does not possess validity; prayer uttered in the name of our Lord Christ has efficacy. "[E]verything hinges on their belief that He was sent for this purpose in accordance with God's counsel and will, in order that they may pray confidently in His name and do everything Christians should do."[35] The demonstration of God's fatherly love for his people through the Son assures us that every obstacle to God is abolished. Thus to be grasped by Christ, whom we love, is the same as being grasped by the Father who loves us.

---

32. LW 24.397 (WA XLVI.88).

33. LW 24.402 (WA XLVI.92). See note 44 which refers to Augustine, *In Joannis Evangelium Tractatus* CXXIV, Tractate 102, *Patrologia, Series Latina*, XXXV, 1897–1898.

34. LW 24.403 (WA XLVI.93).

35. LW 24.408 (WA XLVI.98).

> In brief, Christ is to be known as the Man who is all in all. Whatever He says and does, all this shall be right and well-done. We are to know that God is surely disposed toward us as we see and hear Christ showing Himself toward us with His words, His demeanor, and His miracles. And if God gives us grace, we are to take comfort in hearing this Man gladly, loving Him, and holding Him in esteem. Then there will be nothing but love in the Father, as Christ has just said: "The Father Himself loves you, because you have loved Me." The only thing we still need is a childlike stammering. Hence all depends on our learning to cling to Christ as the One who was sent and given to us by the Father for the attainment of God's grace and salvation. Otherwise all is completely lost.[36]

The love Christ has for his disciples compels him to add these words: "And I do not say to you that I shall pray the Father for you; for the Father Himself loves you, because you have loved Me and have believed that I came from the Father" (John 16:27). Luther saw in this verse the significance of the mediation of Christ as the basis of true prayer. How, then, can Christ say that he will not pray for them, as if he can be dispensed with—as though this honor, right, or power now is completely in our hands? The preceding statement reads: "And I do not say to you that I shall pray the Father for you" (John 16:27a). Immediately after this, Christ declares: "The Father Himself loves you, because you believed that I came from the Father" (John 16:27b). These two statements must be kept together, without confusion or mingling: Christ's prayer and ours must be merged into one, the former being the basis of the latter. "It is true that now we have been given the right to come directly to God with our prayers; yet direct prayer means not that we no longer need a mediator but rather that Christ is a mediator, not of fear, but of freedom and comfort before God."[37] It is obvious that Christ did not wish to be eliminated, and we are not to pray without any reference to him. "For we already have Christ's prayer, in which he interceded for us with the Father. Thus he offered up once, but it is eternally in force, and because of it our prayers are pleasing to God and heard."[38] Prayer is heard solely for the sake of Christ, "our only Mediator and High Priest."[39] Luther linked Mediator with High Priest in declaring that Christ's enthronement works for our good. Christ "will not sit idly up in heaven and forget you."[40] From

---

36. LW 24.411 (WA XLVI.101).
37. Siggins, *Martin Luther's Doctrine of Christ*, 227.
38. LW 24.407 (WA XLVI.97).
39. LW 24.393 (WA XLVI.85).
40. LW 24.103 (WA XLV.555).

his ascended throne, where he resides at God's right hand, Christ continues to apply the eternal power and efficacy of his priestly atonement to us; apart from him is nothing but wrath and judgment. Since we have Christ as our Mediator in our hearts believing that he was sent from the Father to redeem us, we can approach God without fear and hindrance. Such prayer is efficacious because of this Man, who mediates between the Father and us. Because Christ prayed for us, our prayers are acceptable through his.

> Accordingly, we must weave our prayer into His. He is forever the Mediator for all men. Through Him we come to God. In Him we must incorporate and envelop all our prayers and all that we do. As St. Paul declares (Rom 12:14), we must put on Christ, and everything must be done in Him (1 Cor 10:31) if it is to be pleasing to God.[41]

To offer the disciples greater comfort, Christ reminds them of "this great distinction"[42]—that "Christ makes us equal to Himself in all things"— in which they should glory. When our conscience is beset by sin, we cling solely to Christ—his humanity—as he goes through death to the Father from whom he came as the only way to find God (John 16:28). Christ unites us with himself, puts us on a par with him, and blends his prayer and ours into one. The Second Article of the Creed (God the Son) speaks of our right and privilege, as God's new creation, to pray. God may require prayer in the commandments, but as desperately wicked sinners, we may hold back or even flee from him, having been crushed by the law for our innumerable sins. As a remedy, Luther, in his *Exposition of the Lord's Prayer for Simple Layman* (1519), turned to the christological basis of prayer, the knowledge of God as our true Father and his promises to hear us belonging to us solely on account of the Son of man: "In his skin and on his back we too must ascend."[43] Just as God has chosen to meet us in Jesus of Nazareth, "in his skin," so we come before him in his name, ascending "on his back" to the inner world of the divine. Grasp God not in his naked Majesty, knowledge of which will surely terrify and annihilate us, but in his clothed deity, knowledge of whom forms the basis of true trust in God, making "the ascent of the mind to God" possible.[44] Just as faith in Christ constitutes us as God's

---

41. LW 24.407 (WA XLVI.97).
42. LW 24.407 (WA XLVI.98).
43. LW 42.23.
44. See LW 10.121, where, in his first lectures on the Psalms, Luther designated "especially earnest prayer" as the "ascent of the mind to God." The same phrase also occurs in WA TR 2.447: "Thus, the ancient [Christians] well defined prayer: *Oratio est ascensus mentis ad Deum*" (prayer is the ascent of the mind to God)." See Wengert,

beloved, as he is, so also our prayers uttered in his name are pleasing to God, as his are.

> What greater honor could be paid us than this, that our faith in Christ entitles us to be called His brethren and coheirs, that our prayer is to be like His, that there is really no difference except that our prayers must originate in Him and be spoken in His name if they are to be acceptable and if He is to bestow this inheritance and glory on us. Aside from this, He makes us equal to Himself in all things; His prayer and our prayer must be one, just as His body is ours and His members are ours. Thus St. Paul says in Ephesians 5:30: "We are members of His body," of His flesh and bone.[45]

God comes to us in Jesus Christ, as man, vicariously performing for us and in us what we cannot do for ourselves. All that God has accomplished through Christ remains obscure unless it is communicated through the Holy Spirit to our hearts. As proclaimed in Joel 2:38 and Zechariah 12:10, Christians are promised that after Christ's resurrection God will pour out his Holy Spirit on all people; this Spirit is called "a Spirit of compassion and supplication." Just as the Spirit of compassion leads us to the knowledge of the Father's will and what he has accomplished through Christ for us, so also the Spirit of supplication enables us to call upon God from the heart in Christ's name. "Thus these two, grace and supplication, are tied together in such a way that no one can pray properly unless he prays in the Spirit of grace, who assures the heart that it has a merciful God in Christ and that it can joyfully call Him Father."[46] This is borne out in Roman 8:15–16, where St. Paul declares that the Spirit does not strike terror in the hearts with sin and God's wrath, with the result that they flee farther away from God; rather he is the One who causes those frightened hearts that feel their sin and God's displeasure (the negative effects of the law) to flee to the God of forgiveness and mercy in Christ (the positive effects of the gospel). If the Holy Spirit himself does not clarify the knowledge of God's great and heartfelt love for us, it will be of no benefit to us. Not until such knowledge is elucidated in our hearts through the Holy Spirit do we approach him in supplication. "If you believe this [God is a gracious Father in Christ], you

---

Pastoral Luther, 179, note 28, where he derived from Melanchthon that the phrase has its root in Pseudo-Dionysius. See Melanchthon, *On Christian Doctrine*, 24:830.

45. LW 24.407 (WA XLVI.98).
46. LW 24.405 (WA XLVI.95). LW 43.28.

can open your mouth and pray properly to God for what you want, with the confidence that He certainly hears you."[47]

Prayer in Faith: "Amen"

Faith must be present for the command, promise, and words of prayer to be efficacious.[48] It is summed up in our willingness to say "Amen," believing that our prayers will surely be heard. This was previously taught in Luther's *Large Catechism*:

> But the efficacy of prayer consists in our learning also to say "Amen" to it—that is not to doubt that our prayer is surely heard and will be granted. This word is nothing else than an unquestioning affirmation of faith on the part of one who does not pray as a matter of chance but knows that God does not lie since he has promised to grant his requests. Where such faith is wanting, there can be no true prayer.[49]

True prayer is done in faith, wholeheartedly adding "yes" to it, and boldly believing against all appearances that our cries reach heaven. We come by faith, trusting in the strength of these words "in My name." Christ's words reveal the futility of both: neither can our own unworthiness deter us from prayer, nor can our worthiness demand that we pray or achieve fulfillment.[50] They show that our prayer is made effective for Christ's sake alone; it has attained its goal, as it is concluded with the Amen by which Christ confirms his Word. In his sermon on John 16: 23, Luther reiterated what he has taught before:

> Cling to Christ, make your prayer dependent on Him, and bring it before God by asking Him to accept and hear it for Christ's sake. By no means be in doubt or uncertain when you pray; but believe confidently that your prayer has come before God, has reached its goal, and has already been granted. For it has been offered in the name of Christ and has been concluded with the amen with which Christ Himself here confirms His Word.[51]

A Christian ought to be as certain of the fulfillment of his prayer as he is of the reliability of God's character. Even if God does not grant our

---

47. LW 24.405 (WA XLVI.95).
48. LW 24.88 (WA XLV.541).
49. "The Large Catechism," in Tappert, *Book of Concord*, 436.
50. LW 24.387 (WA XLVI.80).
51. LW 24.393 (WA XLVI.85). See also LW 24.88 (WA XLV.541).

prayers in accordance with our wish, we dare not doubt that God has heard them. Prayer can be spoken in the assurance that its petitions are acceptable and heard by the heavenly Father, for Christ has commanded us to pray and promised to hear us. It is precisely because of our unworthiness that we become the object of God's love; for this reason, we fall on our knees and cling to Christ's worthiness, the basis of the fulfillment of our petitions. It would be a sin of blasphemy, the worst one, if one prays because of God's command and promise, and in Christ's name, and yet in doubt and unbelief that God hears it. This is not proper praying; it is sheer sin and mockery (Ps 109:7). Such doubting is a denial of God, and naturally such prayer is vitiated. "For what interest should God have in a prayer which you yourself offer in doubt and unbelief, thereby stating in words of your own that both you and God are liars?"[52] Even when our faith is not strong enough and we fail to do and live as we should, this should not detract from the efficacy of God's Word. We must fulfill the obligation to do what God has enjoined and render obedience proper to God and according to the Ten Commandments. We should come before him not with doubts and on the off-chance that God would heed our prayer but with a firm confidence that he is our "Dear Father in heaven." "He who can gain such confidence in grace even to a small degree has already crossed the highest mountain and has begun to pray. Then everything goes as it should."[53] Although we do not deserve divine favor, Christ, in whose name we pray, is indeed very worthy. Because of the strength of Christ's worthiness, the unworthy and insufficient prayer is found acceptable and worthy before God. "And do not doubt that such a prayer is pleasing to God and that it is heard as surely as the name of Christ, God's own dear Son, is pleasing to Him, and as surely as God must say yes and amen to all that Christ asks for."[54] Luther followed Bernard, his confessor, who admonished his brethren not to refrain praying because of our unworthiness and frailties. "For as soon as we begin to pray," Bernard said, "the words are already counted and recorded in heaven."[55] Thus those who conclude their prayers with a firm "Amen" do not remain awake, tossing back and forth on the pillow, worrying about whether God hears them. The true meaning of "Amen" already appears in Luther's exposition of the Lord's Prayer:

---

52. LW 24.394 (WA XLVI.86).
53. LW 24.386 (WA XLVI.79).
54. LW 24.393 (WA XLVI.85).
55. LW 24.395 (WA XLVI.86). The quotation is Luther's paraphrase. He did not provide a reference for it.

Therefore, take note that a prayer is not good and right because of its length, devoutness, sweetness, or its pleas for temporal or eternal goods. Only that prayer is acceptable which breathes a firm confidence and trust that it will be heard (no matter how small and unworthy it may be in itself) because of the reliable pledge and promise of God. Not your zeal but God's word and promise render your prayer good. This faith, based on God's words, is also the true worship; without it all other worship is sheer deception and error.[56]

True piety consists in obeying God's command, believing God's promise, using the words God offers, and expressing the faith God gives. The power of our prayer rests not on human accretions or subjective conditions, but on the four modalities in which prayer occurs: God's command, his promise, the Lord's Prayer, and faith. God's command and his promise are one; the God who commands us to pray is the one who wants to help us. Just as God's command that we ought to pray obliges us to come, so also his promise that he will hear us draws us to pray. At God's command and promise, we prostrate ourselves before God, raise our countenance to heaven, and plead for help; we invoke God by his mouth, that is, with the words Christ himself taught, which assures us that our prayer is found pleasing to God. We pray in obedience to divine command, and in faith, believing that his promise is no empty solicitude; in so doing God is honored as the true God. The sinner must first encounter the moral imperative of the law and be crushed by it prior to being ready to hear the gospel, and cry to God for mercy. The Lord's Prayer, then, is the exercise of faith, which responds to the creedal announcement of the word of grace in the gospel. Being a human act,[57] prayer is an appropriate response to God's drawing near to his people in his Word; it is an occasion to receive God's grace rather than to earn his favor. Every hindrance to God is abolished through Christ's mediation, and this is communicated to our hearts by the Holy Spirit. "In this way you will discover that you can do nothing, but that everything [including prayer]— both the beginning and the end, the willing and the doing—must be sought

---

56. LW 42.77.

57. Kolb and Arand, *Genius*, 212, where the authors rightly explain why prayer is not a means of grace: "Luther did not list prayer among the 'means of grace' since they serve as instruments for the Holy Spirit's delivery of God's life-giving Word of recreation to his people. Prayer, in contrast, is the human reaction to God's coming near to his people in his Word.... Luther did not regard our act of praying as a means of grace because it is our act, whereas the means of grace are God's instruments administered through his people to bestow forgiveness on others."

from Him and be given by Him."[58] Prayer as such is not our creation, but is a gift of God. In prayer, God remains the causative factor; we remain the responsive factor; both God, that he is the active giver, and we, that we are the passive recipients, are revealed.

---

58. LW 24.384 (WA XLVI.77).

CHAPTER 9

Alternation Between Suffering and Sweetness

The Shape of the Christian Life

A theologian of the cross anticipates shameful persecution as the direct consequence of the confession of the Word of God. "Wherever Christ is," Luther wrote, "Judas, Pilate, Herod, Caiaphas, and Annas will inevitably be also, so also his cross. If not, he is not the true Christ."[1] Suffering is not denied; rather it is placed upon Christ who hallows it as a negative proof of a genuine faith. The fallen world is "a veritable vale of tears, an abode of sadness, a cheerless desert."[2] Though believers encounter sorrow as an existential concomitant of their Christian life and their vocations, they may rest assured that it will not become the ultimate reality, for, as Christ promised, it shall be replaced by joy. The shape of the Christian life is an ever-recurring alternation between sadness and gladness, lament and praise, much like the inevitable movement of the seasons, from summer to winter and back.[3] The shift from sorrow to sweetness occurs not by self-devised means but by God-ordained means: God's promise, prayer, and meditation on God's Word. The true Church awaits eagerly the "Dear Last Day,"[4] when

---

1. LW 43.62–63.
2. LW 22.119 (WA 46.639).
3. LW 24.378 (WA XLVI.71), where the metaphor of summer and winter occurs.
4. The expression "Dear Last Day" appears in *Briefweschel*, WA 9.175, 17 as quoted in Heinz, "'Summer that will Never End,'" 181–86. This article is based on Luther's sermon, "A Comforting Sermon on the Coming of Christ, and the Preceding Signs of

the winter of sadness ends, but the summer of joy never ends. Sin and its concomitants—wrath, death, and all opponents of life will reach a qualitative end; while righteousness and its concomitants—mercy, life, and all goods—reach the consummation. Christ's victory is now present in faith; it is hidden, awaiting its full revelation only in the life to come. Justification sets in motion the beginning of the eschatological process of the end of sorrow so that sadness is not the last word, but joy—the eternal concomitant of justified saints in the life to come. We now live in a paradoxical tension between law and gospel, sadness and gladness, which will be resolved in the end for those who believe. Christians must look forward to the Last Day, when that which is hidden—joy and comfort—will be fully revealed, and thus fully enjoyed. All of this inheres in Luther's exposition of John 16.

Persecution and the Bitterest Suffering

In his previous sermon on John 15:17–18, Luther specified a two-fold reason why suffering is inevitable: first, we have merited suffering on account of our person as a sinner; secondly, being a servant of the Lord, Christ's disciples share the same fate as his Lord, namely, hostility of the world.[5] In his sermons on John 16, Luther continued the theme of suffering, focusing not on the sinful condition which gives rise to it but on the office as bearer of the Word of God where it arises. Because Christ is the shape and substance of our faith and life, the pattern of the cross is intrinsic to our way of being in the world. Just as the shadow of the cross falls on Christ's entire ministry, so it falls on his disciples. While the desire to adhere to and preach the word is a positive sign of a genuine faith, persecution is a negative sign of the Word of God at work. Just as faith seeks understanding, so faith seeks its confession, as David said in Psalm 116:10, "I believe, therefore I speak." God's Word must not only be believed, but also confessed so that the world may hear it. Characteristic of true believers is the inner compulsion to preach the Word and desire for the salvation of God's people; but this is intensified by persecution, as Christ's thirst on the cross was exacerbated by gall and vinegar. The devil and the world plague them with weariness, despondency and doubt. Yet the tried Christians feel like Jeremiah, who though reviled and vilified by his own people, felt as if there were a burning fire in his heart (Jer 20:8–9) that could not be stopped even when tempted. They were so terrified by the world and heartsick by the devil that they felt as though they

---

the Last Day, Luke 21," see WA 34.I.459–82. The inspiring metaphor of summer and winter recurs in this sermon.

5. LW 24.268–69 (WA XLV.706).

were lying in a heated stove, thinking that they would surely perish if they kept silent.

The enemies—the devil and his cohorts—afflict Christians, making their sufferings exceedingly bitter, supplying a strong rationale for derision and defection. The words, "They will put you out of the synagogues" (John 16:2), are nothing else than being severed from the people of God, cast aside as a useless and condemned member. The devil pronounces a sentence: we do not have any part in God's people, debarred from God and salvation, do not participate in prayer and the abundant blessings in Christ. "In brief, it would amount to nothing else than damning God's people, God's temple, His ordinance, and His Word, yes, God Himself in addition."[6]

Christ repeatedly attributes the hostility rendered against Christians by the holiest and the most exalted servants to loathsome blindness. Thus he says in John 16:3: "And they will do this because they have not known the Father, nor Me" (cf. John 8:42–43; 15:21). As prophesied by Christ himself, whoever does not know the Father and Christ will surely stir up lies and murder against believers. Not one doctrine has caused so much bloodshed and begotten so many martyrs as that of Christ and his mediatorial work. As St. Paul says in 1 Cor 2:8: "If they had understood, they would not have crucified the Lord of glory." Now they act in accordance with their blindness. Their doctrine and actions testify against them, though they boast of knowing the truth. Lies are the first weapons with which the devil assails Christians. He adorns his lies with the holy names of God, Christ, and the church, and in so doing changes it into a lie. Failing to attain his ends with lies, he resorts to other means such as murder. This befits the nature of the devil, who is the murderer from the beginning (John 8:44). Thus Christ says: "The hour is coming when whoever kills you will think he is offering service to God" (John 16:2). The devil embellishes his killing with the beautiful trappings of piety and worship of God, just as he adorns his lies with the truth of the Word and of God himself. As proclaimed in this text, Christ's disciples will endure the raging and raving of dreadfully and devilishly evil people. Like St. Paul, they would be treated as "the refuse of the world, the offscouring of all things" (1 Cor 4:13), as so evil that they deserve to be executed in the most ignominious manner. Just as the enemies do not know Christ, so they cannot know and treat a Christian aright but must condemn and persecute the true church.

Where the authentic doctrine of Christ is proclaimed, there will be persecution by the unhinged devil, and by the world inflamed with bitter rage against those who preach the Word of Christ. "Participation in the

---

6. LW 24.303 (WA XLVI.4).

apostolic mission of Christ leads inescapably into tribulation, contradiction and suffering."[7] Christians not only suffer persecution under the physical sword of temporal power, but also excommunication in the name of God and the church. Here Luther applies John 16:2: "They will put you out of the synagogues" to his own context, that is, the papal excommunication of those who preach God's Word.[8] He decries papal sins, but he did not deny that the Christian church abides in the papacy. This reflects his conservative nature, as he was keenly cognizant of the tradition that has been preserved in the Roman church, from which Christians have inherited true treasures. Thus he wrote in *Concerning Baptism* (1528): "The Christianity that now is under the papacy is truly the body of Christ and a member of it. If it is his body, then it has the true spirit, gospel, faith, baptism, sacrament, keys, the office of the ministry, prayer, holy Scripture, and therefrom have received our Christian treasures."[9] Here Luther maintained that Holy Writ, faith, Christ, and the Holy Spirit must also be found among them, although errors and devious paths appear. Since "not all are children of Abraham because they are his descendants,"[10] he held that not all who lay claim to the title "Church" are the church, for there is a chasm between name and the reality.[11] For the church encompasses many scoundrels and rascals who repudiated God's Word and acted contrary to it. Yet they remain heirs and successors of the holy patriarchs, priests, and prophets. They indeed possess God's law and promise, the temple, and the priesthood. The people of God, in the past, practiced idolatry so freely under the cloak of the name "church" that God was compelled to say: "This shall be no longer My temple and priesthood. My people shall no longer be My people. But to those who are not My people it shall be said 'You are sons of the living God'" (Hos 1:10; 2:23). Both true and false church use the beautiful names of God, Christ, the Holy Spirit, the Christian Church, God's Word, his commandments, forgiveness of sin, etc. They are in agreement with "words," but "not in substance and understanding."[12] This has always been since the beginning, and will continue to be the case. But we can know who of those using the name are genuine and false by the "touchstone"[13] Christ himself offers: "And they will do this because they have not known the Father, nor Me" (John 16:3).

7. Moltmann, *Church*, 361.
8. LW 24.330 (WA XLVI.29).
9. LW 40.231–32 (WA 26.147.13–40).
10. LW 24.305 (WA XLVI.6.7). Cf. Romans 9:7.
11. LW 24.305 (WA XLVI.6.7).
12. LW 24.330 (WA XLVI.28).
13. LW 24.306 (WA XLVI.8).

True Church and the Knowledge of Christ

The essence of the church is shaped and determined by the knowledge of Christ. The true church is identified by believing in Christ, that she receives forgiveness of sins and salvation solely through his blood and that this faith reflects the will of God the Father. The true bride of Christ adheres faithfully to his pure Word and has no other comfort than this Savior, whom she has received and confessed in baptism and in whose name she has a part in the Sacrament. For these, the name and the reality are one. On the contrary, those who do not tolerate the pure doctrine of Christ suppress Christ and replace him with humanly-devised doctrine of works and deeds. They teach that adults have long since lost baptism and that they must now atone for their sins and be saved by good works. They deny the plenary view of the atonement, that Christ atones not only for original sin but also for our actual sins. They have deviated from the faith, leading people away from Christ to human performance as ways to expiate their sins and attain forgiveness. Thus they convert Christ into nothing but a stern and irate Judge, "seated on His judgment seat on a rainbow, with his mother Mary and John the Baptist on both sides as intercessors against His terrible wrath."[14] Christ, viewed in such a light, is of no help to us; we cannot but flee from him and seek refuge with other means such as Mary or other saints. In consequence, Christ is completely removed from us, and so is the Father. Not only is he not known but simply kept completely out of sight. He is no longer viewed as the One sent by God the Father for our redemption.

The true, catholic, universal Christian Church may be physically separated and scattered here and there throughout the world, but its members are gathered and united in Christ. In appearance, though they look most rejected by God, they are most loved by him; in reputation, the world considers them insignificant and a pile of refuse, yet the truth lies in its opposite, that they are embraced as the bride, worthy to be loved by the Father for Christ's sake. For Luther, the true church "will not excommunicate or persecute the true believers; it will gladly confirm our doctrine and consider us as dear brethren."[15] If a true believer incurs condemnation, he can bear this joyfully. He awaits the eschatological verification of the Judge, our Lord and Savior, who will separate us from the false church, console us, and confer upon him the name of the church; and Christ will expose these opponents publicly as "the devil's church,"[16] its bride, eternally separating them from

---

14. LW 24.306 (WA XLVI.8).
15. LW 24.310 (WA XLVI.11).
16. LW 24.310 (WA XLVI.11).

his kingdom. This truth is already assured for the true church; it is hidden to the world's eyes but revealed to the eyes of faith. It looks as though the world has the name and honor; the truth lies precisely in the contrary, that it is already decided by Christ that we are the true church, for we possess his Word and know him. Since false brethren segregate and separate themselves from God's people as chaff is separated from grain (Ps 1:4), they end up destroying themselves and leading others with them to perdition. The invisibility of faith is to be affirmed alongside the hiddenness of the true church. It is significant that the true church will endure any trials and storms, for the gospel that saves it will sustain it. Where the Word is, there the church abides till the end. Luther writes: "a Christian holy people is to be and to remain on earth until the end of the earth. This is an article of faith that cannot be terminated until that which it believes comes, as Christ promises, 'I am with you always, to the close of the age.'"[17] The church gathers through the gospel in the Holy Spirit, and is so nourished, comforted, fed and taught by it. God's Word is effective in creating God's people, even when the number is small; and God's people cannot be without God's Word or else they perish. The devil cannot win, as Jeremiah 18:18 declares: "The Law shall not perish from the priest, nor counsel from the wise, nor the Word from the prophet." The triplet ordained by God sustains us: the priests, who teach the Law correctly, the prophets, who will not prophesy God's Word falsely, and the elders and the wise men who will counsel wisely. No one can endure retracting or ceasing true preaching, when we know that God's Word is true.

The doctrine of Christ is "the chief doctrine,"[18] upon which all other doctrines stand and fall; it subsumes all others. "He who errs in the others certainly errs in this one too. Even if he holds to the others, still all is in vain if he does not have this one."[19] Where the knowledge of Christ disappears, everything disappears altogether; all heresy and error abound; doubt and despair must follow. Thus Christ impresses upon the hearts of his disciples the significance of abiding by this article diligently and earnestly: "For where this knowledge of Christ has vanished, the sun (Christ) has lost its brilliance, and there is nothing but darkness. Then one no longer understands anything aright and cannot ward off any error or heresy of the devil. And even if the Word concerning faith and Christ is retained—as it has remained in the papacy—the heart has no foundation for a single doctrine."[20]

---

17. LW 41.148 (WA 50.628.16–19).

18. LW 24.320 (WA XLVI.20).

19. LW 24.320 (WA XLVI.20). Luther utilizes the scholastic term *fides acquisita et informis*.

20. LW 24.321 (WA XLVI.21).

Where the sun (Christ) is shining and illumining the heart, there occurs a true and certain understanding of all things, for the Holy Spirit is surely inherent in it. One can maintain the purity of doctrine in every detail, and judge all other doctrines clearly and definitely. The believer is able to defend this article of faith against heresy and error, for he is imbued with the true Teacher, the Holy Spirit, who alone reveals this doctrine from heaven and is given to all who hear and accept this Word concerning Christ. Those who govern their lives by the Word might stray and stumble occasionally in some place or the other, but they will not defect from this doctrine. "For this light consumes and banishes clouds and darkness; it teaches and consoles him anew. But if he loses this light, he is beyond help."[21] This explains why Christ inculcates this doctrine so emphatically on the hearts of the apostles, commanding them to teach it, and warning them against all offenses that would lead them astray. He wants them to cling to it as the fundamental and chief article of faith, and be found in the lap of the Holy Spirit, who arms them against all error, and aids them against all attacks. "For this knowledge does all these things. It affords us all wisdom; it gives us God with all His goods; it opens heaven; it shatters hell, the devil, and the world with their wisdom and might, lies and murder."[22]

Christ's Departure and the Greatest Joy

Because Christ is going back to the Father who sent him (John 16:5), he offers words of comfort to aid his disciples to withstand the test. Their hearts were so troubled, however, that they did not understand what Christ was saying to them (John 16: 5), nor did they inquire about what his departure really means. Thus Christ says: "But now I am going to Him who sent Me; yet none of you asks Me: Where are you going? But because I said these things to you, sorrow has filled your hearts. Nevertheless, I tell you the truth: it is to your advantage that I go away" (John 16: 5–7). Earlier, Christ's disciples inquired about the road of his departure. Here, however, Christ speaks "not of how He will leave them, but how extraordinarily advantageous His departure is."[23] Christ's disciples are consumed with his departure, the worst thing they feel can happen to him. On the contrary, Christ wants them to focus on the advantage his going to Him who sent him might accrue to them. Undoubtedly his departure grieves them, as is natural. But hidden in this highest sadness that his most shameful death elicits is their

21. LW 24.321 (WA XLVI.21).
22. LW 24.322 (WA XLVI.21).
23. LW 24.333 (WA XLVI.31).

"greatest joy."[24] For if Christ were to remain with them on earth, what they have is nothing but a physical and natural comfort; they can never attain the high, spiritual comfort of the eternal existence. The words "if I do not go away" (John 16:7) refer to the suffering and death of Christ, as proclaimed in Scriptures and foretold by all the prophets. That Christ suffer, die, be buried, and rise again must be fulfilled, or nothing will be accomplished. Christ's kingdom cannot be ushered in, nor can the Holy Spirit be given, until Christ dies and gives up this physical life and existence. The disciple's joy and salvation are now beginning; but he must forget about Christ's physical presence for a little while and look for the Comforter, the Holy Spirit: "For if I do not go away, the Comforter will not come to you; but if go, I will send Him to you" (John 16:7). Christ wants his disciples not to be occupied with his departure, which would sink them into deep depression; rather they should be concerned with where Christ is going and what he is doing, so that they will receive sheer comfort, joy, and life, in lieu of the sadness and sorrow they now feel because of his impending death. Their comfort lies not in dwelling on Christ leaving them desolate, but on the treasure and glory Christ's departure brings: he will receive power from his Father, will be Lord over all, and will bestow upon us the Holy Spirit, who will glorify Christ in the world.

The meaning of Christ's descending from the Father is this: that he, the Son of God from eternity, became a true man and revealed himself on earth in human nature, essence, and form; that he lived and died like any other human being. On the other hand, his ascending, returning to the Father, means that through his resurrection from the dead it is declared that he is now seated at God's right hand, reigning with him forever as eternal and omnipotent God. By his descent from the Father Christ proved himself true and natural man; but by his ascent to the Father he proved himself true and eternal God, proceeding from God the Father. Both God and man co-inhere in one Person, and as such he must be known and believed. Christ's dear apostles could not comprehend the knowledge of Christ's descending from heaven into death and hell, and his ascending to the Father through which he assumes complete possession of, and governance over, everything. Of ourselves, it remains difficult to know Christ as he is and to apprehend him in his lowliness and in his ascension, in order that everything in heaven, on earth, and under the earth may be under his dominion (Phil 2:10). These are "dark words,"[25] unless the Holy Spirit comes to reveal and clarify them. Neither his coming nor his going, neither suffering nor dying is required

---

24. LW 24.334 (WA XLVI.32).
25. LW 24.376 (WA XLVI.69).

of him; he has no lack. Not out of deficiency of being but purely out of our need that he does it, going through the horrible death to the Father in order to confer upon us help, joy, and comfort.

Whilst the Christian will have to weep and lament, entirely without joy and comfort, the reverse will be true of the world, who will laugh and be in high spirits. But the utter suffering, weeping, and lamenting over Christ's death will cease and turn into joy, for Christ says: "A little while, and you will not see Me, and again a little while, and you will see Me. Truly, truly, I say to you, you will weep and lament, but the world will rejoice; you will be sorrowful but your sorrow will turn into joy" (John 16:19-20). Thus an ever-recurring alternation of "a little while" and "again a little while"—sadness and joy—is the shape of the Christian life. God has ordained this "little while" to be "a concomitant of all vocations,"[26] if we were to lead a godly life in them and remain morally upright. "God has arranged matters very well:"[27] that he places people in diverse callings and offices in which they come face to face with grief and sadness. For instance, he who desires to be a pious spouse will surely discover what this "little while" means. The devil is an experienced teacher, who will surely teach this in such a way that one need not learn it from elsewhere. Pious and God-fearing people will soon learn what sadness and misfortune are. Our old Adam must continually be crucified so that the shape of the cross becomes a visible part of our own being as it was of Christ. Mortification does not necessarily occur in deserts, among religious hermits, away from the society of human beings. It can happen in everyday life: in schools, offices, homes or areas where God places us. Suffering is an existential concomitant of all vocations, through which we are constantly reshaped into someone new through our participation in common life. There we often engage an internal battle between self-interest and the good of others, but are constantly brought back to repentance and forgiveness as we become aware of the needs of those around us. The shape of a true theologian consists in seeking to serve and not be served, preferring sufferings to glory as a sign of obedience to God.

> The person who wills to obey God, for that reason receives more crosses and suffering in his vocation than does a man who, before God, is cold though honest. These sufferings, rather than being self-imposed, are imposed by God; not that God brings them upon him from without, through divine direction

---

26. LW 24.377 (WA XLVI.70).
27. LW 24.377 (WA XLVI.71).

of affairs and dispensations. They are brought upon him from within, through God's direction of his heart.[28]

Illness and pain press upon us, accompanying us as existential concomitants of the stresses of living. But all this is trivial and child's play compared to the real, bitterest suffering that godly Christians engage in their battle against the devil and the world. Just as God inflicts some of the same sweat that was inflicted on Adam on people in their vocation, so also God inflicts toil and hardship upon Christians who confess Christ, help preserve Christianity, and maintain faith in their conscience. But the latter is far more sublime and difficult. Just as sorrow is a concomitant of all vocations, so suffering is a concomitant of all godliness. Godly Christians must suffer the "little while," the heinous suffering hurled by the devil and the world. The magnitude of grief is unbearable if God himself is excised from a heart that could derive comfort in his grace and would gladly surrender all temporal things in order to be found in him. The weak and inexperienced could not help but lament, flounder and quake in a most miserable manner. For they have incurred no greater misery, suffering or grief than this: they have lost God himself. "And he who loses God has, of course, lost all. He can no longer have comfort or joy."[29]

Christ knew his disciples had to undergo such indescribable sorrow. He announces to them what the "little while" really means. The hour is heavy with grief, knowing that in a little while they will see Christ no more. So Christ comforts them with the same word *modicum*, "a little while," assuring that such sorrow and grief will not endure forever. Thus he says: "Again a little while, and you will see Me" and "Your sorrow will turn into joy." It seems as though comfort and help disappears and the weeping, which is different from weeping over earthly things, will last forever. In the case of physical lamenting, the loss may be compensated for with something else, or at least forgotten. In the case of spiritual lamenting, however, hope and help are no longer available, "for when God is lost, all is lost, and one cannot hope for another god or savior."[30] This lamenting is eternal; it is without any discernible end or sensible purpose. When God himself is gone, there is "no address for its cry of lament. The lament would be without direction or orientation; it would become an aimless . . . lamenting and sooner or later fall silent."[31] Grief directed to God will find relief, culminating in doxology. On

---

28. Wingren, *Luther on Vocation*, 66.
29. LW 24.380 (WA XLVI.74).
30. LW 24.381 (WA XLVI.74).
31. Bayer, "Toward a Theology of Lament," 218.

the contrary, this eternal lament cannot be healed, for Christ, the remedy, is lost.

> For God is the only God, and He is eternal. Therefore this lamenting must be eternal. There can never be any help. For when one can still hope for an end or know that there is an end, the battle is already half won, and no matter how long the lamenting lasts, one can have the comfort that it has to come to an end sometime. But an end to this weeping and lamenting is inconceivable and cannot be hoped for, because here Christ is lost, and God Himself is gone. According to our feeling and thinking, therefore, this is not a light suffering or one that is short-lived. No. it is eternal and interminable. Here one cannot hope or think that it will ever be possible to obtain Christ again, but one is convinced that now all is over and lost forever.[32]

Christ does not repeat these words "a little while" in vain. With them, he counteracts the idea of lamenting that has no end, and lasts forever. "The present distress is not made insignificant or covered up, but it is taken seriously without becoming the ultimate reality or leading to resignation or cynicism."[33] Christ says that he will return to see them, and see them in a such a way that their troubled hearts will find comfort. For hidden in the "little while" (sorrow) is "again the little while" (joy), just as summer follows winter. With this, he assures them that the time of mourning, which appears eternal and unbearable to them, will have been but a little and brief duration. It is like a woman in childbirth,[34] when all is anguish and anxiety, with no foreseeable end during the hour of endurance. But the table is turned at the moment when the child is born into the world. Anguish is immediately forgotten because of the happy sight of the new life. Likewise, a change like this occurs in the Christian life. Their mourning will be replaced by joy, which knows no end and abides with them. Though we do not see nor can we determine the end, we trust and wait for him who assures us that sorrow is not the last word; it shall come to an end. For even after his departure from them and his death he will return, never to die again and forever be with them again. He will live eternally at the right hand of God the Father; he will be and reign with them. He who clings to Christ's words, that sorrow will end, is enabled to move from sorrow to sweetness.

> Now it is dark night; soon it is day again. Therefore the lamenting does not have to last forever, even though it seems and feels

---

32. LW 24.381 (WA XLVI.75).
33. Bayer, "Toward a Theology of Lament," 218.
34. LW 24.382 (WA XLVI.75).

that way when we are in it. But even though we cannot see or determine the end, Christ has already done so. He points out to us in advance that we must bear this suffering, no matter how bad and unpleasant the devil makes it. Even though we do not see the end, we must wait for Him who says: "I will put an end to it and will again comfort you and give your joy."[35]

Transition from Sorrow to Sweetness

1. *The Promise of Comfort: "The Father is with Me"*

No matter how imperfect and weak the disciples' understanding and faith is, still the suffering which awaits will not harm them, for they remain his disciples, not his enemies. Christ felt the wretchedness, loneliness, and forsakenness far more severely than we would; it inevitably issued forth deep sighs and hot tears from him. At the most painful and frightful period, when death is facing Christ, and a small group of disciples deserts him, Christ will not be forsaken; he draws comfort from his Father. He says in verse 32: "The hour is coming, indeed it has come, when you will be scattered, every man to his home, and will leave Me alone; yet I am not alone, for the Father is with Me." As a true man, it pained him to face the misery of being forsaken by the world, even by his closest allies, but he received comfort from his Father. Likewise, when friends stand aloof from our plague, and the world afflicts our weak souls, we must equip ourselves with the certainty of God's promise: "I will not leave you orphans; I am coming to you" (John 14:18). "St. John Huss,"[36] for instance, was burned at the stake in Constance; he had to comfort himself and overcome his fear with the same verse with which Christ consoles himself: "I am alone; yet I am not alone, for the Father is with Me." Even if his friends, the apostles, and the whole world forsake him, Christ knows that that he is not alone, for he has a Father who does not forsake him. He suffers and dies, as an act of obedience to the Father who sent him for that very purpose, and who promises to uphold him, even if this is not apparent. This grants him support that is greater than heaven and earth. When anxiety and distress befall him, the Father is the source of comfort. So when similar experiences occur because of his Word and our confession of it, we should acquaint ourselves with Christ's words, learning to be sustained by this comfort: though profoundly forsaken and terribly

---

35. LW 24.382 (WA XLVI.75).

36. LW 24.413 (WA XLVI.103). Luther considered Huss worthy of the title "Saint," thus "St. John Huss."

afflicted by all, "the Lord will take us up" (Ps 27:10). And we can declare with Christ: "I am not alone, for the Father is with Me." No matter how long the lamenting lasts or how severe the affliction is, we possess the comfort that it will terminate sometime. God never ceases to be our God, and we are not god-forsaken, even if it seems that way. The transition from sorrow to joy occurs, if we cling to his promise, that the Father is with us, as he is with Christ. Then our identity of being God's beloved is bound up with and preserved in God's promises and faithfulness, just as Christ's identity is linked to and derived from his Father, who has not forsaken him during his journey on earth.

2. The End of Prayer: Droplet and Fullness of Joy

Sorrow, a negative sign of obedience to the Word of God, does not stay as a perpetual state; rather it moves us from the articulation of our hurt, as we place our woes and wailings beneath God's feet, to the joyful appropriation of these fruits inherent in Christ's words: peace, comfort, and victory. Christ commands us to pray, and promises to draw near to those who lament to him. The end of our prayer in Christ's name is "that your joy may be full" (John 16:24).[37] With these words, Christ offsets the earliest reference to the sorrow which the disciples will encounter in the world. "You will weep and lament, but the world will rejoice" (John 16:20). Although Christ has assured them that they will regain their enduring joy, he also knows that their joy on earth will be imperfect and mingled to such an extent that the feeling of sadness often outweighs the joy. For this reason, Christ commands them to pray and ask that joy may be felt increasingly stronger, and concurrently, "comfort may taste better to them and they become all the more desirous of joy."[38]

The perfect joy to be sought in prayer is not a worldly kind, but is closely linked to what promotes the three elements Christ teaches in the Lord's Prayer: that God's name be hallowed, his kingdom expanded, and his will be done. The godly Christian has no greater joy than when these are promoted. What Christ taught here is aimed at false petitioners who reverse this order, seeking only their own self-interest. This is false striving from those who want to be called Christians, but have no genuine love for Christ in their hearts. Here Luther resorts to the scholastic distinction between

---

37. Cf. LW 69.84 (WA 28.156–57) where the theme of joy recurs in his sermon on John 17:13: "But now I am coming to You, and these things I speak in the world, that they may have My joy made full in themselves."

38. LW 24.400 (WA XLVI.91).

"the love of concupiscence" and "of friendship."[39] He quoted Augustine, who describes them as "use" and "enjoyment."[40] Whilst some love God with good intentions, others do so for selfish gain. The love of the latter is "the love of concupiscence," likened unto a whore who loves another because of her rascality. But genuine love of God is like "true conjugal" union of marriage, or "the natural love"[41] between parents and children, where one person has pleasure and joy in the welfare of another without begrudging their happiness. There are two kinds of lovers: one who loves God solely to escape pain and punishment, completely indifferent to the advancement of God's kingdom. This is insincere love, like that of a thief who, for fear of the gallows, feigns love for the judge and the hangman. But the one who manifests true love for Christ has no greater desire and purpose than seeing God's kingdom promoted, God's name hallowed, and God's will followed by all. Thus "the fullness of joy is directed primarily to the sublime matters pertaining to God's name and kingdom, which will have to prosper if joy is to be full."[42]

In this life, however, joy is never felt fully at once, because of the perennial assaults of the devil, the world, and the flesh; this triadic enemy rages against God's name, his kingdom, and his will. The Christian's "chief part of heartache and sorrow"[43] is this: he must see God's name so shamefully desecrated, his kingdom persecuted, and his will scorned and trampled underfoot. It is only in the eschaton we experience nothing but perfect joy; there we shall no longer feel even "a droplet of sadness."[44] There sin no longer oppresses us, temptation no longer weakens the heart, the devil no longer fills us with thoughts of unbelief, blasphemy, and despair; the Old Adam is killed and death no longer holds us captive. We are no longer weighed down with sadness and a heavy conscience, as we are in this life. In faith we are refreshed with only "a droplet of this joy; this is a beginning or foretaste which includes comfort"[45] offered to those who sincerely delight in nothing but the promulgation of God's kingdom. For those who have been refreshed by the first taste of joy will not quench their thirst but yearn for more of it. The bitterness and sorrow which fill our hearts outweighs the joy of which

39. LW 24.398 (WA XLVI.90). See note 41, where this scholastic distinction between *amor concupiscentiae* and *amor amicitiae* appears.

40. LW 24.398 (WA XLVI.90). See note 42, where it indicates that Augustine speaks of this in his *De doctrina Christiana*, Book I, ch.22.

41. LW 24.399 (WA XLVI.90).

42. LW 24.400 (WA XLVI.92).

43. LW 24.400 (WA XLVI.91).

44. LW 24.400 (WA XLVI.91).

45. LW 24.400 (WA XLVI.91).

we taste so little. But by prayer, those who love Christ and whose sole desire is to see God's will done are enabled to make some progress into it, so that their joy may finally be purified and complete. All the joys we gather from this world would not help us stand against temptation and misfortune. For worldly joy rests solely on temporal possessions and unstable foundation; it can endure only in-so-far as honor, pleasures or material things are present, disappearing when these are absent. But the kind of joy Christ promised in his words lasts forever, since its foundation is eternal; it endures and increases amid outward distress. Thus we are able with a joyful heart to forfeit all the world's joys in order that we might be found in him, the fountain of perfect joy.

The justified saint steers in between "both to have and at the same time not to have, to be and at the same time not yet to be."[46] Forgiveness and all graces are ours by faith, even though they are hidden and will be revealed only in the life to come. Likewise joy is present only in faith; the full meaning of it will be grasped at the end. Joy and comfort are founded upon the victory Christ has wrought: "The world, the devil, and the death have been defeated and lie prostrate. Heaven, righteousness, and life are victorious."[47] Christ emphasized this to strengthen the believers so that they might abide in Christ until the end, when all enemies of life are ended not only quantitatively but also qualitatively. The never-ending summer of sweetness, to which our prayer is aimed, lends us wings to soar beyond all temporal losses and relinquish them so that we may be found in Christ. Unbelievers will suffer eternal lamenting and receive no comfort. They are held hostage in the never-ending winter of sadness and lament, for God in Christ is lost. However, the believers know that the winter of sorrow will not last forever; they will be ushered into the summer of joy that has no end, for they have the blessed Trinity. He who has Christ has everything, joy included. A droplet of joy is begun in faith; it increases as we advance in faith; it awaits the full revelation of it at the end, when all is sweetness, and not even a droplet of sadness remains. We wait in the hope that very soon dark night will turn to day again.

We now feel the paradoxical tension between law and gospel, the two contradictory activities of one and same God. Through law, God discloses human miseries (sin, wrath, and death); through the gospel, he discloses the true delights (forgiveness, mercy, and life). Sin and its punishment abound in daily life, which are abundant cause for sorrows and the frailty of faith. Even so, the good news prevails: "When our hearts are troubled with

---

46. Althaus, *Theology of Martin Luther*, 404.
47. LW 24.421 (WA XLVI.110).

sorrow, truly God Himself sorrows, who died that we might be justified, and full of joy."[48] The cognition of sin and just deserts under law is causally useful, as it causes us to cling to the oceanic mercy of God, our hearts filling with joy. The sadness resulting from the revelation of sin via the law surely depresses us; there is no healing unless we cling to Christ as the remedy against it. Just as death precedes life, so gladness follows sadness. Just as law must be accompanied by gospel, the repulsive picture of sin as misery's cause must be followed by the delightful offer of divine mercy as its cure. Faith finds itself caught in the tension between law and gospel, which will be resolved at the end. Likewise the corresponding tension between sadness and gladness, miseries and delight, abides in this life until the end, when it shall be resolved crucially for those for believe. The gospel has come; it has broken into our lives, and has broken down all barriers to God. This is done by Christ's movement of descent and ascent, drawing us up through his death and resurrection to where his kingdom is the Father's and vice versa. Though we are constantly afflicted with lingering residual sins, they no longer reign over us on account of Christ's victory. "The winter" [of sin, death and wrath] has "lingered long enough," but now "a beautiful summer [of righteousness, life and mercy] will approach—a summer that will never end."[49] Thus we take comfort in the coming victory; we trust in hope for the coming of the blessed summer that will never end. We will become what God has declared us to be, perfectly righteous as Christ is. Just as incipient righteousness gives way to the perfect righteousness on the Last Day, so incipient joy gives way to the perfect joy of the coming future.

3. Magnify "One Little Word": The Capitalized Word, "I."

Christ concludes his sermon with his last words in John 16:33, "I have said this to you, that in Me you may have peace. In the world you have tribulations, but be of good cheer: I have overcome the world." Already in *The Large Catechism*, Luther has taught: "Nothing is so effectual against the devil, the world, flesh, and all evil thoughts as to occupy oneself with the word of God, talk about it, and meditate on it."[50] The Christian life does not merely consist in a passive reception of enlightenment from God; it includes active meditation on the Word.[51] Christ's whole sermon has been directed

---

48. LW 13.138.

49. WA 34.I, 481.25–27 as cited in Heinz, "'Summer that will Never End,'" 186. The brackets are mine.

50. "The Large Catechism," in Tappert, *Book of Concord*, 359–60.

51. Trueman, *Luther on the Christian Life*, 119.

toward peace and consolation, "the sum and substance of everything."[52] His words are not spoken in vain; their express purpose is to fortify his disciples against the oppression of trials and temptations. He is keenly aware of the natural tendency of our flesh to give in and immediately forfeit these beautiful promises. Thus Christ cautioned them so often and diligently by clearly informing them in advance that tribulations shall be their lot in the world. When assailed by stress and sorrow, Christ exhorts them never to let these gain the upper hand, but to draw strength from assurance that the battle has already been won. Be of good cheer, for Christ has overcome the world. We too contemplate the victory Christ has wrought: When we feel anxiety and distress, when we lie on our deathbeds, or when we are condemned to die by whatever means God might summon us. In this way we can be victorious over the devil and death; all this occurs as a result of "one little word"[53] spoken by Christ: "I have said this to you."

The shape of the Christian life involves learning the art of occupying oneself with the substance of Christ's speech—"I have said this to you" and "I have overcome the world"—more than heaven or earth. Magnify these words in our thoughts; capitalize the word "I" so that we will see it well and hold it dear to our heart. In light of the big letter "I," the word "you" in the statements "I have said this to you" and "you will have tribulation" would become so small, as small as a single speck of dust in the sun. We consider Christ over us, magnifying his greatness so that all else loses its grip over us. Cling to these words. Christ does not say: all the holy angels, all creation, and the emperor are making these statements; instead he says: "*I, I*, am making these statements."[54] "This should be and mean more than can be measured and grasped."[55] Knowing how weak we are in ourselves, and how frightened and terrified we are by these great giants—death, the devil, and the world—, Christ inspires in us courage and faith in him. Christ wants to attach us to him, and himself, in turn, to us so that we might take comfort in him, for he has already overcome the world. A Christian must cultivate the vision which enables him to become indifferent to the terrible spectacle and the outward appearance of death, and the devil, and everything that would assail or frighten him, and instead seeing Christ seated on high, saying: "I am the One who spoke to you." "Then a Christian can let his foes divest him of this garment, that is, of flesh, bones, skin, and hair. For if he retains this

---

52. LW 24.414 (WA XLVI.104).

53. LW 24.420 (WA XLVI.109). On Luther's doctrine of the Word of God, see Kolb, *Martin Luther*, 131–51.

54. LW 24.416 (WA XLVI.105). Italicized "*I*" is Luther's.

55. LW 24.416 (WA XLVI.105).

Word and takes it with him, then this garment will be restored to him on the Last Day, and it will be more beautiful and glorious than it is now. That is the peace contained in this Word."[56]

The wonder of the Christian life consists in a two-fold conversation: "the one which we carry on with God and the one which God carries on with us."[57] Christians are given two glorious privileges: that the Sublime Majesty stoops to our level, permitting us poor worms to open our mouths that we might pray to him, who gladly listens; and that he speaks with us. On the one hand, prayer is our response to God's drawing nigh to us in his Word; we speak with him, reflecting God's voice back to him as his overflowing love is echoed in our praise and pleadings. On the other hand, God continues to speak with us through his words, and we listen to him. A Christian enjoys these two good astounding benefits conferred by God, which Scripture speaks of as the "Spirit of compassion and supplication" (Zech 12:10). There is a double divine action: first, God draws us to converse with him through prayer; second, God also speaks with us through the Spirit of grace, in order that we may hear him, and by hearing him we may be healed. But to hear his voice is "a far more precious privilege."[58] Unlike the Aristotelian God, Luther's God is "never speechless": "It was in the very nature of God to want to speak and to be able to speak."[59] He wrote: "Hear, brother: God, the creator of heaven and earth, speaks with you through his preachers... Those words of God are not of Plato or Aristotle but God himself is speaking."[60] The faithful hearers will respond: "Pay attention, we are hearing God's speech."[61] God's Word not only describes God's action but also serves as his instrument for achieving his will.[62] With these words, "I have said this to you," Luther extolls the power of Christ's words in conferring peace and consolation. God's speech is indeed God's act; that which he speaks becomes real.[63] God works causatively in his speech so that there remains for us only hearing, heeding and appropriation. "This

---

56. LW 24.419 (WA XLVI.108).
57. LW 24.419 (WA XLVI.108).
58. LW 24.419 (WA XLVI.108).
59. Pelikan, *Companion Volume*, 50.
60. WA TR 4.531, no. 4812. Also quoted in Wilson, "Luther on Preaching," 100.
61. LW 51.76 (WA 10.III.15).
62. Kolb, *Pastoral Luther*, 210.
63. Bayer, *Theology the Lutheran Way*, 129, where he understands "the gospel as a performative speech act, or as an 'effective word.'"

speech-act is effective,"⁶⁴ as it causes things to happen: the transition from an aggrieved heart to a joyful heart.

> God's speech is far more comforting than ours, for it is the kind that brings peace and a calm and joyful heart. No other speech or power on earth, not even the world with all its skill, learning, and intelligence, can do this, not even Moses himself, who, although he speaks in behalf of God, does not put peace in the heart. The Man who is God Himself must do this, as stated in Ps 85:8: "Let me hear what God the Lord shall speak, for He will speak peace to His people."⁶⁵

Our rest and peace are to be found nowhere but in what the Lord Christ says. He who has Christ's Word in his heart becomes so bold and unafraid that he can hold his ground against the devil's wrath and assaults. Such courage results from no other source than one little effective word: "I have overcome the world": the battle is already won. Christians must accustom themselves to contemplate Christ's victory, in which everything has already been accomplished, and in which we possess all that are rightly accrued to us—heaven, righteousness, and life. To conquer the jaws of the devil and the abyss of hell, we are to attach ourselves to Christ, even as he attaches himself to us. "For this Victor has accomplished everything. There is nothing for us to add to what He has done—neither the blotting out of sin nor victory over the devil and death."⁶⁶ We make proper use of Christ's victory by singing about it, glorying in it, and proclaiming it. On account of union with Christ, the fight is no longer real; suffering, ours and the blood of the martyrs, "is only a prize or a part of the glory of such victory."⁶⁷ In Christ, we experience the joyous exchange: Christ's victory is ours, received by faith. Joy is felt incrementally here on earth but fully in the eschaton. Not eternal lament but eternal praise is the concomitant of those whose identity is hidden with Christ in God, and this is sealed in our hearts by the efficacious Spirit.

---

64. Bayer, "Luther as an Interpreter," 76: "This speech-act is effective, active word that establishes community and therein free and makes certain. It does what it says. It says what it does."

65. LW 24.419 (WA XLVI.108).

66. LW 24.422 (WA XLVI.110–11).

67. LW 24.422 (WA XLVI.110–11).

CHAPTER 10

The Glory of the Holy Spirit's Office
The Economic Actions of the Holy Spirit

Luther devoted the period from roughly Easter to Pentecost of 1537 to the exposition of John 14–16 from the pulpit, not an academic, lecture hall.[1] This accounts for the significance Luther's exegesis puts on the doctrine of the Holy Spirit, given the season of the church calendar. Traces of Augustine's interpretation of the *filioque* doctrine, that the Spirit proceeds from the Son, are discernible in Luther's sermonic materials on the Holy Spirit. However, Luther did not engage his audience with the discussion of the infamous *filioque* clause, a doctrine which divides the East from the West.[2] He shuns the polemical discussion about the intra-trinitarian relationship the Spirit has with the Son, and leads them to see the glory of the Holy Spirit's office and activity, from which we apprehend his deity.[3] Just as in Christology, where Luther's focus is not how Christ can be fully God

---

1. With minor variations, some of the materials in this chapter appear in my "Economic Actions," 22–34, a Festschrift dedicated to the celebration of J. I. Packer's ninetieth birthday.

2. For a major study of the *filioque* doctrine, see my *Apologetic for* Filioque *in Medieval Theology*. See also Bray, "The *Filioque* Clause in History and Theology," 91–144; Daley, "Revisiting the '*Filioque*,'" 31–62 (part I), 95–212 (part II).

3. See Arand, "Luther on the Creed," 161–64, where he rightly observes that of the two approaches, Luther's writings, especially the catechisms, focus more exclusively on the economic than on the immanent Trinity, i.e., more on the Trinitarian self-turning toward the world than on the intra-trinitarian relations of the three persons in the one Godhead. For Luther, the former leads us to a knowledge of God's nature. The same contour appears in Luther's sermons on the John's gospel.

and fully man, which he accepts, but what that person—fully God and fully man—does for us (*pro nobis*), so also in pneumatology: Luther's emphasis is not so much on how the Spirit relates to the Son and the Father in the Divine Majesty, as it is on what the Person of the Holy Spirit does in us (*in nobis*). To this end, this chapter dwells on those materials in Luther's sermons on John related to the economic actions of the Holy Spirit. More specifically, it investigates how the economic operations of the third Person of the Trinity form the basis of God's great and heartfelt comfort, the property of all Christians. Luther's theology of the cross requires that "our thoughts of God and our mode of dealing with Him begins where He begins and directs us,"[4] that is, in his Beloved Son, in whom the Father is well-pleased (Matt 17:5). To know God aright we must fix our gaze on Christ and be led by his words; likewise Christians must be proficient in the art of learning to know and believe what Christ depicts about the Holy Spirit, an eternal Comforter who is sent by the Father through the Son's intercession for the purpose of fortifying Christians against all kinds of error and terror. This chapter will focus on the materials from his sermons on John 14–16 and 20, which speak of the glory of the Holy Spirit's office.

Correspondence: Act and Being

John 14:11, "Believe Me that I am in the Father and the Father in Me; or else believe Me for the sake of the works themselves," evinces a correspondence between the works of Christ and his identity—the former leads to the latter. For Christ advises that we proceed from his works to an apprehension of his being as God. These works done publicly before all eyes—healing the blind and the deaf, forgiving our sins, casting out devils, and raising the dead—are not human but are exclusively divine. From these works he does, which are divine, Christ reveals his identity as God. The identity of God is inseparable from his operations. Accordingly, Luther's theology prohibits any attempt to seek "the inner nature of God in some remote sphere above and beyond the structure of God's operations in and upon the world."[5] For the God at work is the God revealed. This spells the death of speculation on who God is in essence, for what can be known of God is in the acts he performs for us. Not only are the works Christ does divine, but they are also witnesses of God the Father. Therefore whoever sees and hears these sees God the Father in them, for "the Father who dwells in Christ does His works." By his works, Christ has aptly demonstrated to us that the Father is

4. LW 24.58 (WA XLV.514).
5. Braaten, "Problem of God-Language," 31.

in him and wants to be known through him. From this, we are persuaded not only that God is in Christ and that Christ is in God, but also are assured of God's fatherly disposition towards us, by which we are comforted. "Thus we become assured not only of the doctrine that Christ is true God with the Father, but also that He is a merciful God and Savior; and we can recognize and apprehend the Father's heart and will in all the works of the Lord Christ, for the true and blessed consolation of all wretched and aggrieved hearts and consciences."[6]

Divine Essence: Names and Works

As it is with Christ, the same procedure applies to the Holy Spirit. Just as the Son's operations are the ground of his being God, so also the Spirit's operations are the ground of his being God, neither an intermediary nor a creature. As regards this, Christ mentions personal works that the Holy Spirit does which God alone does, as the revelation of his divine essence. So when Christ declares that he will bear witness to Christ—"He will teach you all things" (John 14:26)—these works are peculiar to God, and so it is proof that the Spirit is true God. Furthermore, the Spirit illumines hearts inwardly, impressing upon them the true knowledge of God. He does the works of kindling, creating, and strengthening faith in the faithful, and of comforting terrified consciences and keeping them steadfast in the face of the terrors of devil and the world. These words are strong and convincing enough to prove this article regarding the deity of the Holy Spirit.

Christ gives the Holy Spirit the name "Comforter"; it is a personal word, which implies that He is a Person. The statement, "the Father shall send you another Comforter," speaks of the Holy Spirit as a Person distinct and separate from the Father and the Son. This is borne out in John 15:26: "But the Comforter comes, whom I shall send to you from the Father, even the Spirit of truth, who proceeds from the Father, He will bear witness of Me." Here Luther finds "the entire Holy Trinity recorded and named, all three Persons of the Divine Essence and Majesty: the Father, the Son, and the Holy Spirit."[7] Just as the Son comes from within, not outside, the Godhead, as from the Father, so also the Spirit proceeds from within, not outside, the Godhead, as from the Father through the Son's intercession. In terms of his deity, he is also God and of one essence with the Father and the Son.

---

6. LW 24.74 (WA XLV.527).
7. LW 24.290 (WA XLV.726).

[T]he Holy Spirit is not a mere spirit—a creature, for example, or something apart from God and yet given to man by Him, or merely the work of God which He performs in our heart—but that He is a Spirit who Himself is God in essence, who has His essence from the Father, and who was not created or made but proceeds from the Father and is sent by Christ.[8]

Christ speaks of the distinctive Person of the Holy Spirit, as well as of his divine essence, which is one with the Father and the Son, when he says: "Whatever He hears He will speak" (John 16:13). Here Christ refers to an ontic conversation that occurs in the Godhead, in which no creatures can participate. He imagines a pulpit in which the Father is the preacher, the Son is the spoken Word, and the Holy Spirit is the Listener. In reference to His divine nature, Scripture calls our Lord Christ a "Word" (John 1:1) which the Father speaks with and in Himself. This Word has a true, divine nature from the Father. The Word spoken by the Father is unlike a physical, natural word spoken by a human being, whose voice or breath does not remain in him but proceeds from him and remains outside him. However the Word remains in the Father forever.

> For it stands to reason that there must also be a listener where a speaker and a word are found. But all this speaking, being spoken, and listening takes place within the divine nature and also remains there, where no creature is or can be. All three—Speaker, Word, and the Listener—must be God Himself; all three must be co-eternal and in a single undivided majesty. For there is no difference or inequality in the divine essence, neither a beginning nor an end. Therefore one cannot say that the Listener is something outside God, or that there was a time when He began to be a Listener; but just as the Father is a Speaker from eternity, and just as the Son is spoken from eternity, so the Holy Spirit is the Listener from eternity.[9]

Though Luther's emphasis is on the office of the Holy Spirit, this does not mean that he says nothing of the Spirit's relationships in the Godhead. John 16:15 bears this out: "All that the Father has is Mine; therefore I said that He will take what is Mine and declare it to you." The Holy Spirit is God, but he does not derive his divine essence from himself; he receives it from both the Father and the Son. For Christ says here that the Holy Spirit takes "that which is His," namely, the eternal, divine essence, not only from the Father but also from Christ and thus remains one Godhead with three

8. LW 24.297 (WA XLV.732).
9. LW 24.362 (WA XLVI.57).

distinct Persons. "All that the Father has is Mine" means Christ's deity is his by nature and right; it is not borrowed, or purchased, or earned; it is inherently and completely Christ's from eternity, and yet it is the Father's. Thus Christ is almighty and eternal God, just as the Father is. Both share the same glory and majesty. Christ ascribes to himself all that the Father possesses, for both are One God; there is no difference, except that he is born of the Father.

From the preceding statement, "All that the Father has is Mine," Christ concludes that the Holy Spirit is true God, since the Spirit takes his essence from Christ. Of the following statement, "Therefore I said that He will take what is Mine," Luther writes:

> Here the circle is completely closed, and all three—the Father, the Son, and the Holy Spirit—are embraced in one divine essence. Christ says: "From that which is Mine, which is the Father's, namely, the fact that I am one God with Him, the Holy Spirit also takes what He is and has. Therefore He is and has exactly what both the Father and I are and have. For if He takes and has what I have, it follows that He must be of the same nature and essence, since what I have for Myself and call My own cannot be ascribed to any creature."[10]

"To take what is Mine" does not entail a division or partition of divine essence. For God is indivisibly One; the Godhead cannot be dismembered and divided; it is a perfect, complete, and indivisible essence. "Accordingly, where there is a part, there God Himself is; there the whole Godhead is certainly present."[11] Therefore these words, "to take what is Mine," contain no other meaning than that the Holy Spirit himself is also true God, without any distinction except that he derives his essence from both the Father and the Son. Thus Augustine's *filioque* doctrine finds approval in Luther:

> Earlier we heard (John 14:26; 15:26) that the Holy Spirit is sent not only by the Father but that He is also sent by, and proceeds from, the Son. Therefore this Listener [the Holy Spirit] must be called the Listener of both the Father and the Son, not of the Father alone or of the Son alone. Christ stated plainly: "The Comforter, whom I shall send to you from the Father." The expression "to send" has the very same connotation that the expression "to proceed from" has. For he who proceeds from someone is sent. Conversely, he who is sent proceeds from him who sends him.

---

10. LW 24.373 (WA XLVI.68).
11. LW 24.373 (WA XLVI.68).

Consequently, the Holy Spirit has His divine essence not only from the Father but also from the Son.[12]

The Office of the Holy Spirit: The Functional Significance

Just as the Holy Spirit receives his essence from the Son, he too receives his office from the Son. Luther gravitates toward the functional significance of the Holy Spirit in us; the polemical dispute over the *filioque* doctrine does not surface in his sermon.

1. *The Comforter*

The name "Comforter" refers to a specific office and activity, that is, what the Spirit does in us. What Christ does for us the Holy Spirit does in us. Knowing that his bodily absence would create unrest in Christendom, Christ assures them that he will compensate them for their loss; he also will ask the Father to grant them the Comforter, who will remain with them forever. He will strengthen and embolden us, far better than Christ would by his physical presence. Nothing in this life can deprive us of him. There is no lack in him, true God together with the Father and the Son in one divine essence yet distinct in person, and thus we will not lack for comfort, courage, and wisdom. Christ assures them of his prayer, as he states in John 14:16: "And I will pray the Father." This again assures the disciples that they will not suffer lack; nor will they be forsaken. He will pray and implore the Father to give them the Holy Spirit, who will console, strengthen, and preserve them, that they may remain in his love and be able bear all trials with joy. The ascended Christ is not inactive, sitting idly in heaven, but serves us as our dear Priest and Mediator.

Christ depicts the Holy Spirit as a Comforter, who enables us to engage in daily combat with the evil spirit who rules in the world. The two weapons the devil uses in assailing the Christians are sin and the penalty for sin. The devil is "a past master and an excellent theologian"[13] at inducing terror in our hearts, in the hour of death or at other times. The devil comes along with God's Law, by means of which he cites and magnifies sin to the extent that he renders the heart fearful and despondent; more than this, he can turn our good conduct and our best works into many kinds of sin and shame, so that we no longer remember a speck of them. Just as the devil magnifies the

12. LW 24.365 (WA XLVI.59).
13. LW 24.291 (WA XLV.727).

gravity of sin, in the same way he magnifies the severity of penalty for it, that we have rightly deserved judgment a hundred times for this or that sin, and eternal hell as the outcome. But God has been gracious to us and has given us a Comforter as a remedy against this spirit of terror. This Comforter is God himself, who is much stronger with his comfort than the devil is with his terror. His ultimate purpose is to communicate and whisper consolingly to our aggrieved hearts that we are justified not on account of our beings, but purely by the imputation of Christ, our Righteousness.

> "Be of good cheer and unafraid. Go, preach, do what you have been commanded to do; and do not fear the terrors of sin, death, or the devil, even if these terrors present themselves in the name of God. God does not want to be angry with you, nor does He want to reject you; for Christ, God's Son, died for you. He paid for your sins; and if you believe in Him, these will not be imputed to you, no matter how great they are. Because of your faith your works are pleasing to God; they are adjudged good and well done even though weakness does creep in. Why do you let your sins be falsely magnified? Christ, your Righteousness, is greater than your sins and those of the whole world; His life and consolation are stronger and mightier than your death and hell."[14]

The Holy Spirit thus inspires a confident and staunch heart that can scorn the devil with his terror and torment, and defy all his fiery might; thus we could declare with courage: "For Christ is mine with His suffering, death, and life; the Holy Spirit, with His Comfort; and the Father Himself, with all His grace. He sends the Holy Spirit to preach Christ into my heart and to fill it with His consolation. This is the main glory and prerogative of the Holy Spirit."[15]

2. *The Spirit of Truth*

Second, in addition to calling him Comforter (John 14:16), St. John here adds another definition, that he is "the Spirit of truth" (John 14:17; 16:13), the remedy against all lies and false arguments. This is the Holy Spirit's specific office, by which we can apprehend the content of Christ's speech and discern all other doctrines. "Thus He will not only make you warriors and heroes, but He will also confer the doctorate on you and call you doctors and masters who can determine with certainty what is true or false doctrine

---

14. LW 24.292 (WA XLV.727).
15. LW 24.292 (WA XLV.728).

in Christendom."[16] This is the promise, that the Spirit of truth will make our faith certain, remove all doubt, and enable us to judge all other spirits. "And it is a sure sign of the presence of the Holy Spirit and of His power when faith is preserved and is victorious in a real battle and trial."[17]

Luther cites a proverbial saying: "Wherever God erects a church, the devil builds his chapel or tavern next to it."[18] The devil works in us inwardly with his terror—by terrifying us with sin and fear of God, resulting in a restless conscience, which finds no relief unless the Comforter comes; he also works in us outwardly with torture—by frightening us away from the true doctrine with persecution, causing many to go astray in their faith. He arouses many sects, factions, and many false spirits, who deck themselves with the glory and the name of Christ and his Church. To counteract this, Christ says in John 14:26: "He will teach you all things and bring to your remembrance all that I have said to you." Christ bestows the Spirit who makes you sure and convinced of the truth, and calls all Christ's words to mind and applies them to our hearts till the Last Day. "With the Spirit's advent is promised the fulfillment of teaching the community, and leading it in the knowledge and truth of Christ."[19] The Holy Spirit dwells with Christendom and sanctifies it, namely through Word and Sacrament, the external means through which he continues to effect faith in it and the knowledge of Christ, and make sinners pure and holy. This is our comfort and trust: Christians are made holy before God, not by virtue of what we are or do but purely because the Holy Spirit is given to us. The Holy Spirit brings Christ's words home to us and impresses them onto our hearts that we are not holy through ourselves but through Christ's blood, with which we have been sprinkled, washed in baptism, and through his gospel, which is preached to us daily. Thus a Christian can confess with certainty: "I believe in the Holy Spirit and the holy Christian Church."

As the Spirit of truth, he leads his people to bear witness to Christ. Christ said in John 16:27: "and you also are witnesses, because you have been with Me from the beginning." When our mind is made certain of the truth, he will also impel us to testify about Christ, as borne out in Psalm 116:10: "I believe, therefore have I spoken." He does this in two ways: first internally, he bears witness in our hearts that Christ is my Lord and Savior;

---

16. LW 24.292 (WA XLV.728).
17. LW 24.360 (WA XLVI.55).
18. LW 24.292 (WA XLV.728).
19. Helmer, *Trinity and Martin Luther*, 156. For further study of Luther's doctrine of the Holy Spirit, see Prenter, *Spiritus Creator*, 52; and Silcock, "Luther on the Holy Spirit."

second externally, he does so by means of miraculous signs, and through his messengers, the instruments of divine power.[20]

A. Internal Witness of the Holy Spirit: No Other Content but Christ

He will enable the dear Christians who were with Christ from the beginning to proclaim what they have heard and seen. For with them Christ defined the work of the Holy Spirit as Christo-centric; his teaching and testimony is to exalt none but Christ (John 15:26). Christ wrote: "For He will not speak on His own authority, but whatever He hears He will speak;" "He will glorify Me, for He will take what is Mine and declare to you;" "All that the Father has is Mine; therefore I said that He will take what is Mine and declare it to you" (John 16:13–15). Just as the Holy Spirit receives his divine essence from Christ, so his office and his message consist of nothing but glorification of Christ. Luther has Christ say:

> "He will bear witness of none but Me. This will be known as the Holy Spirit's sermon. Therefore He will not be a Moses or a preacher of the Law such as you have had and still have; but I will put into His mouth another and more sublime sermon than the one Moses gave to you. Moses taught nothing but the Law or the Ten Commandments, which he had received from God; he told you what to do and what not to do. But this One will make of you preachers and confessors who tell and testify, not of their own deeds and life but of Me."[21]

In his *Heidelberg Disputation* (1518), Luther held that he who bypasses the person of Christ is charged with what he calls "the theology of glory," the precise opposite of what he calls "theology of the cross," in which God is to be sought nowhere else except beneath the weakness of the flesh.[22] St. Philip, representative of the disciples, is a theologian of glory, who for Luther seeks to find God outside Christ (John 14:8–9). The devil seeks to convert us into a theologian of glory who flits elsewhere and speculates beyond Christ. His aim is to sever us from the testimony of the Holy Spirit so that he may banish our vision from the life of this Man who died for us. He tempts us to

---

20. LW 24.374 (WA XLVI.68): "You can read more about them [the two ways of the Holy Spirit] in Augustine and others who have dealt diligently with such statements." See footnote 35 where Augustine, *In Joannis Evangelium tractatus* CXXIV, Tractatus 96–97, Patrologia, Series Latina, XXXV, 1873–1880, is cited.

21. LW 24.295 (WA XLV.729).

22. LW 31.53.

emphasize the importance of our good works at the expense of faith. He has the upper hand with the Law, or the Ten Commandments; he used it to work in us the opposite of justification—God's wrath, death and damnation. He holds only Moses before our eyes, and proclaims God's command, from which we hear a word of condemnation: "You are a sinner, who deserves to be damned." This is to tear us away from the testimony of the Holy Spirit, an art in which "the devil is a master and an excellent theologian."[23] On the contrary, the Spirit holds Christ before our eyes and proclaims God's promise, from which we hear a word of consolation: "Christ shed His blood for us, forgave my sin, overcame death, conquered God's wrath and hell." This is the Holy Spirit's message that the devil cannot undo. The presence of the Holy Spirit with us is not verified by some intense or ecstatic feeling, or inner experience. Rather it is attested by the fact that, despite the evils without and turbulence within, we retain our faith in Christ. This is attributed to the Holy Spirit, whose office is to kindle and preserve faith in Christ. The Holy Spirit is not a separate deity, bringing to us some new or different revelation. The God who came to us in Christ is the same God who comes as the Holy Spirit. While a theologian of the cross held that God came hidden in the human form of Jesus who died on the cross, a theologian of glory affirmed that in the Holy Spirit he meets God face to face, no longer veiled and hidden in the human form. Luther's theology of the cross is not so much opposed to Christians' religious experiences as it is opposed to a triumphant confidence in experience as an unmediated means to the divine power, wisdom, and glory. His theology applies just as surely to God the Holy Spirit as it does to God the Son. The Holy Spirit does not enlighten us with an unearthly glory; he establishes faith in Christ, contrary to reason and all appearances. Faith, a gift of the Spirit, is justifying faith, whose object is the crucified Christ.

It is the Holy Spirit's office to fill our hearts with no other glory than the glory of the cross. His role is to confer in our hearts the assurance that God's mercy has triumphed over his wrath, and that what Christ has accomplished via Calvary and Easter is ours if only we believe. The objective work Christ accomplishes on the cross becomes a subjective reality in us through the inward witness of the Holy Spirit. With Calvin,[24] Luther affirms that the Holy Spirit "teaches us to understand this deed of Christ which has been manifested to us, helps us receive and preserve it, use it to our advantage and impart it to others, increase and extend it."[25] The Holy Spirit is a Person

23. LW 24.291 (WA XLV.727).

24. Calvin, *Institutes*, 1:79, where he said the same thing: "For as God alone is a fit witness of himself in his Word, so also the Word will not find acceptance in men's hearts before it is sealed by the inward testimony of the Spirit."

25. LW 37.366 (Confession Concerning Christ's Supper). Cf. "The Large Catechism,"

who reveals, and he reveals Christ as a Person who truly redeems. What we gain from Christ is the revelation not just of the true God but of the real heart of God. The heart of God is mirrored in the face of Christ, and from this, we know for sure God does not look at anyone with a sour face. There abides a correspondence between God's face and God's heart; this unity assures us that God is the One who turns himself towards us with acceptance and kindness. God comes as a lowly servant, ready to help and comfort. God allows himself to be crucified for us and freely sheds his blood to redeem us. The "look"[26] that Christ manifests is nothing but "friendly, gracious, a loving and kind look," which corresponds to the heart, glowing with "sheer favor and ardor of ineffable, fatherly, and sincere love."[27] In Christ, God does not appear as an angry judge, but as a gracious God who desires to be our Father, and this is communicated to our hearts in the power of the Holy Spirit. Consequently, believers are made joyful and confident, free and secure in their conscience.

B. External Witness of the Holy Spirit: Word, Sacraments, and Absolution

Externally, the Holy Spirit bears witness to Christ through confession and proclamation. After he has strengthened the faith of the disciples, the risen Christ now commits the office of preaching to them and confers upon them power and authority to remit and retain sins (John 20:23).[28] He sends them just as the Father sends the Son, and bestows upon them the Holy Spirit for this mission and office. Thus Christ says in John 20:22: "He breathed upon them and said to them, 'Receive the Holy Spirit.'" This is one of the main texts where Augustine argues that the Holy Spirit has to be thought of as proceeding from the Son. There he observes a correspondence between the temporal mission of the Holy Spirit and the eternal procession of the

---

in Tappert, *The Book of Concord,* 419. See Peters, *Sin Boldly!,* 278: "On the one hand, God's Word comes objectively as a word addressed to us. On the other hand, God works from within our subjectivity to seal the contract, so to speak, to establish and maintain our relationship."

26. LW 24.61 (WA XLV.516). Luther uses the word "look," which is synonymous to "face."

27. LW 24.61 (WA XLV.516).

28. For a series of Easteride sermons on John 20:23, see LW 69.327–436. These sermons gave Luther opportunity to articulate the power of the Word of forgiveness in preaching, in the spoken Absolution, in the Sacraments and the Scripture. A central theme of Luther's preaching on John is his emphasis on the external, oral, physical Word as the source of Christian faith and assurance.

Spirit from the Son in the Godhead, the former reveals a divine person in his eternal origin. In his *De Trinitate*, Augustine asserted: "For that bodily breathing, proceeding from the body with the feeling of bodily touching, was not the substance of the Holy Spirit, but a declaration by a fitting sign, the Holy Spirit proceeds not only from the Father, but also the Son."[29] With Augustine, Luther held that the works of Christ and the Spirit reflect who they are in eternity. However in this text, Luther's focus is not on the immanent relation within God's triune life but on the economic power of the Holy Spirit Christ endows the disciples with for the mission and office of preaching.[30] The Holy Spirit works in unity with the Word and sacrament to accomplish his saving purpose:

> It is certainly true that the office of preaching the Gospel and of forgiving sins belongs to no one but to the Holy Spirit alone. Insofar as the Holy Spirit is present, so far does the forgiveness of sins also extend. If the Holy Spirit is not present, there is no forgiveness. Thus also to administer the Sacrament, to baptize, to feed with the body and blood of Christ belongs to no one but to the Holy Spirit alone. It is also the office and work of the Holy Spirit to exercise the external, oral Word in Christendom, as St. Peter says (1 Pet 1:12), that the Gospel is proclaimed through the apostles through the Holy Spirit sent from heaven.[31]

God who comes to us by way of the cross deals with us in a two-fold manner: first outwardly and then inwardly. God approaches us through these earthly forms of expressions—preaching, sacraments and the written Scriptures—just as God came to us in the human person of Jesus. Only through this does the inner experience of the Holy Spirit have its basis. "God has determined to give the inward to no one except through the outward."[32] Luther binds the Holy Spirit to the created forms: the Lord's Supper, baptism and absolution—external means through which we know for sure that it is the Holy Spirit who has proclaimed the gospel to us, baptized us, and absolved us from sins. The intention is not to restrict the freedom of God's activity; rather it is the "order"[33] God has established through which he

---

29. Augustine, *De Trinitate*, IV.20, as cited in Daley, "Revisiting the '*Filioque*'," 41.

30. LW 69.353 (WA 28.466).

31. LW 69.353–54 (WA 28.466–67). LW 24.67 (WA XLV 522). See Lohse, *Martin Luther's Theology*, 238: "Due to his teaching concerning God, his distinction between the *Deus absconditus* [hidden God] and the *Deus revelatus* [revealed God], as well as his Reformation distinction between law and gospel, Luther disputed the fanatics' right to appeal to special inspirations apart from revelation or Word and sacrament."

32. LW 40.146.

33. LW 40.146.

sends forth his holy gospel. The work of the Holy Spirit is to create faith in Christ, by hearing (*ex auditu*) the Word which in proclamation comes from outside of us (*extra nos*). Luther's quarrel with Karlstadt, Müntzer and others is that they invert the order. "Dr. Karlstadt and these spirits replace the highest with the lowest, the best with the least, the first with the last. Yet he would be considered the greatest spirit of all, he who has devoured the Holy Spirit feathers and all."[34] These spirits are what Luther call theologians of glory, according to whom the Holy Spirit has spoken to them directly and offered them direct instructions for action and assurance of salvation. Triumphalism espouses that baptism is of no effect in cleansing us; only the Holy Spirit can do that. The basic question is not whether you have been baptized with the Word and water, but whether you have been baptized by the Holy Spirit and his accompanying phenomena. The triumphalist, Luther sums up, "wants to teach you, not how the Spirit comes to you but how you come to the Holy Spirit."[35] He relies on a direct vision and experience of God in divine glory to banish all doubts and fears. This is not possible on this earth, and against such, Luther writes:

> When we get to heaven, we shall see God differently; then no clouds and no darkness will obscure our view. But here on earth we shall not perceive Him with our senses and our thoughts. No, here, we see Him, as St. Paul states (1 Cor 13:12), "in a mirror dimly," enveloped in an image, namely in the Word and the sacraments. These are His masks or His garments, as it were, in which He conceals Himself. But He is certainly present in these, Himself working miracles, preaching, administering the sacraments, consoling, strengthening and helping. We see Him as we see the sun through a cloud. For now we cannot bear to see and look at His brilliant Majesty. Therefore He must cover and veil Himself, so to speak, behind a heavy cloud. Thus it has been ordained that he who wants to see and apprehend both the Father and the Son glorified and enthroned in majesty, must apprehend Him through the Word and through the works He performs in Christendom by means of the ministry and other offices.[36]

---

34. LW 40.83. See Lindberg, *Third Reformation*, 113ff, for a discussion of Luther's understanding of the Holy Spirit in his response to the charismatic challenges to his understanding to the doctrine of salvation.

35. LW 40.147.

36. LW 24.67 (WA XLV 522). See Lohse, *Martin Luther's Theology*, 238: "Due to his teaching concerning God, his distinction between the *Deus absconditus* [hidden God] and the *Deus revelatus* [revealed God], as well as his Reformation distinction between law and gospel, Luther disputed the fanatics' right to appeal to special inspirations apart from revelation or Word and sacrament."

Luther warns against confusing the person with the office. The office remains even if some godless persons assume the office and misuse it. Attention must be given not so much to the person but to the office and the Word. "Now to the extent that the person deals with the Word and carries out the ordinance of the Holy Spirit, to that extent the Holy Spirit, forgiveness of sins, and everything good is there. However, insofar as the person deals with you without the Word and disrupts the ordinance of the Holy Spirit, to that extent the devil and everything evil is there."[37] The efficacy of preaching lies not in the person, but in God's Word. For God's Word is causative, effectively speaking reality into being, as he did to creation. "The Words of God are embodied realities," Jenson writes, "and not mere language."[38]

Luther further clarifies that one can receive the Holy Spirit in two ways: first, for himself and for his person, whom the Holy Spirit through the Word enlightens, justifies and saves, even if he is not in the governing office. "That is the best and most blessed way to have the Holy Spirit."[39] Second, he can have it neither for himself nor for his person, just as Balaam, a wicked man, abandoned the right path, except for his office that he carried out the task of proclamation stoutly. This is borne out in Numbers 23:5: "The Lord put the word in Balaam's mouth and said, 'Return to Balak and speak thus.'" The office is not that of human beings, but of Christ, who places it upon the disciples and invests it with the efficacy of the Holy Spirit. As regards our person, preachers, because of their weaknesses, may not have the Holy Spirit always; as regards our office, if we preach the gospel, baptize, absolve, and administer the Sacrament according to the ordinance of the Holy Spirit, the Holy Spirit is with us always.

C. Reproving of Sin, Righteousness, and Judgment

Third, in his sermon on John 16:5–15, Christ locates the divine judgment under the rubric of the Spirit's office.[40] When the Spirit comes as judge, he exposes human captivity to sin and our complete ineptitude for good. This he does through the agency of his messengers, whom the Spirit has invested with this office. At the same time, however, Christ reassures them that the Holy Spirit will undergird what they do and make their reproof effective, for this is precisely what he comes to do. The Holy Spirit will not keep silent,

---

37. LW 69.355 (WA 28.467–68).
38. Jenson, *Systematic Theology*, 159–60.
39. LW 69.355 (WA 28.467–68).
40. Helmer, *Trinity and Martin Luther*, 154.

even if the world vehemently opposes his office and work. He will not put an end to his reproofs until they have to stop or perish. In John 16:8–11, Christ enumerates three things the Holy Spirit is to reprove:

> First, "of sin, because they do not believe in Christ."

Christ is not speaking of the external sins that the world recognizes and punishes, but of sin as unbelief in Christ, as indicated by these words: "because they do not believe in Me." This is something that the world cannot uncover. The sin for which all people are reproved by the Holy Spirit is far different from the sins that are public and reproved by the world. Sin, in a nutshell, is without faith or the knowledge of Christ. Unbelief is "conclusively identified in one word as sin,"[41] which makes sinners of them all and also condemns them. All share everything in common and without distinction: the sin of being without Christ or without faith, which is reproved by the Holy Spirit in the same way in everybody. In his Commentary on Psalm 51:6, Luther attributes the knowledge of sin to the work of the Holy Spirit. The Holy Spirit pronounces this judgment through St. Paul, who places both Jews and Gentiles under sin and wrath, and proclaims that the gospel was revealed from heaven and that all the world stands guilty of sin (Rom 1:18–32; 3:22–23).

The sin, which is reproved by the Holy Spirit, has nothing to do with outward life and conduct, which the world can judge and condemn. Christ goes to "the very core, namely, to man's heart, which is the fountainhead and the source of the chief sins":[42] false worship, contempt of God, unbelief, evil lust, resistance to God's command, hostility to God, and inability to obey God's Law. The world sees only the outward manifestations of evil; it cannot penetrate the stem and source of all other sins, unless the Holy Spirit reveals this. Experience teaches that no matter how hard we try to restrain, improve, and heal the outside, we cannot ever heal the stem, the root, and the source from the inside. "Much less can the world remove the sin that inheres in human nature and is really the basic sin but is unknown to the world."[43] Unbelief, the principal sin of mankind, implanted in human nature since Adam's fall in Paradise, has to be revealed for what it really is by the Holy Spirit, and healed by Christ, who "erected a new heaven of grace and forgiveness, so that this sin inherited from Adam will no longer keep us under the wrath and condemnation of God if we believe in this Savior."[44]

---

41. LW 24.340 (WA XLVI.38).
42. LW 24.341 (WA XLVI.39).
43. LW 24.342 (WA XLVI.39).
44. LW 24.343 (WA XLVI.41).

He who is damned can no longer complain about Adam and his sin inherited from Adam, for Christ has appeared, atoned for this sin, and vanquished the condemnation. But he must accuse himself, because he did not accept and believe in this Christ, who has achieved redemption for him. Thus each one is responsible for his own destruction. He is damned, not because he is a sinner and worthy of damnation on account of original sin and his own former unbelief but because he refuses to accept Christ the Savior, who abolishes our sin and our damnation. Original sin in Adam damns us all, leading both himself and us into sin and into the devil's power; but now Christ, the second Adam, who was born without sin, removes this sin, and conquers God's wrath. Thus both salvation and damnation hinge entirely on faith or unbelief. Heaven is denied to all who have refused to accept this faith in Christ, and this sentence has already been pronounced with finality. "In brief, without Christ all is damned and lost; in Christ all is good and blessed."[45] Nothing, not even the sin inherited from Adam and the remainders of indwelling sin, can harm or damn us, if only we adhere to Christ. Though sin cannot be completely rid of in this life and still remains even in the holiest person, believers enjoy the comfort that this is not reckoned for their damnation but covered by Christ's forgiveness.

God commands that both law and gospel be proclaimed throughout the world so that sin may be exposed in all its starkness, and that Christ be made known to all as the remedy against sin. "Accordingly, when God's Spirit speaks through the law, his work in the heart is quite different and even opposite to what he does when he speaks through the gospel."[46] The Holy Spirit is a consoling agent to those terrified by the weight of the law; he fills a saddened heart with laughter and joy toward God, and brings God's smile upon us. However, the Spirit is a crushing agent to smug and callous hearts; he acts like a Moses or law-giver, a terrible judge who frightens them with the devil, death, and hell, for they disregard God's Word. They would be better off coming under the threat of God's Word so that they would be frightened enough to flee to God for mercy. Rather than being cheerful and happy, they should really be fearful and terrified, for to them the Spirit is a consuming fire. The cheerful should really be fearful, because of the terror of God's threats; the fearful should really be cheerful, because of the comfort of God's mercy. Therewith the transition to the gospel has taken place.

> Second, "of righteousness, because I go to the Father, and you will see Me no more."

---

45. LW 24.344 (WA XLVI.42).
46. Althaus, *Theology of Martin Luther*, 256.

The righteousness of which Christ speaks here is not of outward, secular righteousness, which the world could discern, teach and practice in this life. Just as Christ was not referring earlier to the world's understanding of what sin is or that which the world reproves, he is referring here to a righteousness recognized by God, one that differs from that acknowledged by the world. This righteousness is not in us, but entirely outside and above us; it is centered only in Christ: "My going to the Father is righteousness." His going to the Father encompasses his suffering, resurrection, and ascension. His righteousness is concealed completely from the sphere of our senses, as Christ avows "You will see Me no more." Though we cannot see and feel it, it can be grasped by faith in the Word preached about him, which informs us that he himself is our righteousness. As support, Luther quotes favorably St. Paul who says in 1 Cor 1:30: "Whom God made our Wisdom, our Righteousness and Sanctification and Redemption."

This righteousness is not bestowed by an infusion of grace, as the scholastics promulgate, as something that is poured into our hearts. In us there is no righteousness of our own of which we could boast and on which we could rely—not a thought, a word, or a work in ourselves. Christ's going to the Father or his ascension is the ground of a righteousness, not conferred upon us as a reward for our obedience or good work, but given to Christ alone and placed entirely in his Person. "Our work is not Christ, and His going is not our doing or work."[47] There is no lack or flaw in Christ's righteousness inherent in his ascension, which he has presented to us as a gift from heaven, and by which it delivers us from sin and death. To seek everything in ourselves, as the heathens do, is to place ourselves outside Christ, and thus make of him a terrible judge. Christ's ascension has propitiated the Father so that no propitiation with our works and through the intercession of Mary and the saints is needed. The blindness and misery with which we were formerly afflicted is now healed in Christ's ascension. We now seek everything not in ourselves but in him. The Holy Spirit confirms this in our hearts: "There is no other consolation than Christ's going to the Father. This is our chief possession and inheritance, our ultimate trust and eternal righteousness."[48]

Third, "of judgment, because the ruler of this world is judged."

Again, the reproving office of the Holy Spirit differs sharply from that of the worldly judgment; the former pertains to the domain of souls and consciences; the latter pertains to matters on life, property, country, people,

---

47. LW 24.348 (WA XLVI.45).
48. LW 24.349 (WA XLVI.46).

etc. The Holy Spirit pronounces a spiritual judgment, which the world cannot do. Things become serious when the Holy Spirit peels off the mask of sin and proclaims that all people without distinction are under sin and wrath, from which there is no help nor escape, for there is no righteousness before God without Christ. The world could exert its power over life and property, and we must obey it, as it is its proper jurisdiction. However, if it exceeds its own jurisdiction and trespasses into God's power, sitting in judgment over divine matters when they should let themselves together with all creatures be judged through his Word, we must do the exact opposite, that is, oppose it in order that we may be found obedient to God. Were we not to do so, we would condemn ourselves and others through God's Word. To prevent us from being frightened by the power of the world and the threats of the devil, Christ decrees, in Luther's rendering: "Any judgment that the prince of the world pronounces in spite of God's Word is already condemned. And anyone who presumes to condemn you in spite of the God's Word is also sentenced and condemned by God."[49]

Christ offers us the comfort that the Holy Spirit has sharper eyes to discern and to punish than any prince or creature, and his judgment will prevail against the judgment and condemnation of the world. What God pronounces remains efficacious: that the ruler of this world is already condemned, so no further judgment and sentence are necessary. What remains to be revealed is the sentence of condemnation which is finally carried out before the whole world, when the devil and his adherents will be hurled into the eternal hell, where they no longer attack God's Word and Christians. Just as Christendom has served as the reproving agency in the past against the devil and the world through the Word, it shall remain the same in pronouncing judgment and sentence upon them.

The Indwelling Presence: The Holy Spirit Concealed in Opposites

The Holy Spirit, concealed to human reason and experience, is revealed to the eyes of faith. Despite contrary appearances, faith grasps the promise of Christ, who says in John 14:17: "You know Him, for He who dwells with you, and will be in you." Those who adhere to Christ in faith and believe his Word will have "a guarantee, a formal promise and a strong consolation from Christ"[50] that they will never, till the end of days, be without the Holy Spirit. For just as Christ remains our Lord and is believed in until the Last

49. LW 24.352 (WA XLVI.48).
50. LW 24.125 (WA XLV.574).

Day, so the anointing which we received from Christ abides in us forever; he will preserve his church on earth, even when this is not apparent. There will always be people who believe and confess the faith through the Holy Spirit. No matter what the numbers are—great or small—Christ's church is on earth and will not perish; thus the Creed says: "I believe in the holy Christian church." The following statement: "I believe in the forgiveness of sins," is also valid, and will not cease as long as the world stands. This, too, has already begun now, through Christ and in Christ, but is now continued through the Holy Spirit. Even though the world does not know the Holy Spirit, it cannot restrain him. Thus the Holy Spirit cannot find room in them who cannot tolerate or hear his teaching; nor can he enter their hearts or eyes, even though he appears before them openly. Unlike the papists of Luther's day, who boasted of their numbers and strength, as if the church as institution were "a mountain of pure iron," the Holy Spirit "makes Himself so extraordinarily small and weak that the world takes offence"[51] in such a small and insignificant group of believers—unworthy, weak, forsaken, poor, and wretched people. It is precisely in these, so destitute of all reputation and all outward appearances, and so condemned by the world, that Holy Spirit dwells. Thus John 14:18: "I will not leave you desolate; I will come to you." God is hidden in the opposite of appearances and feelings. This is indeed a consolation to a small group of Christians who in the eyes of the world appear to be forgotten and forsaken by God and Christ, since God permits them to be exposed to the wickedness and might of the devil and the world. Herein lies the theology of the cross, in which God contradicts the world's estimation and our personal feelings: those whom the world perceives as forsaken are befriended by God, and those whom the world considers as orphans have, God as their Father (Ps 68:5).[52] As God comes unexpectedly in the human form of Jesus, so God comes unexpectedly as the Holy Spirit whenever our feelings convey to us that we are abandoned. Contrary to our personal feelings, those who feel most cursed of God are most cradled by God; those who feel most suppressed or subdued are most comforted by God. "Despite everything they feel and see, they should cling to the promise He gives them here when he says: 'I will not stay away from you . . . I will return to you soon and be with you forever.'"[53] Faith believes Christ's promise to be true, even when reason and conscience oppose it. Faith trusts in the truth of the testimony of God, even contrary to the

---

51. LW 24.126 (WA XLV.575).
52. LW 24.130–31 (WA XLV.580).
53. LW 24.132 (WA XLV.582).

testimony of one's heart and understanding.[54] There are so few who believe, and of them, many, because of their weaknesses, possess the Holy Spirit in small and paltry measure, and are tempted to doubt that they have the Holy Spirit. Therefore it is necessary that they be comforted, and be assured that the Holy Spirit abides in them, despite contrary appearances, beginning with the day of the apostles until now.

The Holy Spirit acquaints us with Christ's and his Father's heart, which are one and the same. All three—Father, Son, and Holy Spirit—share no other purpose and intention, and wish for nothing else than to be the God of comfort. And the God who proceeds from the Father through the Son in the Holy Spirit is indeed the God of love. For Christians, there is nothing—no wrath, threat, or terror—but "a friendly smile and sweet comfort"[55] in heaven and in earth. The knowledge of God's eternal love revealed from the "inside-out" of the immanent being in the Son by the Holy Spirit to Christians corresponds to the knowledge of God's fatherly heart communicated from the "outside-in," through the Son in the economic action of the Holy Spirit.[56] The double-movement of the Trinity constitutes the essence of the gospel: God descends to our flesh in the Son, revealing his gracious will in the Spirit; conversely the Holy Spirit draws us through the Son to the divine paternal heart from eternity.

---

54. Zachman, *Assurance of Faith*, 60–61.

55. LW 24.111 (WA XLV.562).

56. Helmer, *Trinity and Martin Luther*, 216, where the categories "inside-out" and "outside-in" appear: "The Spirit reveals on the outside, the inner thoughts of God not accessible by sight or touch. On the outer-side of God, the Holy Spirit reveals what is found on the inner-side, that is, divine wisdom."

CHAPTER 11

Christological Predication
The Usage of Communicatio Idiomatum

The doctrine of the communication of attributes (*communicatio idiomatum*) did not originate with Luther, as it was employed by Cyril of Alexandra in his dispute with Nestorius.[1] Luther adopted both the Chalcedonian formula that preserves the distinction of the two natures in Christ, and made use of the tradition of the doctrine as a mode of theological speech (*modus loquendi theologicus*). The doctrine is, for him, an ontological deduction from the cross and the incarnation. His handling of the doctrine mainly occurs in his polemical disputes with other theologians, such as Nestorius and Zwingli, with the neo-Arianism of Caspar Schwenckfeld, and in the treatise *On the Councils and the Church*.[2] He uses it in a few places in his sermons on John's gospel because he found it to be in harmony with his christological thinking which he believed was rooted in the Bible. He applies this doctrine specifically in his sermons on John 3:13: "No one has ascended into heaven, but He who descended from heaven;" John 3:14: "The Son of man must be lifted up;" John 3:16: "For God so loved the world that He gave His only begotten Son;" John 3:35: "The Father loves the Son

---

1. See McGuckin, *Saint Cyril of Alexandria*, 153–55; 190–93.

2. For a discussion of the Eucharistic theology of Luther and Zwingli, see LW 37:13–150, "That These Words of Christ 'This is My Body,' Etc., Still Stand Firm against the Fanatics, 1527" and LW 37:161–372, "Confession concerning Christ's Supper, 1528." See also LW 38:235–277, "The Disputation on 'The Word was Made Flesh, 1539," and WA 39.II.92–121, "Disputation on the Divinity and Humanity of Christ, 1540." For an extensive study of this disputation, see Hinlicky, "Luther's anti-docetism," 139–81. For historical roots of Luther's theology, see LW 41.3–178.

and has given all things into His hand;" John 6:61-62: "Do you take offense in this? Then what if you were to see the Son of man ascending where He was before?" and John 14:16: "And I will pray the Father." His usage of the doctrine in these sermons has Nestorianism as his primary target. This is, Luther claims, to "adhere to the speech and expressions of the Holy Writ."[3] With this Luther's position sits comfortably with Chalcedon, in which the attributes of both natures are predicated of the person rather than of each other. Leo furnished eloquent expression to this in his *Tome* (3):

> Since then the properties of both natures and substances were preserved and co-existed in One person, humility was embraced by majesty, weakness by strength, mortality by eternity, and to pay the debt of our condition the inviolable nature was united to a passible nature; so that, as was necessary for our healing, there was one and the same "Mediator between God and men, the man Jesus Christ," who was capable of death in one nature and incapable of it in the other. In the complete and perfect nature, therefore, of very man, very God was born—complete in what belonged to Him, complete in what belonged to us.[4]

Descending from, Ascending to, and Remaining in Heaven

Christ's words, "No one has ascended into heaven but He who descended from heaven" (John 3:13), accentuate the unity principle: his two natures dwell in one Person, and this is in line with the Council of Chalcedon.[5] His Father is God, and his mother is human; both have the one and same Son, our dear Lord and Savior Jesus Christ, as our Creed also teaches. "Inasmuch as Christ is God, He is in heaven above from eternity, together with the Father. When He was born of the Virgin Mary, however, He descended from heaven; but at the same time he remained in heaven. He also ascended into heaven, but he was also in heaven before His ascension."[6] With Augustine,[7] Luther interpreted the expression "descended" as God assuming our poor

---

3. LW 24.107 (WA XLV.558).

4. Bindley, *Ecumenical Documents*, 226. Also quoted in Crisp, *Divinity and Humanity*, 7.

5. Kolb, *Martin Luther*, 112.

6. LW 22.324-25 (WA 47.53).

7. Augustine, *In Joannis Evangelium Tractatus*, Ch. III, Tr. XII, *Patrologia, Series Latina*, XXXV, 1488-1490.

flesh, becoming a human son through the Virgin Mary.[8] Not only had he descended into our flesh but also into death, the grave and hell.[9] "The only Person who is called God and who existed from eternity is He who assumed humanity."[10] Thus both statements are true: he dwells in heaven eternally; and yet he descended to earth in our flesh, without any contraction of being. He remains God, even in his incarnate mode of existence.

Of Christ's office, John declared that he descended from heaven; and after having accomplished what he came to do, he ascended again visibly, sits at the right hand of God, and reigns there with might, not only according to his divine nature, which he had from eternity, but also according to his human nature which he assumed. Everything—angels, principalities, and all creatures—is subject to the Son of Mary, very man, for divinity and humanity are now one essence and one Person in Christ. There is only one Son, God's Son and Mary's, who descended, ascended, and remained in heaven above. This is to be explained according to the ancient doctrine of the *communicatio idiomatum*, that the property of one nature is ascribed to person of Christ:

> Therefore it is correct to say that God's Son descended, ascended, and remained in heaven, although this one act, that of descending, was performed only according to His human nature. But since the two natures dwell in the one undivided Person of Christ, one also ascribes to the divine nature what properly pertains to the human nature. For this reason it is not wrong to say: "This Son of God and Mary descended into hell, suffered, and died." Or "The Son of God and of Mary ascended into heaven and sits on the right hand of His heavenly Father."[11]

Just as body and soul are one entity and being, and cannot be divorced of a living being, so also Christ's humanity and divinity together constitute one being, and cannot be separated from each other. Luther provides an illustration: "It is also said that a highwayman has struck down a person when he may only have inflicted a wound or cut off an arm. And when speaking of a person as slain, one does not say: 'His soul was run through with a

---

8. LW 22.325 (WA 47.53).

9. LW 22.325 (WA 47.53). See note 38, where Luther here identifies the descent into hell with the death of Christ, when ordinarily he distinguishes these two actions. See his *Torgau sermon* of April, 1533 (WA 37.62–67).

10. LW 22.325. (WA 47.54).

11. LW 22.327 (WA 47.55).

dagger'; one mentions only to the body. And yet we say: 'The whole person was injured'; for body and soul are united in one person."[12]

> Although this really applied only to the human nature, by virtue of the personal union in Christ it is also ascribed to the other nature. "That which applies to one nature, applies to the entire person in the concrete." We differentiate between the natures as we do between body and soul; however, there remains but one Person. Thus Christ suffered for us not only with body and soul but also as the Son of God, . . . And this Son, born of Mary, is also God's Son, our Lord, who later suffered, was crucified, ascended again into heaven, and seated Himself at the right hand of the Father. It is not two sons, but one Son.[13]

For Christ did not say: "No one ascends into heaven but the Son of God." Ascension is predicated of the Son of man; Christ's ascension is his home-going to the Father, but this time with a glorified humanity that is his. Earlier he said that the Son of God had descended from heaven. And then he stated: "No one has ascended into heaven but the Son of man." Thus it is proper to say that "the Son of man, that is, the Son of the Virgin Mary, ascended into heaven, descended from heaven, and remained in heaven."[14] The Christian faith harmonizes the Son of man on earth with the Son of God in heaven. As the Son of man, Christ performs his office on earth; he suffers and dies. God became man and debased himself to death on the cross; later he ascended again into heaven, where, being God, he had always remained. Although he was born man, he is concurrently God's Son in heaven. He has not forfeited his divine nature, but remains in heaven. This is the sublime article of faith: Jesus Christ, our Savior, has two natures but is one indivisible Person, who is God with the Father and the Holy Spirit from eternity, and that in time he also became man through Mary. Whoever learns this article well and retains it can harmonize three items: to descend, to ascend, and to remain in heaven. "These words have no other contents and significance than the words we confess in the Creed: 'I believe in Jesus Christ, the Son of God and of the Virgin Mary, God and man, who remained in heaven and comes down to this earth as God's Son, becomes man, and dies.'"[15] This

---

12. LW 22.328 (WA 47.56). See Posset, *Luther's Catholic Christology*, 162, where the whole person as God-man is Luther's starting point: what is attributed to one part of the person is attributed to the whole person.

13. LW 22.328 (WA 47.56). Cf. LW 22.491–98 (WA 47.199–205).

14. LW 22.329 (WA 47.57).

15. LW 22.332 (WA 47.59).

article deserves to be stamped and sealed in our hearts so that we can combat not only heresy but also despair.

Council of Ephesus 431: Nestorians and Theotokos

Nestorians both ancient and modern are Luther's target as he deals with the biblical exposition of John's gospel. The Nestorians ascribed the title "*Christotokos*" to Mary as the mother only of the man Jesus, who by nature was only her son. In so doing, they made two sons of one. However for Luther, Mary was the mother of God (*theotokos*), the title that found official approval in the Council of Ephesus in 431. This, for Luther, is the foundation of our faith:

> But there is only one Son; and yet there are two natures, which gave Mary the right to say: "This Son Jesus, whom I bore and suckled on my breasts, is the eternal God, born of the Father in eternity, and also my Son." And God says likewise: "Mary's Son is My only Son." Thus Mary is the mother of God. And Christ, together with God the Father and the Holy Spirit, is very God from eternity who became man in time. So God the Father does not have a son apart from Mary's, nor does Mary have a son apart from God the Father's. . . Christ has two natures even though He is one indivisible Person. These are not two sons and two persons; there is one Son and one Person.[16]

The attributes of both natures are predicated of one subject, so that there is no risk of Nestorianism.[17] If one differentiates two sons in Christ, then it must follow that there are also two persons, in which case salvation is lost. The two natures must be the one Christ, or else there is no satisfaction for our sins. If Christ were only man, his suffering would have been futile, since no man's suffering could vanquish sin, death and wrath. "Therefore it was necessary for Him to be God, and, in order to suffer, also true man. Furthermore, if there were two persons, He would not be able to sit at the right hand of God as merely a human being."[18] The person must not be divided, for there is only one Son, the Son of both God, born from the Father from eternity, and of Virgin Mary, born in time. Christ is one Person, with two eternally inseparable natures. This provides the greatest comfort in every distress that God and man are one and not two.

---

16. LW 22.323–324 (WA 47.52).
17. Siggins, *Martin Luther's Doctrine of Christ*, 232; Lienhard, *Luther*, 170.
18. LW 22.324 (WA 47.52).

A Date in History: According to Christ's Humanity

This Man Christ is Mary's Son, and is "not older than 1,539 years,"[19] at the time Luther wrote this sermon. God has a date in history,[20] that he was 1,539 years old according to his humanity. To be born and to be suckled are distinctive of the human nature; not to be born is distinctive of the divine nature, for God does not drink milk. Because the two natures are so united in one Person, it is correct to say: "The mother of God is a virgin; God is born." Since God and man are one Person, the properties characteristic of humanity alone are imputed to the deity, for the properties of the two natures are also united. It is correct to say that the Child who drinks his mother's milk is eternal; he existed before the beginning of the world and he created the universe. This is clearly stated in the Creed: "Who was conceived and who was born" is peculiar to the human, and "sits at the right hand," is characteristic of the divine, although it may also be human. The indissoluble union of the two natures in one Person effects a union of properties. Against the Nestorians, who refuse to concede a communication of properties between the two natures, Luther elaborates:

> Since the two natures are united in one Person, the effect is that the properties are also united. Admittedly, the properties of the divine nature have nothing in common with human nature. I shall go beyond this and say that there is still less relation between God and man. Yet these natures are so united that there is only One God and Lord, that Mary suckles God with her breasts, bathes God, rocks Him, and carries Him; furthermore, that Pilate and Herod crucified and killed God. The two natures are so joined that the true deity and humanity are one. Now if the true God dwells in Christ, who was born of Mary, that is, the God who made and created all, we must say that the deity and humanity jointed not only their natures but also their properties, except for sin.[21]

---

19. LW 22.492 (WA 47.199).

20. Cf. Sayers, "Shattering Dogmas," 14, where she says that only the God of Christianity has a date in history.

21. LW 22.492–93 (WA 47.200).

Soteriological Imperative: The Person, God-man, Suffers, and Dies

"The Son of man must be lifted up" (John 3:14) is a particular reference to Christ's humanity, that he must be hung on the cross, suffer and die. But a crucified man could not impart eternal life, unless the Son of man is God. It is a soteriological imperative that the one who was nailed to the cross is Mary's Son, endowed with power to save, since he is also the Son of God. Thus Christ's saying, "No one has ascended into heaven but He who descended from heaven, the Son of man who is in heaven," pertains only to the divine majesty.[22] The Gospel of John unites wonderfully the two natures in the undivided Person of Christ. The power to save, to deliver from death, and to confer eternal life is exclusively of God, but is communicated to man in Christ. When John declares that the Son of man was lifted up that all who believe in him might have eternal life, he does not separate the two natures. He does not say, "Whoever believes in the Son of God has eternal life," but "Whoever believes in the Son of man." This is precisely the point of the *communicatio idiomatum*:

> The two natures are united in the single Person of Christ, and this Person is both God and man. The two natures, deity and humanity, are found in one Person; and the attributes of each nature are imputed to the other, so that whoever believes in the Son of man believes not only in a human being but also in God. Otherwise the man Christ could not save anyone... But of this Person it is said that He can save. For the two natures are so united in His one person and essence that he who believes in the Son of man also believes in the Son of God. Whoever comes in touch with the man Christ also comes to touch with the Son of God. In fact the whole Trinity is found in this Man.[23]

Just as Christ stated that the Son of man must be lifted up, he now speaks of the Son of God who was delivered to be crucified. John 3:16: "For God so loved the world that He gave His only Son, that whoever believes in Him should not perish but have eternal life." It is love that prompts God to give his only Son. Earlier, Mary had given her Son, and now John says: "God the Father gave His Son to be crucified." God's Son and Mary's son are only one Son, thus one Person. "He appropriates both natures for the work of salvation and redemption from eternal death."[24]

---

22. LW 22.346 (WA 47.72).
23. LW 22.346 (WA 47.72).
24. LW 22.351 (WA 47.76).

The Nestorians alleged that only Mary's Son, not God's Son, died for us. This is contrary to what John said: "God gave His Son for the world." This Son is not only Mary's Son but also God's Son, and yet one Son (one Person). Not only the man Jesus but also the Son of God was crucified, for there is one indivisible Person. Therefore St. Paul said in 1 Corinthians 2:8: "If they had understood, they would not have crucified the King of glory." Suffering, proper only to the Son of man, since God cannot suffer, is now communicated to the Son of God, for there is one Son. Hence it is proper to say that God's Son was conceived by the Virgin Mary, suffered and died, was buried, descended into hell, and rose again from the dead. God gave his only Son into death for us and the Son of man died for us, and yet there are not two Sons, the one descending from the Father and the other born of Mary. There is only one Jesus. The attributes of both natures are predicated of the whole person of Christ "in the concrete,"[25] so that the attributes of the one nature are shared with the other. Each nature has its own peculiar character. This one Person, God and man, suffered, that is, the Son of God and of Mary was crucified. Thus mortality, which is exclusively of the human nature, is now attributed to the divinity via the communication of properties in the concrete. Thus we can say: "God became man, God suffered, and God died."[26]

25. LW 22.352 (WA 47.77).

26. Renowned Luther scholars concur that God in Christ suffers, not just his humanity. See Rittgers, *Reformation of Suffering*, 117: "in Christ God had willed for his deity to be united with human nature in such a way that the divine nature could be said to suffer"; Althaus, *Theology of Martin Luther*, 197: "Luther holds that the deity of Christ, because of the incarnation and of its personal unity with the humanity, enters into the uttermost depths of its suffering. God suffers in Christ ('deipassionism')"; Lienhard, *Luther*, 341: "Luther turns himself resolutely away from the Platonic image of a God who is immutable and impassible... God has truly suffered in Christ." Lohse, *Martin Luther's Theology*, 229–30, holds the same view, that the divinity of Christ is not evacuated from the cross; instead, it withdraws his power and hides in the humanity so that humanity is left alone to fight. McGrath, *Christian Theology*, 223: "Jesus suffered on the cross. Jesus is God. Therefore God suffered on the cross." Bayer, *Theology the Lutheran Way*, 236: "The Christological concept of the communication of attributes ... intends to say that the general attributes of the human being take part in the divine nature in the concrete person Jesus Christ and that the reverse is true as well: in Christ, the human being, God suffered, died, and was victorious over death; in Christ, who is God, the human nature has become omnipotent, omniscient, omnipotent." Likewise, Kolb states in *Martin Luther*, 117: "Within Christ's person, however, 'those things that are attributed to the human being may rightly be asserted with respect to God; and on the other hand, those things that are attributed to God may rightly be asserted with respect to the human being. So it is true to say: this human being created the world and this God has suffered, died, was buried, etc.'" For a contrary position, see Luy, *Dominus Mortis*, 119–62, where he argues that Luther did not commit to a two-way communication between the two natures, thus denying the divinity of Christ's sharing of suffering

Christ is Lord and Made Lord Over All: The Communication of Properties

How does one reconcile these two assertions: Christ is Lord over all and at the same time, a human being? According to his humanity, Christ is 1,539 years old, and is not eternal. This Man Christ suffered death on the cross, and if this is so, how can he possess all in his hands? If he is already God and owns all, how could God give him all? Since Christ is God, he possesses all that nothing more needs to be added unto him. If he has all, he must have possessed it prior to his incarnation. How could it be given to him who is God? This is to be explained according to the doctrine of the communication of properties: two natures dwell in the Lord Christ, and yet he is but one Person. Two natures retain their distinctive properties, and each also shares its properties with the other. For instance, mortality is peculiar to human nature; now that the humanity is united to the one person with the divine, suffering and death are predicated of the divine nature. Thus we can assert: "God became man, God suffered, and God died."[27]

Whenever Holy Scripture speaks of Christ as a human being, it does not exclude his deity. In Ps 110:1, we read: "Sit at My right hand." Ascension is exclusively of the human nature, which can now be applied to the divine nature, for the two natures are one. Christ began to sit at the right hand after his ascension. His humanity had not occupied this locus before ascension, but it does not follow from this that Christ had not formerly sat there as God, for he was there all the time. Thus Christ, true man, is now called Lord over all; for he is true God. This, Luther argues, is contrary to Arius: "If He is ascending into heaven now, it must follow that He was not there before."[28] He was in heaven before his descent to the earth; but then he was not yet a man. Since his incarnation the two natures are so united in one person that the divine nature communicates its properties to the human, and vice versa. Throughout the gospel, John teaches that Christ was born, was baptized, and has disciples, is a real human being; at the same time he confesses that all that is God's alone was given into his hands. The term "given to Him" is predicated of the human nature. Luther elaborated:

> Thus the two natures are united in one Person, and there are not two Christs. Therefore, when you hear it said that God gave all things into Christ's hands and that He raised Him from the dead, remember that this is spoken of Christ as man. Then

---

in his humanity.
27. LW 22.492 (WA 47.199).
28. LW 22.493 (WA 47.200).

again, when we hear the expression: "He is seated at the right hand of God the Father," bear in mind that the human nature is united with the divine. To be in heaven and to be on earth are one thing, just as to be crucified and to live are one thing. . . If you are perplexed by the statement that Christ died and that He is alive, you might find it still stranger to hear that Christ is God and man in one Person, that Christ died on the cross as a man, and that He nonetheless remains Christ in eternity.[29]

According to his deity, Christ possesses all, and does not receive anything; but God gave all to Christ inasmuch as God and man are one Person. Since the Son was man, what was God's was imparted to the man. "And now, since it is given to the man, it is simultaneously given to God. Whoever apprehends and worships this man, also worships God; for He is God in essence."[30] A proof of this is John 14:9: "He who beholds the Son also beholds the true God." The Person whom Thomas beholds declares: "I am the Way, the Truth and the Life" (John 14:6). These divine properties—the Way, the Truth, and the Life—which only Christ as God has, are now attributed to Christ as man, for the person is indivisibly one, fully divine and fully human. When John said in John 3:35: "The Father has given all things into His hands," he was referring to the incarnate Son; it is this Man to whom was given all things. To have all in his hands is equivalent of being God, for God "gives his glory to no other" (Isa 42:8). But here he gives all to the Son, born of Mary, so that he may possess everything in his hands. How so? Even before this Christ in his divinity already owns everything, and is Lord over all. Previously he had not been incarnated or descended in the flesh; but now, all things are given to the Son. Thus it is proper to assert that he who was crucified on the cross is Lord over all. Now that Christ is glorified, he receives "the dominion effected by the union of the two natures." Luther expands:

> Thus the human nature in Christ shares in the glory of all the properties which otherwise pertain to God. Since the human nature, which did not possess these properties formerly, now receives them, the text properly states that all things are given to Him. Therefore it is true and proper to say that the Son of God and of Mary was from eternity; that Christ, the Son of God and of Mary, is still Lord over all; and that Christ, the Son of God, received all from the Father. Outside this Man Christ, who was born of the Virgin Mary and who suffered, you must not seek

---

29. LW 22.493 (WA 47.201).
30. LW 22.492 (WA 47.201).

God or any salvation and help; for He is God Himself. . . Yet in this one God there are three Persons, one of whom is Christ, of whom we heard earlier that the whole fullness of deity dwells in Him (Col 2:9). "Of His fullness we all receive grace upon grace" (John 1:16). And "he who believes in the Son has eternal life" (John 3:36).[31]

From the very moment when God and man are united in one Person, Luther could speak of the transfer of divine power to Christ's human nature. Christ began to sit at the right hand of God after the ascension; his human nature had not been seated there before. He was glorified through the resurrection as Lord, that he might be also for us Lord over all things in heaven and earth.[32] This is borne out in his comment on John 3:13, where he declares that the descending of Christ while he still, with respect to his divine nature, resides forever at the right hand of God, pertains only to his human nature, but without asserting that his body had also been at the same time in heaven.

Proper Speech of Christ: According to Each Nature

Christ promises the disciples of his prayer, as he states in John 14:16: "And I will pray the Father." This again assures the disciples that they will not suffer lack; nor will they be forsaken. The ascended Christ is not inactive, sitting idly in heaven, but serves us as our dear Priest and Mediator. He will pray and implore the Father for them to give them the Holy Spirit, who will console, strengthen, and preserve them, that they may remain in his love and be able bear all trials with joy. The preceding statement, "Whatever you ask in My name, I will do," is an assertion of his identity as true God, who is able to give and do all things, for his nature demands it. Here the statement, "I will pray the Father," pertains to Christ who spoke here as the lowliest man on earth, as a servant amongst all people, although he is true God and Lord over all, and who is worthy of our worship. Thus it is not to be understood as the true God, petitioning someone else, for God cannot be subject to someone else and be obliged to him for things received. To gain the proper sense of the text, Luther prescribed this rule:

> You must look at the entire text, inclusive of the words that follow and those that precede. Then you will find that Christ speaks

---

31. LW 22.494 (WA 47.202).

32. Köstlin, *Theology of Luther*, vol. 2.385: "According to this, the exaltation of Christ in his ascension appears . . . to have been only a revelation of that which had been previously transferred to the human nature."

both as God and as man; this will be a powerful evidence, as we teach and believe, that Christ is both true man and true God. For how can one express in any words that He speaks as God and as man at the same time, since He has two distinct natures? If He were to speak as God at all times, one could not prove that He is also true man. And if He were to speak as true man at all times, one would never be aware that He is also true God.[33]

The same Person who said: "Whatever you ask, I will do it," also declares here: "I will pray the Father." These two statements combined make certain this article: that in this undivided Person there is neither purely deity nor purely humanity; but that both the divine and the human nature are inseparably united in one Person. Just as the nature of the Father and the Son remains unmingled, so also the Person of Christ remains undivided here. Since Christ is one God, fully God and fully man, it is appropriate to speak of him as each nature requires, with some words reflecting his human nature, and others his divine. Neither should we collapse the distinction between the two natures nor confuse what Christ says according to his human nature with what he says according to his divine nature. This is to be explained via the doctrine of the communication of attributes, for the sake of the personal union. This Luther elaborates:

> Therefore the attributes of each nature, the human and the divine, are ascribed to the entire Person: "This Man Christ, born of the Virgin, is omnipotent and does all that we ask—not, however, according to the human but according to the divine nature, not by reason of His birth from His mother but because He is God's Son." And again, "Christ, God's Son, prays the Father, not according to His divine nature and essence, according to which He is co-equal with the Father, but because He is true man and Mary's Son." Thus the words must be brought together and compared according to the unity of the Person. The nature must always be differentiated, but the Person must remain undivided.[34]

All that Scripture speaks of Christ is predicated of the whole Person, just as though both God and man are one essence. "Often it uses expressions interchangeably and assigns the attributes of both to each nature."[35] Thus Luther can assert: "The Man Christ is God's eternal Son, by whom all creatures were created, Lord of heaven and earth"; likewise, he can assert: "Christ, God's Son (that is, the Person who is true God), was conceived and

33. LW 24.104 (WA XLV.555).
34. LW 24.105 (WA XLV.536).
35. LW 24.106 (WA XLV.557).

born of Virgin Mary, suffered under Pontius Pilate, crucified and dead."[36] He does not do this according to his divine nature; but because this is done by one and the same Person, it is proper to say that God's Son is performing it. This is how St. Paul's statement in 1 Cor 2:8, "If they had understood this, they would not have crucified the Lord of glory," is to be understood: though this is truly spoken of the divine nature which was with the Father from eternity, but it is also said of the Person who is true man.[37] This is also the meaning of Christ's statement: "What if you were to see the Son of man ascending to where He was before?" (John 6:62)—it is truly said of the Person, whose divine nature is one with the Father, but it is also spoken of him who is true man.

By way of illustration, when a member of the body is injured, the whole person is wounded; when someone strikes a person on the head, we would say that the whole person is wounded, even though only his head is injured. This is in line with Chalcedonian Christology, in which the distinction of both natures and their properties are maintained in Christ. To comprehend this doctrine aright is to assign the functions of each nature to the one undivided Person. According to the divine nature, he was not born of a human, nor did he inherit anything from the Virgin. God is the Creator and a human being is a creature; but here the two have joined together in one Person, and now God and man are one Christ. Mary bore a Son, and the Jews crucified a Person who is God and man; if he were only a man, as other saints are—our salvation is at stake; for mere flesh and blood could not erase one sin nor extinguish one little drop of hell's fire with all his holiness, his

---

36. LW 24.106 (WA XLV.557).

37. LW 24.106 (WA XLV.557). Köstlin, *Theology of Luther*, Vol. 2, 382: "Nor does [Luther] only declare that the attributes of both natures are to be ascribed to the person, but he holds, also, that the attribute of one nature is ascribed to the other nature, that being attributed to the divine nature which belongs naturally to the human. He then, indeed, at once again substitutes the name of the person for 'the divine nature,' or, instead of the declaration that we are to ascribe attributes of the human nature, such as dying, to the divine nature, the simple statement: "The Son of God has died. The Church, he declares, believes that 'not only the human, but also the divine nature, or *the true God* suffered for us. And, in meeting the misunderstanding of this which would infer 'a mortal divinity,' he says more precisely: 'The person existing as God, or having a divine nature, is mortal' . . . Luther declared that he would object if it were thereby meant 'that divinity was separate, and suffered separately because it is also in the humanity.' He himself proposes, in order to avoid all misunderstanding, to express the doctrine as follows: 'That the person, consisting of a divine and a human nature, truly suffered.'" See also Pannenberg, *Systematic Theology*, 388–89: "On the cross the Son of God certainly died and not just the humanity that he assumed. Nevertheless, the Son suffered death in his human reality and not in respect of his deity"; and Fiddes, *Creative Suffering*, 29: "while God suffered in the incarnation he could not suffer in his eternal nature."

blood, and his death. Mary, the mother, does not just give birth to, suckle, and nourish only the man, but she carries and nourishes a son who is God's Son, because the Person is not divided. It is always one and the same Son of God, our Lord. Thus it is correct to call Mary "Mother of God."[38] This is contrary to the Nestorians, who refused to say that Mary had given birth to God's Son, and asserted that Mary is the Mother of Jesus, not of God. With the Creed, we confess: "I believe in Jesus Christ, God the Father's only Son, our Lord, born of the Virgin Mary, suffered, was crucified, died."

The angels in heaven worship him and call him Lord as he lies in the manger, as Luke 2:11 states: "To you is born this day . . . a Savior, who is Christ the Lord." Because Christ is worshipped as God, he must be true God. When we speak of Christ, we speak of him as the undivided Person, in whom both God and man dwell, who is worshipped by the angels. We find him not above in heaven but here below, lying in the manger and on his mother's lap. Luther concluded: "Wherever we encounter this Person, there we surely encounter the Divine Majesty."[39] This knowledge of Christ, who is true God and true man, is the basis of our consolation in all trials, and victory against all enemies of life:

> [All] this makes it possible for us to withstand the devil and to vanquish him in the hour of death and at other times when he terrifies us with sin and hell. For if he were to succeed to persuade me to regard Christ as only a man who was crucified and died for me, I would be lost. But if my pride and joy is the fact that Christ, both true God and true man, died for me, I find that this outweighs, eclipses all sin, death, hell, and all misery and woe. For I know that He who also is true God suffered and died for me, and also that this same true man rose from the dead, ascended into heaven, etc., then I can conclude with certainty that my sin was erased and death was conquered by Him, and that God no longer views me with anger and disfavor; for I see and hear nothing but tokens and works of mercy in this Person.[40]

Luther avers that the fathers contended fervidly that the two natures dwell in the Lord Christ, and he is but one Person, not two persons. Both natures retain their properties, and each communicates to the other.[41] This

---

38. For a discussion of Mary as the Mother of God, see Pelikan, *Companion Volume*, 79; Kelly, *Early Christian Doctrines*, 311ff.

39. LW 24.108 (WA XLV.558).

40. LW 24.108 (WA XLV.558).

41. LW 22.492 (WA 47.200). See note 176. This teaching emerged most succinctly in the controversy over the Lord's Supper, in which he had occasion to reflect on how the properties of each nature are ascribed to the other, so that it is correct to say that

is how Scripture teaches us to speak: Christ was crucified according to his humanity, and he created heaven and earth according to his divinity. Since this one Person is God and man, it is correct to assert that the Man Christ is the Creator, and God's Son was also crucified. Thus the Savior we have must be more than a saint or an angel; if otherwise, we would not receive help from him. Because Christ is God, the treasure we have not only outweighs and cancels sin and death but also grants eternal life. This is something mere humans cannot do, except this person who is the God-man *in toto* (wholly). The ascription of the properties of each nature of Christ to the person means the person is treated as carrying divine and human attributes at one and the same time, yet without confusing or commingling the two natures or a generation of a *tertium quid* (third). This same idea recurs in his comments on John 14. We shall cite a few quotations that show how the properties of each nature are attributed to the person of Christ:

> And now since He is believed as one Person, God and man, it is also proper for us to speak of him as each nature requires. Some words reflect his human, others His divine nature. Therefore we should consider what Christ says according to His human nature and what He says according to His divine nature. For where this is not observed and properly distinguished, many types of heresy must result, as happened in times gone by.[42]

> This is done for the sake of personal union, which we call "the communication of properties." Thus we can say: "Christ, God's son (that is, the Person, who is true God), was conceived and born of the Virgin Mary, suffered under Pontius Pilate, crucified and died." . . . He does not do this, of course, according to the divine nature. But since this is done by one and the same Person, it is correct to say that God's Son is doing it. Thus St. Paul declares in 1 Cor 2:8: "If they had understood it, they would not have crucified the Lord of glory."[43]

> Whatever this Person, Christ, says and does, is said and done by both, true God and true man, so that all the words and works must always be attributed to the whole Person and are not divided, as though He were not true God or not true man. But this

---

Jesus of Nazareth is the Son of God; thus Christ's humanity could be present in the Eucharist, just as his divinity, for the two are one.

42. LW 24.105 (WA XLV.556).
43. LW 24.106 (WA XLV.557).

must be done in such a way as to identify and recognize each nature properly.[44]

This chapter demonstrates that Luther uses the doctrine of the *communicatio idiomatum* in a traditional fashion, ascribing to the person in his concrete existence that which rightly belongs only to the one nature.[45] Accordingly Luther holds that God suffers in the person of his Son, not in his divine nature but according to his human nature. He believes that this teaching is yielded by the Scripture. Thus when he uses the phrase "according to his nature," he does not use it in a Nestorian sense, to deny that God's Son [the Person who is God] suffered. On the one hand Luther uses the phrase "according to his nature" in accordance with the early fathers, to assert that "each nature, of course, has its own peculiar character," on the other hand, however, he uses the phrase to indicate that there is a communion between the two natures since the Person of Christ cannot be divided. The peculiar property of suffering which rightly belongs to the human nature is predicated of the person who is true God; thus Luther asserts: "God suffers or dies." This is the way he approaches the doctrine of the communication of properties, according to which the proper properties of each nature are attributed, not to each other but to the person of Christ. The application of the communication of attributes is the point of Luther's soteriological focus of his Christology.[46] His Christology serves the proclamation of the mighty acts of God for the salvation of all people. The gospel deals with not God *per se*, who is an abstraction but God in the concrete, namely, God in the flesh, who is the only God we know; for outside of Christ there is no God. Thus the Son of God [the person] is impassible in the abstract, but passible only in the flesh of God.[47]

---

44. LW 24.106 (WA XLV.557).

45. Calvin also maintains that the communication is indeed real with respect to the person, designated by the deity or humanity. See his *Institutes*, II.xiv.2ff. See also Dorner, *History of Development*, 104: "In one word, he used the formula to denote a real mutual communication, not merely of attributes, but, with the attributes, of the substance of the natures. For example, application to the humanity of attributes which strictly and originally pertained to the deity alone, he considers to be justified, not on the ground that the two natures are in the one Ego, but that they are conjoined by the *Unio*; for the word 'Man' now includes the deity also, in that it has become 'another and a new word,' with a new signification."

46. Lienhard, *Luther*, 372.

47. Cf. Silcock, "Truth of Divine Impassibility," 205–6. Silcock argues that with the Patristic theologians, Luther affirms that the axiom of divine impassibility holds only in relation to the divine nature in itself, but not when we speak of God for us (*pro nobis*). Thus it is correct to say that God suffers, but only within the context of the gospel which speaks of God's action in the economy of salvation. Hence the paradox of the suffering

The homiletical function of these sermons is not to argue whether God suffers or cannot suffer, but to inculcate the salvific purpose of incarnation. These sermons bring into focus that the God of the Bible is not the God of the philosophers, but the God who lives, suffers, and dies in the flesh. This is indeed God's way of being for us (*pro nobis*), that is, in the efficacious activities of the suffering and dying of the Son on the cross. This too befits Luther's theology of the cross, in which God is most himself in his opposites: not in majesty but in humility, not in glory but in lowliness, not in power but in weakness.

---

of the impassible God lies at the heart of Luther's soteriological Christology.

CHAPTER 12

Bind to Christ's Mouth
No Other Intercessor than Christ

Luther preached on John 17 in 1528/1530, and had catechesis as his orientation. He expressed considerable fondness for this chapter: "It is a beautiful address, a chapter and prayer the like of which Scripture contains none other, for there is no other such person and intercessor, for it is the prayer of our Savior and Head, for our comfort and the Christian faith."[1] Not only did Christ teach us to bind ourselves to his mouth, from which we receive many words of great beauty and sweet comfort, but he also offers us a compact summary of the heart of the Christian faith: "I know of no other [chapter] that treats this chief article of all Christian doctrine so richly, all gathered together in one place, and sets it forth in such powerful words, to wit, that in Christ we have all we need and not in ourselves or in any other human beings."[2] Christ's prayer revolves around the three unities that Christ has been teaching. The Father and the Son are so thoroughly agreed in being, will, word, knowledge, glory, and love that his prayers will surely come to pass. God and man are not separated but so united in Christ that he wills to draw us up through this lowly Man to the Father, not through speculation about God in his majesty, or through secret private revelations without means, or through works or merits of ours. Through union with Christ, which the Word creates through faith, we are given a participation in the Son's essential unity with the Father, and together with this, we are made partakers of all divine blessings and salvation. Those whom the Father gives

1. See LW 69.119, n. 468 as quoted in Introduction to John 17.
2. LW 69.107 (WA 28.185).

the Son will find themselves on the lap of his Savior, enjoying the comfort of being included in Christ's prayer. Believers will behold the matchless, divine glory the Father has given his beloved Son, set forth constantly in Word and revelation, which we apprehend by faith in part, but in yonder life in full, without any concealment. Those who cling to Christ's mouth will reap the power of Christ's priestly prayers, that the God who seizes us in Christ will sustain and strengthen us in this pure knowledge and unity of faith until the day of his glorious coming.

The Pattern of Prayer: Three-fold Glorification

Following Cyril of Alexandria,[3] the virtue of this prayer, for Luther, lies in three distinct parts: we must begin to offer up thanks, praising God and recounting the benefits derived from him, just as Christ here indicates what the Father has bestowed upon him: "Dear Father, you have given us Your precious, gracious, holy Gospel and showered indescribable graces upon us,"[4] and so on. Second, the petitions and our need are laid bare: "Dear Father, help us also to retain it and to remain steadfast in it."[5] And third, we should hurry with it into the world, and pray that everyone should be saved.

Christ's prayer evinces a trinitarian doctrine of glorification in which the Father is glorified in the Son, whose glory is communicated to our hearts in the efficacy of the Holy Spirit.[6] To glorify means "to praise and exalt, to magnify and make known."[7] To glorify the Father, then, means nothing else than that we acknowledge him and know who he is, what his dispositions are and how we stand with him. And this knowledge is found nowhere else but only in and through Christ. There abides a proper order in which the Father cannot be glorified unless glorification happens to Christ first. Then the Holy Spirit must come and preach the gospel, without which no one knows the Father, who is revealed in the Son. This underscores the doctrine of grace alone (*sola gratiae*): "Christ himself does not want to be praised except by the Father and wants to praise Him in return, so that the people may forsake themselves and boast solely of His grace and goodness."[8]

---

3. Cyril of Alexandria, *Commentary on John* 11.3 [17:1], as cited in LW 69.20, n.30.
4. LW 69.15 (WA 28.73).
5. LW 69.15 (WA 28.73).
6. LW 69.23 (WA 28.83).
7. LW 69.21 (WA 28.79).
8. LW 69.24 (WA 28.83).

Christ began with thanking God and acknowledging what the Father has granted him. With a heavy heart, he spoke these words in John 17:1: "Father, the hour has come for you to glorify your Son that your Son might glorify you." He simply prays: "Dear Father, I pray, glorify Me." Then he gives the reason: "that I may glorify you." Abiding in the words "Your Son" is "a bit of thanksgiving,"[9] namely, he confesses and boasts of his identity as the Son of God who has received everything from the Father. "The time is coming," indicates the horrid circumstances, in which he was to suffer and die the most shameful of deaths, cursed and cast out of this world as the worst of devils. The Son of God manifests himself incarnately in the opposite of who he is eternally: "From eternity He is His Son in one majesty, might, and glory; but now He is in the world, in misery, weakness, shame, and death, as if forsaken by the Father and by everyone."[10] Christ has completed the redemptive purpose for which he was sent or given, namely, to extol and gloriously proclaim the Father's honor and glory. Thus verse 4: "I glorified you on earth and accomplished the work that you gave me to do." For our sake Christ assumes upon himself all shame and disgrace, suffering and death, to the glory of the Father, so that we might be redeemed and have eternal life. This includes abandoning all his own honor and glory for the sake of the Father's praise. After having completed this work, he prays the Father would not allow him to be shrouded in darkness but would deliver him out of shame and death and bring him to honor and into light, that is, crown him Lord and King over all creatures. "In sum, the two are intertwined and interlocked—the glory of the Father and that of Christ—so that by glorifying Christ, the Father glorifies Himself, and when Christ is glorified, He thus glorifies the Father. And there is one undivided glorification of both, so that the Son must be glorified by the Father, and the Father in and through the Son."[11]

Next comes the third glorification, for which he had originally prayed: that he might further glorify the Father throughout the world in his Christians so that his glory might shine brighter than before he died. Luther sums up: "See how all three follow upon one another: first, that by His life He glorifies the Father yet comes to ruin because of His glorious preaching, so that the Father must again glorify Him, so that He, too, might extend His glory further and make it still more glorious through His kingdom and Gospel."[12] As Christ our Head now prays that he would glorify himself in

9. LW 69.22 (WA 28.81).
10. LW 69.23 (WA 28.81).
11. LW 69.46 (WA 28.109).
12. LW 69.46 (WA 28.108).

us. Of verse 2: "Just as you have given Him authority over all flesh, to give eternal life to all whom you have given Him," Christ continues with the second and third part of his prayer. His chief purpose of prayer is not that he might retain glory for himself but his glory would be extended and serve us for the attainment of eternal life. Such prayer produces in us comfort and confidence in the face of all adversaries that we who believe in Christ and cling to his Word are the very ones whom the Father has given him.

Luther's concept of prayer includes not only asking God to help but also committing the one praying to act as the Holy Spirit moves him. For his sake, we glorify him and praise him by our doctrine and life, and as a result we incur shame, condemnation, cursing, and death. Just as Christ has suffered and died, passing through shame and disgrace to arrive at eternal glory, so also Christians shall pass through the same experiences to everlasting glory and honor. Thus Christ prays to be glorified not for his own person alone but for our sake, to strengthen our faith against the great offense that the gospel encounters. He prays to be glorified in and through all who will believe in him that the Father be magnified, who through this prayer continually displays in Christians the same power he did in Christ (Eph 1:19–20). As proof of the triumph of the gospel, Luther cited John Huss,[13] a historic antecedent who was condemned and killed in a most shameful way. Despite his martyrdom, the Word of God he preached prevails and shines in the whole world and puts his foes to shame with all its glory. This prayer is effective with God, as the gospel advances unhindered against the world's raging and attacks. Just as the glorification began, so it continues forever within Christendom by the efficacious power of this prayer.

Arianism Repudiated: Know Christ, whom the Father Sent

By his very own confession that he possesses the authority to bestow eternal life to his own and yet has received this from the Father, Christ clearly indicates that he is of one essence and power with the Father, though they are two distinct persons. He clarifies further in verse 3: "And this is eternal life, that they may know you, who alone are the true God, and Jesus Christ whom you have sent." Historically this was the text Arius used to assert that Christ was the highest creature and not true God. Athanasius pressed this passage against the heresy of the Arians and adduced "our highest, most excellent article of faith, yes, the foundation and rock upon which all other

---

13. See Haberkern, *Patron Saint and Prophet*.

articles must rest."¹⁴ The Arians interpret the word "alone" as an exclusive reference to the Father's divinity. Though they truly and correctly taught that there is no other God than the Father alone, they refuse to accept the consequence, that Christ makes himself co-equal with the Father in every respect and speaks as one who is also the same true God. The word "alone" is used not to divide the persons, saying that the one is God [Father], and the other is not [Jesus], but only one God who sent Christ. Christ locates eternal life in the knowledge of himself and of the Father alike. Stressing "You, who alone are the true God," reveals Jesus' custom to give glory to the Father, who has given him all, and so through himself to draw us to the Father. Those who shun Jesus Christ cannot know the Father.

The whole of the Christian life consists in knowing this man well, the one sent by the Father. This is "Christian knowledge and doctrine. Whatever else can be taught outside or alongside this should not be regarded as Christian knowledge."¹⁵ It is imperative that a true theologian occupies himself with this knowledge, "the sole subject"¹⁶ of all study and thought as prescribed by Christ. Luther emphasized: "Do not look for something different and better."¹⁷ No knowledge of God as the Creator, no observance of the Ten Commandments, and no human accretions could confer eternal life; nothing but Christ can make a Christian out of us. What Christ says here: "that they know You, who alone are the true God, and Jesus Christ whom You have sent" has no other content than this: that "there is no other way, method, or means than by knowing the Father, the only true God, through His Son, whom He has sent."¹⁸ The word "knowing" does not refer to human agency or any works humans perform to achieve righteous standing before God. Earthly righteousness lies within the grasp of human capability; it cannot produce nor procure eternal life. But the heavenly and divine righteousness lies outside us, and comes from knowing. "Therefore salvation lies in knowledge,"¹⁹ which we receive by faith.

> In sum, knowledge is not a work but precedes all works. For works follow after and out of knowledge. Or, again, works are defined as what we do. But knowledge is what we receive and take in. This one word "know," then, like a mighty thunderclap,

---

14. See LW 69.30 (WA 28.90), note 73. In the Latin West, Hilary and Ambrose opposed Arian teaching.

15. LW 69.35 (WA 28.96).
16. LW 69.35 (WA 28.96).
17. LW 69.35 (WA 28.96).
18. LW 69.35 (WA 28.96).
19. LW 69.39, note 122.

strikes down all doctrine based on human work, spiritual orders, and worship, as if by these means one could be freed from sins, become reconciled to God, and obtain grace.[20]

His words "whom You have sent" is where he directs us, and by which he accomplishes everything in us. In carrying out the command of the Father who sent him, Christ descended from heaven into our flesh; he assumed the sin of the world upon himself and died for it to "propitiate the Father's wrath."[21] Through himself in his own person he overcomes death and devil and reconciles us with the Father. Being sent by God thus is not insignificant and futile; it is accompanied by such "a significant mandate and task, so necessary and great,"[22] that no angel or saint can establish an eternal relationship between God and us except by the only Son. The real treasure is hidden altogether in the word "sent": "the mind, heart, and will of the Father toward us and . . . all that Christ did, preached, suffered, accomplished, and brought or gave" are revealed.[23] By the knowledge that Christ was sent by the Father for our sake, we rest assured that God is our gracious and kind Father, who has banished his wrath entirely out of mind. And this knowledge is of such great efficacy that it dissipates every force that assails us, and that it impels us to draw nigh to God without fear.

Verse 5: "And now, Father, glorify Me in your own presence with the glory that I had with you before the world existed" highlights again Christ's deity. Luther paraphrases: "Glorify Me, dear Father, I who am Your only Son from all eternity, equal God with You, in one essence and glory."[24] The way in which he arranges in prayer shows how he wants to be glorified, namely, that he is the one who shares the same glory with his Father from eternity. "He is true God, the Father's Son by nature."[25] Unlike the earthly king whose majesty is among and with his subjects, since it cannot be anywhere else, Christ's glory is entirely in God, outside of all creatures. These two words "with You" encompass both unity of nature and the distinction of persons within the Godhead. The glory Christ had was with his Father who is from eternity, not among or with creatures in time. Luther paraphrases Jesus' prayer: "Dear Father, I have now done My task in the world, for which you sent Me. Now, for the sake of your glory, I go to humiliation; I must allow Myself to be oppressed and condemned as the most wretched man

20. LW 69.39 (WA 28.100).
21. LW 69.36 (WA 28.98).
22. LW 69.36–37 (WA 28.98).
23. LW 69.36–37 (WA 28.98).
24. LW 69.46 (WA 28.110).
25. LW 69.46 (WA 28.110).

the world has ever borne. Therefore, glorify Me again, so that the world will have to hear and acknowledge that I am Your Son from eternity."[26] Of itself, no human heart could believe that the crucified Christ, the lowliest of all people, is the true almighty God, except by revelation. The prayer is heard and fulfilled, so that Christ is honored as true man, born of the Virgin, and also the true Son of God, whose glory is identical with the Father from eternity. He now has revealed the Father through the gospel and drawn people to knowledge of him, as indicated by the following verse: "I have revealed Your name to the people whom You gave Me from the world" (v.6). Christ is the revelation of the Father, "the name" of the one who sent him; he does this by proclaiming him as a gracious Father, who has entered us into his favor and forgives all sins, delivers us from death and the devil, helps and sustains us through every trial. This is not out of any work or merit we achieve, but out of pure, boundless goodness, through Christ, his dear Son. The Father is "the proper name,"[27] by which he is to be known, and in which his heart, will, and work is comprehended. The wicked trick of the devil is to dissolve Christ's flesh, tearing it from the Godhead as useless, thus separating the single indivisible person of Christ into two persons. He inspires us to draw a line of demarcation between God and Christ so that we think in two different ways of seeking God: Christ on the cross and God high above in heaven. A theologian of glory tears asunder the person—God and man; he bypasses Christ's humanity and gapes into the naked God, the image of wrath, and thus is totally incapable of healing this affliction. A theologian of the cross seeks God not in the bare Majesty which terrifies us, but in his concrete unity of God and man, beginning from below, that is, from Christ as man, the image of grace.

> On the cross or in the bosom of His mother, one sees nothing but a man in whom there is no anger or terror but sheer kindness and heartfelt love to help us. But if you abandon this sight and climb up into the Majesty, then you must stumble, be terrified, and fall back, because you turn your back on the sight of grace and gape at the bare majesty, which is too high and hard for you. For outside of Christ, nature cannot see any grace or love in God nor obtain them, since apart from Him there is nothing but sheer wrath and damnation.[28]

God refuses to be found in any other way, except in the place where he has intended, namely, in the baby on the Virgin's lap and on the cross, and

---

26. LW 69.48 (WA 28.112).
27. LW 69.49 (WA 28.113).
28. LW 69.52 (WA 28.116).

wherever Christ reveals himself in the Word. The devil is "the world's master and god,"[29] who climbs so high that he seeks to be honored in majesty in the place of God (Isa 14:12–14). On the contrary, the omnipotent God hides in the lowliest of forms, as in the lap of the Virgin, and in the suffering of the cross, a place where the devil cannot follow, for he is a proud, vainglorious spirit. "Therefore, no one can deceive him any better than by binding himself to the stake to which God nailed [Christ]."[30] If we allow the devil to lay hold on us anywhere else than the lowly man (Christ), we are lost; he will tear us away, as a hawk does a chick that has strayed beyond the hen's wings. We must "remain with the man and know that it is God who is speaking, doing, and giving all things through Him so that both God's Word and His work are to be sought in Christ. And Christ is disposed towards you and deals with you—promises, invites, comforts, sustains, gives—all this the Father does."[31] God is so buried and hidden deeply in the poor "crucified God,"[32] bearing and suffering the judgment of sin, eventually dying on the cross. There our faith and salvation stand immovably certain, for we are the ones for whom Christ dies and prays.

Being Included in Christ's Prayer

Conscience cannot remove the oppressive, bitter, and horrifying thoughts about God; it cannot help but feel that God is the enemy of sinners, and there is no help unless Christ must come with power. When afflicted with high temptations concerning predestination, the terrified, poor souls should simply look to the mouth of Christ and be assuredly the ones given to Christ by the Father. Those who are given to him God will uphold and preserve, as he says in John 6:39: "This is the will of the Father who sent Me, that I should lose nothing of all that He has given Me." He later reaffirmed in John 17: 6: "Yours they were, and You gave them to Me;" in verse 9: "I am praying for them . . . for they are yours;" and in 12: "Those whom You have given Me I have guarded and not one of them has been lost except the son of perdition." They are surely God's elect, chosen from the beginning; otherwise, they would not have opened their hearts and received this revelation. Christ lumps together his own words with the Father's: "They have kept Your Word." The words Christ speaks are his, thus "My Word" is appropriate.

29. LW 69.68 (WA 28.136).
30. LW 69.68 (WA 28.136).
31. LW 69.67 (WA 28.135).
32. LW 69.67 (WA 28.135). The "crucified God" is a reference to the Son who was crucified.

Instead he puts "Your Word," by which Christ intends to attribute his words to the Father, thereby drawing himself entirely into the Father. Since he is making both into one loaf, they are hearing Christ's word, yet not his but the heavenly Father's. Those who "have kept Your Word" are children of the Father and the Son, who are one God. We need not fear any wrath, but know for certain that we are his own elect child, sitting on his lap and having everything that the Father has given Christ. We depend on Christ's mouth alone, out of which flows the Word of the Father, by which we cast aside all human thoughts, raise up the fearful conscience, and lighten the burdened hearts. So Christ's prayer will surely be heard, not only because he has merited it by the act of self-humiliation, completing what the Father has sent him to do, but also because both the Father and Son are so thoroughly agreed, as is borne out in verse 10: "All mine are yours, and yours are mine," that what Christ is praying for will certainly come about. Those for whom Christ prays will certainly be preserved against the devil's fiery attacks, as well as against sin and every temptation. It would not have been significant if Christ had merely claimed: "All that is Mine is Yours." For anyone can say that whatever he has comes from God. But a greater significance lies in the next confession: "All that is Yours is Mine." No creature can claim this before God, unless he is one essence with the Father. This text, Luther avers, speaks not only of what the Father has given him on earth but also of his consubstantiality with his Father. "For He is not speaking solely of His disciples and Christians (whom the Father gave him), but lumps together everything that is the Father's: an eternal, almighty essence, life, truth, righteousness, etc."[33] Those whom the Father gave him are those to whom the Father's name is revealed. The elect child is the Son's, as much as the Father's, for they are one. Thus to be included in Christ's prayer is to be received into the Father's kingdom, from which we harvest "an almighty, divine, invincible power and an eternal treasure of grace and salvation."[34]

After having prayed that his Father would glorify him, and having recounted at length how he had glorified the Father among his own by his oral word and revelation, he now commends the believers to the Father as those in whom he must be glorified, so that he would keep them steadfast in the world with the Word they receive. He says: "I am glorified in them" (v. 10), that is, through faith and confession: "Now they know that everything that You have given Me is from you. For I have given them the words that you gave Me. And they have received them and have come to know in truth that I went out from You, and they believe that You sent Me" (vv. 7–8, 10).

33. LW 69.66 (WA 28.135).
34. LW 69.106 (WA 28.185).

All this occurs through the Word that declares that Christ was sent by the Father and possesses all that is the Father's. Not by reason but by revelation we hold firmly that he is God's Son, eternal and true God, Lord over the tyrants of life: the world, devil, sin, and death. And whoever has him has the Father and all grace, divine goods, truth, eternal life, and righteousness, even though the world sees nothing but a miserable, poor, forsaken man, utterly despised and most disgracefully hung on the cross. This is a source of great comfort that Christ boasts of us before the Father, how he is glorified in us.

Christ prays for his disciples: first, because they belong to the Father, whom he has given to Christ. They have come out of the world into the Father's kingdom and possession. Second, Christ is glorified in them, causing them to praise and confess Christ as the one in whom the Father is glorified. Now he adds the third reason: "and I am no longer in the world, but they are in the world, and I am coming to You" (v. 11). "No longer in the world" does not mean being separated from his creation that he no longer can be found. The fanatics taught that Christ has ascended and is seated in heaven above, as if he is circumscribed in one place at a time, and cannot at the same time be anywhere else. So they conclude, according to the physical eye and sight, that Christ cannot be present everywhere with his body and blood in the sacrament. But Scripture furnishes a different meaning of the words "in the world"—it refers to an "outward existence, perceptible to the senses, that is, in this life that the world uses and lives, called a natural life, in which one must eat, drink, sleep, work, and have house and property."[35] Christ speaks as one who is "cut off from the land of the living" (Isa 53:8), no longer living this life but an altogether different life, which is meant by his "going to the Father." Otherwise the following words do not stand: "I am coming to You." The Father is everywhere, in and outside the heaven and earth and all creatures; he cannot be confined to any particular place, as the stars are fixed in the heavens. He is with us wherever we call upon him: in prison, in fire, and all afflictions. If Christ is going to the Father, he must be everywhere the Father is.

Here he expresses the content of his prayer: "Holy Father, keep them in Your name." Verse 12 says: "While I was with them, I kept them in Your name." Since he is going away from them and leaving them alone in the world, he prays that the Father would preserve them just as he did while he was with them. With a vehement ardor of a burning heart, he cries, "Holy Father." With this word "holy," he sets the Father apart from the opposite— all wickedness in which the world participates, yet under the guise of the

---

35. LW 69.72 (WA 28.141).

greatest holiness. He prays that the Father might separate his little flock from all this, and that they will be kept under "Your name." Christ prays for the Father to preserve "the ones You have given Me," and to enable them to keep the Word pure and unadulterated in their hearts.

On the contrary, it is terrifying when Christ says, "I do not pray for the world." The inevitable consequence of being excluded by his prayer is death and hell. This seems to contradict what he taught in Matthew 5:44, that we are to pray for our enemies, for the persecutors and blasphemers. Here Luther proposes that "to pray for the world and not to pray for the world must both be proper and good."[36] The difference lies in this: he does not pray for the world in the same manner nor in the same measure that he prays for his own. This is borne out in verse 20: "I do not ask for these only, but also for those who will believe in Me through their Word." For Christians he prays that they would abide, increase, and continue in true faith, and not apostatize; for the not yet believers, he prays that they would depart from their ways and come to faith. The world in its present condition is at enmity with God; he in no way wants prayers to be uttered as if God would sanction wicked conduct, allowing evil to persist and triumph. Rather he prays the opposite, that God would restrain their wickedness, thwart the sinister plans, and reduce them to nothing. This sort of prayer is not so much against the person as it is against the kind of life that is in opposition to God's Word, which hinders them from conversion. When Christ prays for his own, he does not pray only for their person but for their office and entire estate. Both are so intrinsically linked that "for however and wherever the estate fares and endures, so must their person also fare and endure."[37] With respect to the person, we ought to pray for everyone and make intercession for all without distinction, both enemy and friend, praying that those who are our enemies might enter divine favor and become our friend. But if they are not, then we should pray that their cause would fail and that the person should go to ruin rather than the gospel and kingdom of Christ. The purpose of Jesus' prayer is that truth should triumph and lies be brought to shame; the gospel be praised; and the persecutors of the Word perish. The enemies of the gospel are not those for whom Christ prays, for they are not "Yours" [Father's]. "For they are excluded by this prayer, this is what will strike and overthrow them—provided that our Lord Christ remains their superior in heaven."[38] Therefore their actions and plans will perish, and they along with it, no matter how firmly they are established at present. The elect

---

36. LW 69.62 (WA 28.130).
37. LW 69.63 (WA 28.130).
38. LW 69.63–64 (WA 28.130–31).

are given the treasure, which is Christ in his Word. Whoever perseveres in this treasure, takes thought for it, and prays for it is assured of the comfort derived through Christ's prayers that he will remain steadfast in it, and nothing can undo it.

"That They May Be One"

Those who obey his Word will face persecution, and be scattered and snatched away. Having foreseen this peril, Christ prays: "That they may be one, even as We are one" (v. 21). These words "that they may be one, [even as we are One]" have become an ammunition for Arians to deny the deity of Christ, and reinforce their falsehood. They concede that the Father and the Son are not of one essence, since among ourselves we cannot be of one essence. For each one has his own nature, that is, a body and soul, for himself. Therefore, they said the phrase "be one" means nothing else than to be of one and the same mind, as we are, not of one nature. Against this, Christ does not concede that the Father and the Son are "of one will or understanding," but "that they may be one substance."[39] He uses himself and the Father as a likeness to explain the kind of unity that the people of God must have. Just as the body is and is called "one substance," so all Christians are one body, not only because they possess similar or same thoughts, but much more they possess the same essence. But the unity of essence between a member and the body is a much sublime and greater kind than between your thoughts and those of others. Christians are so attached to each other that they are and remain altogether one indivisible substance, just as the Father and the Son are one (v. 22). He repeats it in verses 22–23: "And I have given them the glory that You have given Me, that they may be one even as We are one. I in them and You in Me." Christ speaks of "this matchless glory,"[40] whereby we become one substance with Christ and through him with the Father in such a way, that just as Christ is never severed from the Father, so all Christians are never separated from him. "This is the extraordinary, precious treasure and well-spring—yes, the true rich mine of all divine blessings, life, comfort, and salvation for whoever can but believe it."[41] By faith, believers are drawn into the unbreakable unity with Christ and the Father, to partake of God's invincible power and eternal blessings.

The unity, that we are members of one single body, is not acquired or merited by our works and worthiness but through the Word that he has

39. LW 69.76 (WA 28.148).
40. LW 69.108 (WA 28.187).
41. LW 69.108 (WA 28.187).

given us. With this, we are given the privilege that whatever affects one member affects the whole body, something that does not occur in the case of similarity. Through this unity, Christendom is called the communion of saints (*communio sanctorum*), that all saints are one lump.[42] In this external life and government, where there are different offices and estates, each performs his distinctive function and lives his own life. But through the Word, all distinctions collapse into one in a single faith, and through this faith everything becomes one loaf and spiritual body, even though the works of the individual members vary. It is the nature of such unity that each shares life and feeling with the rest; the work of each member serves all the members and the entire body together. "That is how it is here. Faith holds and binds works together and makes them one, because all hearts together cling to one Christ and Father, and all their work and life flows and proceeds from this unity of faith."[43] The communion of saints is most active when the Christian is at his weakest. When facing the devil's temptation and the world's assaults, Christians may find support in the fellowship and faith of the church. All Christendom on earth, and all the angels in heaven together with Christ and the Father are joined in upholding and bearing their sufferings. When the devil attacks the lowliest members, immediately the whole body aches and is roused, so that he knows that he is not suffering alone, and that the whole body feels it. Christ, our Head, also hears and feels it in the same way, as though his whole person suffers together with the wounded member. This is verified in the story of St. Paul. When Saul was persecuting the church, Jesus did not say: "Why are you crushing My toes or persecuting my poor flock?" Instead he asks, "Saul, Saul, why are you persecuting Me?" (Acts 9:5; 25:12). For our Head, Christ, feels it first; for it is from the head that the body's power to feel and to sense issues and derives.[44]

Christ's Word is the power of the unity of the Christians; nothing on earth is so great that it could outdo the communion of the saints in Christ's prayer. The Word holds us together, so that we as one body remain under one Head and cling to him alone, seeking no other holiness as efficacious before God except only what is found in Christ. God's innumerable treasures are hidden in this communion, for this is the body to which God has given himself, together with all his gifts. This is revealed to the eyes of faith:

> In sum, she is a powerful lady and an empress in heaven and earth, at whose feet the devil and the world, death and hell must fall when she speaks a word. For who will hurt or harm a person

---

42. LW 69.78 (WA 28.149).
43. LW 69.109 (WA 28.188).
44. LW 69.79 (WA 28.150).

who has such an assurance, knowing that when he sustains the smallest hurt, both heaven and earth, all angels and saints will cry out. If a sin assails him and wants to terrify, gnaw, and oppress his conscience, threatening him with devil, death, and hell, God says together with the wide assembly: "Dear sin, I tell you, do not gnaw him; death, do not slay; hell, do not devour!" But here faith is required, since in the eyes of the world and of reason everything seems to be much otherwise—indeed, the very opposite.[45]

External Means: Preservation and Sanctification

"And now I am speaking these things in the world" means Christ is leaving them these enduring words as an external means of comfort: that "they may have My joy made full in themselves" (v. 14). He wants to point them to another definite place where he could preserve them much better, that is, with the Father, since he himself is going there so that he might inaugurate his kingdom and to be able to be with them everywhere, even though he is departing from this visible, worldly existence. He commends them to the Father, so that through the Holy Spirit and divine power the Father might strengthen and keep them. The end of Christ's prayer is that "His joy may be full in themselves." Joy, a lasting kind, is derived from his Word, in which we take comfort in his most precious promise to us: that Christ and the Father will be with us and protect us, and nothing of this world will harm us. And yet the Word Christ offers is the "Father's Word," as stressed again in verse 14: "I have given Your Word." The Word is the only precious gift, and the greatest treasure Christ has brought from heaven so that after his death they will be able to confess that they have the Word of my Lord Christ, which is the Word of the almighty, heavenly Father. It is given for their joy and comfort against all afflictions, and if they cling to it, they will know they are held in the grip of God's almighty hand and fatherly protection, from which no one can tear them away. They are "not of the world, just as Christ is not of the world, (v. 14). By that, Christ does not ask that they might depart the world along with him (v. 15), but that he has still more to accomplish through them. They are to extend his Word and bring those who will believe in him through it (v. 20). Then Christ repeats "one little Word": "They are not of the world" (v.16), to engender our faith that we are the Father's inheritance, not of the world. The world has no power over us; his Word preserves us from evil. For the sake of the Word we must endure

---

45. LW 69.105 (WA 28.182).

all manner of hardship; but for the sake of the little flock we remain in the world of conflict and battle, and faithfully proclaim the Word, so that it may not be entirely lost, and the devil cannot win. That which keeps us from evil and enables us to endure against so many abominable blasphemies without despair is nothing but the efficacy of Christ's mouth:

> It is surely not human might or wisdom. But here stands one little Word that accomplishes it. Above all there sits One who remembers this prayer and says, "My Christ once prayed for them. Therefore they shall be protected and preserved." This is our comfort, our bulwark and defense—that they [enemies] cannot do to us what they desire, even though they swell to bursting with malice and anger until they wear themselves out persecuting and pursuing us, and God will snatch us out of their teeth and they shall come to ruin.[46]

The way to preservation is not by running into the wilderness or the cloister; rather he says in verse 17: "Sanctify them in Your truth. Your Word is truth." This means preserving them by the Word which is truth; preserving them so that they remain holy in his Word. The world is striving after great holiness; false teachers erect their own holiness. Christ prays that the Father will protect them from such specious and hypocritical holiness so that their "genuine, pure, true holiness,"[47] a product of abiding in his Word, might shine. "For that is the art: to attain this aright without being deceived by the appearance of holiness."[48] For Luther, it is not fasting, ascetic life, special exercises, and great suffering or any human accretions, but the Word, "the touchstone,"[49] that begets real holiness. So "whatever is not the Word or not contained in the Word is not holy but is undoubtedly false and deceptive."[50] Looking only to Christ's mouth is the same as to looking to the Father's truth, by which believers are sanctified. Where there is genuine faith, there is true humility. And then comes true patience and love toward the neighbors, so that he becomes a little Christ to them. The believer knows that true holiness springs from a true faith in Christ's words, by which God continues to strengthen and increase it. From this, then, all good fruits proceed and daily increase. And yet this is not our doing but God's.

Christ points to himself as the source of our holiness, as in verse 19: "I sanctify Myself for them." He will sanctify them through the Word, the

---

46. LW 69.89 (WA 28.163).
47. LW 69.91 (WA 28.165).
48. LW 69.91 (WA 28.166).
49. LW 69.91 (WA 28.166).
50. LW 69.91 (WA 28.166).

agent of sanctification. The content of proclamation cannot be the Ten Commandments, for they cannot bestow true holiness before God. They reveal our inability to keep what they demand of us. They cannot purify the heart, though the works are outwardly accomplished, of which even hypocrites and scoundrels are capable. But Christ's answer is this: "This is the preaching through which they must become holy: I sanctify Myself for them, etc."[51] Not our works and merit, but rather Christ's works and gifts make us holy. Of this, Christ says: "I sanctify myself for them." The phrase "sanctify Myself" is not a negation of his holiness, for it is intrinsic to his person. He does not need to become holy; he was holy in his mother's womb: "What is born in you will be called holy" (Luke 1:35). "To sanctify" is a reference to his priestly office which he is to exercise.[52] Christ needs nothing at all for himself, since he is already holy; he exercises his priestly work in order "that they also may be sanctified in the truth" (v. 19). Christ, our Priest, intervenes in our stead to offer himself on the cross to God the Father to achieve reconciliation with God and make us truly holy. All forms of worship and all boast of holiness are repudiated, because they lack the power to glorify the Father, to bring anyone to the knowledge of grace and to achieve righteousness before God. There are no other means of achieving true holiness save Christ's own sanctification.

> Christ is our Priest, and steps forward Himself in our stead to offer Himself on the cross to God the Father, so that through such an offering and death we are reconciled with God and made holy as well. This is our chief article and the fount of all consolation and the treasure of all Christian knowledge. He must bring all this to bear in this passage, for since He is speaking of the Word and truth whereby we become holy, He cannot remain silent about the means by which we attain all this, namely, that it is He Himself who has merited or obtained it for us and who gives it to us. Whoever apprehends and believes this Word is truly and genuinely holy.[53]

Where Christ is acknowledged as our sanctification, there is the holiest estate of life on earth. "Christ alone is our holiness, and through this capital holiness everything that we have, live, and do is called 'holy,' since the person is holy."[54] Not because we are without sin that we are called holy; nor do we become holy through good deeds. The truth lies in the opposite, that in

---

51. LW 69.98 (WA 28.173).
52. LW 69.98 (WA 28.174).
53. LW 69.98–99 (WA 28.175).
54. LW 69.100 (WA 28.176).

us there is nothing but sin and damnation; but in Christ there is nothing but sheer holiness and forgiveness. We become holy through an alien holiness, that of Christ the Lord, which through faith is bestowed on us and becomes our own. "This holiness is so mighty and powerful that it covers and wipes away all the sins and iniquities that remain in human flesh and blood."[55] Christ's kingdom is nothing but sheer grace, which shields us against sin and constantly combats it, covers it, and cleanses it; it purifies the sinners who in themselves are not worthy of the blood and death of Christ.

Proclamation: Being Sent

Verse 18: "As you sent Me into the world, so I am sending them into the world" reveals proclamation as the purpose for which Christ prays: "So that the world may believe that you have sent Me" (v. 21). Christ's Word will be heralded abroad and be received as God's Word. With this he confirms the beloved apostles as doctors and preachers of the gospel. Just as Christ binds to the Father's Word, so also he binds us to his Word. Thus he said: "I am sending them just as You sent Me." As the apostles have heard Christ's words, so others should hear them, on whom the Lord Christ has placed his words. The preacher is the servant of Christ, who speaks not out of his own initiative and inventiveness but by God's command or mandate. He is to bind himself to Christ's mouth, from which he receives the same testimony as the apostles of Christ did. "In short, in (the Word) are contained all our salvation and blessing, help, comfort, protection, and victory amidst all afflictions and temptations. To this Word, everything must yield—heaven and earth, the devil, and the world, together with all creatures."[56] This message must be proclaimed so that our hearts may rest on it and embrace it as surely as if we are hearing God himself speaking with his own voice.

Verse 20: "I do not ask for these only, but also for those who will believe in Me through their Word" refers to the extent of his Word, upheld not only by his apostles but also expanded into the world. This elevates the preaching office of the apostles, contrary to the sectarian spirits who distain the external means: "Outward things and signs and oral preaching are of no use to faith in the heart; the inner man must have an inner word."[57] They claim that the Holy Spirit alone must do everything, without the oral, external Word spoken with a bodily voice by Christ. "In this way, they draw themselves

---

55. LW 69.101 (WA 28.178).
56. LW 69.94–95 (WA 28.169).
57. LW 69.102 (WA 28.179).

away from God and Christ to the devil."[58] We should simply follow Christ's way: "Who will believe in Me through their Word," and write them in large golden letters and inculcate them in our hearts. Faith constitutes through the Word the inner man (2 Cor 4:16), the one who believes in his heart and places his confidence entirely in God. The external Word is beneficial and necessary not only to the ears but also to the heart; it penetrates through the ears to the heart. The seed does not always take root and sprout, and this is not the fault of the seed, but of the soil. Likewise, not all who hear believe, even though faith must come by the Word.

Word and Faith: Unity

Everything relies on these two articles: on the Word and faith, through which Christ accomplishes everything. Where the unity disappears, so Christ disappears, and consequently there is no knowledge of the Father through him. He prays that the Father will fulfill his "desire," that "those whom the Father has given him" (v.24) shall abide "where he is," that is, in the arms and bosom of the Father (John 1:18). This place "has no name and cannot be pointed out with the finger or depicted; it must be grasped in the Word through faith."[59] We should consider Christ's promise as "the pillow and feather bed for our souls,"[60] and lying upon it, we depart with a firm faith at the final hour when we shall be delivered from the world's misery and the devil's power, and brought to eternal rest. Christ speaks resolutely to the Father, asking him to grant his desire: not only his own will be with him, but also will behold the clear and bright vision of his glory. The glory the godly saints will see is Christ, God's only Son, whom "the Father loved before the foundation of the world" (v. 24). This is now constantly set forth through the Word and believed; it remains obscure or hidden, likened unto a thick cloud hiding the bright sun. But yonder a different light will dawn, where we no longer preach and convey glory in the Word. There faith shall be sight; we shall behold it in all its radiance before our own eyes with ineffable, eternal joy.

He only now begins, at the end of his prayer, to address the Father as "righteous Father," rather than "gracious," or "merciful," or "holy Father." Verse 25: "O righteous Father, the world does not know You." For his heart burns earnestly for the world that categorically repudiates the knowledge of God revealed in Christ. Christ has given us the Word through which the

---

58. LW 69.60 (WA 28.126).
59. LW 69.112 (WA 28.193).
60. LW 69.113 (WA 28.194).

Father's name and all he possesses has been heralded so that we know how to regard him. To know the Father means not only to know him as the Creator of heaven and earth and as the provider of temporal goods, but as the one who sent the Son into the world for our redemption. "This is the sum of Christianity."[61] Of verse 26: "I made known to them Your name, and I will continue to make it known," Christ not merely makes a beginning in the knowledge of the Father, but continues to impress this very thing through both the Word and the Holy Spirit, so that no one need seek God elsewhere. Just as in the beginning, Christ here concludes his prayer, exhorting us to occupy ourselves with understanding this better and more firmly, so that the heart may not flounder but be seized by "a superabundant, eternal love"[62] and be cemented with a joyful confidence in his favor and grace, not fearing any wrath. We are to constantly cling to Christ's mouth through which we feel the force of his prayer: "That the love with which You have loved Me may be in them, and I in them" (v. 26).

---

61. LW 69.118 (WA 28.199).
62. LW 69.111–12 (WA 28.192).

CHAPTER 13

The Power of Christ's Passion
Simplicity of Word and Magnitude of Substance

In simple words St. John describes the account of Christ's Passion to confirm our faith concerning the article (Christ suffered under Pilate, crucified, died and was buried). "If the history is lacking and forgotten, then faith is lacking and extinguished as well."[1] But more crucial than the historical account is the magnitude of its substance, that Christ's merit and suffering is so efficacious and so infinitely priceless in God's eyes that it conquers all sin, appeases God's wrath, and destroys death, the devil, and hell. The retention of Jesus before Pilate highlights the contrast between Christ's innocence and the guilt of the adversaries, and between secular kingdom and spiritual kingdom. To meditate upon Christ's Passion aright is to be acquainted with the knowledge of our sinful nature, and to be devastated by it, as in law, so that we may be acquainted with the knowledge of Christ's grace, and be comforted by it, as in the gospel. Revelation is given for the sake of redemption, in the same way a frank diagnosis prepares a patient for a cure.[2] We could possess great and excellent knowledge if we could keep Christ's sufferings before our eyes: on the one hand, Christ's passion exposes the world's diabolical hostility against the truth; on the other hand, it exposes the cross and tomb as the place in which the world's sin, misery, and wretchedness are borne and buried, if only we believe. The exemplary aspect of Christ's passion is an outflow of the power of Christ as sacrament.

---

1. LW 69.272 (WA 28.415).
2. Koester, "Passion and Resurrection," 91.

Preface to Christ's Passion: Christ's Arrest and Death

Having completed his prayer for his disciples in John 17, Jesus becomes a priest and offers himself as the true sacrifice on the cross. This is the Passion St. John describes in John 18–19. He provides a preface to the Passion. In John 18: 1, he writes, "He went out with His disciples across the brook Kidron where there was a garden, which Jesus and His disciples entered" (v. 1). It may seem unnecessary to mention the brook Kidron, however St. John does this to show the way Christ wanted to approach his death.[3] The heathen consider it an omen of something bad to come. Likewise, St. John particularly mentions this brook to foreshadow Christ's arrest and impending death. He cited the place and name, *"Kedar,"* which in Hebrew means *pullatus, tenebricosus, denigrates*—dusky, dark, and black.[4] He said nothing of the Mount of Olives and the beautiful garden; instead he focused on this dark brook. A small stream, Kidron is very near Jerusalem, and lies so deep and dark, so overlaid with bushes and hedges, that barely anyone can see the water. And Christ had to cross it, indicating the cruelty of the cross that was soon to descend upon him. The garden is called "Gethsemane: *vallis pinguis,* a fertile valley [Matt 26:36; Mark 14:32],"[5] and lies between the Mount of Olives and the city of Jerusalem. The evangelist wants us to contrast the brook Kidron, over which Christ crossed and which indicates Christ's suffering, and the fertile, fruitful valley, running with fat, which he and his disciples entered for nourishment. In the first place, he stresses the poverty in which Christ comes and lives on earth, with no house or room of his own, even though he was King and Lord both of the Jewish nation and of the entire world (Matt 8:20). In the second place, it was customary that whenever he was in Jerusalem, the Lord went into this garden or to Bethany in the evening. Jesus could have traveled a mile or two from the city, but instead he followed his ordinary path. Similarly, we should not seek out misfortune and evil, but must yield readily to God's will should he send evil or misfortune.

Christ is forsaken by the angels, and by all worldly powers (vv. 2–3). "Truly, Christ ought to be our example,"[6] who taught us where to obtain help when affliction and trouble happen. Just as the Father abides with Christ and has not abandoned him, so Christ is with every afflicted Christian. Our strength lies not in princes or any creaturely aids, but in Christ; it

---

3. LW 69.147 (WA 28.205).
4. LW 69.148 (WA 28.205).
5. LW 69.148 (WA 28.205).
6. LW 69.151 (WA 28.215).

is through his grace we possess the necessary strength within ourselves to face trials. This constitutes "the first part of the Passion: that we learn how to be abandoned and alone and to be forsaken by all men."[7] Christian suffering begins in solitude, as did Christ's, who was left alone in his cross and afflictions. Therefore, we must equip ourselves with God's promise, for he who said: "I will not leave you orphans; I am coming to you" (John 14:18).

As part of his preface, St. John also teaches us how to meditate, moving from Christ the person (who) through the work he does (what) to the reason of Christ's passion (why). First, we are to ponder on this word, "I am He," to reap the fruit of comfort from Christ. Verses 4 and 5 say: "Now as Jesus knew all that would happen to Him; He came forward and said to them, 'Whom do you seek?' They answered Him, 'Jesus of Nazareth.' Jesus said to them: 'I am He.'" Proper meditation on him would never fail to produce fruit, causing us to feel ashamed of our own sufferings. Considering every part of Christ's suffering leads one to conclude, "Compared to (Christ's) suffering, the suffering of all men on earth is nothing but a child's game—yes, nothing at all."[8]

Secondly, we are to ponder what his will or intention is, and how great he is who was taken captive, crucified, and put to death. We consider "of what sort, and how great Christ is, that is, what He did to deserve such suffering."[9] According to his person, Christ is truly God essentially; so his deeds—healing the sick, raising the dead, and so on—are also divine. These works attest to the supreme nobility and beneficence of Christ the person; and yet he is condemned by the world, indeed, by his own people. "But all of this is still the least of His works. It is a much greater work when He enlightens men's hearts, destroys the works of the devil, and redeems them from his power, etc."[10]

> In sum, in Christ there are nothing but indescribable works and blessings. And this noble, beneficent person has to endure such suffering that He dies a most shameful death on the cross, the likes of which no man on earth has ever experienced, etc. His obedience, sufferings, and death should deservedly strike down all our suffering and produce true patience in us. For what are the men of earth compared to this person? What are all our

---

7. LW 69.153 (WA 28.217).
8. LW 69.156 (WA 26.225).
9. LW 69.156 (WA 26.226).
10. LW 69.156 (WA 26.226).

works and good deeds compared to the works and good deeds of Christ?[11]

Thirdly, we ponder on why Christ suffered and died. There are two reasons for his suffering. First, humans are so poisoned with hatred of Christ that they cannot tolerate him, even though he lavishly showers upon them the greatest blessings. The second reason lies with Christ himself, whose innocent and obedient suffering secures for believers eternal life, righteousness and forgiveness. It is not out of merit or human works, or out of any deficiency of being but purely out of his great, infinite love that Christ comes to us in his capacity as our Redeemer. Nor did he die for the sake of justice, for no debt or duty obliges him to do so either for himself or for us. No one, except Christ dares claim to have died for our sake; no suffering of the holiest saints or martyrs can render satisfaction for sins, or effect for us righteous standing before God. Christ alone, the Lamb of God, possesses the glory of washing away our sins (cf. Rev 5:2–9).

On the one hand, Christ through his person and his wounds should lead us to "contemplate His willing heart, how He presents himself in obedience to the Father and in kindness to us. Here His heart is not hidden but is extended to us in ready and manifest love and to His Heavenly Father in willing obedience (Cf. Phil 2:8)."[12] On the other hand, no one knows of his own corrupt nature, and its remedy, except by divine judgment. Christ's passion is to be understood through the dialectic of law-gospel. As law, it reveals our inability to please God with our works, and as gospel, it reveals the remedy for our ailment. The proper outcome of meditation on Christ's passion is not compassion for Christ, as was taught in medieval Passion preaching,[13] but terror at our sins which were the cause of Christ's suffering. With this, Luther rejected the medieval emphasis on Christ's passion as a model for penitential imitation.[14] Instead of stressing the meritorious fruits of meditation on the Passion, Luther emphasized the fruit of the Passion: forgiveness of sins.

---

11. LW 69.157 (WA 26.227).

12. LW 69.164 (WA 26.238).

13. See Ludolph of Saxony, *Vita Jesu Christi*, as cited in Introduction, LW 69.126.

14. Ludolph, *Vita Jesus Christi* 2.57.3 (vol. 4:3): "We should bear the Lord's cross and help him to carry it: namely, in our hearts, through memory and compassion; with our mouths, through frequent and devout thanksgiving; in our bodies, through flagellation and mortification, so that we may give thanks to our Savior with heart, mouth, and works." Cited in LW 69.127–28, n. 28.

The Power of the Word: "I am He"

St. John dwells on the person who suffers more than the other evangelists. He alone records the words "I am He" before which "they [the cohort, along with the servants of the chief priests, and Judas] drew back and fell to the ground" (v. 6). By this assertion, St. John wants to show that Christ was not a mere man, but is really who he claims to be, the Son of God. This provokes us to reflect on what kind of a person it is who suffers for us, in order that Christ's wounds and suffering are not, as the world regards them, trivial, inconsequential, and contemptible. Christ's passion also highlights what a terrible thing obduracy is, so that we learn to remain in the fear of God. Even though the chief priests witnessed this great sign of being cast down by Jesus with a word, and had seen Christ perform many miracles, they did not recoil from their intent and evil scheme. Instead of heeding this great miracle and extraordinary warning that Christ did in their presence, they persisted in their raging against him; they choose to remain under the intolerable burden of the law. We too should keep watch and pray God to safeguard us against obstinate hearts, which may ultimately lead, such as the scoundrel Judas, to the abyss of hell, from which there is no return. When afflicted by sin, we rely on his proper work of forgiveness so that we may not despair; when tempted by presumption and arrogance, we submit to his alien work of mortification so that we remain humble.

A two-fold power animates from the word "I am He": the power to cast to the ground all the might of his adversaries, as in law, and to deliver those who are given to Christ, as in gospel. Christ did this while he was in a state of weakness, when he was ready to suffer. This reflects Luther's theology of the cross, in which God's power is hidden in its opposite, that is, in the depths of his weakness that he manifests his might and power, as he struck his enemies to the ground and freed his disciples from the snare of death. "So He asked them again, 'Whom do you seek?' And they said, 'Jesus of Nazareth.' Jesus answered, 'I told you that I am He. So, if you seek Me, let these go.' This was to fulfill the word that He had spoken: 'Of those whom You give Me I have lost no one'" (vv. 7–9). Here Christ gives another sign, saying, "If you seek Me, let these go." Just as he is able to strike his enemies to lay them upon the ground, so too he is able to defend his disciples with a single word, that they might be preserved as a fulfillment of the word he had spoken to his heavenly Father: "Those whom You have given Me I have guarded, and not one of them had been lost" (John 17:12). To the soldiers and servants he says, "Let My disciples go." By these words, he freed them so that none of them would be held, even though Peter and John entered the house of the high priest (John 18:15–16). For the evangelist Christ is their protector, verified by his "I am He" and by his word to the soldiers, "Let these go."

Christ's words, "Of those whom You give Me I have not lost one," are consoling. When people receive Christ and his Word, they are given to Christ. This was borne out before in John 17:6: "Yours they were, and You gave them to Me, and they have kept Your word." Faith lays hold of Christ's Word, which possesses an inherent power to accomplish its own purpose. In whatever weakness Christ is found, he nonetheless possesses such wisdom, might, and power that he is able to thwart the evil schemes of his enemies. He also sets the limit that the tyrants shall not exceed (Job 14:5) and by which they are restrained. Though the enemies fall, we remain secure under Christ's protection. Hell and every power combined still could not harm Christ and those who are his. But if they do suffer, it is not because they must, but because they are willing to do so gladly. Yet nothing of this is visible; only faith perceives it despite appearances to the contrary.

St. Peter's Fall and God's Command

Verse 10-12: "Then Simon Peter, having a sword, drew it and struck the high priest's servant and cut off his right ear. (The servant's name was Malchus[15]). So Jesus said to Peter, "Put your sword into its sheath; shall I not drink the cup that My Father has given Me?" Christ saw that it would come to pass that those who are his, who bear the name of the Christian, would be provoked to wield the sword for themselves, especially for being treated unjustly before God and the world. Peter is an example that we should do nothing unless God sanctions it. It is folly of the old Adam to relinquish what has been commanded to seize upon what has not been commanded. What stirred Münzer to action, for instance, is nothing but this compelling pretext: "The government is unjust; therefore, we must make things run in a Christian way."[16] Even when everyone says, "It is right to draw a sword," we must first determine whether this is commanded, so that we do not sully our

---

15. See LW 69.173 (WA 26.254). Malchus, Caiaphas's servant, is an allegory of the figure and type of the Old Testament. For Luther, the people of old were not a filial but a servile people, who served God primarily under the coercion and compulsion of the law. Malchus means *regius*, a royal servant; he is representative of the servile people of the law who are preoccupied with works. All the works-righteous saints boast of themselves as nothing less than kings and princes, and thus must be called Malchus. In sum, the allegorical interpretation of this servant reflects the distinction between law and gospel. As a figure of all those who serve under the Old Testament, he has lost his right ear, and cannot hear the gospel unless Christ restores it to its place.

16. LW 69.168-69 (WA 26.247).

own hand, as Peter did. God's command should govern our action, rather than "a compelling pretext, premise, and rationale"[17] that everyone should oppose injustice. We must let God's majesty reign supreme in such matters. "God will rather tolerate a government that commits injustice than the common mob with a just cause."[18]

Verse 13: "First they led Him to Annas, for he was the father-in-law of Caiaphas [who was high priest that year]." That Annas was the old priest, and Caiaphas the high priest that year shows that they exercise the high priest's office in turn (cf. Luke 3:1–2). This is contrary to God's ordinance, as they divided their priesthood amongst themselves. Though they behaved like knaves, the priesthood remains holy, for it belongs to God, instituted and ordained by God; it was not evil nor to be rejected, even though the priests made light of it. The general rule remains: "Abuse does not destroy the substance of a thing."[19] The abuse and the divine estate or office must be distinguished, such that even if the estate is abused its essence remains. Annas and Caiaphas occupy the summit of dignity and sit on a greater throne than do the pope and the emperor. Luther employs to denounce the maxim of papal infallibility: "It is not to be presumed that the pope in such a lofty station can err."[20] None but the God of the First Commandment, "a jealous God" (Exod. 20:5), is the one whom we are to trust. God demands that we fear and trust God alone, even if he speaks to us through a donkey (cf. Num. 22:28–30). This leads us to confess: "Whoever clings to Christ cannot err; whoever does not cling to Christ must err, even if he were greater than a pope."[21]

Luther commends to the scholars to determine whether Peter made his denials in the house of the high priest Annas or Caiaphas.[22] His main concern here is the fruit that can be reaped from Peter's denials. All the evangelists most diligently describe Peter's fall and clearly depict all three of his denials. "In truth, I [Luther] believe that nothing in the whole Passion is so painstakingly described and depicted as is Peter's denial."[23] For no article of faith is more difficult to believe than the remission of sins.

> The reason is that all of the other articles apply outside of ourselves and do not enter into our experience, nor do they affect

17. LW 69.169 (WA 26.248).
18. LW 69.171 (WA 26.251).
19. LW 69.177 (WA 26.259).
20. LW 69.178 (WA 28.260).
21. LW 69.180 (WA 28.263).
22. LW 69. 183 (WA 28.267).
23. LW 69.185 (WA 28.271).

us, as when we believe that God, Creator of heaven and earth, is our Father; also that Jesus Christ, God's Son, suffered and died; and so on as it says in the symbol, or Children's Creed. All of this goes by us as if it were something that affects someone else. For everyone thinks: "That applies to St. Peter and St. Paul; who can tell whether it applies to me?" But forgiveness of sins does affect and apply to me and to you.[24]

All other articles affect someone else, but this article "affects us and enters into our experience, and causes other articles to affect us and enter our experience."[25] By comparison, the other articles are "more difficult"[26] to understand and comprehend. For instance, we are to believe that the bread in the Lord's Supper is Christ's body and the cup or the wine is Christ's blood. But this article is "the most difficult thing"[27] to grasp because not only are we supposed to talk about and understand this article but also to accept it and apply it to each one of us as certain. Not until we are touched by the strength of this article for us do we apprehend the benefit of other articles: "What benefit do I receive from God's creation of heaven and earth if I do not believe the forgiveness of sins? Indeed, what is more, what benefit do I receive from Christ's death and the coming of the Holy Spirit if I do not believe in the forgiveness of sins?"[28] Thus it is necessary for our sakes that St. Peter's fall is recorded for our instruction and comfort (cf. Rom 15:4). When terrified by sin and God's wrath, we should look at Peter, and be assured of God's grace. We will not find any sin that can equal his, except for obduracy and presumption, "a sin unto death" (1 John 5:16). When we hear that Peter disowned Christ and swore on pain of his salvation that he had no relation with this man, we confess, "this is a sermon for us."[29] Peter, "the greatest and best apostle,"[30] fails more shamefully than the rest and yet is restored, and receives the "fruit and benefit of Christ's suffering:" the forgiveness of sins.[31]

---

24. LW 69.185–86 (WA 28.272). See note 150, where Luther describes the article of resurrection as the most difficult to believe. Cf. LW 69.286.
25. LW 69.186 (WA 28.272).
26. LW 69.187 (WA 28.272).
27. LW 69.188 (WA 28.273).
28. LW 69.185–86 (WA 28.272).
29. LW 69.188 (WA 28.276).
30. LW 69.186 (WA 28.272).
31. LW 69.186 (WA 28.273). Luther did not preach a separate sermon on John 21, where Jesus reinstated St. Peter.

The Interrogation: Innocence and Guilt

Caiaphas, the high priest for that year, interrogated Jesus about his actions, his disciples, and his doctrine (v. 19). This text presents two issues. The first is that Christ confessed before the high priest that he spoke nothing in secret, but taught openly in the synagogue and the temple (v. 20). Just as Christ instructed his disciples publicly in the boat, on the plain, on the mountains, in the synagogues, and in the temple, he also taught them in secret and individually. In response to the general question about his doctrine, Christ directs the high priest's question to his hearers, and Luther paraphrases Christ's reply: "There is no part of My doctrine about which I am ashamed either before you or before the world. I am not ashamed of My doctrine on account of your Majesty; rather, I appeal to My hearers."[32] This causes the servant to strike him on the cheek. But when Christ says, "If I have spoken evil, prove that it is evil; but if I have spoken right, why do you strike Me?" (vv. 20–21, 23), people have used this text to "make counsels out of God's commandments."[33] This is the other issue that demands attention. As is borne out in Matthew 5:39–41: "But if anyone strikes you on the right cheek, turn to him the other also. And if anyone sues you and takes your tunic, let him have your cloak as well. And if anyone forces you to go one mile, go with him two miles," the gospel categorically enjoins us not to draw a sword, not to repay evil with evil, but to do good even to our enemy and forsake all. Matthew 5:39 says, "Do not resist the one who is evil. But if anyone strikes you on the right cheek, turn to him the other also," has no other content than this: "My [Christ's] doctrine does not pertain to the emperor but to those who want to be willingly righteous and to be called the children of God, to them I give this teaching."[34] What he intends to stress is "overcome evil with good" (Rom 12:21). Christ's answer to the servant, "If I have spoken evil, prove that it is evil" (v. 23), brings into focus a distinction between offering the other cheek and rebuking the one who strikes us. When dealing with injustice, we must separate mouth and hand from each other. We should not yield our mouth to approve of wickedness, just as Christ speaks out against what is unjust. But the hand should keep still and not repay evil with evil. Christ does not teach that we must command the one who strikes us on the cheek that he should do the same to the other. Instead, he holds that if anyone wants to strike you, do not defend yourself

---

32. LW 69.189–90 (WA 28.279).
33. LW 69.190 (WA 28.279).
34. LW 69.192 (WA 28.282).

nor wield a sword against him, do not take revenge but rebuke him as an act of mercy and a clearance of your conscience.

> But above and beyond this, even though you suffer injustice and do not take revenge and pray for your enemy, you are also obligated to bear witness to what is right and wrong and to rebuke what is wrong. For you ought not approve your adversary's sin, but should warn and rebuke him. This is what it means to show great mercy in the midst of evil, namely, to show your enemy his sin. In this way, your own conscience is safe; and yet this is not revenge, but wholly and purely a good deed.[35]

Christ's saying to the servant, "If I have spoken evil, prove that it is evil; but if I have spoken right, why do you strike Me?" is not spoken out of arrogance. "Instead, it is a fine, steadfast earnestness, which was written down for our imitation and comfort, that we, too, in such a case might be steadfast and earnest."[36] Proud Caiaphas' sole reason for interrogating Jesus was to entrap him so that he might abase himself and confess his error. Despite the high priest's invidious plan, Jesus replied earnestly: "I have made no secret of My teaching. Ask those who have heard what I said to them." As far as his person is concerned, Christ will gladly suffer; as far as his doctrine is concerned, he remains unshaken, earnestly testifying to it before the world. In holding fast to his doctrine, Christ sets a beautiful example for us to imitate: just as he in his weakness answers before the high priest concerning his doctrine, so we, despite our frailty and infirmity, should insist upon the Word that we have once accepted and taught, and declare staunchly our faith, even at the risk of being bound (cf. 2 Tim 2:9).

The villains appear before the judgment hall, casting Jesus there, and yet they find no just cause to execute him, as Pilate three times reproaches them. Yet they want to be completely holy and will not enter the judgment hall; they want to preserve themselves from being defiled so that they might partake of their precious Passover (v. 28). This text first addresses the Jews, who displayed great holiness by refusing to enter Pilate's house. They possessed scrupulous conscience on this lesser matter, yet the great matter of crucifying the Son of God they passed over without any qualms of conscience. This characterizes a faithless hypocrite, who makes a show of a little holiness, but neglects the weightiest matter of the Law, and breaks all the Commandments of God without any hesitation. The hypocrites are like the ostrich (Lev 11:16; Deut 14:15) that covers its head under a small branch and foolishly assumes it has concealed its entire body. They adorn

---

35. LW 69.195 (WA 28.285).
36. LW 69.196 (WA 28.287).

themselves like the ostrich with some little thing such as tithing, and yet they practice the greatest villainy. Their holiness, when exposed to the light, is nothing but the kind that "does not want to enter the judgment hall." False saints want to conceal their wickedness under the show of holiness. The secular government by itself can produce only hypocrisy and outward obedience without the proper attitude of the heart. It needs the spiritual government, in which "the Holy Spirit exposes them here and shows us what they are."[37]

This text also highlights an insidious, pernicious temptation of the devil. When the devil finds a poor soul that longs to be righteous, he assails and plagues the conscience, by causing them to ignore strong sins and transgressions, but to make much of small sins, such as someone speaks or laughs.[38] He is skilled in the art of covering up great sins and the coarse "knots,"[39] such as doubting and wavering faith, so that we ignore them, and do not desire forgiving grace. When tormented by wrongdoing and stumbling along with the other infirmities and sins, we should lay hold of the article of the Creed, "I believe in the forgiveness of sins," and the Fifth Petition of the Our Father, "Forgive us our trespasses." We confess humbly: "I am a poor sinner; I know of no holiness nor comfort of my own; my holiness and comfort is Christ alone."[40]

When Pilate asks the people what sort of accusation they are laying against Jesus, they waver, for they do not want their charge to be brought into the open. They know full well that their accusation lacks legal basis, and yet wish Jesus condemned to death privately, without receiving a just hearing. But Pilate denies their request. So they answer: "If this man were not an evildoer, we would not have delivered Him over to you" (v. 40). Implicit in such an answer is the presumption that holy fathers, like the chief priests and scribes, would not condemn anyone who is not already guilty. But the secular governor Pilate will have none of this. So in verse 31 he said, "Take Him yourselves and judge Him by your own law." Since the Jews know the accusation and the grounds for execution, Pilate reverted the judgment back to them, but they say to him, "We are not permitted to condemn anyone to death" (v. 31). Had the Romans not taken jurisdiction over capital punishment, they would have condemned Jesus to death at once. Luther used this text because he knew what his adversaries did to him in opposing

37. LW 69.201 (WA 28.295).

38. For speaking and laughing as sins, cf. the Rule of St. Benedict 4:52–55; 6;7.56–61 (9th–11th degree of humility) as cited in LW 69.202, note 209.

39. The word "knots" means sins. Cf. Luther, Sermons on the Mount (1530/32), LW 21.62, as cited in LW 69.202, n. 208.

40. LW 69.203 (WA 28.298).

the truth and his evangelical cause. Bishops, priests, and the papal clergy expend every effort to prevent any "free, Christian council"[41] from taking place, lest the cause of the gospel be given a hearing.

A Gentile, like Pilate, knows nothing of God, and, moreover, deals with blood and capital punishment. On the contrary, the Jews have God's Word and the prophets, which should enable them to make just judgments without appealing to a Gentile for the verdict. Yet here they fail to do justice, and in their hatred they perceive less than Pilate does. The irony lies in that this Gentile, who is far inferior to the Jews, must pronounce his judgment on the Jews themselves, who should know better than others. John supplies another reason why the Jews and Pilate were conferring with each other, that is, "to fulfill the word that Jesus had spoken to show by what death He was to die" (v. 32). The accounts in Luke 18:32–33 and Mathew 20:18–19 indicate the kind of death Jesus would die: that the Jews would put the Innocent One to death, but the Gentiles would exact the sentence and execute condemnation. While the high priests make the initial move to take Jesus captive and condemn him to death, the Gentiles mock, ridicule, spit on him, and kill him. In this way both Jews and Gentiles are the agents of the Lord's death.[42]

John does not indicate how Jesus was accused before Pilate; Luke, however, indicates the charge: "The whole company of them arose and brought Him before Pilate. And they began to accuse Him, saying, 'We found this one misleading the people and forbidding them to give tribute to Caesar, and saying that He is Christ, a king'" (Luke 23:1–2). Then Pilate "entered the judgment hall again," and queried: "Are you the king of the Jews?" (John 18:33). The accusation is about Jesus being a rebel against Caesar. "That is the title and the guilt He must bear."[43] Pilate accepts this accusation, but denies the charge that Jesus stirred up the people with his teaching throughout Judea, beginning in Galilee (Luke 23:5). The arch-scoundrels and godless knaves know all too well that it was not true that Christ wanted to be a king, for when they wanted to capture him by force and crown him as king, he shunned it and withdrew to the mountain alone (John 6:15). When he was asked whether or not to pay taxes to Caesar, he showed his obedience to

---

41. LW 69.206 (WA 28.301). See LW 69.206, note 230: "Luther had appealed from the pope to a 'free Christian council' as early as 1518 (WA 2.36–40; WA 7.75–90). At the time of these sermons, Luther was at best indifferent to the prospect of a council: 'A council cannot do much harm, if it should take place, though it does not seem likely or credible that one will take place' (letter to Amsdorf, March 15, 1529, WA Br. 5.540, no. 1396)."

42. LW 69.208 (WA 29.303).

43. LW 69.208 (WA 28.304).

him, and said: "Render to Caesar the things that are Caesar's, and to God the things that are God's" (Matt 22:21). Having known that this charge would claim Pilate's attention, they pressed the accusation most vigorously. The Gentiles called the accusation as a rebel "a crime in which the royal majesty is attacked."[44] Christ defends himself against the charge, by speaking to Pilate: "Do you say this of yourself, or did others say it to you about Me?" (v. 34). Christ and his Christians are peaceful people, preaching that everyone should be subject and obedient to the authorities. But the gospel does not run its inexorable course without tumult. A distinction exists between God's kingdom and Caesar's kingdom; physical rebellion against the established authority (Rom 13:2), and spiritual rebellion which does not interfere with the secular government. "Hands, body, possessions—these we leave in obedience to the established authority, as is proper, but the hearts of men we lead to God, that they may be under obedience to God."[45] In Christ's kingdom, the gospel is preached, but as Christ says in Luke 12:52, "In one house there will be five divided"; and yet the house does not collapse. Spiritual rebellion happens, not because children rebel against their parents nor obey their government, but because they share a different faith from each other. Christ is a King, but not a worldly one.

Verse 37: "Then Pilate said to Him, 'So, you are a king.' Jesus answered, 'You have said it. Indeed, I am a king. For this purpose I was born and for this purpose I have come into the world—to bear witness to the truth.'" To "bear witness" means to "preach," as St. John often uses the word.[46] With it the Lord indicates briefly the nature of his royal office, that he does not come riding on a great and majestic warhorse and wielding the sword; but preaching the spoken word by which he rules his kingdom. "Truth" encompasses "the virtue and power of his Word,"[47] through which the gospel is heralded. Everything Christ testifies before Pilate is "the pure truth."[48] It is his royal office to preach the truth, to which we bear witness, and through which we are justified before God. Everyone who is of the truth hears Christ's voice. His voice is the Word of the gospel, which must be grasped with heart and faith.

---

44. LW 69.209 (WA 28.305).
45. LW 69.212 (WA 28.312).
46. LW 69.213 (WA 28.314).
47. LW 69.213 (WA 28.315).
48. LW 69.214 (WA 28.317).

The Way of the World

The world reverses the truth of what the gospel declares: the righteous One in God's eyes the world regards as the wicked one, and vice versa. This is epitomized here in the contrast between two figures: Barabbas (guilt) was considered good, and Christ (innocence) was counted as the worst scoundrel (v. 40). This reflects what Luther had previously taught in his *Heidelberg Disputation* (1518), "A theologian of the glory calls evil good, and good evil."[49] In the world, truth is condemned, and falsehood exalted; evil extolled and innocence crucified. The blessings of God—temporal blessings (peace, health, and beauty), and sublime gifts (the gospel, divine truth, and life)—that God bestows suffer privation, distortion, or misuse in the world that repudiates "the truth" that delivers from sin and death. This is the power of Christ's passion, from which we know the way of the world, the very antithesis of Christ's.

Pilate complies with Roman law and custom in which no one can be executed unless he had been previously tried, and arraigned. Hence he delays his judgment as long as he can, particularly because the charge against Jesus him lacks legal grounds. Just as the tribune had Paul flogged and examined the case against him (cf. Acts 22:24), so Pilate had Jesus scourged hoping this would appease the crowd.[50] Those assembled cry out, "Crucify Him, crucify Him" (John 19:6). This is "an even larger piece of the portrait of the beautiful, dear world"[51] than what we have seen. In the previous chapter, we read that the world does not tolerate the just and innocent, and second, it prefers the rebel and murderer, Barabbas, to Christ, the bearer of truth. "These are hard and coarse knots [sins]."[52] "But the third is much more coarse: the darling, beloved world is not satisfied or satiated even when the truth is punished in moderation."[53] This is the pattern of the world: an evildoer often receives mercy, as did Barabbas. But those who persecute the truth would not cease raging against Jesus. "And the soldiers plaited a crown of thorns and put it on His head and arrayed Him in a purple robe and said, 'Hail, King of the Jews!' and struck Him on the cheek" (John 19:2–3). The soldiers exploited Jesus' confession, and began to act out a "Carnival play."[54]

---

49. LW 31.45.

50. The idea that Pilate intends the flogging of Jesus to satisfy the Jews so that they will cease demanding Jesus' execution is universal in the preceding exegetical tradition. See *Collected Works of Erasmus* 46:337, n. 7, as cited in LW 69.222, n.6.

51. LW 69.222 (WA 28.332).

52. LW 69.222 (WA 28.332).

53. LW 69.222 (WA 28.333).

54. LW 69.224 (WA 28.335). For the Carnival dramas of Nürnberg's Hans Sachs,

With such bitter, malevolent, unpardonable mockery they pressed a crown of thorns upon his head, and dressed him in an old purple robe. Flogging is painful, but such diabolical slander hurts even more, for God's truth is not only horribly disdained but also shamefully maligned with contempt.

Along with the other evangelists, John stressed the malice of those hostile to the truth; and how Christ was condemned to death, even though he was innocent. It was Pilate's duty to pronounce the sentence in accordance with Roman law. The Jewish religious leaders knew they punished Jesus unjustly, and yet they insisted that Pilate should sentence Christ and put him to death. Pilate should have rebuked Annas, Caiaphas, and the chief priests, when they lied before the Roman Emperor's governor and authority. Instead, he spoke discreetly and politely: "Take Him yourselves and crucify Him, for I find no guilt in him" (John 19:6). Christ's passion unveils the knowledge of how the world operates: the wisest, most learned, and holiest of people become sheer devils with respect to Christ and his gospel. For even though Pilate defends Christ for a while, he, too, opposes Christ. He has him scourged, and continues to hold him hostage until he finally gives in completely and has Christ condemned to death. No accusation is more absurd than the Jews' declaration: "We have a law, and according to that law He ought to die because He has made Himself the Son of God" (v.7). Yet Christ was not to die under the Jewish law but by the authority of Caesar on the charge that he had made himself king and usurped Caesar's reign. This is attested by the superscription placed on top of Jesus' cross: "Jesus of Nazareth, the King of the Jews" (John 19:19). The Jews considered it blasphemy to claim to be the Son of God (cf. Matt 26:65), and that such a person should be stoned (Lev 24:16), though not crucified. The Lord Jesus had vindicated himself sufficiently concerning the charge that he said, "I am the Son of God" (cf. Matt 26:64; John 8:28), but it was of no avail. This is characteristic of the way of the world, in which evil is extolled, and good renounced.

"Crucify Him": Innocence in Exchange for Guilt

Christ's passion highlights the wretchedness and wickedness of the world; it also brings to light the glory of the gospel. Christ could well have extricated himself from such an accusation and condemnation, but for our sake he endures it. The false judgment brought upon him has salvific bearing for us, and thus applies to us. Hidden in the negative voice, "Crucify Him," is

---

see Aylett, *Translations*. Also cited in LW 69.224, n. 10. In popular piety, Carnival plays function as a mirror image for the early modern biblical play, and serve as a paradigm for human expression in general and religious experience.

the positive voice of the gospel: Christ, the innocent Lamb, bears for us the guilt that should have been ours, for the false indictments brought upon him apply to us. The cross reveals the great love of Christ, who for our sake endured such suffering; he bore the curse of the law to give us the blessing of the gospel. Christ's suffering has delivered us from the burden of sin, law and death. And "this is our glory and the glory of our holy Gospel."[55]

> Moreover, the words that Christ must die because He made Himself the Son of God are also a good teaching and prophecy for us. For the Law is death and the devil for us, and the guilt of having made ourselves sons of God lies on all of our heads. Moses' text [Lev 24:6] is certainly right: whoever makes himself the Son of God ought to die. All of us human beings have made ourselves sons of God, and so we are all deserving of death; this is the very burden from which Christ has delivered us. Thus He received His just punishment, inasmuch as He had taken our place and wanted to pay in our stead. For His own person, to be sure, He is innocent, and the Law of Moses that condemns blasphemers to death does not apply to Him. But because He had undertaken to stand in the place of all human beings, He must also expect the punishment.[56]

The "greatest and the gravest of sins," from which all others derive, is pride.[57] Luther quotes Sirach 10 (Ecclus 10:12–13), *Principium peccati apostatare a Deo*, "The source of pride is when a man falls away from God and turns his heart from his Maker. For pride impels a man to all sin."[58] Desiring to be God, that is, when a person puts his confidence in his own works and righteousness as the basis of justification, is the chief sin. Such a person does not need forgiving grace nor the Lord's help. But to forgive sins, justify, and save is exclusively divine work. Whoever attributes these works to himself and his own merit and righteousness elevates himself as God. Now the law says: whoever is arrogant and makes himself God's Son ought to be condemned. Therefore to interpret this text as meaning that Christ was supposed to die because he is the Son of God is not altogether wrong; rather, "it is good."[59] However, the Jews do not concede that he is the

55. LW 69.230 (WA 28.347).

56. LW 69.230 (WA 28.348).

57. One might note the contrast to Genesis 3, where Luther defines doubt as the gravest of all sins, the original sin. See LW 1.147–48 (WA XLII.111): "In short, all evils result from unbelief or doubt of the Word and of God. For what can be worse than to disobey God and to obey Satan?"

58. LW 69.231 (WA 28.349), n. 28.

59. LW 69.231 (WA 28.350).

Son of God nor that God's Son, according to the prophesy of the Law, had to die for the sins of the world. Instead of saying, "He was supposed to make Himself the Son of God and die in accordance with the prophesy of the Law," they say, "He has made Himself the Son of God. That is why He ought to die according to the Law as a blasphemer."[60] Yet what the Law declares of someone who makes himself the Son of God does not trouble Pilate at all. The Gentile Pilate had to bear witness of this—Christ in innocence condemned to death—against the most learned and holiest people on earth. This highlights the gospel of joyous exchange, in which Christ's innocence stands in the place of, and absolves, our guilt.

> For even though in innocence He is condemned to death, nevertheless He is guilty before God according to the Law, not for His own person but in our stead. He stands before Pilate not as the Son of the Virgin Mary but as an evildoer, and that not on His own behalf but on behalf of you and me, on the ground that he wanted to be the Son of God, that is, because we wanted to be the Son of God, that is, to be equal to God. Thus Christ is innocent on his own behalf, but on our behalf he is guilty. For He has taken our guilt upon Himself in order to pay our debt.[61]

Pilate did not regard Christ as the Son of the true, living God, because he knew nothing of that God; rather, since the Romans worshipped many and various gods, he thought Jesus might be one of these. He was not afraid of violating Jewish law, but he was fearful that he might stumble upon one of the heathen gods (John 19:8). Thus he leads Jesus back into the judgment hall and asks, "Where are you from?" (John 19:9). Since Jesus has claimed to be the Son of God, Pilate wants to know which god's son he is, because he would not have wanted to cause an offense by passing sentence on someone who might be a god, or the son of a god. Christ did not give any answer because he had made his glorious confession before Pilate, testifying to the purpose for which he was born, namely, to bear witness to the truth (John 18:37). Since Pilate was indifferent towards the truth (John 18:36), Christ regarded him as unworthy to be given additional information and gave him no answer. This irritates Pilate: "Will you not speak with me? Do you not know that I have power to crucify You and power to release You?" (John 19:10). At this point, Christ can no longer keep silence and answers, "You would have no power over Me unless it had been given from above" (v. 11).

---

60. LW 69.231 (WA 28.351).

61. LW 69.231 (WA 28.351). What Luther taught here parallels to his *Commentary on Galatians* 3:13 (1531/35): Cf. LW 26.283-84 (WA XL.443-44) where he dealt with Galatians 3:13 in 1531/1535.

Previously, when Pilate inquired of his origin, Christ had kept silent, but now, when Pilate lashes out thinking that he is the one who has the power, Christ sees that it is necessary to rebuke him for his presumption and arrogance, and tells him that he has no jurisdiction over him. For Luther, just as Christ comes to bear witness to the truth and rebukes Pilate's injustice, so we should also confidently rebuke our own Pilates as well as their insolence and pride, for one should not keep silent about injustice nor let sin go unrebuked.

Holy Scripture applies the singular to the plural and, conversely plural to the singular.[62] So, upon "the one who delivers Me over to you," Christ pronounces a fearful sentence and severe judgment upon the entire group, guilty of "the greater sin" (John 19:11). He speaks here of Caiaphas, Annas, Judas, and the Jews, all those who delivered Christ over to Pilate. This is "an astounding statement and strange way of speaking"[63] that those who delivered Christ to be crucified "have the greater sin" than the one who commits the deed. Only Christ dares to pronounce such a judgment, as he judges the deed according to what lies in the heart, not according to outward appearances. Though Pilate has authority from above, nevertheless, Christ does not exonerate him but exposes him to his own guilt. Pilate's deed goes against nature and reason, which teach that we should not do harm to anyone on behalf of another.

"You are not Caesar's Friend": Worldly Righteousness Ceases

The moment Pilate learns there is no ground for executing Christ he is the holiest man on earth, because his mind is set on releasing Christ. But the people cry out, "If you release this man, you are not Caesar's friend" (John 19:12). The mob makes the first accusation that Jesus wants to be a king in opposition to Caesar, but Pilate quickly dismisses that accusation. Then they accuse him of making himself the Son of God, and this too was suppressed. Now they return to the first accusation that he made himself a king. They sharpen their accusation a little more by saying that "whoever makes himself a king is opposed to Caesar" (v. 12). The accusation of blasphemy does not affect Pilate; the accusation that Christ made himself king of the Jews held his attention. If Pilate were to release this man, the Jews would charge him with sanctioning rebellion and that he was disloyal to the emperor. Human nature is so inclined to have Caesar as a friend, rather than as a foe,

62. LW 69.238 (WA 28.363).
63. LW 69.238 (WA 28.363).

for no other reason than the preservation of body, life, property, and home. Once Pilate hears words "you are not Caesar's friend," he clings to his own life and property and keeps Caesar as his friend, and has Christ crucified, even though he knows an injustice is being done. He issues the verdict upon the innocent, "It is better for one man to perish than for myself and everyone else, together with all we possess, to be endangered and destroyed" (cf. John 11:50). In the person of Pilate we see negatively what "human holiness and righteousness is capable of, what its foundation is, and how securely it stands when the body must suffer or be placed in danger."[64] Before the terrifying words, "You are not Caesar's friend," all Pilate's righteousness crumbles into pieces. Hence it is called "a temporal worldly righteousness."[65] Even the Gentiles who boast of such righteousness do not extend it any farther than when their life, authority, and honor are in jeopardy. Where these end, then virtue ends as well. In the wake of the gospel, the children of God no longer govern their lives by merit or reward. They have no part in "a transitory, childish and servile"[66] righteousness, which crumbles when the advantage ceases. They should do good to others without seeking their own advantage, to glorify God and for the benefit of neighbor.

The evangelist indicates the time, person, location, and the occasion concerning Jesus' trial. This was done for the sake of the Jews, so that they could be convicted beyond all shadow of a doubt. Pilate sits down on the judgment seat and does not question Jesus any further (John 19:13). The judgment hall is facing the street, with a raised platform in front of it like a terrace. Pilate sat on that terrace when he presided in judgment so that everyone could see him. The judgment is held in public so that Christ was in sight of everyone, not off in a corner. It was "on the day of Preparation of the Passover and about the sixth hour of the day" (v. 14) when the judgment occurred.

Pilate delivers Jesus over to the Jews, not in accordance with the law, for he was innocent as Pilate himself acknowledges, but, as Luke 13:25 says, in accordance with their will. In this act, Pilate makes himself an agent of all the sins of the Jews and becomes guilty of the blood of this righteous man, even though he has given witness to his innocence and often spoken of him without any guilt in his person. But worldly justice endures so long as there is no threat or danger. The Lord has foretold of the verdict that falls upon him when he said to his disciples, "The Son of man will be delivered over to the Gentiles" (Mark 10:33). Gentile power and authority will sentence

---

64. LW 69.241 (WA 28.370).
65. LW 69.242 (WA 28.370).
66. LW 69.243 (WA 28.371).

Christ to death because he has set himself up as a king. Neither did Christ desire to be the physical king of the Jews nor did he want to be a seditious rebel against Caesar. But this is the guilt he and his followers must bear: Christ with his gospel, along with all those who desire to live under his gospel, is condemned as a rebel, guilty of crime against the imperial majesty of Caesar. Whoever wants to serve the gospel and bear the cross of Christ must endure the charge that he will be called seditious. "For the passion assigns Christ the sentence of dying as a rebel, and Holy Scripture calls the Gospel a seditious, tumultuous teaching, as St. Paul says in 2 Corinthians 6:4–5: 'Let us commend ourselves as servants of God: by great endurance, in afflictions, hardships, calamities, beatings, imprisonments, tumults, labors,' etc."[67] As Psalm 2:1–2 says, "Why do the nations rage and the people speak so vainly? The kings of the land rise up and the rulers take counsel together against the Lord and against His anointed." The heavenly Father and his Son, Christ, "cause"[68] tumult in the world, so that kings and emperors rage and the people prattle about it. Here Luther further clarified that the guilt for such turmoil lies not with the heavenly Father and the Son but with the kings and emperors who will not tolerate Christ with his gospel. Of the spiritual kingdom, Christ never encourages rebellion nor preaches it. It is true that the Christian doctrine is tumultuous, because its contents are in conflict with what people want to hear. It suffers tumult, but it does not incite it for we do not preach that one should wield the sword, but rather that each is to be obedient and subject to Christ's government. Those who cannot tolerate the gospel and condemn it are those who stir up tumult. It is they who use the sword simply because the Christians preach and confess the truth, and yet they have the reputation of being seditious. The verdict that Christ is a rebel also falls upon us. From this we draw comfort and joy, because we are faring just as our Head, Christ, fared, for "a servant is not above his master, nor a disciple above his teacher" (Matt 10:24).

Redemption: Christ Bore His Own Cross

"So they took Jesus and led him away," (v. 16) and "he bore his own cross" (v. 17). Jesus speaks as though it were the custom of the land that each one had to bear his own cross and gallows; so Christ too bears his own, and no one can bear it but Christ alone. St. Paul has his own cross, as he says in 2 Corinthians 12:7: "A stake was given me in the flesh, a messenger of Satan to beat me with his fists, to keep me from being too elated." The word "stake" means

67. LW 69.248 (WA 28.380).
68. LW 69.250 (WA 28.381).

"cross,"[69] which is placed upon St. Paul, that no one but he alone should bear it. Some of the fathers[70] suggest that Christ became so exhausted under the weight of the cross that he was unable to continue and that Simon of Cyrene was forced to bear the cross for him. Artists paint it as though Simon helped the Lord Jesus carry the bottom of the cross, with Christ bearing the upper portion of the cross.[71] That, Luther avers, is not correct: "Simon did not help Jesus carry his cross; rather, Christ, condemned to death, went forward, not with empty shoulders but bearing His cross and gallows upon His own neck."[72] This is how it occurred: Christ began to carry his cross from Pilate's palace onward, through the whole city, and right up to the gate. Then, in front of the gate, they seized Simon of Cyrene, a lowly and common man who was on his way in from the field (Luke 23:26). They compelled him to carry the cross after Jesus up to the place of execution. With Augustine,[73] Luther contends that the evangelist Luke did not say that Simon helped Jesus carry the cross but rather clearly indicates that they "laid the cross on Simon, to carry it after Jesus" (Luke 23:26). Just as Jesus was not relieved of his cross, so also Simon was not exempted from it.

Christ was led to the place where criminals were executed; it is called the place of a skull, full of corpses and bones. Jesus' death did not occur in a separate, secret place, but in the ordinary public place deliberately so it would appear that he had obtained what he had really deserved, and had to suffer punishment just as any other evildoer. John 19:18 says, "There they crucified Him, and with Him two others, one on each side, but Jesus between them." That Jesus was crucified with the two rebels and violators of the peace is a fulfilment of the Scripture, as the other evangelists quote from the prophet: "He was numbered with the evildoers" (Mark 15:28; Luke 22:37; Isa 53:12). The soldiers are so poisoned with malice that they are not satisfied with Christ's crucifixion but also make it more horrific, that he be crucified between the two criminals, as if he were the worst rebel, though Pilate had not commanded this. This they did to serve the chief priests. Added to physical torment Christ received all the derision and scorn from those who passed by him, wagging their heads and saying, "If You are the Son of God, come down from the cross" (Matt 27:40; Mark 15:30). "That is

---

69. LW 69.252 (WA 28.384).

70. See Gerson, *Ad deum vadit*, 102; Lyra John 19:17, "Et baiulans sibi crucem," Matt 27:32: "Exeuntes autem," as cited in LW 69.253, no. 102.

71. Despite Luther's remarks, the woodcut of Jesus carrying the cross in the Passional in Luther's 1529 *Personal Prayer Book* shows Simon carrying the bottom of the cross. See LW 43.42–45.

72. LW 69.253 (WA 28.386).

73. Augustine, *Harmony of the Gospels* 3.10 as cited in LW 69.253.

[truly] suffering—to say nothing of the torment of the soul about which we know nothing."[74]

> In short, everything that Christ encounters in His suffering is sheer diabolical hatred and spite. Whatever He does is pure poison and gall to the devil's servants. If He opens His mouth, He is mocked. If He wants to drink, they give him vinegar. When He prays, they sarcastically twist His words in mockery. . . Only this Jesus, who is condemned in His innocence, experiences this. So it is meant to happen: all ruthlessness is meant to fall upon Christ and His Gospel, so that the devil pours out all his wickedness and all his power upon Christ and in Him becomes powerless, for the salvation and comfort of us who believe in Christ.[75]

Christ's passion reveals the horror of sin, not his sin for there is none, but ours for which he suffers and dies. It costs the loss of God's Son, who is condemned to the most shameful death without any guilt of his own, and nailed to the cross as the worst of malefactors, and, moreover, must endure the cross himself to expiate our guilt.

> So Christ is now crucified and hangs on the cross as the worst thief, scoundrel, rebel, and murderer who has ever been on earth; and the innocent Lamb, Christ, must bear and pay for someone else's guilt. For it applies to us; those are our sins that burden His neck. We are this kind of sinners, thieves, scoundrels, rebels, and murderers; for even if we are not all so coarse as to carry them out in deed, we are still guilty of them before God. But now Christ comes to our place and bears our sins and pays for them so that through Him we are delivered. For if we believe in Him, not only will those of us who avoid gross outward sin be saved through Christ, but also those who fall into gross outward sin will be saved if they genuinely repent and believe in Christ. For many murderers are saved, as the histories of the Passion demonstrate when the malefactor on the right is converted and saved (Luke 23:39–43).[76]

Each convict had a sign on his cross upon which was written the misdeed he had committed. Pilate put an inscription over the Lord's cross, "Jesus of Nazareth, the King of the Jews" (John 19: 19), indicating that Christ was crucified because of his disobedience and rebellion. The title on the

74. LW 69.264 (WA 28.404).
75. LW 69.264 (WA 28.406).
76. LW 69.256 (WA 28.391).

cross was written in Hebrew, Greek, and Latin (v. 20) ensuring that everyone could see, read, hear, and understand why he was crucified. In this way, Pilate intended to excuse himself, as if he had no part in Christ's death, and reproached the Jews for having crucified their King. Just as Christ was slandered as a worldly king, a rebel against Caesar, so we are slandered as seditious in the world because we gladly take our stand under this title, and confess Christ as king. "[T]his false charge has now been transformed into pure innocence and truth. We take this title in earnest, though for Pilate it is mockery."[77] The Jews cannot concede him the whole title, "Jesus of Nazareth, the king of the Jews." So they petition Pilate, "Do not write, 'Jesus of Nazareth, the King of the Jews,' but rather, 'Jesus of Nazareth said He was the King of the Jews'" (v. 21). Pilate refuses and answers: "What I have written, I have written" (v. 22). It is of God's decree, Luther intimates, that the title applies to Christ alone, thus no new inscription is needed.

> Thus the Lord's title must remain on the cross, not because of Pilate's prudence but because of God's decree, because this title is due Christ alone. And whoever would live under this King must be a Jew: one who confesses, praises, and gives thanks. Many formerly signed and blessed themselves with this sign in the morning. Now, the words in themselves are good, but the abuse whereby they have been made into an idol is evil. The words should be understood aright and believed; that is their proper use.[78]

Accordingly, Christians could benefit from the proper use of the title of honor, "Jesus of Nazareth," through which we trample under foot the devil. To unbelief, the devil is a prince, or a god of this world; to faith, he is powerless. With the one word "Jesus of Nazareth," a Christian utters with true faith, the devil collapses as if struck by a thunderclap.

The soldiers who crucified Christ split his garments and divided them among themselves (John 19: 23). They left his tunic in one piece and gambled for it. The evangelist inserts this for the sake of the spiritual interpretation located in Psalm 22:18, "This was to fulfill the Scripture that says, 'They divided My garments among them'" (v. 24). St. John does not forget the historical account, and he concludes, "So the soldiers did these things" (v. 24). The account discloses how confident, unyielding, and audacious the behaviour is of these presumptuously confident soldiers who crucify Christ. Christ has nothing else on earth, neither tunic nor clothing; rather he hangs naked upon the cross. He has nowhere to lay his head and hangs

---

77. LW 69.258 (WA 28.394).
78. LW 69.259 (WA 28.395).

suspended in the air. Now he departs from the world entirely; he gives away his mother and his most beloved disciple, who nestled on his breast at the Last Supper (John 13:23). Christ suffers immense pain without concerning himself any longer with either mother or disciple or any earthly things. To his mother, he says, "Woman, behold, this is your son" (v. 26). To his disciple, he says, "Behold, this is your mother" (v. 27). From that moment, John the disciple took Jesus' mother as his own, looked after her, a solitary widow now stripped even of her only Son.

Papal preaching of Luther's day on the Passion esteemed Mary, namely that she has been given and committed to us as our mother. Luther did not disdain Mary, but hailed her, the dear Virgin and holy mother, in all honor, provided only she is not honored with the honor due to Christ. For neither was she crucified nor did she die for us; neither did she pray for us on the cross. It was Christ who suffered and died for us and with tears offered up supplications and prayers for us (Heb 5:7). Only Christ's merit and suffering on the cross covers all our sin, appeases God's wrath, and overcomes death, the devil, and hell. Christ forsakes everything—earth, his mother, his disciples, his comfort—to save us. For since he separates himself from his mother on earth, and does not cleave to her, we should not attach ourselves to her and abandon the Son. If we cling to her, we tarnish Christ's honor and office, transferring them to his mother. This is to turn Mary into an idol. To do so is to deny the sufferings of Christ and the fruit that results from it. We should adhere to him alone and render him the honor that is due to no one else.

When the Lord uttered in John 19: 28, "It is accomplished," he meant all Scripture was fulfilled. The world and devil did all that they could to Christ, and Christ suffered all that was required for the redemption of humanity, all that was prophesied and proclaimed in Scripture through the prophets. Christ's passion sets up an insurmountable barrier to all attempts to amass merit from human deeds, or assign merit to it. For this reason Luther insists that Jesus bore his own cross all the way to Calvary, reducing Simon of Cyrene to a minor role. In this, Luther's theology evinces a fundamental theological shift: that Christ's passion presents him as a unique substitute for sin rather than as an example of penitential imitation for sin-burdened Christian. Atonement is achieved: Christ, the Lamb of God is slain and offered for the sins of the world [John 1:29; Rev 13:8]. "Everything is fulfilled and completed, and no one may dispute, as if anything yet remained to be fulfilled and accomplished."[79] Christ's atoning work is so

---

79. LW 69.265 (WA 28.406).

thorough and complete that there is nothing left for humans to do, except praise him and his grace.

Whereas the ancient Mosaic Passover Lamb was only a figure, type, and shadow of the future, Christ on the cross is "the true, substantial Passover Lamb."[80] St. John cites Zechariah's prophecy of Christ's future suffering (1 Pet 1:10–11) in v. 37: "They will look on Him whom they have pierced" (Zech 12:10). He refers this to the present sign and miracle, that "blood and water" (v. 34) flowed out of his opened side. Generally the early fathers refer water and blood to the Holy Sacraments: the water is Holy Baptism and the blood is the Lord's Supper.[81] With Paul,[82] St. John calls "blood" the grace of Jesus Christ; he calls "water" the gift of Holy Spirit. He puts the two together to show and testify what Christ has poured out into the world. It is grace that justified us, through which we enter divine favor for the sake of Christ's blood. The gift of the Holy Spirit purifies and preserves us; it keeps us in true faith until sin is put to death. Though we are redeemed by the blood, the old Adam, with its evil lusts and sins sill remain, and is at war with the Holy Spirit. So it is necessary that we be continually and daily washed, cleansed, and purified. The twin benefits—forgiveness and purification—belong to those who cling to the pierced side with faith. Christ as gift must be embraced by faith before Christ as example is undertaken in works.

Christ's Tomb: Comprehended in Word and Faith

The burial of Christ is attested by Joseph of Arimathea and Nicodemus who buried him as well as by the new tomb in which he is laid (John 19:38–39). Joseph, a disciple of Jesus, was a respected member of the Council, who was also waiting for the kingdom of God (Mark 15:41); he had not given in to their counsel and deeds (Mark 15:43). He was accompanied by Nicodemus, a Pharisee and ruler among the Jews, who formerly had come to visit Jesus by night (John 3:1–2). Joseph and Nicodemus did not want Jesus' body to remain on the cross, allowing it to decay. The extravagant anointing is performed not only once but repeatedly, as a sign of love. Myrrh and aloes are preservatives; they are expensive, and extraordinarily fragrant, preserving

---

80. LW 69.272 (WA 28.416).

81. Cf. Augustine, *Tractates on John* 120.2 [NPNF1 7:434]; Cyril of Alexandria, *Commentary on John* 12, 48:1645. Others interpret it as referring to redemption and purification. Cf. Ambrose, *De benedictionibus Patriarchum* 4:24 (PL 14:681). Erasmus interprets them as signifying that Christ's death begets washing from sin [water] and eternal life [blood]. See his *Paraphrase on John*, in CWE 46:214.

82. For Luther's contrast of grace and gift in the preface to Romans in the 1522 translation of the New Testament, see LW 35.369–70.

the body and clothes that were coated with them. Though the Lord Jesus endured a disgraceful and shameful death, he was not only buried but also to be buried in honor and splendor by reputable and prominent persons at great expense. He was laid "in a new tomb in which no one had ever been laid (v. 41). Joseph and Nicodemus placed him there, and the Jews secured the tomb with a stone and seal as testimony that Christ was buried and placed in the earth for our sakes. St. John indicates this to make us certain of the article of faith that Jesus indeed died and was placed in the tomb. It was a courageous act for Joseph to approach Pilate for the body, and for Nicodemus to accompany him and help bury it. Their fearless and open confession of Jesus is the fruit and power of the death of Christ and his prayer on the cross.

The salutary use of Christ's burial through faith is "the foremost and most necessary part"[83] of Christ's passion. His tomb is a purely external thing, and is of no avail; but when it is regarded in the Word with faith, it is also salvation and blessing. Proper contemplation of Christ's passion should not remain with the external cross and empty tomb, but must progress to the inward contemplation of them by faith. The external elements "should and must come first, but the inward should come afterward and follow through the external."[84] Christ's tomb should be contemplated so that each may confess: "Christ's tomb is for our benefits." Just as he took all our sins with him to the cross and bore them in his body, so also he brought with him all our sins into the tomb and buried them in it. Christ's tomb is holy, not because of its external architecture, but because all the world's sin, misery, wretchedness, death, and damnation lie buried in it and because it makes our own tomb holy. His tomb, with which we join, becomes our treasury through which we are completely sanctified from our sins. "This is a salutary, blessed tomb,"[85] from which we inherit everything, namely, redemption from sin, death, and every evil. Only the eyes of faith can distinguish between Christ's tomb and the tombs of all others, including Abraham, Isaac, and Jacob. None but Christ was buried for us, as the Children's Creed teaches: "I believe in Jesus Christ our Lord, who suffered, died, was buried..." The words "our Lord" means everything that Christ did becomes ours.[86] Thus Luther heightens the phrase "for us" (*pro nobis*)[87] as the true meaning of the Creed:

83. LW 69.275 (WA 28.418).
84. Cf. Against the Heavenly Prophets (1525), LW 40.146.
85. LW 69.278 (WA 28.421).
86. LW 69.276 (WA 28.419).

87. For Luther's emphasis on the phrase "for us," see his Lectures on Galatians (1531/1535), LW 26:32-39 (WA XL.83-94); LW 26.176-79 (WA XL.295-300).

"Christ was conceived and born *for us*, suffered and was crucified *for us*, died and was buried *for us*."[88] The real Christian pilgrimage and true kiss of the holy sepulcher is not a physical but a spiritual kind. Thus Luther repudiated long and expensive pilgrimages many had made to the holy tomb in Jerusalem to earn indulgences and the forgiveness of sins. St. Jerome, Luther claimed, should have remained in Rome; instead he abandoned his duties at home and traveled to Jerusalem to see the holy sepulcher.[89] Nothing more is accomplished except to make the tomb into an idol.[90]

Through faith we make Christ wholly and completely our own, along with his suffering, dying, death, and tomb, and become sharers in his merit, death, and tomb for the forgiveness of sins, eternal righteousness, and salvation. For in Christ, there is no lack; all miseries—sin, wrath, death, and hell—are wiped out and buried. Thus he is most worthy of our worship and salutary kiss. "And that is the true prayer, the true kiss, and the highest honor"[91] that we can render to the whole passion: suffering, dying, and burial.

---

88. Italics are mine.
89. LW 69.279 (WA 28.421).
90. LW 69.279 (WA 28.421).
91. LW 69.277 (WA 28.420).

Chapter 14

Resurrection and Flame of Love

Christ our Brother and His Voice

St. John carefully portrays the history and event of the resurrection to make certain the foundation for the article of our faith, "I believe that Jesus Christ rose from the dead."[1] The contrast between cross and resurrection is not that one celebrates defeat and the other victory. Easter is not a joyous day, preceded by Calvary, a day of doom; rather it means resurrection renders the cross effectual such that the victory is nothing else than the victory of the crucified.[2] The Word of God is the causative agency of one's conviction and confession of it. Christ's voice is the flame of love in Mary Magdalene, creating faith in Christ the "Brother." The gospel of joyous exchange between our sin and Christ's righteousness is comprehended in Christ our Brother, in whom we are included in the Father's eternal love for the Son, which is communicated to our hearts in the efficacy of the Holy Spirit. This dear and friendly word "brother" is a word of the gospel to the

---

1. LW 69.287 (WA 28.431).

2. Hermann Sasse counteracted the charge of one-sidedness in preaching: "The theology of the cross obviously does not mean that for the theologian the whole church year shrinks to Good Friday. It rather means that one cannot understand Christmas, Easter, or Pentecost without Good Friday. Luther was alongside Irenaeus and Athanasius, one of the great theologians of the incarnation. He was that because he saw the cross behind the manger. He understood the victory of Easter as well as any theologian of the Eastern Church. But he understood it because he understood it as the victory of the Crucified. The same can be said of his understanding of the activity of the Holy Spirit." Sasse, "Theologia Crucis," in *Letters*, 387–88. Also cited in Pless, "Cross-bearing and Life in a Lutheran synod," 185.

faithless and forsworn people, who have felt the intolerable burden of the law. Though we are not as pious as Mary Magdalene, we now experience Christ to be more intimately present with us as we walk with him daily than he was with Mary then, but only for a brief period. The whole weight of the Christian faith is wrapped up in this confession of Christ, the risen Christ our Brother, who has overcome death and the grave, and his righteousness is reckoned unto us in exchange for our sin. Faith grasps the salutary fruits of Christ's resurrection: redemption from sin and death, consolation and joy—all of this is due to the superabundant greatness of God's power, not human power.

Resurrection: The Most Difficult Article

In his sermon on John 19, Luther declares: "No article of faith is more difficult to believe than 'I believe the forgiveness of sins,'"[3] for no other reason than this: not until the article of the forgiveness of sins enters our experience and affects us personally do we ever grasp the power of other articles. However here in his sermon on John 20, he propounds:

> [Resurrection] is the highest and foremost article, along with other articles of our Christian faith upon which our salvation rests. For this has been and still is the most offensive article and the hardest to believe. The other articles of our Christian faith are also hard to believe, but this article is the hardest. The reason is that no other article is so repugnant to our experience as this one. For we see right before our eyes that the entire world is being snatched away by death and is dying.[4]

Resurrection of the dead is most difficult article to believe, for no other reason than this: not only does it contradict outward appearances and experience, but also human reason.[5] It is problematic both at the level of personal experience and at the rational level. However faith in God's Word triumphs over contrary appearances. The certainty of this article rests not upon human reason, but the testimony of Holy Scripture, which we apprehend by faith:

> In sum, if someone takes the counsel of reason and judges by outward appearances and experience, faith will collapse, and a

---

3. LW 69.185 (WA 28.271).

4. LW 69.286 (WA 28.429).

5. LW.28.59, where Luther said reason "perverted this article [resurrection] into tomfoolery." See Scaer, "Luther's Concept of the Resurrection," 109–24.

human being will abandon this article. Therefore, it is necessary for every Christian to keep before the testimony of Holy Scripture concerning the resurrection of the dead, according to which the Lord Christ's resurrection is proven and attested through undoubted revelation as well, and to take a sure stand upon this, abandoning outward appearances and the experience of reason. And this is also the reason why St. John, like the other evangelists, so carefully described the history of the Lord's resurrection and left nothing out that might serve to confirm this article.[6]

For Luther, the Jewish leaders of the time, such as the Pharisees opposed such faithful testimonies of the Lord's resurrection, even when confronted with manifest signs. But both friend and foe bore witness to it. The women and the disciples themselves confessed that the Lord was not in the tomb. This is borne out in St. Luke [24:22-24]: "Some women of our company amazed us. They were at the tomb early in the morning, and when they did not find His body, they came back, saying that they had seen a vision of angels, who said that He was alive. Some of those who were with us went to the tomb and found it just as the women had said, but Him they did not see." St. Matthew reports that the story had been circulated among the Jews to the present day, and would have been spread throughout the common people. The Lord's adversaries—the governor Pilate, the chief priests and Pharisees, and the common people—also attest the Lord's resurrection. This article also has the testimony of the Great city of Jerusalem and the populace, though none in it had seen Christ rise from the dead. For God raised Jesus on the third day and caused him to appear, not to all but to those who were the appointed witnesses. Peter and John, Mary Magdalene and all the other women and disciples went to the tomb, and discovered the truth, just as the angels had said. The Lord himself appears among them; he eats, drinks, and talks with them. He even allows them to touch and behold him; and says, "See My hands and My feet, that it is I Myself. Touch Me, and see. For a spirit does not have flesh and bones as you see that I have" (Luke 24:39). Forty days before his ascension, Christ convinces them so that none can deny, but all must confess, that the Lord has truly risen, just as he said. This is also in perfect agreement with the testimony of the dear prophets. In this way, "the event itself as well as the Scripture"[7] certify in our hearts the historical veracity of such testimonies. Any kind of special revelation and attempt to see Christ in person through personal visions do

---

6. LW 69.287 (WA 28.431). Janz, *Martin Luther*, 116–17.
7. LW 69.288 (WA 28.434).

not stand, for very often the devil disguises himself in the form of Christ. The testimonies of Christ himself, his enemies, the apostles, the prophets, the event, and Holy Scripture are more than enough to convince us than any secret revelation.

Secular and Spiritual Kingdom

St. Luke (24:2–3) indicates that when the women saw that the stone had disappeared from the tomb, they went inside the tomb and did not find the Lord's body. St. John portrays it differently, that as soon as the women found the stone rolled away from the tomb, they returned home to tell the other disciples about it. Thus verse 2 says, "So she ran and went to Simon Peter and the other disciple, the one whom Jesus loved, and said to them, 'They have taken away my Lord from the tomb, and we do not know where they have laid Him.'" Her words disclose the passionate heart she exhibits for Christ, indicating her deepest longing and desire with which her heart is full. The two disciples, Peter and John, are consumed with such great love for the Lord Jesus, more than all the other disciples. That is why they rush to the tomb first, and are ahead of all the rest. Still, John, being younger and stronger, makes his way to the tomb faster than Peter. The narration from verses 3–7, indicates that these two run together. John reaches the tomb first, yet did not enter the tomb, but Peter, who followed him, entered the tomb and saw the linen cloths lying there and the towel folded up nearby in a place by itself. In Luther's day, this sequence of events was employed to argue for papal authority. Since John gives way to Peter to enter the tomb first, they argued, this establishes that Peter, the successor to whose throne is the pope, is the lord of all the apostles. This is not so, Luther avers, for Christ came to accomplish more urgent things on earth than to establish a secular kingdom. Christ had commended the physical, worldly government to Adam, to whom God said in Genesis 1:28, "Be fruitful and multiply and fill the earth and subdue it and have dominion over the fish of the sea and over the birds of the heaven and over every living thing that moves on the earth." On the contrary, Christ came to ordain and establish the spiritual government, in which the Word and preaching of it, by which we are redeemed from sin and death, reign. Every Christian should aspire to be "the greatest and foremost"[8] in the office of Christ and the apostles, which consists in nothing else than "service, namely, the care of souls, serving human beings with the word of grace, so that they are delivered from sin, death,

---

8. LW 69.294 (WA 28.442).

and hell and are saved."⁹ They should not govern as lords in the worldly manner, but that they should hold out the Word of life and lead people to heaven by such preaching. "Now whoever does this . . . he should rightly be called pope and supreme."¹⁰ But such authority of service, which Christ commands in his kingdom, does not gain acceptance in those who quarrel over worldly authority of power and sovereignty. Such so-called leaders of the church teach nothing but external ceremonies, human commandments, and performance of good works as the way to salvation. In so doing, they abdicate Christ's office and abandon the authority of service characteristic of the apostles, martyrs, and all genuine Christians. These ceremonies and commandments do not remedy sin and death. Eating, drinking, and clothing belong to the worldly kingdom; they cannot help us obtain eternal life. In the spiritual kingdom, the soul needs nothing of these temporal goods, but the gospel, which frees him from sin and death and ensures eternal salvation.

Peter went into the tomb first, even though he arrived at the tomb after John. The other disciples allowed Peter to have the pre-eminence, because he was the oldest and was the first to be called by Christ. Even so, Peter allows himself to be commissioned to Samaria by the rest of the apostles to preach the Word of God (Acts 8:14). Each willingly gives preference over himself. What is indicated here in this text is how John esteemed Peter, and not how Peter was the chief of the apostles. In the world, the order and distinction must be kept and preserved, so that those in secular authority are more honorably esteemed than the subjects; otherwise the stronger would trample the weaker underfoot, eventually converting the world into a wasteland. But here in the spiritual kingdom where Christ rules and there are only pious children, such a distinction disappears, nor is it necessary. So the more profoundly a Christian abases himself and serves another, "the best and highest"¹¹ he is in the kingdom of heaven. The measure of greatness is humble service and not lordship, weakness and not power, suffering and not glory. These radical reversals are integral to Luther's theology of the cross and are programmatically opposed to worldly standards.

> Therefore, this and other Gospel texts should not be applied to external, physical reality, . . . but rather to inner, spiritual reality, meaning that all who occupy the office of Christ and the apostles should care for the salvation of men's souls. For secular authority rules over body and possessions, but Christ rules over

---

9. LW 69.295 (WA 28.443).
10. LW 69.294 (WA 28.442).
11. LW 69.295 (WA 28.443).

souls through His apostles and disciples with the Word. Therefore, with this text St. John neither institutes nor confirms the power and sovereignty that the pope arrogates to himself over all Christendom and the whole world as head of the Church and god of the world. Rather, he shows here the kindness, love, and humility that obtained among the dear apostles.[12]

Mary Magdalene and The External, Physical Word

Although the dear disciples saw the physical tokens of resurrection, they still could not believe in it. Instead they concluded the opposite, that the Lord's body had been stolen by his adversaries and removed from the tomb. They reasoned that the people in authority and power might have committed such an outrage, tearing off the linen cloths and the towel from the dead body and folding them up. Had friends done this, they would have had carried away the body together with the linen cloths and towel and rolled the stone back in front of the tomb again. In their weakness, they conceive what should have attested the Lord's resurrection as evidence against it. Their unbelief was further compounded by what they heard from Mary Magdalene, when she said: "They have taken the Lord away out of the tomb, and we do not know where they have laid Him" (v. 13). Of themselves, the disciples cannot believe in the Lord's resurrection. This is because they are without the external Word; verse 9 says, "they did not yet know the Scripture, that He must rise from the dead." Not until they receive the Word, and hear Christ expound the Scriptures to them and open up their understanding do they believe. No testimonies, of the three angels Gabriel, friend or foe, can convert or move the hearts to believe, unless they are accompanied by Christ's voice. Holy Scripture is "the best and strongest testimony,"[13] for it possesses an inherent efficacy, not to be borrowed from any extraneous factors such as human experience, philosophical reasoning or rationalistic apologetic, or human deeds. The Word of God bears "a performative authority" that has the power to transform lives and create new situations.[14] The Word accomplishes its own mission when it is preached and truly heard by the people. As with Mary Magdalene, the Word spoken by Christ kindles a "flame of love"[15] in the heart.

12. LW 69.296 (WA 28.446).
13. LW 69.298 (WA 28.447).
14. Lischer, *Theology of Preaching*, 71. Cf. Bultmann, *Faith and Understanding I*, 308: "His works are his words [and] his words are his works."
15. LW 69.300 (WA 28.451).

St. John singles out Mary Magdalene and applauds her for her faith. Mary saw the open tomb (v. 1), and "two angels in white sitting in front of her inside the tomb" (v. 12) who converse with her, ask why she was weeping. And then the Lord himself appeared in the guise of the gardener, saying: "Woman, why are you weeping? Whom are you seeking?" (v. 15). She would have been frightened by such a sight and fled from the tomb with trembling, as St. Mark [16:8] wrote concerning the other women, who, when they saw a young man dressed in a long white robe in the tomb, would have taken flight from the tomb with fear. But Mary was so drunk with love that she neither heeds any of this nor is afraid of angels or anyone else. The day after Sabbath, she came alone, and early, scarcely waiting till dawn broke. She forsakes all household cares and work, and races to the tomb, without any thoughts of what people might say about her, or what danger might befall her, since many of the governor Pilate's and the chief priests' guards are stationed at the tomb. If only she could find the dead Christ she would be satisfied. Mary, from whom Christ drove seven devils, is so full of love for the Lord that she can think of nothing but Christ's deed of kindness and their daily fellowship. This is what naturally happens, that when friendship is severed by death, it results in immeasurable pain; this is what happens to Mary's friendship with Christ.[16]

Though Mary is consumed with love for the Lord, she does not possess faith in Christ's resurrection; she mistakes the Lord for the gardener. "Supposing Him to be the gardener, she said to Him. Sir, if you have carried Him away, tell me where you have laid Him, and I will take Him away" (v. 15). It is amid her fervency for the Lord that he calls her by name, and says in verse 16, "Mary." The Lord spoke to her with his natural, usual voice, known to the disciples and women around him. It was not until Jesus addressed her by name did she recognize him, no longer as the gardener but the risen Lord. "His voice bears witness to her concerning Him, that He Himself is present and alive."[17] Immediately she turns around, races to him, and wants to touch and kiss him. Now he is alive, no longer dead to her, he whom she wanted to take away from the tomb. Seeing, for Mary Magdalene, is not believing;[18] rather the Word of Christ she hears evokes a faith that illumines what she has seen. There abides a sequence that begins with unbelief through the conviction of truth to its confession. Thus verse 18: "Mary Magdalene went

---

16. Luther's teaching echoes classical discussions of friendship and favor in Cicero, *De amicitial* 2.8, 9.29 and Seneca, *De beneficiis* 1.11 as cited in LW 69.299.

17. LW 69.304 (WA 28.455).

18. See Koester, "Passion and Resurrection," 91.

and announced to the disciples, 'I have seen the Lord, and this is what He said to me.'"

How can Mary proclaim the promise of future life with God? The word of God in the form of command in verse 17: "Go and tell" is the action of Mary. She can only speak of the resurrection because Christ has commanded her to do so, that is, to proclaim the Word of the One who does not lie but remains faithful. The truth of Christ's resurrection is the predicate of the Word of address from Christ himself, who is true. "This is the theological sequence which Luther develops. Its premise is that God is true because God cannot negate God's self. The living God cannot abandon us to death, or God would be contradicting God's self."[19] Preaching is the condition of possibility of an awakened hope, which has God as its origin. It declares to us what we could never tell ourselves, nor could we invent, that is, hope of future life with God. The risen Christ, who calls Mary by name, commissions her to preach; he supplies the conviction and contents of her preaching. Not of free will but God's creative act, her lips are opened and mouth loosed for the proclamation of the praise of God, despising the dangers that may confront her. The knowledge of the truth, fused with the Holy Spirit, brings with it an inward compulsion to speak of what she has experienced. Those who are justified are compelled to say with David: "I believe, therefore have I spoken" (Ps 116:10). Public confession is the "the highest work"—"the virtue of virtues,"[20] for there is no greater work than confessing the name of the Lord. The Word of God that grasps Mary is the flame of her love for Christ; or, the voice of Christ addressing her is the ground of the certainty concerning himself, that he is present and alive, and certainty concerning "all who die in the faith, [that they] have their 'place' in God's Word and promise in Jesus Christ."[21] And yet faith does not create the word; rather it hears and receives it. Faith is "drawn from the Word of God,"[22] and does not follow the dictates of human reason and the senses. Once created, faith takes leave of itself and simply permits God to take the lead and reign over us.[23]

The same experience Mary had with Christ is predicated of us: that we possess his holy Word, which we read, hear, and preach. Christ is the common guest among us and abides with us daily, just as he was with Mary.

---

19. Sauter, "Luther on the Resurrection," 102.

20. LW 12.394.95.

21. See Karl-Heinz zur Mühlen, "Luther II. Theologie," as cited in Sauter, "Luther on the Resurrection," 102, n. 9.

22. LW 12.22.

23. Paulson, *Lutheran Theology*, 122.

Some might argue that Mary found it easy to love Christ, for she had the Lord with her in person, and he was her guest. Likewise it would be easy for us to love him, if Christ were also our guest in person. Luther challenges such an assumption, "What advantage would it be even if He were here with you in person and was your guest?"[24] He cites the Pharisees, who had Christ in person, and he was their guest. But they did not befriend Christ, but bit him like poisonous vipers. The same applies to us, that if Christ were to be physically present, we might not befriend him. Mary loved Jesus Christ not because of his appearance, nor because of his physical presence alone; rather, she bound herself to his mouth and attuned her ears to hear him speak. "That very Word which she heard from Him was the flame of her love, which she had burning in her heart."[25] The Word that ignited in her fervent love and ardent faith towards Christ will do even more for us, for we hear him speaking now longer and clearer than Mary, who heard him speak for a short while. By comparison, the flame of love burns brighter and greater in us than in Mary Magdalene.[26] Our intimacy with Christ thus is greater than Mary's.

Nevertheless no one loves Christ as much as Mary did. So, then, in her we have a picture of a fine, beautiful heart that is so disposed to the gospel that "in her sight, everything else is dead and deceased; only Christ, dead and buried, lives in her heart."[27] She is convinced that when she has the gospel, she has everything; without it, she has nothing. Anyone who hears this example should explore if his heart is burning with such fervent, earnest love for Christ. For we too are the recipients of inexhaustible blessings from God, which should impel us to serve him with reciprocal love and earnest zeal. We may have heard the gospel for many years now, and we act as if we had always possessed this treasure, and need no more instruction. We regard the dear Word with laziness,[28] carelessness, contempt and persecution. Though Christ abides with us, and accompanies us with all his love and friendship, it is folly of us not to lay hold of the Word by which we learn to know God aright. Terrible blindness and horrible darkness befall those who show disdain for God's Word and ingratitude for God's great kindness, and what they have is nothing but troubled, unstable hearts and consciences. We

24. LW 69.300 (WA 28.451).
25. LW 69.300 (WA 28.451).
26. LW 69.301 (WA 28.451).
27. LW 69.302 (WA 28.453).
28. On laziness, see Luther's discussion of the Third Commandment in his *The Large Catechism* (1529) I.99 in Tappert, *Book of Concord*, 378: "This is precisely the sin that used to be classed among the mortal sins and was called *acidia*—that is, indolence or satiety."

too will be repaid for this, as Solomon says in Proverbs 1:26 (cf. Prov. 10:24): "What the wicked dreads will come upon him."

Resurrection and Ascension

Once Christ had ascended to the Father, he could no longer be touched. But Jesus forbad Mary to touch him, even while he was with her on earth. Christ says, "Do not touch Me, for I have not yet ascended to the Father" (v. 17). With these words, Jesus wanted to rebuke Mary, who understood the Lord's resurrection to mean he will return to this mortal life as he was before. That explains why she wants to touch him and enjoy his fellowship, kiss him, and serve him as before in this life of time, of sense, of nature, and of death. In that case, his existence would not be any different from that of Lazarus (John 11:1–44), or the son of the widow (Luke 8:41–56), who were reawakened by Christ. Mary's opinion is "false and incorrect."[29] Christ was risen, in order that he might go to the Father. Luther paraphrases the meaning of Christ's saying:

> I have not risen from the dead so that you might touch and kiss me as before. Neither am I any longer in the same existence and life as before. By My resurrection I have not stepped back into My former existence and life in order to use them as I formerly used them and as Lazarus and others use them after they had been reawakened by Me. Rather, I have risen from the dead in order to ascend to My Father and begin a different, eternal life. Lazarus did not rise in this way, for Lazarus did not ascend to heaven.[30]

Latent in Christ's words is a distinct purpose borne by his resurrection, different from that of Lazarus and others who were raised from the dead: "namely, that through it He would ascend to heaven and take up the kingdom as King and Lord over all."[31] What truly concerns Christ is not Mary's touch, but that his resurrection be properly understood as that which guarantees entrance into a different existence, that of eternal life. Christ says: "But go to My brothers and say to them, 'I am ascending to My Father and to your Father, to My God and to your God.'" Resurrection is the presupposition of Christ's ascension to the heavenly throne, where he resides with

---

29. LW 69.304 (WA 28.455).
30. LW 69.304 (WA 28.456).
31. LW 69.304 (WA 28.456).

his Father, presides over all, and heals us by imputing us his righteousness through the Holy Spirit, whom he asks the Father to send (cf. John 14:16).[32]

It is proper to affirm that the human nature of Christ has died a real death. "And yet, it is right to say that the Son of God has been put to death."[33] Since Christ is one Person, fully God and fully man, it is proper to say the Son of God dies. But, at the same time, we must also affirm that Christ could not die "because he was himself the living God."[34] Since Christ is of one being with his Father, his Father is also our Father through our union with Christ. The glorification of Christ consists in his resurrection and entry into another life, where he is no longer under the jurisdiction of hell, sin, and death, and the law is rescinded. Believers who are in Christ are made lord over all, just as he is, and co-heirs with Christ in the possession of a heavenly kingdom and eternal inheritance. In Christ, risen from the dead and exalted to the right hand of the Father, believers receive a new life, a new situation, and a new creation; they participate in the divine life itself, so that "God lives in us, and make us partakers of His life, to live through Him, and from Him, and in Him."[35]

Fruits in the Word "Brother"

Christ says: "But go to My brothers and say to them, 'I am ascending to My Father and to your Father, to My God and to your God.'" Christ committed to Mary the task of preaching to strengthen his disciples' faith in his resurrection. The beauty of this text, "Go and say to My brothers," preached almost every Easter consists in this: the risen Christ desires to be called the brother of his disciples and all believers. There is no more friendly, lovely word than the word "brother." But whenever it lands on a self-sufficient, shameless, wicked, and ungrateful heart, it is a shame. "These words [Go and say to My Brothers] ought to be written with large and golden letters—not merely on paper or in a book but in our hearts so that they live within."[36] Christians of all sorts could deduce the confidence and consolation that are comprehended in this word "brother." Peter denied the Lord three times, and the other disciples had fled from him and left him forsaken in his affliction and suffering. And yet to these faithless and forsworn people, who have come under the terrible burden of the law, Christ did not speak a nega-

32. WA 726.24–30 as cited in Lienhard, *Martin Luther*, 364–65.
33. WA 40.III.721, 27 as cited in Lienhard, *Martin Luther*, 364.
34. WA 721.28 as cited Lienhard, *Martin Luther*, 364.
35. WA 10.I.1, 199, 25 as cited in Siggins, *Martin Luther's Doctrine of Christ*, 169.
36. LW 69.305 (WA 28.456).

tive word of judgment. Moreover Christ, "God's eternal Son, the Creator and Lord of all things,"[37] speaks a word of the gospel: "Go and say to My brothers." Whoever understands how rich and comforting these words will become drunk with joy and delight, just as Mary Magdalene is drunk with fervor and affection for the Lord. The great King and Lord of all creatures calls us "His creatures,"[38] of which we are not even worthy. But he also wants us to be and to be called "His brother,"[39] which is awe-inspiring. There is cause for joy, since the man, who might call us his creature but now calls us his brother, is a great King and a Lord over heaven and earth, sin and death, the devil and hell, and any creatures in this world and the world to come (Eph 1:21). "But our hearts are too small and narrow and the comfort is far too great and altogether overwhelming for us to grasp it firmly, even though we hear and learn about it daily."[40] But whenever the word "brother" enters a heart and is firmly believed, such a heart would become eager and joyous as an outcome.

The fruits that proceed from this word "brother" are great and glorious beyond all measure. If we are Christ's brother, just as Christ assuredly promises us in his words, then it must follow that we are heirs with Christ of all his possessions and of equal inheritance, sharing all things in common with him (Rom 8:17). Through Christ our Brother, his Father is also our Father, and his God is also ours. Believers are wrapped up in the eternal love the Father has for the Son, for both are found pleasing to God. The Father's love for the sinful world initiates the Son's descent into the flesh; the Son's obedience to the Father effects our inclusion in him through the way of God-forsaken death on Golgotha and Easter in his ascent to the Father. Just as Christ our brother draws us up into the heavenly Father in his ascension so that we may participate in his righteousness and life, so also he bestows his Holy Spirit to bring the Father's love to fulfillment in us and heal us by the joyous exchange of our sin for his righteousness in a free act of grace.

A vast distinction occurs between Christ the person, the righteous One, and his disciples, the sinners. But he wills to share his entire inheritance with them so that there is no distinction between him and them in so far as their common blessings and identical inheritance are concerned. The friendly, lovely word "brother" places a crown on our head, and together with it all the gospel privileges, for we are included in the Father's eternal love for the Son.

37. LW 69.306 (WA 28.458).
38. LW 69.306 (WA 28.458).
39. LW 69.306 (WA 28.458).
40. LW 69.306 (WA 28.458).

When, however, this word "brother" is properly applied to me, comes from the heart and is firmly believed, it then follows that I belong to paradise and the kingdom of heaven, where Christ is Lord, for I am to be His co-heir, to live and rule together with Him. Indeed, He gives us not merely the bare name but also the inheritance with it. Thus every Christian and believer is called the Lord Christ's brother because he is an heir together with Christ of all heavenly blessings.[41]

Christ also stresses in Matthew 12:50: "Whoever does the will of My Father in heaven is My brother and sister and mother." "Doing the will of the Father" does not mean the religious duties we perform; rather it means nothing other than clinging to Christ and believing with certainty that Christ's promise to be our Brother is true. Concerning this, Christ himself provides an interpretation of what God's work and will are, in John 6:29, "This is the work of God, that you believe in Him whom He has sent." Shortly after, he says, "This is the will of Him who sent Me, that everyone who looks on the Son and believes in Him should have eternal life, and I will raise him up on the last day" (John 6:39–40). Those who cleave to Christ and believe in him are his mother, brother, and sister, and God's children and heirs. All share the same heavenly kingdom and blessings as Christ does—not through merit or deeds of their own, but purely by way of imputation.

The fanatics claim otherwise, that we should abandon the Word and "advance higher."[42] They make this case by appealing to the inner word apart from or beyond the external word and oral preaching. "Thus it is the devil himself who is among the sectarians and fanatics who profess that the preaching of the Gospel is nothing: that one must reach even higher."[43] Because they advance higher than the external Word, the fanatics end up producing their own thoughts and disgraceful dreams.[44] For no one could produce better and loftier preaching than Christ who descended from heaven to earth: "Here, however, is the best and loftiest Doctor and Teacher who has ever come or will come upon the earth; He brings this doctrine that He is our Brother."[45] No matter how great our sins are, the word "brother" can absolve them if we cling to Christ and believe that his promise to be our brother is efficacious; it possesses a power greater than all the foreswearing and denial committed by Peter and all the blasphemy and persecution com-

41. LW 69.307 (WA 28.459).
42. LW 69.307 (WA 28.461).
43. LW 69.308 (WA 28.461).
44. Cf. LW 40.101 (Against the Heavenly Prophets, 1525).
45. LW 69.308 (WA 28.461).

mitted by Paul. The preaching of our dear Jesus Christ is not written down for the sake of the disciples and apostles, but for the sake of all believers. Nevertheless, the preaching of Christ's brotherhood is a sermon we are far too weak to preach or believe. "There is nothing lacking in Him; the lack is ours."[46] Not only do we find it difficult to believe such things, but also the apostles themselves heard it and yet did not believe until the Holy Spirit came to teach them. Our conscience can be so tormented by the devil and afflicted with doubts that it cannot tolerate the word "brother."

Luther offers a practical advice on the timing within which we should think about sin and not think about it. The frightening truth of a death-causing God was not intended for a terrified soul; it is to be preached to the smug and impenitent sinners. But once the sinner has been exposed and terrified in conscience by the law of sin, he is now made ready for the reception of God's grace in Christ. "Therefore, here we should forget our sin (for there is a time to think about sin and also a time not to think about sin) and not follow the gnawing and biting of our conscience, nor judge according to what we feel, but rather according to the Word."[47] The phrase "forget our sin" means not judging ourselves, which the devil encourages to rob us of joy, but clinging to the sweet word "brother," wherein joy lies. We should cast our sin anew upon Christ, our Brother, in whom there is no sin but righteousness, no evil but sheer goodness, no death but sheer life. When tormented by sin and bad conscience, Luther vividly repudiates it by the concept of imputation in a monologue: "Hear what My Brother Christ has to say, for He says: 'I am God's Son and heir; you shall be My co-heir if you Cling to Me and believe in Me. You shall not win such a treasure from Me by merit; rather, I give it to you out of grace and freely.'"[48]

On the evening of that Sabbath after Mary Magdalene had carried out the proclamation that Christ had commanded her, the Lord himself appears before the disciples through closed doors, stands in their midst, and kindly greets them with this, "Peace be with you" (v. 19).[49] The proclamation Mary brought to the disciples includes his resurrection and ascension to his God and Father, being constituted as his brothers and co-heirs with him so that the heaven he possesses belongs to them. Now, so that they may be

---

46. LW 69.309 (WA 28.463).

47. LW 69.309 (WA 28.464). See LW 14.85 (WA 31, I.149) where Luther spoke of the art of forgetting oneself as looking away from self and clinging to the right hand of God. Forgetting oneself means not judging oneself according to human perspective, which sees sin, but looking to God's judgment on sin: innocent.

48. LW 69.309–10 (WA 28.464).

49. Luther preached this sermon on John 20:19–23 in Wittenberg, March 30, 1529.

certain of this proclamation, and strengthened in their faith in this article, Christ himself appears in his own Person, and grants them happiness and salvation as their glory and inheritance. Christ offers them "his hands and side" (v. 20) for inspection, so that their eyes and reason are certain of his resurrection. So the Word and the work concur with each other to inculcate faith, the action of the Holy Spirit.

> The Word of Christ goes first, being proclaimed first through the angel, [then] through Mary Magdalene, and finally through the Lord Himself. Through this Word their hearts are inwardly enlightened, comforted, strengthened through the power of the Holy Spirit. Next comes the work: that Christ, in accordance with the Word, appears alive and by His appearing moves the disciples' eyes so that, since are to be the witnesses of His resurrection in all the world, they may not only hear of it but also see and experience it themselves. This is as Christ says to Nicodemus, *Quod vidimus testamir*, "We bear witness of what we have seen" (John 3:11). Therefore, this appearance and revelation should be numbered with His other appearances and should establish and strengthen our faith through the certain evidence of the Word and the work.[50]

Absolution is the concrete, definite locus where the fruit and power of the resurrection of Christ are applied and distributed.[51] The risen Christ entered though closed doors, without damaging them, and stood among the terrified disciples, declaring: "Peace to you." Not only does Christ show himself alive, but he also brings with him these treasures: comfort and peace. Christ appears in places where reason and experience least expect and bids them an amiable greeting. Accordingly, if Christ stands in our hearts as among his disciples, and proclaims an absolution, then we hear his voice. We need not gape toward heaven for the remission of sins, as a theologian of glory does. We should not imagine: "God forgives above, and men [forgive] here below, [but] who knows whether God above (*the absolute God*) wants to forgive."[52] A theologian of the cross does not speculate what the absolute God might do; he moves away from the absolute God to the revealed God, that is, from above to below. For Christ institutes the absolution here on earth; his resurrection will effect it.[53] Absolution administered here on

---

50. LW 69.352 (WA 28.465).

51. LW 69.394, 396, 398, and 416.

52. LW 69.416 (WA 41.445). The "God above" means "the absolute God" or "the naked Majesty."

53. LW 69.416 (WA 41.445).

earth, either through the pastor or a neighbor, is God's. Then we have the Word, which assures us that nothing, neither death nor the devil nor Christ himself, will sever us from God, for Christ has accomplished it by "the superabundant greatness of His power" (cf. Eph 1:19–20).[54] Whether privately administered or publicly spoken, the gospel must be received in faith.[55]

Simultaneity: Cross and Resurrection

The simultaneity (*simul*) of the cross and resurrection is integral to Luther's doctrine of justification. Easter is not a second "happy" message alongside the "sad" message of Good Friday.[56] Rather his resurrection is the declaration of what occurs in the marvellous duel on the cross, where blessing is locked in mortal combat with curse in Christ but triumphs over it.[57] On the cross, Christ assumes our sins, as if they were his very own, to make satisfaction for them. By raising him from the dead, God vindicates him as our righteousness. Commenting on Rom 4:25, "Christ rose for our justification," Luther wrote: "Christ's victory is a victory over law, sin, our flesh, the world, the devil, death, hell, and all evils; and this victory of his he has given to us. Even though these tyrants, our enemies, accuse us and terrify us, they cannot drive us to despair or condemn us. For Christ, whom God the Father raised from the dead, is Victor over them, and he is my righteousness."[58] The same understanding appears in his 1540 Sermon for the First Sunday of Easter, on John 20:19–29:

> Accordingly, we must say that [Christ] rose for this purpose: so that we should be righteous and live through His resurrection, and this is what He has commanded His apostles and everyone to preach unto the end of the world, namely, that a kingdom has been established on earth, which is a kingdom over against sin, death, and the power of the devil, and it brings heavenly and eternal blessings.[59]

---

54. LW 69.352 (WA 28.465).
55. See his Quasimodogeniti sermon of April 23, 1536, LW 69.408–17 (WA 41.541–46).
56. Schroeder, "Why the Cross is at the Center," 56.
57. LW 26.261–62 (WA 40, I.440–41). Schroeder, "Why the Cross is at the Center," 56. "The resurrection is the first reported event in the history of law-free, death-proof new creation."
58. LW 26.21–22 (WA 40.I.65.12–17).
59. LW 69.436 (WA 49.242).

A theology of the cross directs those who feel the effects of their sins and the divine wrath under the law, not to themselves or good works, but to Christ's conquering act on the cross and his victory through his resurrection. Just as the cross happened for us, so the resurrection happened for us, so that we delight in nothing else than that our sin and death are overcome. The law that makes us sinners is abolished; the sin that makes us guilty of death is conquered; and the death that terrifies us is vanquished. Christ's resurrection marks the triumph of the cross; it vindicates the atoning death of Christ by making it effective in securing the justification of believers. Thus St. Paul powerfully declared that Christ's sin-bearing death had become triumphantly effective for the forgiveness of sins (cf. Rom 4:25). By faith, we harvest the salutary fruit of Christ's resurrection: "redemption from sin and death."[60] This resurrection image, Christ the Brother, whose voice we continue to hear more clearly in Scripture than the friendly voice which called Mary Magdalene, suffices to fill our hearts with life, grace, blessedness, and righteousness, and prepare us to face the opposites, the terrifying images of death, disgrace, curse, and sin. The doubting Thomas (John 20:26–29) did not want to believe either Peter or the woman or any of the disciples; he wanted to convert himself through the mark of the nails, which possess no special conversion power. Yet, the risen Christ did not deal with him harshly and frightfully, but kindly and amicably. Precisely by his unbelief he proves himself to be the very person whom God loves. God finds above all the ungodly, who are not worthy in themselves, to be loved. The example of Thomas works good for us, by which we know the Lord befriends us in our frailties, and bears with our unbelief, which is completely opposed to him. Instead of making us go to him, the Lord goes to us, as he did to Thomas, breaks through our unbelief, and offers a comforting word: "Peace to you. Your sins are forgiven." Christ could not wait to apply to us the treasure of forgiveness and eternal inheritances he won through his suffering, death, and resurrection. Faith grasps the power of his voice, and concludes with certainty: "He could not be more friendly. Whoever knows Christ in this way truly knows Him. Therefore, we should look to Him for all good, all kindness in every peril of fire, water, etc. He is the one cornerstone on which we should depend in all our troubles and say, 'Ah, Lord, You will not abandon me; You will bring me aid.'"[61]

---

60. LW 69.289 (WA 28.437).
61. LW 69.404 (WA 37.381).

Afterword

The contrast between the theologian of glory and the theologian of the cross is as fundamental to Luther's theology as anything. Paralleling his dialectic of law and gospel, it goes to the very heart of what it means to be human and what it means to be Christian. And those who claim that Luther is not a systematic thinker, while perhaps correct in a very trivial manner with reference to the fact that he never wrote a systematic theology, would do well to see the consistent presence and systematic impact of the cross-glory distinction in his writings. It points to how we think about God, how we relate to him and, indeed, what we as individuals and as the church can expect to be our experience of God and Christ in this vale of tears.

It is thus a joy and a privilege to write the afterword for Dennis Ngien's wonderful study of Luther's theology of the cross as it is articulated in his sermons on the Gospel of John. If ever there was a match made in theological heaven, it is surely the *magnum opus* of the Bible's most profound writer on the theme of the Word made flesh and the theologian for whom there could be no engagement with God as gracious outside of the flesh of the Incarnate Christ. And here we might say that there is no contemporary writer who addresses Luther on this theme with greater theological and pastoral sympathy than Dennis Ngien, a scholar who has spent a lifetime making Luther the pastor accessible and helpful to the modern church. And it is privilege to commend it to the church at large.

The book you have just read is a gateway to the deep riches of Luther's thought. At a time when the church in the West faces significant changes to its social and cultural status, when her gospel has become not simply irrelevant and implausible to the wider world but downright offensive, the time is ripe for us to draw once again on historic voices from the Christian past who understood what it was to be marginal, to be in a precarious condition and to embrace the cross not simply as an inspiring action of God in the past but as the very criterion of what it means to be, to think, and to live as a Christian in the present.

Theologians come and theologians go. But Luther's longevity is the result of the fact that he, of all Christian writers, seems to have come closest to understanding the breadth and depth not only of what Paul articulates in his Corinthian letters but also of what John points to in his gospel: that the eternal, omnipotent God yet took flesh and made himself small and weak not simply to save us but to be that kind of God towards us, that we might be that kind of Christian for our neighbors. Dennis's book is a worthy exposition of Luther on this theme. May it capture the hearts—and the imaginations—of another generation of believers.

Carl R Trueman
Westminster Theological Seminary

Bibliography

Primary Sources

Luther, Martin. *D. Martin Luthers Werke: Kritische Gesamtausgabe.* 100 volumes. Weimar: Hermann Böhlau Nachfolger, 1883–.
———. *Martin Luthers Werke: Kristische Gesamtausgabe. Briefwechsel* 11 Volumes. Weimar: Hermann Böhlau Nachfolger, 1901–61.
———. *D. Martin Luthers Werke: Kristische Gesamtausgabe. Tischreden.* Weimar: Hermann Böhlau Nachfolger, 1912–21.
———. *Luther's Works.* American Editions. 55 Volumes. Edited by Jaroslav Pelikan & H. T. Lehman. St. Louis: Concordia; Philadelphia: Fortress, 1955–1967.
———. *Luther's Works, Vol. 69: Sermons on the Gospel of St. John Chapters 17–20.* Edited by Christopher Boyd Brown. St. Louis: Concordia, 2009.
Lenker, John Nicolas. *Sermons of Martin Luther.* Grand Rapids: Baker, 1983.
Lull, Timothy, ed. *Martin Luther's Basic Theological Writings.* Minneapolis: Fortress, 1989.
Tappert, Theodore, ed. *Luther's Letters of Spiritual Counsel.* Philadelphia: Westminster, 1955.

Secondary Sources

Althaus, Paul. *The Ethics of Martin Luther.* Translated by Robert. C. Schultz. Philadelphia: Fortress, 1972.
———. *The Theology of Martin Luther.* Translated by Robert C. Schultz. Philadelphia: Fortress, 1966.
Anthony, Neal J. *Cross Narratives: Martin Luther's Christology and the Location of Redemption.* Oregon: Wipf and Stock, 2010.
Arand, Charles P. "Luther on the Creed." In *The Pastoral Luther: Essays on Martin Luther's Practical Theology,* edited by Timothy J. Wengert, 147–70. Grand Rapids: Eerdmans, 2009.
Asendorf, Ulrich. *Eschatologie bei Luther.* Göttingen: Vanderhoeck and Ruprecht, 1967.
Augustine. *In Joannis Evangelium Tractatus,* Ch. III, Tr. XII, *Patrologia, Series Latina,* XXXV. Paris: Migne, 1854.

Ayres, Lewis. *Nicaea and Its Legacy: An Approach to Fourth Century Trinitarian Theology*. Oxford: Oxford University Press, 2004.
Barker, H. Gaylon. *The Cross of Reality: Luther's Theologia Crucis and Bonhoeffer's Christology*. Minneapolis: Fortress, 2015.
Barth, Hans-Martin. *The Theology of Martin Luther: A Critical Assessment*. Minneapolis: Fortress, 2013.
Barth, Karl. *Church Dogmatics*. 4 Volumes. Translated by Geoffrey W. Bromiley and Thomas F. Torrance. Edinburgh: T. & T. Clark, 1956.
Bauckham, Richard. *Gospel of Glory: Major Themes in Johannine Theology*. Grand Rapids: Baker Academic, 2015.
Bayer, Oswald. *Freedom in Response. Lutheran Ethics: Sources and Controversies*. Translated by Jeffrey F. Cayzer. Oxford: Oxford University Press, 2007.
———. "Luther as an Interpreter of Holy Scripture." Translated by Mark Mattes. In *The Cambridge Companion to Martin Luther*, edited by Donald McKim, 73–85. Cambridge: Cambridge University Press, 2003.
———. *Martin Luther's Theology: A Contemporary Interpretation*. Translated by Thomas H. Trapp. Grand Rapids: Eerdmans, 2008.
———. *Theology the Lutheran Way*. Edited and translated by Jeffrey G. Silcock and Mark C. Mattes. Grand Rapids: Eerdmans, 2007.
———. "Toward a Theology of Lament." In *Caritas et Reformatio: Essays on Church and Society in Honor of Carter Lindberg*, edited by David Whitford, 211–20. St. Louis: Concordia, 2002.
Bayer, Oswald and Benjamin Gleede. *Creator est Creatura: Luthers Christologie als Lehre von der idiomenkommunication*. Berlin: de Gruyter, 2007.
Bernard of Clairvaux, *De consideratione*, Book IV. *Patrologia, Series Latina*, CLXXXII. Paris: Migne, 1854.
Biel, Gabriel. *Collectorium circa quattuor libros sententiarum*. 4 volumes. Edited by H. Rückert, M. Elze, R. Steiger, W. Werbeck, and U. Hofmann. Tübingen: Mohr, 1973–92.
Bindley, T. H. *The Ecumenical Documents of the Faith*, 4th edition. Westport, CN: Greenwood, 1950.
Bornkamm, Heinrich. *Luther's Doctrine of the Two Kingdoms in the Context of His Theology*. Translated by Karl H. Hertz. Philadelphia: Fortress, 1966.
Braaten, Carl E., ed. *Our Naming of God: Problems and Prospects of God-Talk Today*. Minneapolis: Fortress, 1989.
Braaten, Carl E, and Robert W. Jenson, eds. *Christian Dogmatics* 2 vols. Minneapolis: Fortress, 1984.
———. *Union with Christ: The New Finnish Interpretation of Luther*. Grand Rapids: Eerdmans, 1998.
Brooks, Peter Newman, ed. *Seven-Headed Luther: Essays in Commemoration of a Quincentenary 1483-1983*. Oxford: Clarendon, 1983.
Bruner, Frederick Dale. *The Gospel of John. A Commentary*. Grand Rapids: Eerdmans, 2012.
Brunner, Emil. *The Mediator*. Philadelphia: Westminster, 1947.
Bultmann, Rudolf. *Faith and Understanding. I*. Translated by L. P. Smith. London: SCM, 1969.

Calvin, John. *Institutes of the Christian Religion*. Translated by Ford Lewis Battles. Volume 20. The Library of Christian Classics. Edited by John T. McNeill. Philadelphia: Westminster, 1960.

Chemnitz, Martin. *The Two Natures in Christ*. Translated by Jacob A. O. Preus. St. Louis: Concordia, 1971.

Collver, Albert B., Jon Vieker, and Bart Day, eds. *Dona Gratis Donata: Essays on the Occasion of the 90th Birthday of Norman Nagel*. St. Louis: Create Space, 2015.

Congar, Yves. "Considerations and Reflections on the Christology of Luther." In *Dialogue Between Christians: Catholic Contributions to Ecumenism*, 372–406. London: Geoffrey Chapman, 1966.

Crisp, Oliver D. *Divinity and Humanity*. Cambridge: Cambridge University Press, 2007.

Cyril of Alexandria. "Commentary on John 12." In *Library of Fathers of the Catholic Church*, 48 vols. Oxford: J. H. Parker, 1838–85.

Dorner, Isaak A, *History of the Development of the Doctrine of the Person of Christ*, Division Second, Volume II. Translated by Rev. D. W. Simon. Edinburgh: T. & T. Clark, 1868.

Eichrodt, Walter. *Theology of the Old Testament*, Vol. 1. London: SCM, 1961.

Elert, Werner. *The Structure of Lutheranism*, Vol. 1: *The Theology and Philosophy of the Life of Lutheranism in the Sixteenth and Seventeenth Centuries*. Translated by Walter A. Hansen. St. Louis: Concordia, 1962.

Fiddes, Paul S. *The Creative Suffering of God*. Oxford: Clarendon, 1999.

Forde, Gerhard O. "Luther's Theology of the Cross." In *Christian Dogmatics*, edited by Carl E. Braaten and Robert W. Jenson, 47–63. Minneapolis: Fortress, 1984.

———. *On Being a Theologian of the Cross: Reflections on Luther's Heidelberg Disputations, 1518*. Grand Rapids: Eerdmans, 2007.

———. *The Preached God: Proclamation in Word and Sacrament*. Edited by Mark C. Mattes and Steven Paulson. Grand Rapids: Eerdmans, 2007.

Gavrilyuk, Paul L. *The Suffering of the Impassible God: The Dialectics of Patristic Thought*. Oxford: Oxford University Press, 2004.

George, Timothy. *Reading Scripture with the Reformers*. Downers Grove, IL: Intervarsity, 2011.

Gerrish, Brian. *Grace and Reason: A Study in the Theology of Martin Luther*. Oxford: Clarendon, 1962.

Gorman, Michael J. *Cruciformity: Paul's Narrative Spirituality of the Cross*. Grand Rapids: Eerdmans, 2001.

Grillmeier, Aloys. *Christ in Christian Tradition: From the Apostolic Age to Chalcedon (AD 451)*. Vol. 1. 2nd edition. Translated by John Bowden. Grand Rapids: Eerdmans, 1977.

Haberkern, Philip N. *Patron Saint and Prophet: Jan Hus in the Bohemian and German Reformations*. Oxford: Oxford University Press, 2016.

Haga, Joar. *Was there a Lutheran Metaphysics? The Interpretation of Communicatio Idiomatum in Early Modern Lutheranism*. Göttingen: Vandehoeck & Rupprecht, 2012.

Hagen, Kenneth. *A Theology of Testament in the Young Luther: The Lectures on Hebrews*. Leiden: Brill, 1984.

Hamm, Berndt. *The Early Luther: Stages in Reformation Reorientation*. Grand Rapids: Eerdmans, 2014.

Helmer, Christine. *The Trinity and Martin Luther: A Study on the Relationship between Genre, Language and the Trinity in Luther's Works* (1523–1546). Mainz: Verlag Philipp von Zabern, 1999.

Hendel, Kurt. "Finitum est capax infiniti: Luther's Radical Incarnational Perspective." In *Encounters with Luther: New Directions for Critical Studies*, edited by Kirsi Stjerna and Brooks Schramm, 161–74. Louisville: Westminster/John Knox, 2016.

Herms, Eilert. *Luther Auslegung des Dritten Artikels*. Tübingen: Mohr, 1987.

Hillerbrand, Hans J., ed. *The Oxford Dictionary of the Reformation*. 4 vols. Oxford: Oxford University Press, 1997.

Hinlicky, Paul R. *Luther and the Beloved Community. A Path for Christian Theology after Christendom*. Grand Rapids: Eerdmans, 2010.

Hinlicky, Paul R. "Luther's anti-docetism in the Disputatio et humanitate Christ." In *Creator et creature: Luthers Christologie als Lehre von der Idiomenkommunikatio*, edited by Oswald Bayer and Benjamin Gleede, 139–81. Berlin: de Gruyter, 2007.

Jansen, Reiner. *Studien zu Luthers Trinitätslehre*. Frankfurt: Peter Lang, 1976.

Janz, Denis R. *The Westminster Handbook to Martin Luther*. Louisville: Westminster John Knox, 2010.

Jenson, Robert W. *Systematic Theology*. 2 vols. Oxford: Oxford University Press, 1997.

———. *Unbaptized God. The Basic Flaw in Ecumenical Theology*. Minneapolis: Fortress, 1992.

Kelly, J. N. D. *Early Christian Doctrines*. New York: Harper & Row, 1978.

Kolb, Robert. "Luther on the Theology of the Cross." In *The Pastoral Luther: Essays on Martin Luther's Practical Theology*, edited by Timothy J. Wengert, 33–58. Grand Rapids: Eerdmans, 2009.

———. *Martin Luther as Prophet, Teacher, and Hero: Images of the Reformer 1520–1620*. Grand Rapids: Baker, 1999.

———. *Martin Luther: Confessor of the Faith*. Oxford: Oxford University Press, 2009.

———. *Martin Luther and the Enduring Word of God: The Wittenberg School and Its Scripture-Centered Proclamation*. Grand Rapids: Baker Academic, 2016.

———. *Teaching God's Children His Teaching: A Guide for the Study of Luther's Catechism*. Hutchinson, MN: Crown, 1992.

Kolb, Robert and Charles P. Arand. *The Genius of Luther's Theology: A Wittenberg Way of Thinking*. Grand Rapids: Baker Academic, 2008.

Kolb, Robert and Timothy J. Wengert, eds. *The Book of Concord: The Confessions of the Evangelical Lutheran Church*. Minneapolis: Fortress, 2000.

Kolb, Robert, Irene Dingel and Ľubomir Batka, eds. *The Oxford Handbook of Martin Luther's Theology*. Oxford: Oxford University Press, 2014.

Korby, Kenneth F. "The Use of John 6 in Lutheran Sacramental Piety." In *Shepherd the Church: Essays in Honor of Rev. Dr. D. Pittelko*, edited by Frederic Baue et al, 129–44. Fort Wayne, IN: Concordia Theological Seminary Press, 2002.

Köstlin, Julius. *The Theology of Luther in His Historical Development and Inner Harmony*, translated by Charles E. Hay, 2 vols. Philadelphia: Lutheran Publication Society, 1897.

Lage, Dietmar. *Martin Luther's Christology and Ethics*. Lewiston: Edwin Mellen, 1990.

Lane, Tony. "The Wrath of God as an Aspect of the Love of God." In *Nothing Greater, Nothing Better: Theological Essays on the Love of God*, edited by Kevin J. Vanhoozer, 138–67. Grand Rapids: Eerdmans, 2001.

Lehmann, Martin E. *Luther and Prayer*. Milwaukee: Northwestern, 1985.

Leroux, Neil. *Martin Luther as Comforter. Writings on Death*. Leiden: Brill, 2007.
Lindberg, Carter. *The Third Reformation? Charismatic Movements and the Lutheran Tradition*. Georgia: Mercer University Press, 1983.
———. *Beyond Charity: Reformation Initiatives for the Poor*. Minneapolis: Fortress, 1993.
Lienhard, Marc. *Luther: Witness to Jesus Christ: Stages and Themes of the Reformer's Christology*. Translated by Edwin H. Robertson. Minneapolis: Augsburg, 1982.
Lischer, Richard. *A Theology of Preaching*. Nashville: Abingdon, 1981.
Loewenich, Walther von. *Luther's Theology of the Cross*. Translated by Herbert J. A. Bouman. Minneapolis: Augsburg, 1976.
Lohse, Bernhard. *Martin Luther's Theology: Its Historical and Systematic Development*. Translated and edited by Roy A. Harrisville. Minneapolis: Fortress, 1999.
Lortz, Joseph. *The Reformation in Germany*. 2 vols. Translated by Ronald Walls. New York: Herder & Herder, 1968.
Lull, Timothy F., and Derek R. Nelson. *Resilient Reformer: The Life and Thought of Martin Luther*. Minneapolis: Fortress, 2015.
Luy, David J. *Dominus Mortis: Martin Luther on the Incorruptibility of God in Christ*. Minneapolis: Fortress, 2014.
Macleod, Donald. *The Person of Christ*. Downers Grove, IL: InterVarsity, 1998.
Malysz, Piotr J., and Derek R. Nelson, eds. *Luther Refracted: The Reformer's Ecumenical Legacy*. Minneapolis: Fortress, 2015.
Mannermaa, Tuomo. *Two Kinds of Love: Martin Luther's Religious World*. Minneapolis: Augsburg Fortress, 2010.
Marty, Martin. *Hidden Discipline*. St. Louis: Concordia, 1962.
McGrath, Alister E. *Luther's Theology of the Cross*. 6th edition. Oxford: Blackwell, 2017.
———. *Iustia Dei: A History of the Christian Doctrine of Justification*. Cambridge: Cambridge University Press, 1986.
McGuckin, John. *Saint Cyril of Alexandria and the Christological Controversy*. Crestwood, NY: St. Vladimir's Seminary Press, 2004.
Melanchthon, Philip. *Loci Communes Theologici*. Translated by Wilhelm Pauck. Vol. XIX. Library of Christian Classics. Philadelphia: Westminster, 1965.
Meuser, Fred W. "Luther as Preacher of the Word of God." In *The Cambridge Companion to Martin Luther*, edited by Donald K. McKim, 136–48. Cambridge: Cambridge University Press, 2003.
Moltmann, Jürgen. *The Church in the Power of the Spirit*. London: SCM, 1977.
Mtata, Kenneth, ed. *"You have the Words of Eternal Life." Transformative Readings of the Gospel of John from a Lutheran Perspective*. Geneva: The Lutheran World Federation, 2012.
Nagel, Norman E. "Martinus: 'Heresy, Doctor Luther, Heresy!' The Person and Work of Christ." In *Seven-Headed Luther: Essays in Commemoration of a Quincentenary 1483–1983*, 25–49. Edited by Peter Newman Brooks. Oxford: Clarendon, 1983.
Ngien, Dennis. *Apologetic for Filioque in Medieval Theology*. Milton Keynes: Paternoster, 2005.
———. *Fruit for the Soul: Luther on the Lament Psalms*. Minneapolis: Fortress, 2015.
———. *Gifted Response: The Triune God as the Causative Agency of Our Responsive Worship*. Milton Keynes: Paternoster, 2008.
———. *Luther as a Spiritual Adviser: The Interface of Theology and Piety in Luther's Devotional Writings*. Milton Keynes: Paternoster, 2007.

———. *The Suffering of God according to Martin Luther's "Theologia Crucis."* New York: Peter Lang, 1995.
Oberman, Heiko A. *Harvest of Medieval Theology: Gabriel Biel and Late Medieval Nominalism.* Durham, NC: Labyrinth, 1953.
———. *Luther: Man between God and the Devil.* Translated by Eileen Walliser-Schwarzbart. New Haven: Yale University Press, 1989.
———. *The Roots of Anti-Semitism in the Age of Renaissance and Reformation.* Translated by James I. Porter. Philadelphia: Fortress, 1984.
O' Collins, Gerald. *Christology: A Biblical, Historical, and Systematic Study of Jesus.* Oxford: Oxford University Press, 1995.
Packer, James I. *Keeping in Step with the Holy Spirit.* New Jersey: Revell, 1984.
Parsons, Michael. *Martin Luther's Interpretation of the Royal Psalms.* Lewiston: Edwin Mellen, 2009.
Paulson, Steven D. *Lutheran Theology.* London: T. & T. Clark, 2011.
Pannenberg, Wolfhart. *Jesus: God and Man.* Translated by Lewis L. Wilkins & Diane A. Priebe. Philadelphia: Westminster, 1968.
———. *Systematic Theology.* Volume 2. Translated by Geoffrey W. Bromiley. Grand Rapids: Eerdmans, 1994.
Pelikan, Jaroslav. *The Christian Tradition: A History of the Development of Doctrine.* 5 vols. Chicago: University of Chicago Press, 1971.
———, ed. *Luther's Works: Companion Volume. Luther the Expositor: Introduction to the Reformer's Exegetical Writings.* Saint Louis: Concordia, 1959.
Peels, H. G. L. *The Vengeance of God.* Leiden: Brill, 1995.
Peters, Ted. *Sin Boldly! Justifying Faith for Fragile and Broken Souls.* Minneapolis: Fortress, 2015.
Placher, William C. *The Domestication of Transcendence: How Modern Theology about God Went Wrong.* Louisville: Westminster John Knox, 1966.
Pless, John T. "Cross-bearing and Life in a Lutheran synod: What can we learn from Hermann Sasse?" In *Dona Gratis Donata: Essays on the Occasion of the 90th Birthday of Norman Nagel*, edited by Bart Day and John Vieker, 183–96. St. Louis: Create Space, 2015.
———. *Praying Luther's Small Catechism.* St. Louis: Concordia, 2016.
Posset, Franz. *The Real Luther: A Friar at Erfurt and Wittenberg.* St. Louis: Concordia, 2011.
———. *Luther's Catholic Christology according to his Johannine Lectures 1527.* Milwaukee: Northwestern, 1988.
———. *Pater Bernhardus: Martin Luther and Bernard of Clairvaux.* Kalamazoo, MI: Cistercian, 1999.
Prenter, Regin. *Spiritus Creator.* Translated by John M. Jensen. Philadelphia: Mühlenberg, 1953.
Reinis, Austra. *Reforming the Art of Dying: The ars Moriendi in the German Reformation (1519–1528).* Hampshire: Ashgate, 2007.
Rittgers, Ronald K. *The Power of the Keys: Confession, Conscience, and Authority in the Sixteenth Century.* Cambridge: Harvard University Press, 2004.
———. *The Reformation of Suffering: Pastoral Theology and Lay Piety in Late Medieval and Early Modern Germany.* Oxford: Oxford University Press, 2012.
Sasse, Hermann. *Letters to Lutheran Pastors.* Vol. 1:1948–1951. Edited by Matthew C. Harrison. St. Louis: Concordia, 2013.

———. *This is My Body: Luther's Contention for the Real Presence in the Sacrament of the Altar*. Minneapolis: Augsburg, 1959.

———. *We Confess Jesus Christ*. Translated by Norman Nagel. St. Louis: Concordia, 1984.

Sauter, Gerhard. "Luther on the Resurrection." In *Harvesting Martin Luther's Reflections on Theology, Ethics, and the Church*, edited by Timothy J. Wengert, 99-118. Grand Rapids: Eerdmans, 2004.

Sayers, Dorothy L. "The Shattering Dogmas of the Christian Tradition." In *Christian Letters to a Post-Christian World*. Grand Rapid: Eerdmans, 1969.

Schaff, Philip, ed. *A Select Library of the Christian Church: Nicene and Post-Nicene Fathers*. First Series. 14 vols. New York: 1886-89. Reprint, Peabody, MA: Hendrickson, 1994.

Schnackenburg, Rudolf. *The Gospel According to St. John*. Translated by Kevin Smyth et al.; 3 vols. New York: Herder & Herder, 1968-82.

Schroeder, Edward H. "Why the Cross is at the Center." In *Gift and Promise: The Augsburg Confession and the Heart of Christian Theology*, edited by Edward H. Schroeder, Ronald Neustadt and Stephen Hitchcock, 37-58. Minneapolis: Fortress, 2016.

Schroeder, Edward H., Ronald Neustadt and Stephen Hitchcock, eds. *Gift and Promise: The Augsburg Confession & the Heart of Christian Theology*. Minneapolis: Fortress, 2016.

Siggins, Ian D. *Martin Luther's Doctrine of Christ*. New Haven: Yale University Press, 1970.

Silcock, Jeffery. "Luther on the Holy Spirit and His Use of God's Word." In *The Oxford Handbook of Martin Luther's Theology*, edited by Robert Kolb, Irene Dingel, and L'ubomir Batka, 294-309. Oxford: Oxford University Press, 2014.

Spitz, Lewis W. "Luther Ecclesiast: An Historian's Angle." In *Seven-Headed Luther: Essays in Commemoration of a Quincentenary 1483-1983*, edited by Peter Newman Brooks. Oxford: Clarendon, 1983.

Stott, John. *The Cross of Christ*. Leicester: InterVarsity, 1986.

Stjerna, Kirsi I., and Brooks Schramm, eds. *Encounters with Luther: New Directions for Critical Studies*. Louisville: Westminster John Knox, 2016.

Tappert, Theodore G, trans. and ed. *The Book of Concord: The Confessions of the Evangelical Lutheran Church*. Philadelphia: Fortress, 1959.

Thielicke, Helmut. *Our Heavenly Father: Sermons on the Lord's Prayer*. New York: Harper and Row, 1960.

Thompson, John. *Modern Trinitarian Perspectives*. Oxford: Oxford University Press, 1994.

Torrance, James B. *Worship, Community and the Triune God of Grace*. Carlisle: Paternoster, 1996.

Torrance, Thomas F. *The Trinitarian Faith*. London: T & T Clark, 1995.

Trueman, Carl. "*Simul Peccator et Justus*: Martin Luther and Justification." In *Justification in Perspective: Historical developments and Contemporary Challenges*, edited by Bruce L. McCormack, 73-98. Grand Rapids: Baker Academic, 2006.

———. *Luther on the Christian Life: Cross and Freedom*. Wheaton, IL: Crossway, 2015.

Vanhoozer, Kevin J., ed. *Nothing Greater, Nothing Better: Theological Essays on the Love of God*. Grand Rapids: Eerdmans, 2001.

Vajta, Vilmos. *Luther on Worship*. Philadelphia: Fortress, 1958.

Watson, Philip. *Let God be God: An Interpretation of the Theology of Martin Luther*. Philadelphia: Mühlenberg, 1948.
Weinandy, Thomas G. *Does God Change? The Word's becoming in the Incarnation*. Still River, MA: St. Bede's, 1985.
———. *Does God Suffer?* Notre Dame: University of Notre Dame, 2000.
Wengert, J. Timothy, ed. *Harvesting Martin Luther's Reflections on Theology, Ethics, and the Church*. Grand Rapids: Eerdmans, 2004.
———. *The Pastoral Luther: Essays on Martin Luther's Practical Theology*. Grand Rapids: Eerdmans, 2009.
———. *Reading the Bible with Martin Luther*. Grand Rapids: Baker Academic, 2013.
Wilson, H. S. "Luther on Preaching as God's Speaking." In *The Pastoral Luther: Essays on Martin Luther's Practical Theology*, edited by Timothy J. Wengert, 100–116. Grand Rapids: Eerdmans, 2009.
Wingren, Gustaf. *Luther on Vocation*. Translated by Carl C Rasmussen. Philadelphia: Mühlenberg Publishing, 1957.
Whitford, David M. *T. & T. Clark Companion to Reformation Theology*. London: T. & T. Clark, 2014.
Wright, William J. *Martin Luther's Understanding of God's Two Kingdoms: A Response to the Challenge of Skepticism*. Grand Rapids: Baker Academic, 2010.
Zachman, Randall C. *The Assurance of Faith: Conscience in the Theology of Martin Luther and John Calvin*. Minneapolis: Augsburg Fortress, 1993.
Zenger, Erich. *A God of Vengeance? Understanding the Psalms of Divine Wrath*. Translated by L. M. Maloney. Louisville: Westminster John Knox, 1996.

Journal articles

Arand, Charles O. "'The Battle Cry of Faith': The Catechism's Exposition of the Lord's Prayer." *Concordia Journal* 21 (1995) 42–65.
Boehme, Armand J. "John 6 and Historic Lutheranism." *Logia* 25 (2016) 7–15.
Boulton, Michael. "'We Pray by His Mouth'": Karl Barth, Erving Goffman, and a Theology of Invocation." *Modern Theology* 17 (2001) 67–83.
Bray, Gerald. "The *Filioque* Clause in History and Theology." *Tyndale Bulletin* 34 (1983) 91–144.
Carlson, Arnold E. "Luther and the Doctrine of the Holy Spirit." *Lutheran Quarterly* 11 (May, 1958) 135–46.
Clark, John C. "Martin Luther's View of Cross-bearing." *Bibliotheca Sacra* 163, no. 652 (2006) 335–47.
Daley, Brian E. "Revisiting the '*Filioque*': Roots and Branches of An Old Debate." *Pro Ecclesia* X (2001) 31–62 (part I); 95–212 (part II).
Davidson, Ivor. "Theologizing the human Jesus: an ancient (and modern) approach to Christology reassessed." *International Journal of Systematic Theology* 3 (2001) 129–53.
Dockery, David S. "Martin Luther's Christological Hermeneutics." *Grace Theological Journal* 4 (1983) 189–203.
Forell, George Wolfgang. "Justification and Eschatology." *Church History* 38 (1969) 164–74.

Fergusson, David. "Theology of Worship." *Scottish Bulletin of Evangelical Theology* 21 (2003) 7–19.

Heinz, Johann. "The 'Summer That Will Never End': Luther's Longing for the 'Dear Last Day' in his Sermon on Luke 21 (1531)." *Andrews University Seminary Studies* 23, (1985) 181–86.

Mueller, John Theodore. "Notes on Luther's Interpretation of John 6:47–58." *Concordia Theological Quarterly* 20 (1949) 802–28.

Olmsted, Richard H. "Staking All on Faith's Object: The Art of Christian Assurance according to Martin Luther and Karl Barth." *Pro Ecclesia* 10 (2001) 135–58.

Pless, John T. "Learning to Preach in Advent and Christmas from Luther." *Concordia Theological Quarterly* 62 (1998) 269–86.

Posset, Franz. "St. Bernard's Influence on Two Reformers: Johannes von Staupitz and Martin Luther." *Cistercian Studies* 25 (1990) 175–87.

Jenson, Matt. "Suffering the Promise of God: Engaging Oswald Bayer." *International Journal of Systematic Theology* 13 (April 2011) 134–53.

Kärkkainen, Veli Matti. "'The Christian as Christ to the Neighbor': On Luther's Theology of Love." *International Journal of Systematic Theology* 6 (2004) 101–17.

Kelly, Robert. "The Suffering Church: A Study of Luther's *Theologia Crucis*." *Concordia Theological Quarterly* 50 (1986) 3–17.

Kleinig, John. "Oratio, Meditatio, Tentatio: What Makes a Theologian?" *Concordia Theological Quarterly* 66 (2002) 255–67.

Koester, Craig. "The Passion and Resurrection according to John." *Word & World* 11 (1991) 84–91.

Krispin, Gerald S. "The Consolation of the Resurrection in Luther." *Lutheran Theological Review* 2 (1989–90) 37–51.

―――. "A Study in Luther's Pastoral Theology." *Logia: A Journal of Lutheran Theology* 10, no. 2 (2001) 13–19.

Krodel, Gottfried G. "Luther's Work on the Catechism in the Context of Late-Medieval Literature." *Concordia Journal* 25 (1995) 364–404.

Lang, Uwe M. "*Anhypostatos-enhypostatos*: Church Fathers, Protestant Orthodoxy and Karl Barth." *Journal of Theological Studies* 49 (1998) 630–57.

Moldenhauer, Aaron. "A Translation and Analysis of Martin Luther's 1528 Catechetical Sermons on the Lord's Supper." *Concordia Journal* 53 (2007) 43–60.

Moseman, C. "Martin Luther on 'Becoming Christ to One's Neighbor.'" *Presbyterion* 26 (2000) 93–105.

Nestingen, James A. "The Lord's Prayer in Luther's Catechism." *Word and World* 22 (2002) 36–48.

Ngien, Dennis. "The Economic Actions of the Holy Spirit in Luther's Sermons on the Gospel of John." *Crux* 52 (2016) 22–34.

―――. "Reaping the Right Fruits: Meditation on the 'Earnest Mirror, Christ.'" *International Journal of Systematic Theology*, vol. 8 (2006) 382–410.

Olmsted, Richard H. "Staking All on Faith's Object: The Art of Christian Assurance according to Martin Luther and Karl Barth." *Pro Ecclesia* 10 (2001) 135–58.

Pfitzner, Victor C. "Luther as Interpreter of John's Gospel with Special References to his Sermons on the Gospel of John." *Lutheran Theological Journal* 18 (1984) 65–73.

Scaer, David P. "Luther's Concept of Resurrection on I Corinthians 15." *Concordia Theological Quarterly* 47 (1983) 209–24.

―――. "Once More to John 6." *Concordia Theological Quarterly* 77 (2013) 47–62.

Schults, F. LeRon. "A dubious Christological Formula: from Leontius of Byzantium to Karl Barth." *Theological Studies* 57 (1996) 431–46.
Schneider, Carolyn. "The intimate connection between Christ and Christians in Athanasius and Luther." *Scottish Journal of Theology* 50 (2005) 1–12.
Silcock, Jeffrey G. "The Truth of divine impassibility: a new look at an old argument." *Lutheran Theological Journal* 45 (2011) 198–207.
Steiger, Johan Anselm. "The *communicatio idiomatum* as the Axle and Motor of Luther's Theology." *Lutheran Quarterly* 14 (2000) 125–58.
Thompson, John. "The Humanity of God in the Theology of Karl Barth." *Scottish Journal of Theology* 29 (1976) 249–69.
Tinder, Galen. "Luther's Theology of Christian Suffering and Its Implications for Pastoral Care." *Dialog* 25 (1986) 108–113.
Turcescu, Lucian. "'Person' versus 'Individual,' and Other Modern Misreadings of Gregory of Nyssa." *Modern Theology* 18 (2002) 527–39.
Tylenda, Joseph N. "Calvin's Understanding of the Communication of Properties." *Westminster Theological Journal* 38 (Fall 1975) 54–65.
Vogel, Winfried. "The Eschatological Theology of Martin Luther, Part I: Luther's Basic Concepts." *Andrews University Seminary Studies* 24 (1986) 249–64.
———. "The Eschatological Theology of Martin Luther, Part II: Luther's Exposition of Daniel and Revelation." *Andrews University Seminary Studies* 25 (1987) 183–99.
Wengert, Timothy J. "Caspar Crucifer Sr.'s 1546 'Enarratio' on John's Gospel: An Experimental in Ecclesiology Exegesis." *Church History* 61 (1992) 60–74.
Yeago, David. "The Bread of Life: Patristic Christology and Evangelical Soteriology in Martin Luther's Sermons on John 6." *St. Vladimir's Theological Quarterly* 39 (1995) 257–79.

www.ingramcontent.com/pod-product-compliance
Lightning Source LLC
Chambersburg PA
CBHW032051220426
43664CB00008B/950